5.95

CHINA:

The Revolution Is Dead — Long Live The Revolution

CHINA

The Revolution Is Dead
Long Live The Revolution

Edited by the 70's
Introduction
by
Kan San

BLACK ROSE BOOKS Montréal

BLACK ROSE BOOKS No. G 35

Hardcover — ISBN: 0-919618-38-3
Paperback — ISBN: 0-919618-37-5

Published by BLACK ROSE BOOKS 1977

Reprinted 1979

Canadian Cataloguing in Publication Data

China:the revolution is dead, long live the revolution

ISBN: 0-919618-38-3 bd. ISBN: 0-919618-37-5 pa.

1. China — History — 1949-1976 — Adresses, essays, lectures.
I. The 70's.

DS777.55.C48   951.05   C79-090023-8

Cover Design: Michael Carter

BLACK ROSE BOOKS LTD.
3981 boulevard St. Laurent
Montréal H2W 1Y5
Québec, Canada

Printed and bound in Québec, Canada

CONTENTS:

Preface / vii
Introduction by Kan San / xi

SECTION ONE
The Great Proletarian Cultural Revolution and the
Reversal of workers' power in China
  by Progressive Labour Party / 5
China: Let a hundred flowers bloom
  by Nigel Harris / 40
On "The Great Proletarian Cultural Revolution"
  by F.H. Wang / 61

SECTION TWO
Mao's China and the "Proletarian Cultural
Revolution"
  by Raya Dunayevskaya / 93
The Explosition Point of Ideology in China
  by the Situationalist International / 105
Theses on the Chinese Revolution
  by Cajo Brendel / 117
"Everything remains the same after so much Ado"
  by K.C. Kwok / 141

SECTION THREE
Whither China?
  by Sheng-Wu-Lien / 153
The Dusk of Rationality
  by Yu Shuet / 171
Introduction To Revelations that move the Earth
to Tears
  by Wu Mann / 193
An Interview with an Ultra-Leftist / 205

Concerning Socialist Democracy and the Legal System
  by Li I-Che / 213

APPENDIX
Some thoughts on the Chinese Revolution
  by Lee Yu See and Wu Che / 242

PREFACE

A very difficult task we face in evaluating social movements is the communications problems between revolutionary movements in the Western world and the Eastern world. An important contribution in overcoming this obstacle is the work of the libertarian communist group called "70s" in Hong Kong. This group is opposed simultaneously to Western capitalism and Chinese state-capitalist bureaucracy. It is a group that includes revolutionaries who have escaped from China.

In the preface they wrote, the "70s" introduce the essays published here in the following way:

The developments in China since 1949 have interested and fascinated many: Hong Kong students who are searching for an identity, academics and careerists in the ivory towers, as well as revolutionaries all over the world who are genuinely interested in the course of humanity.

This book is a collection of essays on the Great Proletarian Cultural Revolution. Readers will be aware of the fact that while the name of the book is entitled "Readings from an Ultra-left Perspective", there is not just *one* "ultra-left" interpretation of the Great Proletarian Cultural Revolution.

The book is divided into three sections. The first section consists of three essays written from an ultra-leftist standpoint which is basically Marxist-Leninist. The four essays in the second section are libertarian communist. (We would disagree with this characterization of these essays. For instance Dunayevskaya describes herself as "Marxist-Humanist" *Black Rose Books)* The third section consists of the views of the Chinese ulta-leftists in their own words.

Needless to say, the 70s Biweekly, being a libertarian group, is much closer to the views expressed in sections two and three, especially the two essays: The Dusk of Rationality and Everything Remains the Same After So Much Ado. In a forthcoming book on Chinese Anarchism, we, members of the 70s Biweekly, shall try to make our views on China more explicit. However, we believe that the analysis of the Marxist-Leninist ultra-left presented here can be quite useful and illuminating.

The purpose of the book is modest: simply to provide some basis for further discussion on the future of China and for the development of a perspective on the ongoing socialist revolution on a world scale.

The experiences of the Great Proletarian Cultural Revolution, we believe, will provide as much inspiration to revolutionaries as the Paris Commune.

We would like to thank the following people for their assistance in the preparation of this book, including the translation of some of the Chinese texts into English, proof-reading, correcting the translation, typesetting the manuscript, making useful suggestions etc.: R. Yiu, S.P. Mok, M. Ho, S.K. Tsang, F. Chan, G.D. Tai, J. Mo.

A Chinese edition of this book is also being prepared.

We at *Black Rose Books* believe that this book has a sweeping eclecticism which leads to a theoretical vagueness. While not wanting to publish a full book review here, we found the critique made by a group called *Bureau of Public Secrets* useful and reprint below part of what they had to say, while welcoming the publication of the book.

"Even leaving aside the three articles written from Leninist perspectives — whose analyses the 70s editors explicitly reject — several of the articles contain dubious formulations which are not criticized. Cajo Brendel's 'Theses on the Chinese Revolution' are determinist and reductionist. His tedious comparison of the Chinese Communist Party with the Russian one reinforces the notion of the inevitablility of the bureaucratic regime. He fails to formulate the *choices,* the contradictions that bear on revolutionary *possibilities.* He plays down the great Shanghai uprising of 1927 (see Harold Issacs's *The Tragedy of the Chinese Revolution)* and reduces its crushing to a whim of Chiang Kai-shek's: 'because he scorned Jacobinism, not because he feared the proletariat' (thesis #22). And all he sees during the sixties is a conflict between the 'new class' (the managerial bureaucrats) and the old-line Party bureaucrats, in which 'the ultimate victory of the 'new class' is the only logical perspective' (#60). The large-scaled armed revolts touched off by the "Cultural Revolution", which burst the bounds of both bureaucratic factions, are mentioned only once, as 'details': 'every detail cannot be fitted into this analytical framework" (#58). An 'analytical framework' in which the proletariat can't apparently play any role but that of a tool for one or another ruling class, or of a 'detail', is a strange one to be taken up by a 'libertarian communist'.

Like many other commentators on China, K.C. Kwok takes the bureaucrats' rhetoric too seriously, accepting the issues as they define them, trying to follow the constantly shifting 'lines' and figure out who is to the 'left' or 'right', etc. His 'Everythings Remains the Same after so much Ado' is a confused hodgepodge resulting from the attempt to blend extensive, ill-digested borrowings from the Situationalist International's "Explosion Point of Ideology in China' (also included in the book) with Yang Hsi-Kwang's 'Whether China'. 'Whether China' and Li I-Che's 'Concerning Socialist Democracy and Legality' are both important expressions of the development, under extremely difficult conditions, of an indigenous critique of the Chinese bureaucracy (comparable in this respect to Kuron's and Modzelweski's 'Open Letter to the Polish Communist Party Members'). Nevertheless, their analyses are seriously distorted by their attempt to follow through with a radical anti-bureaucratic program while stimultaneously holding up the Mao faction as a pillar of the revolution. Taken literally, the articles are merely expressions of the absurd contradictions of Maoist ideology pushed to the explosion point. To a large extent, however, the authors were consciously exploiting those contradictions. Li's article, originally a gigantic wall poster, was allowed to remain up in Canton a whole month because local officials could not be sure that this was not one more government-sponsored attack on 'capitalist roaders'; and when it was finally condemned and certain passages were singled out as 'especially reactionary', Li was able to show that they were exact quotations of Mao. (As a result of their writings, both Yang and Li have been sent to prison camps. The 70s is involved in an international campaign for their release, along with that of those arrested during the Tienanmen riot.)

Yu Shuet's 'Dust of Rationality' and the two pieces by Wu Man contain valuable information and insights, but in both writers there are points where the analyses become vague and ideological. For example, Wu criticizes Mao because he 'did not interpret Marxism through humanism in the endeavor to maintain its best qualities, but interpreted it as a tool for struggle with dialectics as the method". But Marx's dialectical method *is* often a useful tool for struggle. The problem lies in the appeal to an ideological *authority* implied by exegetical 'interpretation,' whether Maoist or 'humanist.' And Yu states that 'in the past, the leadership of revolution ignored the value of the individual'. But in the context of the present revolution this is beside the point; when people eliminate external power over them, it doesn't matter if someone 'ignores the value of the individual' — because he is not in a position to do anything about it. Of course it is natural that amidst the brutal reality of stalinism, where even the most modest human values may become so mutilated as to be conceived only as vague, distant ideals, people cling desperately to such ideals. As Wu notes, the 'alter of high ideals' found in the poems and stories of *Revelations that Move the Earth to Tears* 'is something which they have created to take temporary shelter (in). But as long as radical aspirations remains 'ideals' — spectacular, separate from and 'above life', expressed by an elite of artistic, ideological or religious specialists — this false dichotomy of 'real' and 'ideal' implicity supports the bureaucracy by giving it credit for some sort of 'realism'. Similarly, Yu's reference to 'rationality' is too ambiguous. If a vulgarized rationalism is taken up by the bureaucracy, this scarely masks the delirious irrationality at the heart of stalinism, the bureaucracy's need to falsify all aspects of life in order to cover up the big lie at its origin."

These writings, whatever the limitations within which the authors labour, are even more useful as a guide when examining the forthcoming rapproachment between China and the USA. We see in the analysis presented in these essays the seeds of what many Maoist Sinophiles in the Western world thought impossible, namely the striving to persue their common interests of the ruling groups in Peking and Washington.

Black Rose Books

INTRODUCTION
by
KAN SAN

1.   The Great Proletarian Cultural Revolution – Why is it called "cultural"?

Superficial observations only revealed brutal struggles, large scale rebellion, or a limited civil war in various places. Under the directive of Mao Tse-tung, Yao Wen-yuan published the essay "Criticizing the New Historical Play: The Dismissal of Hai Jui from Office" and this raised the curtain of the Great Proletarian Cultural Revolution. Yet the revolution should not be called "cultural". After the October Revolution the Soviet Union had not travelled on the road to socialism and had become an imperialistic power. Mao Tse-tung had to seek an explanation for this. Of course we ourselves would not think that the foundation for the realization of socialism has been laid if the means of production were nationalized under the leadership of a vanguard party. However, to a stern believer of Bolshevism like Mao Tse-tung, the revisionism of the Soviet Union was puzzling. Subsequently he came to the conclusion that the superstructure has brought about counter-effects to the economic base. Mao said, "We recognize that in the long course of historical development, the material determines the spiritual; social existence determines social consciousness; but we also recognize in turn the counter-effects of the spiritual on the material, social consciousness on social existence, and the superstructure on the economic base". This is to say Mao Tse-tung felt that although the capitalist class had been overthrown, their ideas and ideology were still greatly influencing the superstructure in the arena of theoretical formulation, academic research and artistic creation. According to Mao Tse-tung from 1949 to the outbreak of the Cultural Revolution it was the influence of capitalist consciousness on the cultural front that gave the centre stage to the emperor and his generals and political advisers, to the rich educated youth and his beauty. Such propagation of anti-socialist ideas was making preparations for capitalism to be restored. He further felt that if this problem was not resolved, China was likely to turn revisionist. Mao pointed out that the Hungarian Uprising erupted because the revisionist intellectuals of the Petofi Club had acted as the vanguard to bring about the restoration of capitalism.

In short, Mao Tse-tung ignited the Cultural Revolution because he wanted to resolve the problem of the residual capitalist ideas and consciousness having a counter-effect on the economic base. He wanted to carry out a revolution which would deeply affect the inner soul of mankind, and revolutionize the thoughts of the people so that China would steer clear from the path travelled by the Soviet Union.

Nevertheless, this endeavour of Mao Tse-tung has often been ignored because most so called "China experts" in the capitalist world would never ask the question as to how socialism might be achieved and how revisionism might be avoided. As for the genuine socialist-revolutionaries, they also often neglected this grand design of Mao Tse-tung. Mao was considered chief of the Chinese bureaucratic class and could therefore be written off simply as reactionary. To them Mao Tse-tung could have no ideals and was concerned only with his own power. What I would like to point out is that while it is accurate to identify Mao as the chief of the Chinese communist bureaucrats, however, it is because Mao is the most power-ful bureaucrat with nearly unlimited authority, that he fails to recognise himself to be a bureaucrat. Furthermore, his character and personality possesses a certain amount of romanticism and idealism which makes him disposed to oppose the bureaucratism of others.

It is my belief that unless we understand the aim of Mao Tse-tung in initiating the Cultural Revolution to be more than the resolution of his disputes with the Liu Shao-chi faction, unless we are aware that Mao Tse-tung was seeking to revolutionize the thoughts of the people, we would not be able to explain many of the seemingly incomprehensible occurrences in the Cultural Revolution.

2. A Real Revolution developed from a Sponsored Revolution

Before the Cultural Revolution, the power and influence of the Liu Shao-chi faction had been deeply entrenched, to the extent that, in the words of Mao Tse-tung – "no needle can pierce through; no water can seep through"! Mao, in addition to his control of the army through Lin Piao, commanded respect through his own authority but he possessed nothing else. Moreover, Mao ignited the revolution not purely for the sake of a power struggle. The move in fact embraced a highly idealistic overtone, and this explained why Mao had the courage to mobilise the masses to attack the bureaucrats of the Liu Shao-chi faction by means of "big Link-Up", big character posters and the slogan "attack with pens and defend with arms." At that time, although the people found their material well being slightly better under communist rule as compared to the days of Chiang Kai-shek, they nonetheless felt suppressed in many respects. The youth, in particular, were torn between the education of orthodox Marxism which conferred upon them high ideals on one hand, and their experience in reality which differed greatly from socialism which the Chinese communists preached to be in existence. But they could not see where the problem really lay. The bureaucrats enjoyed special privileges and received special attention. What the bureaucrats advocated was to join the party and become an official. What was prevailing, was elitism. The principle of "from the top to the bottom" ruled and the masses were reduced to small pawns on a chess board and screws in a megamachine, completely obedient to the top leadership. Hence when Mao Tse-tung mobilised the masses to struggle against the Liu Shao-chi faction, they responded most enthusiastically. It is because the masses, tired of bureaucratic rule, naively believed that it was the Liu faction to whom all problems could be traced. They became a formidable force and the Liu faction was completely toppled.

During the course of struggle against the Liu Shao-chi faction, the masses realised their own strength. The bureaucrats, once posited high above, revealed their impotence and cowardice in front of the people. When the masses smashed the governmental machine, they discovered that each individual had a secret file in which a comment made by the bureaucrats would predetermine that individual's whole life. For the sake of the struggle against the Liu faction bureaucrats, the Red Guards went everywhere to link up with one another and organised themselves. Their power of analysis was greatly improved as a result.

After the Liu Shao-chi faction had been crushed, Mao felt that the major problem had been solved, the only remaining one being the reconstruction of peace and order. But most of the masses felt that even though the Liu faction was overthrown, the problem had not been solved. Some who were thoughtful and sensitive, having acquired a better understanding of the bureaucratic system from their struggle against the bureaucrats, persisted to the end. Some were also beginning to cast away the control exerted by Mao Tse-tung's thought, and did what they thought ought to be done. The Shanghai Radio Station broadcast the warning that the rebels must not seize power from the Party, saying: "Some thought-confusing members of our group said, 'Without the Party's leadership, we still managed to achieve for ourselves victory in the January Revolutionary struggle for power. Seize power again in the same way and use it well."

Mao Tse-tung, seeing that the masses were gradually going out of his control, panicked. The more thoughtful Red Guards in particular, by means of link-ups exchanged revolutionary experiences with their counter-parts in other provinces and gradually formulated their own framework of analysis, most notably in the article "Whither China?" by Sheng Wu-lien. They pointed out that the only prospect for the Chinese Revolution was forming the Chinese People's Commune to be modelled after the Paris Commune 1871. For this goal to be achieved, they thought that the precondition was to smash the entire state machinery and the entire bureaucratic system. Ultra-left ideas thus germinated and flourished and groups like the Northern Star Study Society and Kung Shan Tung were established, causing Mao to feel the more uneasy. Furthermore, the outbreak of the Wuhan Mutiny by the military to oppose the masses' seizure of their power further compelled Mao Tse-tung to decide on the suppression of the Red Guards. Through the military, Mao forced the masses to surrender their weapons to join the Revolutionary Committee of the Old, Middle-aged, and the Young, with the Army, Cadres and the Masses, so as to restore bureaucratic rule and to force the masses to surrender their arms seized from the military. He further launched the "Up the Mountain and Down the countryside" campaign, driving the youths up the mountain and down the countryside, preventing the Red Guards from getting together to discuss and learn how to rebel and how to attain genuine socialism. The masses' consciousness and ideas had not yet developed to maturity and they had not been aware of Mao's trickery. This real revolution, developed from the sponsored one was crushed before it could make great strides. The revolution is dead; long live the revolution! The failure was to pave way for the new total revolt.

3. The Development of Ultra-left Ideas

The Revolution failed. The masses, still puzzling over the crux of the problem, had however not yet given up and were eager to clarify it themselves. They pursued their learning more enthusiastically than before. The youths who were to be sent to the countryside all rushed to the bookshops to buy themselves all the relevant reading materials they were preparing to read in the countryside, so that before the mass migration took place, the writings of Marx, Engels, Lenin, Stalin and Mao were sold out. Although the tumultuous mass movement was suppressed, the Cultural Revolution had not yet ended. On one hand, the Cultural Revolution had had an important effect on the superstructure, including literature, education, scientific research, political organisation, and had negated a great part of the establishment — but all these had yet to be reconstructed. Controversies over questions such as the method of production, enterprise management etc. had also not been solved. On the other hand, the conservative faction of the bureaucrats had reorganised their strength and demanded a restoration of the old order of the days before the Cultural Revolution. They thus tried to seize power from the newly instated bureaucrats, causing the contradiction to be deepened and become evident. The disclosure of the Lin Piao affair, the anti-Lin, anti-Confucius campaign, the criticize Water Margin Movement, and the reemergence of certain of the disgraced bureaucrats rendered the vision of the masses clear, enabling them to understand that the Cultural Revolution was yet another trick played by Mao to fool the people. The masses began consciously to boycott the instructions imposed by the bureaucrats. For example, in the field of production, their lack of enthusiasm for work lowered production greatly, and their sabotage further prevented the production target from being reached, tightening the supply of commodities. In the fields of arts and literature, education and scientific research, because of the boycott by the masses, non-cooperation of the old bureaucrats, and the incompetence of the Gang of Four and their followers, Mao's already ridiculously inappropriate policies were to become even more farcical. In the field of arts and literature, only some ten scripts of model operas were accomplished, and all literary works were repeating the same theme and their characterisations were very much the same. The standard of education declined rapidly: those who accused the teachers were hailed as the model of the people, and those who submitted blank answer sheets in examination, heroes. The intensification of all these contradictions made the pursuit of the answer to "Whither China?" all the more urgent.

The above article "Whither China?" by Sheng Wu-lien firstly pointed out that China should head towards the goal of the Chinese Peoples Commune. The way to attain the goal was by means of overthrowing the rule of the new bureaucratic capitalist class through violence to solve the question of political power. It is indeed utopian to neither talk about the seizure of power nor entirely smash the old state machine, but just cry the empty slogan of realising the May 5th directive. The red capitalist class had become a corrupt class hindering the progress of history; their relationship with the masses had changed from that of the leader and the led to the ruler and the ruled, and the exploiter and the exploited, from a relationship based on equality in the course of revolution to that of the oppressor and the oppressed. This class must be overthrown if the Chinese Peoples. Commune were to be realised. The article provoked tremendous response and sparked off further analysis of the essence of the rule of the Chinese communists. The Li I-che poster once again proved with examples the emergence of the new class in China. The essence of the new bourgeois mode of production is "changing the public into private". When the leader of the state or an enterprise redistributes the properties and power of the proletariat in a bourgeois manner, he is in fact practising the new bourgeois private possession of these properties and powers. What has been commonly observed is that some leaders have allowed themselves, their familes, kinfolk and friends special political and economic privileges, even going so far as to swap amongst themselves and push their children into political and economic positions through back door channels. Once the Li I-che poster was pasted up, the people of Canton enthusiastically copied the whole text, and its influence extended more and more. When the Tienanmen Incident erupted, the Chinese Peoples' understanding of the bureaucrats was pushed to the peak, well demonstrated by their words: "China is no longer the China of yore, and the people are no longer wrapped in sheer ignorance. Gone for good is Shih Huang-ti's feudal society!" The Chinese communists mobilised the militiamen to execute the bloody suppression of the masses. After the Tienanmen Incident, the era of Mao Tse-tung finally retreated from the stage of history. The intense infuriation of the masses indirectly led to the rapid downfall of the Gang of

Four and finally managed to force the bureaucrats to stop labelling the Tienanmen Incident as counter-revolutionary. The masses once again became the major determinant of China's politics.

4.   The Lessons of the Cultural Revolution

The richest heritage of the Cultural Revolution was the realisation by the masses of the greatness of their own strength. The head of the State who had been regarded as immaculate as well as many of the leading cadres had fallen within a very short time. The idea that leaders were indispensible was negated. In the past everything had been done as instructed by the leaders as if the absence of leaders would lead to the collapse of the sky. The experience of the Cultural Revolution however convinced the masses that without the directions from above and with the masses themselves managing, planning and executing all administration, steel continued to be produced and the trains were punctual in arrival and departure. Production improved both qualitatively and quantitatively. When the workers controlled and managed production on their own, their commitment to work increased for they not only knew how to produce, but also comprehended what it was they were working for. Work ceased to be alienating and the working morale rose tremendously. The dullness of the past had given way to a situation swelling with life and burning with warmth. The people seemed to have realised in this very moment the meaning of life, the truth of revolution, the prospect of China and the future of mankind.

There were, admittedly, a few who had felt uneasy in the face of such great freedom. But they too looked back to those days of freedom with nostalgia and felt infuriated and disgusted with the existing political conditions. They witnessed the process through which the State Chairman Liu Shao-chi became "a traitor and a spy"; the constitutional successor to the Party and the State, Lin Piao, became a "traitor, a man with ambition and a conspirator" who died without a grave; an unknown young man became the vice-chairman of the Party and was then denounced as "a new born capitalist"; Mao's wife, "student and comrade", Chiang Ching, was condemned as a monster and likened to Wu Ji-tien. The struggle among the bureaucrats disclosed their corruptibility and rendered the People's vision clear, making them realise that "there had never been any saviour, god or emperors to give them happiness and that the happiness of mankind had to be created by man himself." To avoid being fooled again by the bureaucrats, to be freed from the bureaucrats and from the need of morning prayers, evening penitences, the loyalty dance, and the constant threat of struggles and criticisms, the people have to rely on their own strength all the more for the smashing up of the entire bureaucratic system.

The shift of Mao's attitude from making beautiful promises to mobilise the masses in the beginning of the Cultural Revolution, to suddenly proposing "Revolutionary committees are fine!" to deceive the masses into discarding the demand for the establishment of the Chinese Peoples' Commune, and then finally utilising the army to execute the brutal suppression of the masses . . . taught the People an old yet still new lesson: the ruling class would never retreat from the stage of history voluntarily. Without force and violence, they would never be overthrown. To be kindhearted and lenient towards the bureaucrats would only result in being slaughtered by them in the end, and to compromise with the bureaucrats was analogous to offering the bandits weapons. The generation baptised by the Cultural Revolution will be the initiator and backbone of the forthcoming socialist revolution in China.

5.   Conclusion

The Chinese communists recently announced that "the Great Proletarian Cultural Revolution has been concluded by the victorious crushing of the Gang of Four". The real meaning of this is — Mao Tse-tung is dead; the Gang of Four are arrested, and the Chinese bureaucrats no longer have conflicting opinions on the restoration of the old order of society before the Cultural Revolution. All bureaucrats who have lost their positions during the Cultural Revolution have been restored to positions of power, and are ready to avenge the activists of the Cultural Revolution. Does this mean anything but that the Cultural Revolution marked for its anti-bureaucratic overtone has ended? For the rebels of the Cultural Revolution, the Cultural Revolution had failed long ago. Now, it only means that they can no longer make use of the contradictions among the bureaucrats as they have done in the past few years.

On the face of it thus Mao's attempt to initiate the Cultural Revolution in order that China will not become like the Soviet Union has failed, for the Hua-Teng policies now implemented have totally negated this attempt of Mao. Mao's failure however was to be expected and unavoidable. Although Mao Tse-tung was capable of grasping the idea that the superstructure would and could have significant influences on the economic base, influences which if not seriously attended to, would ultimately lead to revisionism, nevertheless as head of the bureaucrats, and deeply imbued with bureaucratic ideas, Mao could not understand that the maintenance of the bureaucratic system itself was the prime factor contributing to revisionism and imperialism. During the course of the Cultural Revolution, Mao had tried hard to maintain the bureaucratic system, as demonstrated by his saying that "Revolutionary committees are fine" and by his insistence on the practice of giving orders to be followed – even to the extent that "those understood by the people must be executed and those not understood must also be executed." How then could the revolution he sought develop from the inner soul of the people? How then could China be saved from travelling the tragic road of the Soviet Union? The failure of the Cultural Revolution is no accident.

But Mao Tse-tung had nonetheless unexpectedly educated the generation of the Cultural Revolution. His repeatedly reactionary measures helped to generate the awareness of the people and they now have found the way for the Chinese revolution. Mao's own practice in the Cultural Revolution destroyed his faked revolutionary image and finally led to his fading out from the stage of history. From now on, no bureaucrat will be able to bring forth theories like the "thoughts of Mao Tse-tung" to fool the masses. The Chinese People have got rid of the chains previously restricting their thoughts and the ideas of the "Ultra-left" can develop in the absence of mystifying fog. The bureaucrats have lost their weapon of ideological control on the Peoples' consciousness.

What the Hua-Teng bureaucrats have proposed are merely the policies and practices rejected by the people during the Cultural Revolution. How then could they get accepted by and satisfy the people aspiring to genuine socialism? It is not a simple process for people who are aware to turn to action. But how long will it take for this process to be accomplished? This can come about only when the "Ultra-left" thoughts and ideas become further spread out and when there are other changes in the political situation in China. As we live outside China, we are unable to contribute much to the two areas mentioned above. On the other hand, the Chinese Revolution is an integral part of the world revolution, and if there is a genuine socialist revolutionary upsurge in any part of the world, it will inevitably affect China in a substantial way. For this reason, I have come to exchange ideas and experiences with you and hopefully this will contribute to the development of the world revolution in a small way, which will then act as a catalyst to the socialist revolution in China. Then will be the day when the aim of "liberation of myself through the liberation of mankind" is attained.

**SECTION
ONE**

THE GREAT PROLETARIAN CULTURAL REVOLUTION
AND
THE REVERSAL
OF
WORKERS' POWER
IN CHINA

In 1962 the Chinese Communist Party openly attacked the Soviet line, and the Communist parties of almost every country split. In the United States the old Communist Party had followed the Soviet position; the group which split from it, Progressive Labor, supported the Chinese position. Initially, Progressive Labor was composed of young people who had been in the Communist Party, but by April 1965, when it formed itself as the Progressive Labor Party, it had won over many students and other youth.

In its 1964 Constitution, Progressive Labor resolved

"to build a revolutionary organisation with the participation and support of millions of working men and women as well as those students, artists and intellectuals who will join with the working class to end the profit system . . . . We will build a socialist U.S.A., with all power in the hands of the working people and their allies."

Progressive Labor leader Milt Rosen wrote in Progressive Labor (May-June 1965):

"Only by destroying the political power of a small greedy ruling class, can our people achieve their aspirations. By travelling the road to revolution we will learn the strategy and tactics necessary to transfer political power to those who build and create the wealth and genius of our country . . . . . The perspective of the ruling class, for oppression, war, and cultural and moral decay, is totally at odds with the aspirations of the world's people. The people will win."

To achieve the people's victory, Progressive Labor based its Party on the Leninist principles of vanguardism and democratic centralism. Progressive Labor also systematically infiltrated into the mass student organisation, Students for a Democratic Society (SDS), which eventually led to the famous

5

split in Summer 1969 of SDS into the Weatherman, Revolutionary Youth Movement 1, Revolutionary Youth Movement 2 and a SDS controlled by Progressive Labor.

Progressive Labor openly admired the Thoughts of Mao Tse-tung. One of them, reflecting the organisation's thinking, explained: "PL is accused of being Maoist and that is true, but we don't want to tail after the Chinese like the CPs tailed after the Soviet Union. We look to the Chinese for illumination. Our aim is to develop a truly American, not a Chinese Communist movement."

It was apparent that Progressive Labor for some time did maintain fraternal relationship with the Chinese Communist Party. Some former Red Guards from Canton reported that they had seen copies of Challenge, the newspaper of Progressive Labor Party, during the heyday of the Cultural Revolution.

However, the Chinese ceased to be illuminating to the Progressive Labor by 1971 when Progressive Labor came out openly condemning the betrayal of the Great Proletarian Cultural Revolution by Mao Tse-tung as well as the counter-revolutionary nature of China's foreign policies in supporting the reactionary governments of Pakistan, Ceylon, etc.

The general line of the Progressive Labor Party is explained in the publication "Road to Revolution III".

The Great Proletarian Cultural Revolution and the Reversal of Workers' Power in China originally appeared in the November 1971 issue of PL magazine, the official organ of Progressive Labor.

The accepted view among Marxist-Leninists is that the Great Proletarian Cultural Revolution (GPCR) was a struggle of the masses, led by Chairman Mao, to defeat the bourgeois, rightists within the Party and thereby prevent their influence from growing to the point where they could reverse the proletarian dictatorship. The "16-point" *Decision of the Central Committee of the Chinese Communist Party (CCP) Concerning the GPCR* (Aug. 8, 1966) defines the struggle in this way:

"Although the bourgeoisie has been overthrown, it is still trying to use the old ideas, culture, customs and habits of the exploiting classes to corrupt the masses, capture their minds and endeavour to stage a come-back. The proletariat must do just the opposite: it must meet head-on every challenge of the bourgeoisie in the ideological field and use the new ideas, culture, customs and habits of the proletariat to change the mental outlook of the whole of society. At present, our objective is to struggle against and crush those persons in authority who are taking the capitalist road, to criticize and repudiate the reactionary bourgeois academic "authorities" and the ideology of the bourgeoisie and all other exploiting classes and to transform education, literature and art and all other parts of the superstructure that do not correspond to the socialist economic base, so as to facilitate the consolidation and development of the socialist system."

The basic assumption is that the GPCR takes place under conditions of proletarian dictatorship, i.e. that the working class holds state power and has successfully carried through the socialist transformation of the material base. A Red Flag editorial of Feb., 1967 made the goals more concrete and defined the enemy:

"Proletarian revolutionaries are uniting to seize power from the handful of persons within the party who are in authority and taking the capitalist road .... Adequate attention must be paid to the role of revolutionary cadres in the struggle to seize power....They can become the backbone of the struggle to seize power and can become leaders in this struggle....A clear distinction must be drawn between those in authority who belong to the proletariat and those who belong to the bourgeoisie....

The overwhelming majority of the ordinary cadres in the Party and government organizations, enterprises and undertakings are good and want to make revolution."

The official documents of the GPCR state that 95% of the cadre are revolutionary, that only a "small handful of capitalist-roaders" have "wormed their way" into the party and that even leading cadres who have made serious mistakes can be re-educated by the masses and allowed to remain in their posts. Thus the GPCR is seen as a struggle between the Left, led by the proletarian headquarters of Mao, Lin Piao, Chou En-lai et. al. and the Right, led by the "black gang": Liu Shao-Ch'i, Teng Hsiao-p'ing, P'eng Chen and T'ao Chu. Victory went to the Left preserving and consolidating socialism in China.

But this picture is confused by a third force on the scene. Mao and official CCP statements refer often to "extreme-leftists" who attack *all* the leading cadre, engage in "bitter armed struggle," deny that the People's Liberation Army (PLA) is a supporter of the Left, despise Chou En-lai and the other bureaucrats of the State Council and launch indiscriminate attacks against China's nationalist allies. What do we know about this "extreme-Left" and what was its program?

Many of the large mass organizations of students and workers formed to overthrow the "capitalist-roaders" espoused "extreme-Leftist" views. In Hunan province, the "Sheng-Wu-Lien," a coalition of 20 Red Guard and rebel-worker groups, claimed 2 to 3 million followers. In Kwangsi, the "April 22 Rebel Grand Army" was one of the two largest mass organizations and came repeatedly into conflict with the PLA and the Central Authorities. In Peking, "extreme-Leftists" were strong in the Red Guard Congresses of Tsinghua and other universities. In Canton, the "Red Flag" was an "extreme-Leftists" group which was for a time the largest organization in the city and the major antagonist of the Military Region Command which ruled the city. Another important "extreme-Leftist" group was the "Red Guard Army," known in Canton as the "August 1 Combat Corps," which was made up of de-mobilized veterans of the PLA and several times resisted orders to disband. Similar organizations existed in Honan, Hopeh, Szechuan, Shanghai and all the major urban areas. The consensus of Red Guard sources and western scholars who have studied the question is that somewhere from *30-40 million* people followed these organizations.

Moreover, these local organizations, based in factories, schools, cities and regions, began to develop an extensive network of connections. Red Guards travelled frequently to congresses where experiences and ideas were exchanged; liaison stations were established in many cities by important local groups, e.g., the Chingkangshang Rebel Red Guard group of Peking University had representatives in Canton, Wuhan and Shanghai. These congresses and stations were the beginning of a movement toward political and ideological unification of the "extreme-Left" which proceeded rapidly until smashed by the government and Army between Sept. 1967 and July 1968.

These facts make it clear that we are dealing here with a polictical movement quite different from the isolated sectarian groups whom Lenin had attacked as "ultra-

7

Left" after World War 1. This is a mass movement which frequently put forward positions in contradiction to Mao/Lin/Chou and came into sharp conflict with the PLA under their leadership.

An article in a Shanghai periodical in late July 1947 characterized the politics of the "extreme-Left" in this way:

"Recently, a sort of so-called 'new trend of thought' prevails in society. Its principal content is to distort the major contradiction of socialist society into one between the so-called 'power-holders,' i.e., the 'privileged persons' who hold 'property and power' and the masses of the people. It demands an incessant 'redistribution' of the social property and political power under the proletarian dictatorship. The new trend of thought has equated the current GPCR with a conflict for wealth and power 'within a reactionary ruling class.' It has equated the headquarters of Mao/Lin with that of Liu/Teng/T'ao. It has branded all leading cadres as privileged persons and thrust them all into the position of objects of revolution." (*CNS*, No. 188)

The "extreme-Left" held that China was already in the hands of a *bourgeois ruling class* at the time the GPCR began, that the vast majority (90%) of the leading cadres were part of that oppressor class, that the PLA was its tool to smash the real Left and maintain power, that the new "red" bourgeoisie had emerged during the 17 years from 1949-66 from the ranks of the revolutionaries themselves and, therefore, that the GPCR was not, as Mao said, a struggle to consolidate proletarian rule, but *the first revolution in history to attempt to take power back from the revisionists.* The basic analysis led the "extreme-Left" groups to carry out the following political campaigns.

1) They demanded the ouster of Chou En-lai as the chief representative of China's "red" capitalists, along with the high-ranking economic and administrative ministers he was sheltering.

2) They demanded that the GPCR be carried into the Army Officer Corps, which they saw as a part of the new ruling class. They engaged in arms seizures from the PLA, raiding depots and arms trains, on the principle that a revolution to overthrow the bourgeoisie had to be an armed struggle of the masses.

3) They looked to the Paris Commune as the model of the institutions of the proletarian state and fought to establish the commune-type of state throughout China (abolition of the standing army, worker's wages for officials, election and right of recall of all officials).

4) They opposed China's foreign policies of alliance with secondary imperialists (France, etc.) and bourgeois nationalist regimes (Indonesia, Pakistan, etc.) To carry this through they seized foreign ships in the harbors, burned the British consulate in Aug. 1967, launched a liberation struggle in Hong Kong, seized Soviet arms going to Vietnam over China's railroad lines and opposed China's nuclear development program.

5) They began to discuss and implement the formation of a new Marxist-Leninist Communist party, given their assumption that the CCP had become the party of the bourgeois apparatus which was restoring capitalism under the ideological cover of Marxism-Leninism.

The "extreme-Left" presented a view of what was going on in the GPCR which was contradictory to the official views of the CCP under Mao. ("95% of the cadres are good" vs "90% of the cadres must step aside"). If their analysis of the political situation in China was correct, if China was at that time ruled by a "red" bourgeoisie, then the "extreme-Left" is, in fact, the *Left* and Mao and his allies are the principal section of the "red bourgeoisie." The attack on Liu Shao-ch'i and a tiny minority of high officials was therefore a struggle *within* this bourgeois class between those who wanted to develop China through dependence on the Soviet Union and those who wanted an independent path. Mao and Lin Piao attempted to mobilize the masses to their side by appropriating many of the ideas and slogans of the Left and presenting them in watered-down versions. We are not arguing that this was, in every case, a *conscious* process of deception; but that the ideology of new-democracy/Mao-Tse-tung Thought *objectively* led the proletarian and peasant masses into an alliance with a part of the bourgeoisie (the 95% of "good cadres"), allowing this part to consolidate its power at the expense of the masses and sacrificing only an especially discredited group of officials as scapegoats.

It is necessary, therefore to make an objective historical analysis of the development of socialism in China, in order to determine whether position of the "extreme-Left" in GPCR was correct.

Throughout the period of revolutionary struggle in the countryside, (1927-1949) the line of the CCP contained two contradictory aspects: on the one hand there was a "poor-peasant" *class struggle* line directed against both the landlords and the capitalist rich-peasants and calling for collective forms of landholding; on the other hand, there was a "rich-peasant" new-democratic *class collaborationist* line directed solely against the most important landlords and the Japanese imperialists and advocating partial reliance on local capitalists. These two lines were in constant struggle, giving CCP policy and practice a vacillating and inconsistent character. The class-struggle aspect was primary during the period of civil war against the Kuomintang (1946-1949) and led to victory and proletarian dictatorship. But the new-democratic line became primary right after the seizure of power.

This new-democratic political line anticipated a transition period during which capitalism was to be allowed to develop further, although under close regulation, so as to create the material and ideological conditions for making the transition to socialism gradually and without further armed struggle. The CCP had promised the people immediate benefits from the elimination of the landlords and the imperialists and the opening up of new opportunities for individual and collective enrichment. On the eve of victory, Mao defined the party's tasks:

"If we know nothing about production and do not master it quickly, if we cannot restore and develop production as speedily as possible and achieve solid successes so that the livelihood of the workers, first of all, and that of the people in general is improved, we shall be unable to sustain our political power, we shall be unable to stand on our feet, we shall fail ....

In this period, all capitalist elements in the cities and countryside which are not harmful but beneficial to the national economy should be allowed to exist and expand... But the existence and expansion of capitalism in China will be restricted from several directions ..... Restriction versus opposition to restriction will be the main form of class struggle in the new-democratic state." (Report to 2nd Plenum of 7th Central Committee (CC).)

There was only one way to bring about an immediate restoration and growth of the national economy: rely on the former ruling class which had learned the methods and skills required to keep the economy functioning. This meant, in particular, enlisting into the service of the new state the large body of technicians, managers, engineers, government administrators and intellectuals who had served the old regime. According to

An Tzu-Wen (*NCNA*, Sept. 30, 1952), the cadre force had quadrupled between '49-'52, from 720,000 to 2,750,000. The bulk of these were the so-called "retained cadres," capitalist managers and ex-Kuomintang civil servants. Some were peasants and workers who had distinguished themselves in various political campaigns, especially the land reform; but the CCP was mistrustful of the many rural activists who had tendencies during land reform to commit "Leftist" errors, meaning that they had carried expropriation into the ranks of the rich peasants, whom Mao wished to preserve as a source of increased production. Another group consisted of recent graduates of colleges and special cadre training schools.

The ideological commitment of the bulk of cadres was thus not to socialism, as a system of social relations among men, but to national economic development, which they would tend, as a result of class background and education, to conceive in capitalist terms. The CCP tried to counter this situation by intensive political education of the new cadres and mass campaigns in which the workers were encouraged to criticize all elements of personal corruption, bureaucratic style of work, etc. that they found in the cadres. But these steps could not in any short period alter the basic ideological orientation of the bulk of the new cadres.

Moreover, many of the cadres were taken into the party, in order to subject them to its discipline and facilitate their ideological re-molding. Party membership rose from 3,000,000 in mid-1948 to 5,800,000 in mid-1951. (Official CCP figures in Schurmann, p. 129.) It was inevitable, given the new-democratic line, that the CCP would attract many whose primary commitment was not to socialism but to the protection and advancement of the interests of the bourgeoisie. The repeated anti-Rightist struggles of the next decade (1954-55, 1957, 1959) testify to the existence of this element within the Party.

The "retained" cadres, as well as the newly trained college graduates, were paid the wages which they were accustomed to receiving. Given their primarily bourgeois orientation, only material reward commensurate with the privileged position of managers and administrators within capitalist society would induce them to serve the new state power. This created a contradiction with the system under which the Communist cadres had lived before liberation, the so-called "supply-system." All cadres, whatever their responsibilities and positions, from the rank-and-file on up to top leadership were provided with the basic necessities of life in kind, plus a little pocket money for incidentals. This created an egalitarian and democratic style of work. It was a concrete application of the communist principle of distribution: "From each according to his ability, to each according to his need." Those who were committed to serving the people by destroying the system of exploitation and creating a new system of socialism should be willing to do the work they were capable of without special material reward. This corresponded to the lesson Marx, Engels and Lenin had drawn from the experience of the Paris Commune: that a fundamental principle of proletarian dictatorship must be that *work for the state be performed at average workers' wages.*

After Liberation, the supply-system for Communist cadres contradicted the wage system under which new cadres were paid, a wage system which necessarily contained large differentials between high and low levels, it being a basic idea of bourgeois society that the mental work of administration and management is superior to manual work and ought to be rewarded correspondingly. The CCP leadership then made the choice to eliminate the supply-system and bring all the cadre, both Party and non-Party, both pre-Liberation and post-Liberation, under a unified wage-grade system. This was completed by a State Council Order of Aug, 31, 1955:

"for the purpose of putting into effect the principle of to each according to his work' and 'equal pay for equal work,' the supply system now applicable to a section of government employees is to be changed into a wage system as from July 1955 in order to unify the system of pay and allowance for governmental employees and facilitate the building of socialism." *(NCNA,* Sept. 14, 1955. Transl. in SCMP, 1134, 1. 12)

At the same time, the cadre wage system was consolidated into a 30-grade scale with the following monthly wages: (from Barnett, p. 191)

REPRESENTATIVE POSITION	GRADE	WAGE (in Yuan/mo.)
Premier, Head of State, etc.	1	600
Deputy Premier, CC member, etc.	2-5	400-500
Central Minister	6	400
Bureau Chief (Central)	9-12	200-250
Division Chief (Central)	13-15	150-200
County-level Magistrate	13-15	130-160
Section Chief (Central)	16-17	100-135
County-level section member	18-23	50-90
Clerical staff	24-27	30-45
General Service personnel	28-30	23-29

For purposes of comparison, here are some representative wage figures for workers and managers: (from Chao Kuo-chun, Vol. 2, p. 73-74 – figures for 1956)

Plant Director – 263, Chief Engineer – 223, Chief Designer – 135, Engineer – 118-191, Technician – 103-166, Chief Accountant – 74-126, Bookkeeper – 45-78, File Clerk – 41-66, Worker in heavy industry – 69-106, Worker in light industry – 56, Worker in construction – 31-51, mis. worker – 23-34. At the same period peasant incomes ran about 8-15.

It is clear from these highly-differentiated wage scales that the principle of the Paris Commune was not being applied. The payments were thought to reflect correctly the principle of distribution under the first stage of socialism – 'to each according to his work.' The official editorials explaining the change presented the following view:

"The supply system was a system of treatment of government employees adopted at a time of the revolutionary war when the financial and economic situation was rather acute. It was built on the premise that the revolutionary workers possessed a high degree of political consciousness. Its special features were: On the basis of the minimum subsistence requirements of revolutionary workers, the state was to supply them with a definite quantity of the essential articles of livelihood ... There was thus little difference between the treatment accorded to cadres at higher levels and the general rank-and-file government workers, insofar as their personal requirements were concerned. It may be described as a measure in keeping with the military communist way of life.

If the supply system has played an important role in ensuring the final victory of the revolution, why should it be replaced now in its entirety by the wage system? ... This is because the supply system is contradictory to the principles of 'to each according to his work' and 'equal pay for equal work.' (Tu Shao-po & Wang I-cheng

11

in Shih Shih Shou Ts'e, Sept. 25, 1955. Transl. in *ECMM*, no. 19, p. 27)

... He who performs better labor and does better work gets a better pay and equal work will earn equal pay. In this way, one can be caused to interest himself, from the standpoint of material interests, in the results of his labor and to link up his personal interests with the overall interest of the state ... " (*Renmin Ribao*, Sept. 14, 1955. Transl. in *SCMP*, no. 1134, p. 13)

The CCP leadership thus saw the supply-system not as a desirable application of the communist principle of distribution but as an expedient adaptation to the conditions of extreme material deprivation which prevailed before Liberation. The coming of socialism, with greater abundance of products, would eliminate the necessity for this kind of egalitarian sharing of difficulties. In this view, Socialism, the first stage in the development of the new society, is separated from communism by a long period of development of the productive forces. Only when there is general abundance, the ability to satisfy the material needs of all the people, could the transition to communism begin. During the first stage, material incentive still played a powerful role, along with other aspects of bourgeois thinking, and had to be harnessed to the needs of socialist development. The supply-system was therefore "utopian" and a violation of the stage-by-stage development toward communism.

The opposing argument was put forward by Left forces during the Great Leap (1958) and again during the GPCR. It acknowledged that distribution according to need for the whole population and for all products could only be introduced gradually but saw the *ideological consciousness of the masses,* not the level of development of the material forces of production, as the main limitation on the rapidity of transition to communism. To the extent that people were won to the idea of "serve the people," as against bourgeois individualism, communism could be introduced in part, even if at a lower level of *shared* subsistence than would be possible with the further development of the economy. In particular, the Party members, as the ideological *vanguard* of the working class, and especially the Party *leaders* should be willing to apply communist distribution to themselves even if the masses as a whole continued to cling, in part, to material incentive.

It was, in fact, the bourgeois road that prevailed. Rather than winning the bourgeois intellectuals to communism, the Party was won to material incentive. This was a consequence of the new-democratic line. Having taken power without a mass force of workers and peasants won ideologically to communism and having committed itself to satisfying the immediate material aspirations of the masses, the party had to rely on the bourgeois technicians to manage affairs of state and economy. If the masses had been won to a greater degree to socialism, a totally different course would have been possible — the creation of new organs of power and administration putting management directly into the hands of the people, under the leadership of the party. This might have meant, temporarily, more "disorder" and stagnation of production as the people learned to fashion and run these new socialist forms, but it would have avoided reliance on bourgeois forces and ideas and eventual reversal of the revolution. Moreover, the new-democratic line welcomed into the Party, during the anti-Japanese War, many forces whose primary commitment was to nationalism and bourgeois land reform. These forces within the Party were strong enough to bring about the elimination of the supply-system and the merging of Party cadres into the privileged stratum of officials. The new wage-grade system provided a framework of material privilege within which a new bourgeoisie could slowly form and become conscious of its class interest in opposition to further development toward communism.

THE QUESTION OF A STANDING ARMY

In summarizing the lessons of the Paris Commune, Marx had pointed also to its abolition of the standing army and replacement by the *arming of the workers,* the proletarian militia. In the third of his *Letters From Afar* (March 11, 1917) Lenin had expanded:

> We need a state, but not the kind the bourgeoisie needs, with organs of government in the shape of a police force, an army and a bureaucracy (officialdom) separate from and opposed to the people. All bourgeois revolutions merely perfected *this* state machine, merely transferred it from the hands of one party to those of another.
>
> The proletariat on the other hand . . . . must "smash," to use Marx's expression, this "ready-made" state machine and substitute a new one for it by *merging* the police force, the army and the bureaucracy with *the entire armed people* . . . the proletariat must organize and arm *all* the poor, exploited sections of the population in order that they *themselves* should take the organs of state power directly into their own hands, in order that *they themselves should constitute* these organs of state power." (*Coll. Works,* Vol. 23, pp. 325-326)

The Chinese revolution was made by armed masses of workers and peasants. After victory was achieved, the decision was made to *disarm* the masses and concentrate weapons in the hands of a standing army which lived in barracks separate from the masses. At the same time there began an intensive program of modernization, both technical and administrative, of the PLA which put increased emphasis on knowledge of military science, on sophisticated weaponry and on professionalism. All of these developments led, in the early 1950s, to significant moves away from the democratic-egalitarian traditions of the PLA. They culminated in the State Council order of Feb. 1955 setting up a system of ranks within the PLA and eliminating the supply-system for military service personnel. This was followed in October by the conferring of the title of Marshal on the ten top leaders of the PLA, the wearing of shoulder badges and insignia showing rank, and the creation and award of several types of military decorations. A *Renmin Ribao* editorial of Sept. 28, 1955 gave arguments for the new rank system:

> "Why must the PLA adopt the system of military ranks at present? This is because with the application of the Military Service Law (conscription), the modern equipment of the armed forces requires that the training and activities of the servicemen should follow strict systems and regulations. The ranking and inter-relation of the officers should be clearly defined, and the organization and discipline of the armed forces should be consolidated . . . . all officers must wear shoulder badges and insignias of their ranks so that there will be clear distinction between officers and other ranks, between the various branches of the armed forces . . . . Only in this way would the units of the armed forces be able to carry out successfully their task of defending the country in a changing situation and under the new conditions of complex equipment, speed of movement and joint action of the different branches.
>
> After the adoption of the military ranks, there will be clear distinction between the

officers and the men . . . . Will this affect the close unity of the officers and the men and of the officers of the upper and lower ranks? The answer is no . . . . There is no clash of class interests between the officers and the men . . . . their interests being the same. The officers and the men would struggle together to defend the country, protect the interests of the people, and safe-guard the cause of Socialism. Therefore the holding of military ranks . . . . implies that the officers are entrusted with an even greater responsibility and should be even more concerned with the men and take better care of them . . . . The military ranking system will also ensure the quality of officers as required by national defense. The modern revolutionary fighting forces require of the officers not only their loyalty to the country and the people . . . . but also accomplishment in the knowledge of military science as well as proficiency in modern military techniques . . . . The conferment of titles is determined on the basis of responsibility, political qualities, abilities, terms of service and contribution to the revolution." (Trans. in SCMP, no. 1147, pp. 3-5)

The new system of ranks also included a wage scale for payment of men and officers, extending the principle "to each according to his work" to the people's army. Our best information on these wages comes from Edgar Snow who visited an army camp in his trip of 1961-62 and was given the following pay figures (*The Other Side of the River*, p. 289. These figures are in \$U.S./month. Snow calculated the monetary exchange himself)

Private	− 2.50	Lt. Colonel	− 51-60
Corporal	− 4.	Colonel	− 62-64
2nd Lt.	− 20.	Senior Col.	− 74-84
1st Lt.	− 24.	Lt. General	− 144-160
Captain	− 29-33	General	− 192-236
Major	− 39-44	Marshal	− 360-400

Why was the principle of the proletarian militia not carried through? In the first place, it requires a high level of ideological commitment of the masses to the long-term goal of the party − communism. Only if that ideological understanding exists will the Party feel that it can rely on the masses to defeat the class enemy during the sharp class struggle which continues under proletarian dictatorship. If, as in the case of the CCP, the Party has won the support of the masses by leading a national liberation struggle with an alliance with the national bourgeoisie, then the concentration of armed force in a standing army directly under the control of the Party (all officers are Party members) is seen as a guarantee against the situation where the Party loses, temporarily or permanently, the support of the masses.

In the second place, the CCP never broke away from the bourgeois concepts of war and did not carry through the revolutionary idea of people's war. While on a number of occasions Mao put forward the idea that men are primary over weapons in warfare, he did not mean by this to deny the role of modern weaponry but only to attempt to control its use by political criteria. In practice, the CCP invested heavily in modern weapons, going all the way to atomic weapons in the 1960s. The logic of positional war with modern weapons corresponds to the kind of professionalism which came to dominate the officer corps of the PLA.

This does not mean that a proletarian militia is totally unable to use weapons beyond small arms. But it would adopt them only to the extent that its organization remained socialist and not elitist. The militia would train in the factories and neighborhoods. Those with technical knowledge would act as teachers but without becoming administratively separate from the masses, nor would this knowledge be kept as a monopoly of the few; rather all the people would attempt to master the more advanced weapons. Military work would be an aspect of political work and leadership would appear here as in all areas of life; but this leadership would not become professional, separate, institutionalized. Such a people's militia, moreover, would have a powerful weapon only rarely used in the past, the appeal to the proletarian class interests of the soldiers of the imperialists. A people's war is as much agitational as military in the narrow sense. And even if defeated temporarily by an army equipped with superior fire-power, the militia would have maintained the ideological consciousness of the masses and prepared them to continue to struggle against all their class enemies, while the standing army under socialism in China became one of the most important breeding-grounds for the new bourgeoisie and eventually became a tool of that class.

Arming of the people requires that the Party be willing to share power with the masses, that the dictatorship of the proletariat be seen as a system of *worker's rule with party leadership,* a version of Left-center coalition under new conditions, rather than as a system in which the party monopolizes all positions of power because it is not willing to trust in the masses and their desire to fight for and defend socialism. This in turn requires that the party win power, leading masses of people who are *consciously fighting for socialism,* not just more material goods or land or peace. And it is precisely this element that the Bolshevik and Chinese revolutions lacked. And the reason that they maintained a standing army under Party control.

THE TRANSFORMATION OF THE ECONOMY

So far we have seen some of the effects on the exercise of state power of the bourgeois aspect of the new-democratic line, the aspect that advocated reliance on the capitalist class as a progressive force in the first-stage of the revolution. But this line, insofar as it was Marxist-Leninist, also had a proletarian aspect, the intention of moving to socialism in a second-stage and the mobilization of the masses of workers and peasants to destroy the power of their class enemies. In 1953, the CCP proclaimed the General Line of the construction of Socialism, sketching out the Party's plan to gradually expropriate all private capital and lead the peasants through a number of stages to collective production. Serious disagreements developed within the CCP around the question of how rapidly and comprehensively to move toward socialism. Liu and others had foreseen a much longer period of new-democracy and ascribed a much greater progressiveness to capitalism. They exerted their influence throughout the fifties to slow down and distort the elimination of the bourgeoisie. The Left in the party, made up primarily of worker and peasant cadres taken in during the sharp class struggles of 1947-52, fought constantly to move to higher stages of socialism.

Mao and his close supporters, applying the new-democratic line, swung back-and-forth periodically between these two groups and, most importantly, refused to break decisively with the Right. This created a complex pattern of economic struggle with distinct stages: 1) a sharp advance by the Left with which Mao associates himself, 2) an attempt by the leadership to restrain the advance and prevent it from passing beyond the new-democractic framework to a decisive break with bourgeois ideas, and 3) counter-attack and victory by the Right putting an end to the advance and often retreating to an earlier position. This pattern characterizes all the major episodes; Land reform (1947-

1950), Collectivization (1955-56), Communization (1958-59) and the GPCR (1966-68).

The first step was Land Reform, initiated as early as 1947 in the old Liberated areas and completed in 1950-51 in the Southern areas. The property of landlords was taken over and distributed to the peasants. In the early stages, Leftist cadres and poor peasants had tended to carry the struggle past the landlords to the rich peasants who owned sufficient amounts of land to require the employment of hired labor. These rich peasants were rural capitalists and often had industrial or commercial interests in addition to land. The CCP leadership quickly put a stop to these "excesses" and Mao summarized the new line in June 1950.

"Carry forward the work of agrarian reform step by step and in an orderly manner. The war has been fundamentally ended on the mainland; the situation is entirely different from that between 1946 and 1948, when the PLA was locked in a life and death struggle with the KMT reactionaries and the issue had not yet been decided. Now the government is able to help the poor peasants solve their difficulties by means of loans to balance up the disadvantage of having less land. Therefore, there should be a change in our policy toward the rich peasants, a change from the policy of requisitioning the surplus land and property of the rich peasants to one of preserving a rich peasant economy, in order to help the early restoration of production in the rural areas. This change is also favorable for isolating the landlords and protecting the middle peasants and small "renters out" of land." (Report at CC meeting, June 6, 1950. Transl. in *CB*, supplement no. 1, p. 3)

The same new-democratic line, with its prime emphasis on *quantity of production*, which required the use of bourgeois "experts" in the factories and state organs, required that the rural capitalists be allowed to flourish, at least for a time. The CCP was well aware, from observing the history of the Soviet countryside in the twenties, that the small-producer economy created by land reform was subject to internal instability; control of draft animals and implements by the richer peasants would progressively lead to the impoverishment of the "new-middle" peasants and their return to the status of wage-earners, i.e., that a petty-property commodity-producing economy generated capitalism rapidly and inexorably. It attempted to counter this development by encouraging, both ideologically and financially, the formation of mutual-aid teams, arrangements in which peasants would use their privately-owned implements to help each other by planning collectively the application of those resources. By late 1952, 40% of rural households were members of such teams, which generally included 7-10 families. In addition, genuine co-operatives, in which land and larger tools were pooled and used collectively, although payment was still made for the property contribution of each family as well as its labor contribution, were formed in many of the areas where land reform had taken place earliest.

But the policy of preserving the rich peasants left them free to use their political influence and economic power to enter the mutual-aid teams and co-ops, turning them into instruments of their individual enrichment, or to destroy them from without. Mao reported in 1955 that there had been "large scale dissolution of co-ops in 1953" as rich peasants convinced the other peasants that the road of individual enterprise was superior to the socialist road of the co-ops. Rich peasants entered the mutual-aid teams in order to share in the government loans and technical assistance which the teams qualified for. They then usually managed to get the lion's share of the benefits for themselves. Thus by 1954-55, the class struggle in China had reached a fateful turning point. If no further mass

16

movement toward socialism could be made, then the countryside would revert to capitalism and the proletarian dictatorship would most certainly be undermined.

But a profound ideological process had been percolating among the peasants in the preceding years. They had begun to grasp Marxism-Leninism under the leadership of the Leftist rural cadres. These cadres had not shared in the privileges of the senior cadres in the cities and lived among and at roughly the level of the peasants. The peasants initiated in 1955-56 a mass movement to form co-operatives. Leadership was taken by the poor peasants and the new "lower-middle peasants," former poor peasants who had received insufficient land and implements from the agrarian reform to be able to survive without continuing, often in disguised and illegal forms, to hire themselves out to the rich capitalist peasants, or go deeper into debt to them. By May, 1956, 91.2% of rural families were members of agricultural producers' co-operatives (APCs). By the end of 1956, 88% were in *advanced APCs,* in which payment to the individual family was based only on labor contributed, while property contributed was not compensated beyond the initial payment for its value. This was a tremendous victory for the Chinese proletariat and demonstrated concretely that *peasants could be won ideologically to fight for socialism.*

While the move along the "socialist road" was the primary aspect of this rural struggle, the Right forces in the CCP were strong enough to enforce certain limitations on the movement, to concede certain positions to the bourgeoisie.

The rich peasants were not compelled to enter the APCs, but had to be convinced that it was in their interest to do so. So, many remained separate, often with the best land and implements and continued to act as a source of temptation to the upper-middle peasants who had often reluctantly agreed to enter the APCs. Moreover, the prices set for subsidiary crops on the free markets were highly favorable and tempted the peasant to divert his labor and fertilizer from the collective endeavour to his private plot.

The principle of income distribution within the advanced APC was payment according to labor performed. Material incentive, transferred now from the level of the individual family to that of the small group, was still the cardinal point. Co-ops with different ratios of labor power to mouths-to-feed or different qualities of land received therefore very different per-capita incomes. The party fought vigorously against the tendency of the poorer peasants to demand more egalitarian distribution in favor of labor-poor families. A complex system of calculating work-points according to the job performed, the quality of the work, etc. was introduced, the equivalent of the piece-rate systems then being introduced in industry. This kind of system, beginning from a situation where the APCs are unequally endowed with labor power and land, would lead to progressively widening disparities in living standards between poor and rich APCs. A kind of "collective" exploitation of poorer co-ops by the richer could eventually result. It was this tendency which led, as we shall see, to the mass movement among the poor and lower-middle peasants to form the people's communes in 1958.

Developments in industry had been very similar. In 1949-50 the state had seized the property of those capitalists who were intimately involved with the imperialists and politically supported the Kuomintang. This had brought a large part of Chinese industry into the hands of the state. In 1955-56 the government moved to convert all remaining bourgeois industrial property into jointly owned state-private enterprise. The state had complete control over the use of the property and ownership of its output while the former capitalist owners were compensated for their property in government bonds paying a fixed rate of interest. Many of the capitalists, in addition to these fixed-income payments, stayed on as plant directors and staff at the high money salaries prevailing in these positions and, through the combination of these sources of income, were able to continue living in a way that was far above that of the average worker and a constant source of corruption of the government cadres.

The system of management used in both state and joint enterprises was known as "one-man management" and had been quite consciously borrowed from contemporary Soviet practice. Its essence was the absolute authority of the manager over day-to-day operations, hiring and firing, use of available resources. This system was modified in 1956 to give a much greater advisory and supervisory role to the Party committee in the factory, made up of the most politically advanced workers, but the managers retained great power.

In June, 1956, the great variety of wage payment schemes which the CCP had inherited from pre-Liberation factories were unified and rationalized in a systematic wage reform. This set up a basic wage scale with eight grades, with the wage in the highest (most skilled) grade being approximately three times the lowest. Roughly 80% of wages was to be base pay, calculated by hours worked according to skill grade, with the remaining 20% being used to spur extra output through piecework or bonus remuneration. Material incentives were the basic technique driving production, as is shown in an important article commenting on the wage reform.

> "This revision will effectively eradicate equalitarianism and the state of unreason-ableness and confusion obtaining in the current wage system and serve as a power-ful material factor setting into motion the extensive masses of workers and office employees to strive for fulfillment of the First Five Year Plan ahead of schedule." (Chin Lin, in *Lao-tung* (Labor), no. 3, March 6, 1956. Transl. in *ECMM*, no. 35, pp. 32-35)

A *Renmin Ribao* editorial of July, 1956, emphasized that piece rates are the most effective way of tying income directly to the individual quantity and quality of work performed and advocated their extensive development in the wake of the wage reform. By 1957, about 42% of all workers in state-operated factories and mines were covered by some sort of piece-rate system. Beginning in 1954, workers were given special monetary rewards for invention and innovation. Workers were given special bonuses of up to 15% of the standard monthly wage for achieving cost reductions or overfulfilling output quotas. In addition, the State Council, in 1955, set down regulations establishing monetary rewards for scientific contributions aimed at "inspiring the positive and creative talents of scientific research workers .... for serving the construction of the country." Monetary rewards to scientists represented multiples of the average worker's yearly income, ranging from 2,000 yuan to 10,000 yuan.

It is fair to say, therefore, that material incentive was the primary idea affecting the ideology of the Chinese working-class through 1957. This kind of reliance on bourgeois thought and habits could only weaken the working class ideologically and prevent it from developing the communist consciousness necessary to enable it to prevent restoration of the state power of the bourgeoisie. The Party led mass campaigns for ideological re-molding of the thought of workers and cadres. But these were vitiated by the incon-sistency of the party line and *could not change the strong bourgeois ideas constantly being generated by the material conditions under which people worked.* Moreover, Mao's reluctance to deal self-critically with the theory of new-democracy which allowed and encouraged the Party's Rightists to devise these schemes, prevented him from breaking the unity of the Party. He compromised repeatedly with Liu and the other Rightists on the

18

most fundamental questions.

The Rightist trend of 1956 also extended to the ideological sphere. Initial Chinese reaction to Khrushchev's speech to the 20th CPSU Party Congress was quite favorable. At the first session of the 8th National Congress of the CCP (Sept., 1956), Liu gave a political report, as Head of State of the People's Republic, which included the following points,

".... The fact that our bourgeoisie has heralded its acceptance of socialist transformation with a fanfare of gongs and drums is something of a miracle. What this miracle shows is precisely the great strength of the correct leadership of the proletariat and the absolute need for the dictatorship of the proletariat.

... During the past few years, the national bourgeoisie has taken part in the rehabilitation of the national economy ... In the course of socialist transformation, the alliance of the working class with the national bourgeoisie has played a positive role in educating and remolding the bourgeois elements. In the future, we can continue our work of uniting, educating and remolding them so that they may place their knowledge in the service of socialist construction. Thus, it can be readily seen that it is wrong to consider this alliance as a useless burden."

In another speech to the Congress, reported years later in a Red Guard tabloid, Liu is reported to have said, "The question of who will win in the struggle between capitalism and socialism in our country has now been decided" and he criticized "some members of our Party who hold that everything should absolutely be 'of one color' " — (i.e., the Left).

THE GREAT LEAP FORWARD AND THE RURAL PEOPLES' COMMUNES (RPCs)

The Great Leap period of 1958-59 is very complex because all the conflicting class forces in society and within the Party participated and put forward very different ideas and goals for the movement. For the Left, it was an attack on all the aspects of "bourgeois right" that had been primary up to that time in Chinese institutions; it put into question and often eliminated material incentives, piece-rates, managerial authority, high pay differentials, etc. It challenged the existence of the standing army and the wage system for cadres. For the Left, the large-scale RPCs, amalgamating the former APCs into units often containing 5,000 to 6,000 households and changing the existing system of income distribution, were the organizational means for beginning the transition to communism. The system of free supply of grain was introduced into the RPCs along with communal mess halls, nurseries, laundries, etc., so that the principle of distribution "to each according to his needs" was no longer a distant goal separated from the present by a long process of economic development, but a living reality. The commune eliminated the private plots of land and raised the socialization of property to a new level. The income earned by any individual household was determined not, as previously, by its own individual performance or that of the small work team of which it was a part, but as a share, based on a political calculation of needs, of the total output of the commune. Working for the commune, rather than for oneself, became, at least in part, a living principle.

It is useful here to quote extensively from some of the Left writings of the period, to show the kind of thinking which lay behind the mass movement of the summer and fall of 1958.

An article which stimulated a lengthy discussion was "Break Away From the Ideas of Bourgeois Rights," by Chang Ch'un-ch'iao (whom we will meet again as a participant in the Shanghai Cultural Revolution in 1967).

"To support the PLA, thousands of militiamen followed the Army in their march to the South. They led the same life of military communism as the Army. They did not aim at becoming officials or getting rich. No idea of wages, let alone "piece-wages" entered their minds .... After the nation-wide liberation, this life of military communism marked by "supply-system" was still very popular .... Comrades who were inured to the life of supply system did not covet the wage system .... but shortly afterwards this system of life was subjected to the impact of the bourgeois idea of right. The idea of bourgeois right has its kernel in hierarchy. In the view of persons imbued with the idea of bourgeois right, the supply system was undesirable .... There was nothing strange in such arguments brought forth by the bourgeoisie. But soon a number of party cadres were subjected to the impact of this idea. Among them were heard more criticisms of the drawbacks of supply system while more talks were heard about the merits of the wage system .... In a word, the communist supply system which ensured victory of the Chinese revolution, was condemned by some people as a serious offense which must be punished.

The main argument against the supply system is that it cannot stimulate production enthusiasm. Its theoretical basis is the "principle of material interests" stressed by economists. It is said that as survivals of the old division of labor still exist under the socialist system, i.e., some distinctions still exist between mental labor and physical labor, between workers and peasants, and between skilled and unskilled labor, the principle of "developing production through the material interests of workers" is represented as a wonderful principle.

.... The arguments seem to be very convincing but reduced to the popular language it is the same as the old saying: "money talks." If high wages are used to "stimulate," then socialism and communism can be bought like a piece of candy. What do we have to say about such a theory? .... It is precisely the workers, who, according to the above-mentioned economists, are the most concerned with the wage levels, who express fundamentally contrary views. Shanghai's workers .... pointed out that advocates of this theory want to "let money instead of politics assume command." These words hit the bull's eye. Of course, we do not deny .... that the inequality in "bourgeois right" cannot be done away with at once .... *but did Marx tell us that bourgeois right and bourgeois hierarchy of inequality must not be destroyed but should be systematized and developed?* Did he not say that the principle of "material interests" should only be partially stressed and that communist education should be intensified politically, ideologically and morally in order to break down the bourgeois right? ....

.... As a result of the attack on the supply system, the living standard which did not show much difference in the past has changed among our party cadre and some who were not inured to hardship have rapidly learned manners of gentlemen, high-class Chinese and old Mr. Chao (a snobby character in Lu Hsun's *Story of Ah Q*). Some cadres feel displeased when they are not addressed as "heads." This indeed stimulates something. But it does not stimulate production enthusiasm but enthusiasm in fighting for fame and wealth .... It stimulates estrangement from the masses. Some elements soon degenerate into bourgeois rightists .... Some cadres expect extra pay when they work for only one extra hour." (Transl. in *CB*, no. 537, pp. 3-5)

Another article of the same period, "Let us Begin Our Discussion with the Supply System," by Hu Sheng, put forward the idea that, while it was not possible to introduce communist distribution "according to needs" generally and completely until the productive forces of society had developed further, it was necessary to fight for communist "aspect":

"Does the enforcement of the supply system mean realization of communism? It is not yet the case. Many people's communes in the countryside now provide free meals; some even provide "three things" (meaning food, clothing, free housing), "five things" and even "seven things." It is not proper to represent this as communism.

But it should be said that it contains the communist factors. At a time when products are not so abundant, the communist "to each according to his needs" principle cannot be fully realized. By communist factors are meant a comparative uniformity for all and the break-up of the "to each according to his work" framework. Under the supply system, one will not set a big store by pay ...." (Transl. in *CB*, no. 537, pp. 33-36)

Under the free grain supply system described in these articles food was provided free of charge in communal mess halls. Often additional necessities of life were provided free by the commune. This meant that the poorer co-ops, who previously had difficulty in providing these necessities, were merged into the larger commune and benefited from the higher productivity of the more advanced co-ops. Conversely, it meant that the peasants in the more advanced co-ops, which often meant the ones which had incorporated a larger number of former rich peasants, had to be willing to share the fruits of their own labor with the less fortunate, i.e. to put the needs of the commune as a whole above their own small group material interest. This transformation was no automatic administrative matter; it was the result of a sharp class struggle led in the countryside by party cadres in which poor and lower-middle peasants struggled for the formation of communes while rich and upper-middle peasants resisted them and tried to undermine the free supply aspects. The communization movement itself had been preceded in the fall of 1957 by a sharp anti-Rightist struggle within the Party in which some of the most prominent figures in economic affairs (such as Ch'en Yun) were demoted because of their opposition to the Great Leap.

A second aspect of the Left view of the Great Leap was the change in the mode of economic planning and organization. Rather than professional managers dominating the factories, with an advisory Party committee, the Left advocated that the Party committee itself combine political direction with day-to-day management, i.e. putting politics in command. This new management system was introduced in a number of factories and generally accompanied the partial elimination of piece-rates, narrowing of the pay differentials among the workers and an increase in the amount of political discussion and struggle within the enterprises. Control over the planning process was taken away from the central Ministries and given over to Provincial and county Party committees who were to involve the workers and peasants themselves much more closely in the process of drawing-up, reconciling and executing the plans. Overall co-ordination was to be maintained not by centralized bureaucratic determination of the details of output quotas and resource use (combined with much reliance on the price-market mechanism) but by de-centralized response by the masses and basic-level cadres to the general line put forward by the Party leadership. This kind of de-centralization was very different from that carried out in the Soviet Union and Yugoslavia, where more power to lower-level units meant more power to managers and technicians, not workers.

But there was a contradiction between the Left view of the RPCs as a new form of organization (with a new ideology) opening up the transition to communism, and the view of the Party leadership, which saw the Great Leap primarily as a *production drive* and the RPCs as a tool which could mobilize labor on a large scale and in a more specialized fashion to complete the industrialization of the country and catch up to the capitalist nations. The communes had been preceded by predictions of enormous increases in production, capital investment and per/acre yields, both in agriculture and industry, for the years 1957-62. It was anticipated that Chinese steel production would "catch up to Britain in 15 years." As part of this plan, the CCP advocated the policy of "walking on two legs," supplementing the large-scale modern factories in the cities with a network of smaller-scale regional and local industries making use of the traditional skills of the workers and peasants and relying on locally-available resources. The communist aspects of the RPCs, especially rejection of material incentives and growth of free supply, were always evaluated by the CCP leadership *in relation to their effect on production.* This cautiousness can be seen in the official editorials which followed the Aug. 20, 1958 Communique of the CC giving approval to the communization movement:

" . . . The establishment of people's communes is shaping up as a new irresistible tide of the mass movement on a nation-wide scale . . . . The existing people's communes have shown ever greater superiority over the farm co-operatives in spurring the initiative of the masses in production, raising the rate of utilization of labor power and labor productivity, enlarging productive capital construction, accelerating the cultural and technical revolutions and in promoting public welfare.

. . . The Chinese peasants, having defeated capitalism economically, politically and ideologically and having overcome right conservatism in agricultural production, have carried out agricultural capital construction on an unprecedented scale, adopted advanced technical measures in farming and thereby are doubling farm yields or increasing them by several, a dozen or scores of times. At the same time, small and medium industrial enterprises are being rapidly developed in the countryside to promote the integration of industry and agriculture and to raise the standard of living of the rural population.

Of course, when the people's communes are established it is not immediately necessary to transform collective ownership into ownership by the whole people and it is even less appropriate to strain to advance from socialism, i.e., the primary phase of communism, to its higher phase." ("Greet the Upsurge in Forming People's Communes" *Red Flag*, no. 7, Sept. 1, 1958. Transl. in *CB* no. 517, pp. 1-4)

CCP editorials and resolutions repeatedly stress that the free supply system should not be taken so far that "production enthusiasm" is affected. As time passed, it became clear that the new forms of social organization and the new communist ideas were leading to sharper class struggle in the countryside and that this struggle was likely to interfere with achievement of the evermore-grandiose production and productivity targets emanating from Peking. When the CC met for its 6th Plenary Session in Dec. 1958, it issued a set of "Resolutions on Questions Concerning People's Communes" which carried the retreat from Leftist views several steps further:

22

"True, the free supply system adopted by the people's communes has in it the embryo of the communist principle of distribution according to needs; the policy of running industry and agriculture simultaneously and combining them carried out by the people's communes has opened up a way to reduce the differences between town and countryside and between worker and peasant; when the RPCs pass over from socialist collective ownership to socialist ownership by the whole people, these communist factors will grow further. All this must be acknowledged . . . . Nevertheless, every Marxist must soberly realize that the transition from socialism to communism is quite a long and complicated process of development and that throughout this entire process society is still socialist in nature. Socialist society and communist society are two different stages marked by different degrees of economic development.

. . . The communist system of distribution is more reasonable, but it can be put into practice only when there is a great abundance of social products. In the absence of this condition, any negation of the principle of "to each according to his work" will tend to dampen the labor enthusiasm of the people and is therefore disadvantageous to the development of production, to the increase of social products and hence to speeding the realization of communism. For this reason, in the income of commune members, that portion of the wage paid according to the work done must occupy an important place over a long period and will, during a certain period, take first place. In order to encourage the labor enthusiasm of commune members and also facilitate satisfaction of their complex daily needs, the communes must strive to increase the wages of their members gradually and, for a number of years to come, *must increase them at a faster rate than that portion of income that comes under the heading of free supply . . .* " (Transl. in *CB*, no. 542, pp. 7-23) (our emphasis-PLP).

The italicized words represent a major turning point in the development of the communes. Many of the more advanced had carried through the practice of giving half of income as free supply; and they had the perspective of gradually increasing that percentage as social productivity increased. But this resolution implied that this per cent was already too high and that the correct perspective was for it to *decrease*. As a result, free supply, in the bulk of the communes, fell to around 30% in the first months of 1959.

Another paragraph of the resolution altered previously held views on the degree of socialization of property:

" . . . Some people think that the switch over to communes will call for a redistribution of existing personal consumer items. This is a misconception. It should be publicized among the masses that the means of livelihood owned by members (including houses, clothing, bedding and furniture) and their deposits in banks and credit cooperatives will remain their own property after they join the commune and will always belong to them . . . Members can retain individual trees around their houses and small farm tools, small instruments, small domestic animals and poultry; they can also continue to engage in some small domestic side occupations on condition that these do not hamper their taking part in collective labor." (*Ibid*)

These may seem like very small concessions to private property, but they were the opening wedge in a retrogressive movement which was to lead, within a year, to the restoration of the private plots and the revival of private sideline occupations.

We have seen that the party leadership justified the new principles of organization as beneficial to achieving great production advances. During 1958 Mao made a trip to Moscow to negotiate the largest Sino-Soviet trade agreement ever, as part of a plan to exchange the increased agricultural surplus for heavy capital goods. Thus, the leadership in no way accepted another cardinal tenet of the Left: that a socialist state should strive for self-sufficiency and avoid becoming dependent on others, especially those whose ideological position has already been put into question. When the great production advances failed to materialize, the CCP (just like the Russians and western commentators) blamed the excessive "Leftism" of the communes and took steps to retreat from those measures. In fact, the production difficulties of 1959-1961 resulted from a combination of severe natural calamities, unrealistic output targets, and especially the incorrect over-emphasis on heavy industry which the CCP had taken over uncritically from the Soviet experience. The Party Right was able to use the production crisis to completely over-whelm the Left and begin to undo the accomplishments of the Great Leap. In 1961-62, as we shall describe in the next section, the retreat turned into a rout as the new ruling bourgeois forces took China rapidly along the capitalist road.

Before moving on, it is important to consider the following question: Was the People's Republic of China a proletarian dictatorship during the period 1949-1959? We have seen that it set up a number of arrangements which violated the teachings of Marx and Lenin on the conditions of workers' rule (standing army, cadre income, etc.). Moreover, its foreign policy during those years was in no essential way different from the type of policy which our party criticizes today. China was the prime mover in the Bandung conference of non-aligned nations, strove at all times to establish diplomatic relations with bourgeois nationalist leaders, upheld unity with the revisionists by signing the Moscow declaration of 1957 and the 81 party statement of 1960, both of which acknowledged the possibility of peaceful transition to socialism, and, in general, put forward new-democracy as the universal strategy for revolution in the contemporary world. Throughout this period, bourgeois authorities dominated culture and education; and the former capitalist class continued to enjoy material privileges through its interest-income and high salaries.

But this is only one aspect. The other is the destruction of the landlord class, the expropriation of the property of the bourgeoisie (who, even if they retained some strong positions from which to engineer a comeback, had certainly become, for a time, subordinate to the workers and peasants), and the destruction of petty bourgeois property and ideas among a peasantry which had launched the commune movement. *The most important lesson of these years is that the poor and middle peasants can grasp Marxism-Leninism and fight for socialism and communism.* Our party's line on the peasants is not an abstract prediction but is based on the accomplishments of the Chinese peasants and the ideological consciousness they reached. A great Left force of workers and peasants had been created which was to re-appear strongly during the GPCR in an attempt to resume the progress toward communism which had prevailed until 1959.

In the Leninist view, state power is an instrument of the class which holds it, used to transform the economic, political and ideological conditions of the society. The question of who holds state power cannot be answered by examining only forms (the Soviet Union, after all, has a Communist Party and state ownership of property) nor by taking ideological pronouncements at face value (the Soviet revisionists still occasionally proclaim their devotion to proletarian dictatorship) but only by determining *which class is transforming society in the direction of its own interests*. There are only two forms of state power possible in the modern world: proletarian dictatorship or bourgeois dictatorship. All theories of third forms: new-democracy, joint dictatorship of revolutionary classes, democratic dictatorship of proletariat and peasantry, etc., are incorrect and correspond to no objective reality. In China between 1949 and 1959, the primary aspect of social change was in the direction of communism, despite the errors of line and policy which were to have such a devastating effect. No bourgeois dictatorship would have created the people's communes or free supply or thoroughly liquidated the landlord class or removed the capitalists from much of their power. In 1949 a workers' state came into existence in China and from its positive accomplishments we can learn much about what socialism is and will be.

THE RESTORATION OF BOURGEOIS RULE

The communes of 1958 had totally abolished private plots of land. It is important, therefore, to look at the available information for the period 1960-66 to see what changes had intervened. In 1964, a delegation of agriculturists and economists from Pakistan toured a sample of communes. Their observations were collected and used as the basis for a book: S.J. Burki, *A Study of Chinese Communes, 1965*. They found that in 1964 the 10 communes they surveyed, which included a large variety in terms of region and size, averaged 7.55% of the total land in private plots. For four communes which made more detailed information available, the following had been the change over time:

YEAR	Per Cent of land under Private Ownership
1958	
1959	1.39
1960	2.79
1961	4.24
1962	6.40
1963	7.61
1964	8.64

The private plots, however, played a larger part in the peasants' lives than these figures indicate because of the higher value of the crops grown on them. The 10 communes showed the following income figures:

COMMUNE	Private Plot Income as% of Total Family Income
1.	20.8
2.	30.2
3.	18.4
4.	22.9
5.	17.1
6.	16.9
7.	20.6
8.	19.4
9.	13.5
10.	8.8
average	19.3

Even this data under-estimates the revival of private agriculture and its role in rural livelihood. More detailed information comes from the Lien-chiang documents, a series of directives and reports concerning communes in Lien-chiang county in Fukien province on the east China coast. They cover the years 1962-63 and were seized during a Nationalist Chinese raid on the coast. (They are translated and annotated in Chen, C.S. (ed.) *Rural People's Communes in Lien-chiang*). We quote from the editor's summary of the statistics provided by the documents:

"The area of private plots, by law, could not exceed five to seven per cent of a team's crop area. (A team, at that time, contained, on the average, 24 households and a brigade, 171 households.) Nevertheless, in the Hu-li brigade the private plots amounted to 9.5 per cent of its crop land. The situation varied from team to team in the brigade. At one extreme, the private plots in one team amounted to 11 per cent of its crop land and at the other, 7.6 per cent. In the Shan-K'ang brigade, the private plots in the individual teams ranged from 12.1 per cent to 15 per cent of the crop area, the average being 13.1 per cent. For the two brigades, the private plots averaged 11.3 per cent of their crop land, which was substantially higher than the limit set by the law.

Besides the private plots, team members might also hold reclaimed land and land for growing animal feed. In addition, some land collectively owned by the team was farmed out to the members for cultivation.

The reclaimed land in the county amounted to 40,000 mou, or 19.6 per cent of the crop area.

Farmed-out land was 4,178 mou, or 2.05 per cent of the county's crop area. Private plots (11.3 per cent), reclaimed land (19.6 per cent) and farmed-out land (2.05 per cent) together constituted the "Small Freedom" land, which amounted to more than 30 per cent of the crop area. In some teams the proportion was more than 50 per cent. Households were permitted to engage in such subsidiary domestic enterprises as embroidery, sewing, knitting and bee-keeping. The products, except for the kinds and quantities subject to state purchase, could be disposed of in the free market. A surprisingly large variety of private activities, which would be thought impossible under a socialist system, was pursued by members of the commune system. Many commune members engaged in peddling. Selling what was produced by oneself was permitted, but re-selling what one purchased from others (er pan shang) was generally viewed with disapproval. Some members did odd jobs ("rat work") outside their own commune units. Half the 106 member labor force of the Lien-teng brigade in the Ao-chiang commune worked outside: 31 in stonemasonry and earth-work, three in carpentry, 44 in peddling and 27 in miscellaneous jobs. The profits from peddling totalled 8,200 Yuan, averaging 196 Yuan per peddler (four of the peddlers made profits of more than 1,000 Yuan each). Members who worked outside the team would have to surrender their earnings to the team. Failing to do so, they would be given no ration and would have to buy food at high prices and be subjected to certain fines. Lending money at high interest was fairly prevalent. It was reported that in three communes . . . 384 households engaged in lending at high interest, involving a total of 72,440 Yuan in principal. The rate of interest ranged from 1 to 1.5 per cent."

He calculates a breakdown of the peasants income sources:

Source of Income	Value (Yuan)
Collective:	
Rations	19.87

Retained fruits	4.50
Work-points	41.88
Income from collective system	66.25

Private:

Private plots.	7.14
Reclaimed land	14.28
sub. dom. enterprise	(unknown)
misc. private income	(unknown)
Total Private Income	21.42
Total income per person/year	87.67

From this table it can be seen that private sources contributed about a quarter of total income, and this does not take into account the miscellaneous and illegal sources, which in some cases could be quite large. Moreover, the high prices paid for subsidiary products, such as livestock and vegetables, grown privately, presented the peasant with the constant temptation to divert his effort from the collective to the private sector. Many cases are reported of peasants attending to their private plots by day and making up by working the collective land at night.

Even more significant for ideological and political trends is the organization of the collective sector itself. A large-scale *desocialization* of the communes took place over the period 1959-62. By this is meant that property and control over its use were transferred downward from higher-level units to lower-level, from the commune to the brigade to the team, in order to bring about a closer relation between individual output and reward and restore the primary role of material incentive. The communes went through three distinct stages, depending on which level of organization was the *"accounting unit."* (An accounting unit, roughly defined, "carries on independent accounting, is responsible for its own profits and losses, organizes production, and distributes income." – Lien-chiang Document VII.) From Aug. 1958 to March 1959, the commune itself, with an average of 5,000 households, was the accounting unit. In March 1959, the CC decided to shift the accounting unit from commune to brigade. Then in Nov. 1961, it issued a directive establishing the team as the accounting unit. (In the meantime, the number of communes had been tripled and their average size reduced to 1622 households. A team had an average membership of 24 households in 1963.) This new arrangement was formalized in one of the most important documents of recent Chinese history, *The Revised Draft Regulations Governing Rural People's Communes,* promulgated in Sept. 1962.

The basic principles of ownership and income distribution are set forth in these regulations:

Article 21.
Land within the scope of the production team is all owned by the production team. None of the land owned by the commune, including the members' private plots, private hills and housing may be rented out or bought or sold.
Labor power within the scope of the production team is all to be controlled by the production team. Transfer of labor power for use by the commune or the production brigade must be discussed with the mass of members. It may not be requisitioned without their agreement.
Large domestic animals and agricultural implements owned collectively by the

27

production team may not be requisitioned by the commune or the brigade. Any agricultural implements, small scale agricultural machines and large domestic animals formerly owned by the communes or brigade which may be suitably owned by and utilized by the production team should revert to production team ownership . . .

Article 22.

The production team has autonomy with regard to production operations and management and distribution of income . . .

Article 31.

For convenience in organizing production, the production team may be divided into permanent or temporary work groups, each to be assigned a section of land to work on a short-term, seasonal or year-round basis.

Groups and individuals who are active in labor, responsible in management, noteworthy in achievements, or who overfulfill their obligations must be given suitable rewards. Those groups and individuals who are not active in labor, are irresponsible in management, and who do not fulfill their obligations must be given a suitable reduced payment for labour or other punishment.

Article 32.

The production team should give reasonable payment for the labor of its members. It should avoid egalitarianism among the members in calculating payment for labor.

. . . Payment for labor requiring technical skills in agriculture or herding should be higher than that for common labor.

The over-all effect of these regulations was to bring back the situation where the peasant's view was limited to producing for the immediate small group of which he was a part. The beginnings of any aspects of communist distribution and communist morality (working for the sake of a larger and larger collective) were reversed completely. Along with this the experiments in free supply of grain on a commune-wide scale were wound up and income differentials between teams reappeared with full force.

These organizational changes were accompanied by an ideological campaign to justify the reversal of the original commune spirit. Private sideline occupations were said to be not only compatible with the collective economy but a necessary stimulus to it. Piece-rates, similar to those prevalent in industry, were encouraged as the best way to tie reward to effort. And the motif, "this is the period of socialism; communism must wait until the full development of productive forces," was dominant once again. The argument was made that private plots and team-ownership did not represent movements toward capitalism for the following reasons: 1) The private plots are owned by the brigades and only assigned to members for use. They cannot be transferred or sold; 2) Collective labor takes up the majority of member's time. 3) Only the collective economy can provide the tools and raw materials necessary for sidelines production; and 4) The markets for private output are controlled by the state. It was also pointed out that individual production is not the same as capitalist production, since the latter requires free purchase of means of production and existence of an expropriated proletariat. (Hsiao Liang, "Is Development of Family Side Occupations Likely to Aid Capitalist Spontaneity," transl. in *CB*, no. 677, pp. 14-17.)

But this is a typical revisionist argument. Nobody claimed that private plots, contracting of land by teams to households, private re-clamation of land, peddling, withholding effort from the collective, material incentive systems and all the other bourgeois tendencies characteristic of this period were already full-blown capitalism. The Left ideologists of the Great Leap had simply pointed out that the entire period of Socialism was a *class struggle between capitalism and communism,* that during this period a fierce and continuous struggle would take place between those who wanted to move forward to communism and those who wanted to freeze the revolution at some particular stage and then reverse it. Those who advocate the compatibility of private and collective tendencies, rather than their fundamental contradiction, will end up *objectively* building bourgeois consciousness among the masses and creating the *conditions,* ideologically, for the restoration of capitalism. Any time the revolution ceases moving forward toward communism as its clear goal, it will immediately begin to turn around towards capitalism. *There is no middle position.* Because of their concern for quantitative levels of production (implicitly defining socialism as material improvement) the CCP leadership created organization and ideology in the countryside which strengthened bourgeois consciousness and weakened proletarian consciousness. A clear example of this position is provided by the following article.

"As we know, the system of distribution of "to each according to his work" enforced in rural people's communes at the present stage represents a sort of material incentive and material guarantee in-so-far as the laborers are concerned. It plays an important part in stimulating the labor enthusiasm of commune members. But does this mean that material incentive is the only way to heightening one's production enthusiasm? No. It must be realized that only with politics assuming command is it possible for material incentive to play its part correctly.

. . . the party's policy is, on the one hand, to make it clear to the masses that their most fundamental interests lie in speeding up socialist construction and, on the other hand, to take the greatest care of the immediate living conditions and material benefits of the masses. In handling the relations between the state, the collective and the individual in people's communes, over-emphasis on the collective and long-range interests is unfavourable to the raising of the production enthusiasm of the masses . . . if the principle of "to each according to his work" is not adhered to, those commune members who have strong labor-power and do more work will feel they are put at a disadvantage. If one simply looks at the superiority of collective labor and collective economy and loses sight of the small freedom permitted within the big collective and the necessity of meeting the diversified needs of members at the same time as increasing social wealth, one is disregarding the present level of production and consciousness of the masses . . . thus, it is not proper to set political command against material incentive. Political command and material incentive are united; they may not be cut apart; nor one be stressed to the neglect of the other." (Chao Hsu-kuang, from *Kung-ren Ribao,* Dec. 1, 1961. Transl. in *CB,* no. 677, pp. 23-25.)

In articles like this and many others of the period the bourgeois principle of material incentive and the proletarian principle of politics taking command are not seen as waging a life and death struggle. Rather, in line with the new-democratic idea of utilizing the bourgeoisie in *constructing socialism,* they are seen as each playing a useful role; *their relation is primarily one of unity and only secondarily one of struggle.* This reversal of the unity-contradiction relations is the essence of revisionism, seen from the standpoint of dialectics.

Nor was the revival of revisionist ideas and politics limited to the rural areas. Major changes took place in industrial management, economic planning and wage payments. The system that began during the Great Leap of transferring managerial control to the Party Committee at the factory level was ended and the managers returned with even greater power than before 1957. The manager is responsible for meeting certain financial targets set by the State Plan. The main ones are profit targets and cost reduction targets. In meeting these he has a great deal of discretion in determining what the enterprise shall produce, in placing orders with other factories or retail agencies and in using advertising to solicit orders for his goods. Contracts between enterprises are widely used and are legally binding. There is a good deal of evidence that the State has surrendered allocational controls over many goods, allowing them to be exchanged through the market. Before 1957, all profits above the set targets were taken by the state, with a portion returned to the enterprise for bonuses. In that year, however, and continuing to the present, a profit-sharing scheme was worked out. Under this, the enterprise was allowed to retain a fixed percentage of all profits above the target. This can be used for bonuses to staff and workers as well as for expansion of the scale of the enterprise.

Closely connected with these changes in management and planning are the return to piece-rates and material incentives in the factories. In early 1961, enterprises were urged to cut down on employment, keeping only the best of their workers. Those retained would share more greatly in the excess profits of the enterprise. Piece-rates were advocated even more strenuously than before the Great Leap. A new device used was team piece-rates, which set groups of workers against one another in production competition.

These new policies were summarized in the so-called *"70 Articles on Industrial Policy"* reputedly authored by Liu Shao-ch'i and Po I-po in Dec. 1961. Here are excerpts from these:

Article 2. The task and target in industry from now on is "the market comes first."

Article 9. All industrial units which show a deficit in "economic accounting," with the exception of those designated, are henceforth to cease operating.

Article 21. The currently enforced eight hours of study and eight hours of meeting each week should be reduced as much as possible in order to avoid interfering with the rest time of the employees and workers.

Article 22. Henceforth no industrial unit is to summon its employees and workers again to engage in "bitter battles."

Article 25. Factories may calculate piece-work wages when feasible.

Article 26. When it is not feasible to calculate piece work, they may implement a collective piece-work system.

Article 52. Carry out the system of the factory manager bearing responsibility under the leadership of the party committee.

Article 65. Unions having 50 or more members are permitted to have a chairman who is half-removed from production. Those with 200 or more members may have a union chairman who is entirely removed from production. Those with over 500 men may have two men who are removed from production.

Special attention should be given to Article 9, which stipulates the domination of profits over production. (During this period Chinese economists began to write about "market socialism"; the content of their theories was in essence the same as that coming forth from Liberman in the Soviet Union, and revisionists like Sik and Brus in Eastern Europe.) The essential effect of a genuinely planned economy is that the production pattern which results, being determined by a social calculation of the people's needs, would differ from the pattern determined by a monetary calculation of costs and profits. This article enforces a market-determined pattern by eliminating enterprises which don't meet the monetary test.

Articles 21 and 22 register the leadership's opposition to the participation of the workers in struggles against managers and technicians and their concern that excessive political study and debate would reduce labor productivity.

Another major bourgeois trend during 1960-66 was the system of temporary and contract labor which came into use. Under this, the number of workers permanently assigned to enterprises was reduced while the number who were temporarily employed when work was available and then let go increased. In this way, enterprise managers had more flexible control over costs of production and could shift social insurance and public welfare costs on to the communes and the State.

It was the Right forces within the party which seized control after the Great Leap. Many of the young cadre who had led and supported the Great Leap were purged or demoted. The party, under the leadership of the Right, became the representative of the bourgeois forces which had been slowly developing and consolidating; the senior cadres, the officer corps, the professional managers and technicians; all those whom the concessions of new-democracy had put into privileged economic positions. Even the old capitalist remnants got a new lease on life when the Party, in 1962, decided to extend their fixed-interest payments for at least five more years.

The dictatorship of the proletariat is itself a form of continuous and sharp class struggle. New bourgeois forces are constantly emerging from the ranks of the people. If bourgeois ideology is not decisively combatted, it is possible *at any stage* in the transition to communism for the movement to be reversed and the bourgeoisie to come back to power. This does not mean that the full economic and political structure of capitalism can quickly be restored; that requires a transition period during which the new bourgeois ruling class undermines and dismantles the socialist aspects of the economic base. What it does mean is that the power of the state is now being used to move the ideological consciousness of the people *away from communism and toward capitalism.* That kind of use of state power is the essential definition of the dictatorship of the bourgeoisie and that is what came to prevail in China in the period 1960-1966.

THE ANTI-SOVIET REVISIONISM CAMPAIGN 1959-66

One factor would seem to contradict the characterization of China, 1960-66, as a bourgeois dictatorship: the split in the international communist movement and the sharp anti-revisionist struggle waged by the CCP. Why would the new "red" bourgeoisie feel it necessary to defend the ideology of Marxism-Leninism against the changes the Russians were advocating? Two fundamental points can be made about this struggle.

1) At no time did the CCP question any of the tenets of Marxism-Leninism as it had always interpreted it, especially its compromises with nationalism and united-fronts alliances with secondary imperialists against "the main enemy." It simply defended Marxism-Leninism against Soviet denials of its basic concepts: proletarian dictatorship vs. "state of the whole people" and armed struggle vs. peaceful transition. Major Chinese documents, such as the *Proposal on the General Line*, 1963, and Lin Piao's *Long Live The Victory of People's War*, 1965, reaffirmed the nationalism-based strategy that had brought the Chinese revolution to power. The practice of Chinese foreign policy did not alter

significantly during the period of the anti-Soviet polemics; in fact; the Chinese re-doubled their efforts to put themselves at the head of an anti-U.S. imperialism coalition of nations. Chou En-Lai made an extensive tour through Africa in 1964, lauding such bourgeois regimes as that of Toure in Guinea and Nkrumah in Ghana. He especially went out of his way to make overtures to the Algerians and Egyptians. 1961-1965 saw the development of close relations between China and Indonesia. Liu Shao-chi' visited Indonesia in April 1963 and stated, "The Republic of Indonesia has become an important force opposing imperialism and colonialism and safeguarding the peace and security of Southeast Asia and Asia as a whole." (Peking Review, April 19, 1963) The Chinese line in Indonesia was to lead the Indonesian Communist Party (PKI) to the disaster of 1965 in which it was virtually destroyed.

Moreover, throughout the period of bitter back and forth polemics, the Chinese continued to maintain *effective unity of action* with the Soviet Union in delivering arms to Vietnam over the Chinese rail-roads. At no time did the Chinese engage in public polemics against Soviet aid.

2) The immediate cause of the split was Russian refusal to provide the Chinese with atomic weapons or even the technical assistance and materials necessary to produce them. One of the purposes of Mao's Moscow trip in 1958 was to persuade Khrushchev to make this available. The polemics heated up considerably shortly after his failure. The Chinese have given this explanation themselves:

"In 1958 the leadership of the CPSU put forward unreasonable demands designed to bring China under Soviet military control. These unreasonable demands were rightly and firmly rejected by the Chinese government. Not long afterwards, in June 1959, the Soviet government unilaterally tore up the agreement on new technology for national defense concluded between China and the Soviet Union in October 1957, and refused to provide China with a sample of an atomic bomb and technical data concerning its manufacture." (*The Origin and Development of the Differences Between the Leadership of the CPSU and Ourselves.* Peking, 1963, p. 26).

This was followed by Soviet refusal to support China in the Formosa straits, the proposed summit meeting of Khrushchev and Eisenhower and Soviet support for India in her border dispute with China. What the Chinese objected to most strongly was Russian rapprochement with the U.S. and desertion of support of Chinese foreign policy goals.

What then, is the real meaning of the dispute? The Russian bourgeoisie had seized power some years earlier and was already well along the way to restoring capitalism. Given the degree to which the Russian workers and peasants had lost confidence in Marxism-Leninism and given the long period during which nationalist ideas had been emphasized (from before World War II), the new Russian bourgeoisie could proceed to the renunciation of Marxism-Leninism without fear of popular reaction and begin to create a revisionist ideology more in correspondence to the new material conditions of bourgeois rule.

The newly consolidated Chinese "red" bourgeoisie, however, was coming to state power at a time when hundreds of millions of workers and peasants still looked upon Marxism-Leninism as a correct guide to social practice. But analysis of the objective historical process has shown us that Marxism-Leninism in the particular version that characterized the line of the CCP and the ideas of Mao Tse-tung, *contained a number of incorrect ideas which led inexorably to bourgeois restoration.* No doubt the Chinese leaders consciously believed that they were defending genuinely revolutionary ideas against Soviet revisionism. Historical experience has demonstrated otherwise. The anti-

Soviet polemics were necessary in order to defend that body of ideas which corresponded to the class interests of the bourgeois class. Had the Chinese leaders gone along with Khrushchevite ideology they would have been exposed before the masses and would have lost the "Left" cover under which capitalist counter-revolution is most likely to succeed.

Moreover, the ideological imperative corresponded to the desire of the new Chinese bourgeois forces to free themselves from excessive economic and ·military dependence on the Soviet Union and create the material and scientific infrastructure for the development of their own atomic arsenal. The attempts by Soviet leaders to moderate the inter-imperialist rivalry with the U.S. opened up the possibility that the Chinese bourgeoisie could displace the S.U. as the leader of a world wide united front of "oppressed nations" against U.S. imperialism (now joined by Soviet social-imperialism).

Nothing in these external struggles contradicts the view, derived from internal evidence, that the bourgeoisie had regained power in China in the early 1960s.

MORE ON THE GPCR

We began this report by summarizing the class forces in the cultural revolution. We then presented evidence to confirm the position of the so-called "extreme-left" that most senior cadres and army officers had become a new bourgeoisie which was carrying out capitalist restoration. We can now look at some of the details of this great revolution in the light of that Left outlook.

The new element created by the GPCR was the existence of a great many *mass organizations* of students and workers. These tended to divide along political lines. Left groups, such as "Sheng-wu-Lien" in Hunan and "May 16 Corps" in Peking, took the leading role in the early days of the GPCR in attacking the high-level power-holders in the municipalities and provinces. These cadres, in turn, organized and supported mass organizations to defend their positions; these mass organizations waged protracted and often violent struggle with one another.

The mass organizations which favored "seizure of power" overthrew the existing senior cadre in many important provinces and municipalities in Dec. 1966 and Jan. 1967. In Peking, Shanghai and Taiyuan, the people moved to set up organs of power modelled on the Paris Commune. The implication of the commune arrangement was that all the existing cadre should be removed and replaced by new leaders elected by the membership of the mass organizations. The students and workers who put forward this demand were quite sure that they had the support of Chairman Mao in proclaiming the commune-type state as their goal. On Feb. 5, 1967 the Shanghai commune was proclaimed and all the leading cadre of the Shanghai municipal Party committee and the Shanghai municipal Council were put on notice that they would be evaluated by the people. A new organ of power, the provisional committee for the Shanghai People's Commune, was established, with members drawn from a number of mass organizations which had participated in the power-seizure. The most important leader of the commune was Chang Ch'un-ch'iao, who had been a prominent Leftist during the Great Leap. Chang left for Peking on February 12 to consult with Mao.

When he returned on February 24th, he reported to a mass rally that Chairman Mao opposed the name Shanghai People's Commune and preferred that it be called Shanghai Revolutionary Committee, on the model of the new organ of power which had been created in Heilungkiang Province (Manchuria) in January. These are the reasons Chang gave:

33

"On the 12th, Chairman Mao called us to Peking, and received us on the same day . . . .

Chairman Mao said: "The present revolution is a revolution under proletarian dictatorship, one that has been organized and started by ourselves." . . . As we understand it Mao showed clearly here that for the past 17 years our country was under proletarian dictatorship and that it was Chairman Mao's revolutionary line, not the Liu-Teng line, that was in the ruling position. Why, then, did we need to carry out a revolution under proletarian dictatorship? Chairman Mao explained: "It is because some of the organs of proletarian dictatorship have been usurped."

. . . he noted that the slogan "Thoroughly Improve Proletarian Dictatorship" is a reactionary one . . . . Speaking correctly, the proletarian dictatorship could only be improved partially.

Can we do without revolutionary leading cadres? No! A combat team cannot do without a responsible man. In seizing power now, we must also have cadres that is, we must have new as well as old cadres. Why do we need old cadres who have assumed leadership work before? The reason is very simple. For instance, some workers perform very well. They dare to break through and rebel; they are able and have made significant contributions to the cultural revolution. But if we turn over to them a city such as Shanghai or a province such as Kiangsu, then they would find it very difficult to manage it because of lack of experience. They may be more adept in the management of one workshop.

Chairman Mao says, "A university student cannot become a university president for he has not graduated yet and is not familiar with the whole university." As I see it, he is not even qualified to become a department head because he has no teaching experience and no experience of leading the work of the whole department. So we should ask a professor or assistant professor to lead the department.

Young comrades present at the forum, don't be discouraged. Chairman Mao also says that young people have made numerous contributions to this great cultural revolution, but they cannot at once be expected to take over the duties of the secretaries of the Provincial Party Committee or the Municipal Party Committee. I myself think so too. The "three-way-combination" provides very good training for the young people. If young people in their twenties follow the old revolutionary cadres and learn from them for seven, eight or ten years, then they are still young when they become secretaries . . . .

There are more than 600 cadres holding the rank of heads of departments (bureaus) and more than 6,000 cadres with the rank of section head in Shanghai. How can we fail to find candidates for the "three-way-combination" from among these? . . . . And the great majority of these comrades are good.

This idea of "doubting all and overthrowing all" is a reactionary one. This is not an idea of us rebels, but it has an influence on us. When we are infuriated to see that many people are so stubborn, we can easily be taken in by the propaganda of others.

. . . Recently the State Council told us that the rebel headquarters of an organ of the municipal party committee issued an order to the State Council demanding the abolition of all posts of "chiefs". Many things said in it were wrong. For instance, it was stated that "for a long time the department heads control the section heads and the section heads control the section personnel." I think that the same will be true in the future also. "The chiefs have always ridden on the backs of the Party and the people." Comrade Lin Piao is Minister of National Defense, and does he ride on the backs of the Party and the people? It is reactionary to say that he does. Chairman Mao explicitly stated: "We shall not be able to survive for a few days if we do away with even deputy section heads."

Chairman Mao said: . . . "names should not be changed too frequently, because the form is only of secondary importance while the content is primary."

"The main thing is: which class is in power? For instance, the Soviet Union has changed, yet its name remains the same . . . .

. . . Now the various provinces and municipalities are learning from Shanghai and calling themselves people's communes. What should the State Council be called? Should the national title be changed? If the state is changed into the Chinese People's Commune, then the chairman of the state would be called commune chairman or director. After the title is changed, there would still be the question of recognition or nonrecognition by foreign countries. I think the Soviet Union would not recognize it because to do so would be disadvantageous to herself."

"Let the Shanghai People's Commune be changed to Shanghai Municipal Revolutionary Committee . . . . Would you not feel isolated because yours is the only commune in the whole country? The *Jen-min Jih-pao* could not publish the news, for if it published it, all would follow suit, and the series of problems mentioned above would arise." (Transl. in *SCMP*, no. 4147, March 27, 1968, pp. 1-19)

Clearly, the Shanghai Commune didn't just have its name changed. The "three-way-alliance" which Chang brought from Mao as the organizing principle of the new Revolutionary Committee — an alliance of army cadre, leading cadre who were "making revolution" (i.e. were willing to denounce Liu), and hand-picked representatives of some of the mass organizations — was incompatible with the view of the Leftists among the students and workers. The Shanghai Commune itself, with Chang and Yao Wen-yuan in the leadership, had already excluded the "Red Revolutionaries," the most Left student group. On January 27, the latter had tried to question several members of the Shanghai Writers Union who had been drafting diatribes against them. They were prevented from doing so by a detachment of troops of the Shanghai garrison, sent on Chang's orders. When they appealed to the Central CR Group in Peking (of which Chang and Yao were members) they were condemned as "ultra-Leftists." This clash between the Left and the PLA was only a small foretaste of things to come.

An important editorial in Red Flag in February clarified the line of the CC further: "Leniency should be adopted in making decisions about cadres who have made even very serious mistakes, after they are criticized and struggled against . . . .

Cadres who have committed mistakes should be given the opportunity to examine, criticize and correct them. So long as they make a self-criticism, correct their mistakes and come over to the side of Chairman Mao's revolutionary line, they can still be given appropriate leading posts. Many of them can even be drawn into the provisional organs of power . . . . " ("Cadres Must be Treated Correctly," Transl. in *On the Revolutionary Three-in-One Combination*, FLP, Peking, 1968, p. 36).

A State Council directive of January 23, 1967 ordered the PLA to intervene actively in the provinces to bring about the formation of Revolutionary Committees. The typical series of events that followed was: 1) revolutionary mass organizations would overthrow the leading cadres as supporters of the Liu line. 2) the PLA would prevent these cadres from offering any kind of armed resistance (through mass organizations that they controlled); 3) some of the leading cadres, often from the second-line of leadership, would denounce their former superiors, make phony self-criticisms and organize mass groups to support themselves; 4) these Right mass organizations would come into sharp and protracted struggle with the Left which wanted to overthrow all the bourgeois cadres, not just a handful; 5) when this struggle passed over, as it generally did, to armed struggle, the PLA would intervene, on orders from the CC and CR Group, to "overcome the contradictions among the people" and bring everybody, including the new group of "Maoist" cadres, into a "three-way-alliance." If the Left persisted in refusing to work with the "red" bourgeoisie, then it was attacked and disarmed by the PLA.

Some examples of the end-result of the process: In Heilungkiang, the co-chairmen of the Rev. Comm. were P'an Fu-sheng, first secretary of the former Provincial Party Committee, and Wang Chia-tao, commander of the Military Region. In Shantung, the chairman was Wang Hsiao-yu, ex-deputy mayor of the province's largest city. In Tsinghai the chairman was Liu Hsien-ch'uan, commander and party secretary of the Military District. In Szechuan, the chairman was Chang Kuo-hua, First Commissar of Chengtu Military Region and the commander of the Tibet operations of the PLA. In Kansu, Hu Chi-tsung, secretary of the former Provincial Party Committee, became a deputy-chairman.

It was this overall movement that the Left later came to call the "February Adverse Current of Capitalist Restoration" or the "Evil Wind of March." The sharpest struggle was in the city of Canton. There the Leftist organizations were so strong that the CC had to place the province under direct military rule. Huang Yung-sheng (presently Minister of Defense) was sent to Canton to take command. The Leftist Red Flag faction attacked the military command several times during the following months, seizing arms, records, etc. and agitating for the removal of Huang. The armed struggle in Canton continued into mid-1968 before the resistance of the Left had finally been suppressed.

Between February and August 1967 the Left forces became more and more conscious and began to focus on the persons and institutions they held responsible for the failure of the leading cadres to "step aside." They directed their fire at Chou En-lai and the Vice-Premiers he was sheltering, Chen I and his Foreign Ministry and the PLA. Red Guards in Peking held several mass rallies denouncing Li Hsien-nien and Nieh Jung-chen, both high-ranking PLA generals who had turned to economic affairs. (The latter was in charge of the nuclear development program). On each occasion Chou personally intervened to rescue his fellow bureaucrats. In July, 1967, Lin Chieh, editor of *Red Flag* (he was purged in August) published an editorial calling for the "dragging out of a small handful of capitalist-roaders in the Army." Even though this formulation was compromising (a "small handful") it was still too much for Mao and Lin Piao who insisted that the members of the CR Group who had connections with the radicals be purged. Chiang Ch'ing (Madam Mao), who had brought these men onto the Group in the first place, was prevailed upon to denounce her proteges in a speech to a meeting of representatives from Anhwei on Sept. 5,

> ". . . Comrades, I am not in favor of armed struggle, and you must not think that I like it, because I'm for 'peaceful struggle, not armed struggle.' . . . Armed struggle always hurts some people and damages state property.
> At present, let us take Peking as an example. There is a bad thing, and I call it a bad thing because it is a counter-revolutionary organization, called the "May 16" corps.

Numerically it is not a large organization, and superficially the majority of its members are young people, who are actually hoodwinked. The minority consists of bourgeois elements ... who make use of the ideological instability of the young people .... The "May 16" assumes an "ultra-Leftist" appearance; it centers its opposition on the Premier (Chou).

Now we come to the second question: the army. Sometimes earlier, there was this wrong slogan: Seize a 'small handful in the Army.' As a result, 'a small handful in the Army' was seized everywhere and even the weapons of our regular troops were seized.

Comrades, come to think of it: If our field Army were thrown into confusion and if trouble occurred, could we tolerate such a situation? ... The slogan is wrong. Because the Party, the government and the Army are all under the leadership of the Party. We can only talk about dragging out the handful of Party capitalist roaders in authority and nothing else .... Even if some comrades, a minority of comrades, some individual comrades in our Army committed serious errors, they need not be dealt with in this way.

I have talked with the young fighters of Peking about this question. Last year you went out to kindle the fire of the revolution and exchange revolutionary experience. But by going out again now, you will only do a disservice. You said that you were unable to drag out the small handful in the Army and that you needed our help in doing this. In some places, this has been done. This is a wrong assessment of the situation, and the result of the fact that you have fallen into a trap set by others.

We must not paint a dark picture of the PLA, for they are our boys and we must protect their honor. (Here she reads out the CC's Sept. 5 Order Forbidding Seizure of Arms .... from the PLA, which instructed the Army to respond with force to attempted seizures.) Do you know what has happened? Military materials allotted for the support of Vietnam have been seized, and the ammunition. Those were ammunitions for striking the American imperialists! ... Some people also seized foreign ships. In Peking a strange thing has happened: some people went to the foreign embassies to make troubles and the office of the British Charge d'Affaires was burned down. We, of course, are determined to hit the American imperialists and reactionaries. But we must not make trouble at foreign embassies, and we must not go aboard foreign ships. It would be childish for good people to do so; and when bad people do so, they want to ruin the reputation of the country."

During August a sharp struggle took place around the Foreign Ministry. Struggle sessions had been taking place against Chen I since June and had forced Chinese foreign policy slightly Leftward. Statements appeared focusing on armed revolutionary struggle against Ne Win in Burma and Sihanouk in Cambodia. In August Leftists, led by Yao Teng-shan, last Chinese representative in Indonesia, seized the Foreign Ministry. The British mission was sacked and burned, rebellion in Hong Kong was encouraged, foreign ships were boarded and cargo seized and editorials began to oppose the Vietnamese negotiations. But this period ended rapidly when Mao personally intervened to "save" Chen I and began to repair the damage the Left had caused to China's "diplomatic position."

After September the formation of revolutionary committees continued in more provinces. But the Left had also grown stronger in several provinces and continued to resist the continuation of bourgeois rule under this new guise. In Hunan, "Sheng-wu-lien" held out until April before being crushed and disbanded by the PLA. The most protracted struggle took place, however, in Kwangsi, the province bordering on N. Vietnam. Here, the Kwangsi "April 22 Rebel Grand Army" had been engaged in seizing arms bound for Vietnam and in preventing the formation of a stable revolutionary committee. A leaflet of June 1968 reveals how the cadres on the preparatory group for the revolutionary committees armed the members of conservative organization to attack "April 22." As a result of the battle, says the leaflet:

"more than 2,000 buildings were reduced to rubble in Wuchow, more than 4,000 inhabitants rendered homeless, hundreds of rebel fighters killed and more than 3,000 April 22 fighers and revolutionary masses arrested, creating a serious situation in which diehard conservatives and capitalist-roaders tried to reverse previous correct decisions on them." (Transl. in *SCMP, no 4213, p.4)*

Leaders of "April 22" and its rivals, along with Army leaders, were called to Peking in July for a meeting to settle the conflict. There, April 22, like the Leftists of Peking, Shanghai and Hunan, found out too late which side Chairman Mao was really on. At the meeting, "April 22" was condemned, the Army was ordered to protect the railway lines to Vietnam (many of which had been closed for months by Leftist railway workers) and the composition of the preparatory group was approved. (The CC Notices on the Kwangsi situation are translated in *URS, Vol. 53, Nos. 1 and 2; the minutes of the above meeting in URS, Vol. 53. No. 9)*

By autumn of 1968 the Left had been defeated everywhere and the new power structure was consolidated. A portion of the cadres had been purged, although many were and will be re-educated and rehabilitated, but the great bulk of the cadres who had carried through the bourgeois policies of 1960-66 remained in power. The role of the military officers had increased, as can be seen in the composition of the new 9th CC, announced at the 9th CCP Party Congress in April 1969. Of the 279 members, 123 are military cadres, 76 are leading political cadres and 80 are former members of mass organizations loyal to the Right. The continuity of political leadership is shown by the fact that eight of all the 11 members of the Standing Committee of the Politbureau of the 8th Central Committee (elected in 1956) are full members of the new 9th CC. Twenty-three members of the new CC had been criticized and repudiated in mass struggles during the GPCR. The Cultural Revolution, as an attempt by the proletariat to take power back from the bourgeois revisionists, has failed and the Right is in firm control of the CCP.

Why did it fail? The basic reason is insufficient mass support and an important factor in that was misconception about the role of Mao Tse-tung. Repeatedly, the Left forces, or at least some part of them, continued to hope that Mao would come over to their side and agree to lead a new Marxist-Leninist party to attack the entire bourgeois class. Because they waited upon his moves and looked to his initiative, the Left constantly found itself unorganized and insufficiently prepared for the sharp attacks made upon it by the Army, with Mao's approval. Behind the weakness lies the long history of the personal cult of Mao, which culminated in the quasi-religious glorification of him during the GPCR. This played an especially big part within the Army, where Lin Piao had been leading a "learn from Chairman Mao" campaign since 1962-63. Their reluctance to admit (or even conceive) that Chairman Mao might be wrong in his evaluation of the situation must have led many Leftists to accept, partially, a Centrist stance. This failure to break with Maoism, ideologically and organizationally, led to their defeat. Moreover, the bourgeoisie had used the period 1960-66 to conduct an intense ideological campaign against Leftist thought which must have weakened the ideological consciousness of the masses to the point where only a minority, though a very large one, was willing to follow the Left into battle.

Since the end of 1968, the Leftist students and workers have been sent away from the centers of power as part of the "hsia-fang" movement of sending young people to live and work among the peasants in remote and difficult regions. (In itself, there is nothing wrong with students going to learn from peasants; but, at this particular time and in this political context, the main aspect of "hsia-fang" is to fragment the Left and remove it from contact with the urban proletariat.

None of the Leftward ideological or economic trends of the GPCR can last. Material incentives are reappearing as the emphasis shifts overwhelmingly in publications and propaganda to technical innovations (see any recent Peking Review). The Draft Regulations for Rural People's Communes of 1961-62 have never been changed; in fact, the CC, throughout the GPCR, emphasized that they would be around for at least 30 years. With the Right in firm political control, these trends will continue.

TRANSLATION SERIES

CB   – *Current Background*, U.S. Consulate-General, Hong Kong
ECMM – *Extracts From China Mainland Magazines*, Hong Kong
SCMP – *Survey of China Mainland Press*, Hong Kong
CNS   – *China News Summary*, Taiwan
URS   – *Union Research Service*, Union Research Institute, Hong Kong

CHINESE PRESS

Red Flag (Hung ch'i or Hongqi) – bi-weekly theoretical magazine of the CCP
Renmin Ribao (or Jen-min Jih-pao) – People's Daily, daily organ of the CC of the CCP
New China News Agency (NCNA) – English-language news service of the Chinese government

OTHER SOURCES OF STATISTICAL DATA

Barnett, A.C., *Cadres, Bureaucracy and Political Power in Communist China*
Schurmann, H.F., *Ideology and Organization in Communist China*
Chao Kuo-chun, *Economic Planning and Organization in Mainland China*, Vol. 2

CHINA: LET A HUNDRED FLOWERS BLOOM OR

"A Host of Dragons Without a Leader"

Nigel Harris

Nigel Harris is a leading theoretician of the neo-Trotskyist group, International Socialists, which is probably the largest of the left groupings today in the United Kingdom.

The origins of the International Socialists are in the Trotskyist movement. Towards the late forties, a grouping within the British Trotskyist movement developed the theory that Russia was no longer a "degenerated or deformed workers' state", but a class society where a new form of capitalism prevailed — "state-capitalism". The main theoretical elaboration was the work of Tony Cliff. As a result, the Cliff Group and other people who held the "state capitalist" position were either expelled or left and late in 1950 began to publish a duplicated paper Socialist Review. The new group, taking its name from the paper, held its founding conference at Whitsuntide in 1951.

Another essential component of IS's basic theory was the idea of the "permanent arms economy", which sought to explain how the prolonged post-war boom was possible. The argument was that it was arms expenditure that was postponing capitalist crisis.

The Socialist Review group was, admitted by its own historian Ian Birchall, throughout the fifties, a purely propaganda group. However the group which became better known as International Socialists began to grow significantly before and after 1968. Members of the International Socialists are trying to build IS into a revolutionary workers' party although they feel that the task is still very far from being completed. (History of International Socialists by I. Birchall; International Socialism No. 77)

Nigel Harris is an economist teaching at Oxford University. He is the author of a new book, India-China: Underdevelopment and Revolution, in which he endeavours to show that neither private capitalism (as in India) nor state capitalism (as in China) can bring off development; and that the effective economic performance of China is not all that different from that of India!

I   The *detente* between Washington and Moscow, the partial 'thaw' in the Cold War, permitted the expression not just of nationalistic polycentrism between nation-States, but polycentrism within each nation-State. The forces of revolt were not merely expressed in a Gaullist foreign policy against NATO, but also in France's May revolt against de Gaulle himself. Nowhere has this double process been more vividly illustrated than in China where the basic problems of survival for the majority are greater. Between the slack expansion of agricultural output and the inexorable pressure of a rising population, in a world overshadowed by the industralised powers, by the military threat of the United States and Soviet Union, there is almost no room for manoeuvre. China, like the other underdeveloped countries, is trapped in a stifling straight-jacket where despair and bold rhetoric mingle on equal terms.

But just because it is an underdeveloped country, China's economy can survive much of the Cultural Revolution when it is isolated to a few urban centres. The rural majority continues its life much as before. The economy does not depend in the same way upon a single integrated structure. The villages depend much less upon the cities than in a more developed country. Thus, in some of the wilder talk about 'civil war', one must be careful to see how many people and places were really involved. Sometimes, it seems, a minor scuffle between two bands of teenage thugs has been duly reported with solemnity on Red Guards posters as a major struggle, and thence transmitted to the world press as a collapse of the social order. The information emerging from China is more fragmentary than that on any other country in the world, and must be treated with a certain initial scepticism.

On present evidence, the Cultural Revolution is drawing to a close. It may still be a long time before the entire country is once more at peace, but the leadership does seem to be committed to establishing peace. Nothing has happened since the climax of January, 1967, to change the basic balance of forces in the country. Up to that time, the central Party leadership held the initiative and set the pace. It was able to escalate its war against opposition forces in the Party in successive phases, until it virtually abandoned the Party altogether. The climax was reached when the students, the Red Guards, were shown to have failed in their task of remaking the Party, and the Peking leadership appealed to the workers and peasants to 'bombard the Party headquarters', 'to seize power'. It thereby released a host of new forces which rapidly came to threaten itself. Despite many short-term zigzags in policy, since January, 1967, the leadership has been trying to draw back from the abyss. It has been forced to devote itself to the problems raised by its campaign, rather than to the purposes of the campaign itself. It first sought to use the army (PLA) to impose a single unified order on the country, and then, when this proved inadequate, to promote conservative deals with whatever local provincial leadership, in collaboration with the army, would co-operate.

But to do this was to deny the earlier rhetoric of the Cultural Revolution, to rehabilitate the discredited Party cadres and reject implicitly the competing demands of Red Guards and Revolutionary Rebels. Peking had too little power over the whole country to secure its will, and sudden spasms of violence and conflict have swept through provincial capitals as new and old groups competed for first place in the new order. Despite the merciless exposure of the old provincial Party leadership, many of them returned to power. The stalemate between Peking and the opposition could not have been illustrated more vividly. Neither side could defeat the other, and in their common interest in domestic order against the mass of the population, both were forced back into co-operation. The crucial problem — namely, the balance of power between Peking and its provinces — remained unsolved. Indeed, if anything, the Cultural Revolution has immensely exacerbated the problem rather than approached its solution.[2]

As the campaign proceeded, it connected different layers of the population and Party in different areas at different times. This immense complexity of issues and loyalties is the background to the twists and turns in Peking's policies. Once opened, the contents of Pandora's Box threatened to take control. But each change in policy ran the risk of inciting new groups of people to begin to compete for the prizes, and ultimately, a real — rather than rhetorical — class war. There are some signs that a few of the rebels made the transition from attacking 'a handful in the Party taking the capitalist road' to war on 'the Red Capitalist Class', a phrase from the manifesto of a Hunan rebel group, Sheng-wu-lien[3]. The rise and fall in Peking's attacks on the 'ultra-Left' and 'anarchism' gives an indirect indication of how serious the threat at times has been, and, perhaps, still is.

The twists and turns in policy embody Peking's search for an agency to replace or reform the Party, to sidestep localised webs of power in each province, and thereby impose a new centralised regime. On the 'Left' swings, it tried to use new forces — Red Guard bands, Revolutionary Rebel groups; on the 'Right', it brought in the army (PLA) in the first instance, and then the Party cadres themselves once again. The PLA is only three million-strong, unlike the 17-20 million cadres in and around the old Party, and provincial PLA units in any case are likely to have loyalties to the province concerned. The stresses within the PLA threatened the sole remaining coherent framework in the country as a whole, as well as exposing China's vulnerability to Soviet or American threats. In the end, Peking was reduced to try to rehabilitate the Party itself. Nothing was solved; two and a half years had been lost with nothing to show — except, perhaps (for 1967 alone) 86.4 million copies of Mao's *Selected Works* and 350 million Red Books.

II. The Centralisation Issue.

The Cultural Revolution was an attempt to overcome the sluggish rate of China's economic growth, and one of the results of that sluggish rate, localised power groups which inhibited central direction. At the beginning of the campaign, the most important of the localised groups were in control of provincial administration. At the end, new groups had blossomed at every level, and, indeed, outside the administrative structure altogether.

The battle is, then, over the distribution of scarce resources. It is partly between town and country, between different provinces, between the provinces and Peking; it is also partly between workers and managers or Party cadres, and, in some areas, between peasants and Party cadres. The first kind of conflict is one between different geographical areas; the second, between different national classes (or fragments of such classes). Territorial conflict is endemic in most underdeveloped countries, and has been central to the pre-industrialization history of the developed countries. However, in developed countries today, interdependence between the different territorial parts of the economically centralised nation-State has long since superseded conflict. There are, of course, some kinds of regional conflict still — Welsh and Scottish nationalisms are currently embodying certain regional demands. But these are only possible on the margins when social and class conflict is relatively mild. When class conflict rises, it tends to eliminate much of the significance of regional clash in modern developed countries. Rather than Welsh employers and workers combining to fight London; Welsh, Yorkshire, Scottish and other miners combine to fight the National Coal Board, part of an employing class which includes Welsh, Scottish and so on employers.

In a backward country, national interdependence is weak, for the economy consists of much more independent segments. National classes are therefore very underdeveloped as well. The ruling class is 'embryonic'; that is, its members have not all identified a common class interest, and particular groups are prepared to press their opposition to the national centre to the point of open rebellion. Thus each territorially defined ruling group is open to pursuing its own narrow interest at the cost of the national ruling class interest; the final stage is pursuing this narrow interest, is to secede from the parent State altogether and create an independent State. Whether or not a group does this depends upon its assessment of its strength (how far it is economically independent in fact, how far its own subordinate classes will follow it) and its assessment of the strength concentrated in the parent-State (if the parent-State has a monopoly of military force and is willing to use it, the local group is unlikely to rebel except where it can get foreign assistance on a comparable scale).

An exacerbating condition in this relationship is the demand the parent State makes upon the local ruling group to relinquish a share of the surplus generated in the group's territory. If the group's territory is economically advanced, its surplus is likely to be an industrial one; in return, it may receive foodstuffs, without which it cannot survive. Thus, the industrialised areas are likely to have, initially, a greater interest in a strong national centre which can provide them with adequate foodstuffs. By contrast, the food-surplus areas are likely to resent central control since their product is taken, yet, in conditions of high accumulation, they see few returns in terms of manufactured goods. If foodstuff is plentiful, these tensions may be minor ones, the real debate surrounding the national distribution of investment resources – which area gets the next steel mill. The foodgrain surplus areas have power to influence national investment distribution when food is short; the food-deficit areas, often (but not always) the industrialised areas, can attract the major share of investment resources when food is easy to obtain because they already provide an infrastructure of previous investment which will maximise the use of such resources.

On the other hand, every local ruling group has some interest in securing as much as possible of the surplus its territory produces in order to strengthen its own power within the territory.

This is a very oversimplified account of a complex issue. There are many other factors at stake in the bargaining between different areas, and between areas and national centre – for example, whether or not the area is also an international boundary; or whether or not communications and distance preclude the centre actually moving force against a recalcitrant province. In China, Peking has, in the short term, to trust the Lhasa administration because it cannot move large numbers of troops into Tibet rapidly. Peking needs to maximise the rate of capital accumulation if China is to develop as a national economy. To do so, it must secure unimpeded control of the surplus generated in every province. To do this, it must prevent provincial Parties from skimming the provincial surplus for their own purposes, and distribute the national surplus as it thinks fit. If Shanghai can make the best use of new investment, then that is where new investment must go, even if it deprives the poor provinces and increases regional differentials in terms of income and power. However, a number of features over the past decade have steadily strengthened local power and thereby progressively inhibited Peking's ability to plan. Overcoming these inhibitions cannot indefinitely be postponed. The longer entrenched enclaves of provincial power are permitted to stand against Peking, the more powerful they become, the more difficult Peking finds it to accelerate the overall rate of development. Thus, the Maoist stress upon the need for poverty and self-sacrifice is a stress on the need for a common subordination to central control, a common sacrifice of consumption for national accumulation.

In Imperial China, the conflict between provinces and centre was one important theme at different times. When the Imperial dynasty was strong, it sought to inhibit the creation of a provincial opposition by keeping the mandarins in circulation between provinces. Provincial mandarins were supposed never to have sufficient time and opportunity to build up a proper base within the province. This circulation of officials has not happened in Communist China. The provincial administration of 1965 was still manned by many of the people who originally took power in the province after the fall of the Kuomintang, and the regional bureaux are still, broadly, the original occupying armies.

Between 1948 and 1957, the country as a whole was steadily centralised, a process culminating in the period of tightest central control during the First Five Year Plan. Yet the unity of the country still depended upon the local Party cadres: indeed, holding the Party together meant holding China together. But there was in this period room for Peking to manoeuvre. A respectable rate of economic growth and rising foodgrains output made central control tolerable. This does not mean there were no provincial tensions. For example, in the 1953-54 rectification campaign (which, at the national level, purged Kao Kang and Jao Shu-shih), the first secretaries in six provinces and two autonomous regions were changed. Again, the purge of 1957-58 affected 12 provinces and autonomous regions. It seems there had been much grumbling among provincial leaders during the speed-up in collectivisation in 1956-57, and the purged were accused of favouring a slower rate of economic growth and qualifying national directives. In Honan, the Party first secretary was said to have argued: 'Honan is different from Peking and Shanghai, and what is marked out by the central leadership can serve only as a guide[4]. Small personal cliques were said to have seized control of some provincial parties for their own benefit, the cliques appealing to provincial loyalties. For example, the purged Governor of Shantung is alleged to have said: 'I am a native of Shantung, I am for the people of Shantung and the cadres of Shantung'; by implication, against the Pekinese. He was accused of packing the party with his own supporters and blocking national directives. But the purge in practice affected mainly the middle ranks of the provincial Parties rather than its top leadership. During the Cultural Revolution, others have been accused in identical language – for example, Peng Chen, the Peking Party leader until 1966, was accused of making Peking an " 'independent kingdom' ", watertight and impenetrable".

Perhaps one of the motives of the central leadership in the Great Leap Forward was to break the provincial leadership's power by decentralising the economy to the under-province level, to the county (*Hsien*) and Commune. Peking relinquished substantial controls over management, finance, grain procurements, price control and planning. There was some decentralisation of control and planning. There was some decentralisation of control over new capital projects, and in some parts of the economy, control was divided between the province and the centre ('dual control' of the railways, for example). Peking remained in control of interprovincial grain balances, even if not of grain procurement.[5]

From 1960, Peking tried to reverse the results of this disastrous loss of power which, far from destroying the provincial leadership, had only strengthened it. But the agricultural disasters of 1960-61 made it, in the short term, even more dependent upon provincial co-operation. Any slight variation in local administrative control could produce famine in such conditions. Peking concentrated on a cautious, conservative economic policy, described earlier by Cliff as a phase of 'neo-NEP'[6]. The margins were far too narrow to gamble, even though permitting the situation to continue only made it more difficult to solve later on. Differentials between rich and poor, advanced and backward areas, town and country, between social strata, widened, underpinned by the provincial

Party's toleration of its own friends and supporters. The longer Peking permitted local power to continue unhampered – or rather, checked by little more than Peking's propaganda rhetoric as in the 'socialist education campaign' – the more powerfully entrenched provincial leaders might become, the more slippery Peking's grasp of provincial surpluses. The threat implicit in the shifting power balance was that Peking might become just a servicing centre for real power groups in the provinces or the front for a coalition of powerful provinces. Indeed, it has been argued that Peking's purchase of grain on the world market was not so much to meet a general deficit at home as to give it an edge in the hard bargaining over the distribution of interprovincial grain balances[7]. Peking imports about six million tons of foodgrains a year, which is a mere three per cent of China's total grain output, but 12 per cent of central procurements and probably much more of interprovincial balances. However, the grain is not solely for domestic use; it has been used as an instrument of foreign policy – grain was exported to Egypt last year so that China could compete with Soviet foreign policy.

However, breaking the provincial leadership is only one part of the problem. Once the web of control at the provincial level is broken, it might merely be that a multiplicity of groups would be created at the under-provincial level, each vying for power in the province, each exhibiting what the Peking press calls a 'mountain stronghold' or 'small group' mentality. At least, in the old situation, Peking had only to deal with 28 local authorities (provinces, autonomous regions, autonomous municipalities). Destroying that level of administration could create thousands of different groups to be dealt with. In addition, both the central leadership and the provincial leaderships were not necessarily united. At the centre, within the small leadership groups, different perspectives were available, and as the struggle outside developed, so it connected with this inner struggle, fragmenting the inner cliques, which in turn fragmented the forces outside. At every level, factionalism threatened to dissolve what unified structure remained, producing an immensely complex picture where easy identification of the forces became impossible. And the disagreements came to range over the whole spectrum of foreign and domestic policy – from the best way forward for the economy, to China's relationship to Russia, the US and Vietnam.

The PLA seemed to be the sole force left to hold the whole together. Securing the sowing and harvesting of crops was one of its persistent responsibilities. Yet it was too small to take up the burdens of the Party properly. If the rural Party administration weakens, the peasants may fail to relinquish the grain. Honan radio, for example, rebuked selfish peasants for hoarding grain, for 'economism', in mid-1967. But once the grain is hoarded, a force as small as the PLA cannot possibly find it. Fortunately, 1967 seems to have been a very good year – officially, 10 per cent above 1966's output. But the limitations of PLA control were vividly illustrated. The centre of necessity had to begin the process of rebuilding the Party, whatever the economic cost.

The central leadership – or the dominant faction within it – closed all educational institutions in mid-1966 in order to make available an extra-Party scourge of the cadres. It was ironic, since earlier Mao had said the youth was the weak factor in China's progress since it had not experienced Kuomintang rule. At every stage, the Red Guards needed official encouragement and support for survival – for transport, telegraphic services, food, accommodation, newsprint, etc. – and were subject to subversion by different factions in the central and provincial leaderships. By November, 1966, it was clear the Red Guards were no longer a useful instrument for the central leadership, but, on the contrary, merely engendered factionalism and violence. From that date, the Peking leadership began the long task of trying to get the students back to school and University.

In February, 1967, primary schools were officially reopened, with secondary schools and universities supposed to open in March: all, despite earlier promises, unreformed. By June, it was clear work had not been resumed in the schools. They were used as faction headquarters, as dormitories; the teachers were often too demoralised to risk returning to work; university textbooks had been denounced, but no new ones written. One correspondent[8] estimated that on average a half to two-thirds of all school pupils attended school for one or two hours per morning to read or sing Mao quotes and undergo military training.

The summer violence of 1967 sucked in the Red Guards groups once more and made them, at particular times and places, briefly important. The campaign in the Party had little effect — the Red Guards were determined to get their foot in the door before the old order returned. Hsieh Fu-chih, Minister of Public Security, reproved the youth for squabbling in October[9], and said some of them might gain admittance to a reformed Party after a probationary period.

None of this had very much effect, and the summer of 1968 found bands of Red Guards again awaiting the opportunity to participate in the struggle for power. However, throughout 1968, the central leadership shifted its emphasis almost entirely away from youth — the 'working class' should now be the main element in the Cultural Revolution. The Party recruited squads of 'workers and peasants' to do the task the PLA had failed to do, and moved them into all educational institutions to reimpose discipline. The first such team entered Tsinghua University in late July, and was rewarded with a basket of mangoes from Mao himself[10]. A much greater stress appeared in the Party press on the errors of 'intellectuals', and the need for them to submit to discipline.

However, there were some suggestions that the more radical elements in the Cultural Revolution Group in Peking still saw the youth as a possible replacement for the Party. On September 7th, a rally to celebrate the end of the long agonising process of forming Revolutionary Committees in all provinces was held in Peking. But it was not held before the famous Tienanmen, nor did Mao or Lin Piao attend. And Chiang Ch'ing, Mao's wife and one of the most important members of the Cultural Revolution Group, gave a most curious speech to the assembled students which included the following ambiguous comment on her predecessor's speech: 'You will notice that — unlike Chou En-lai — I have pointedly omitted to mention the workers and peasants who are trying to break you up'. It had other waspish asides, and ended with an injunction to the audience to keep its spirits up. Clearly, someone had been defeated.

III. The Cultural Revolution in 1967 and 1968

The brief climax to the Cultural Revolution in January, 1967, was followed by an immediate and rapid retreat by the central leadership. A central directive of January 21st ordered the PLA to intervene and restore order, seeking to create conservative coalitions, the 'triple alliances', between the PLA, reformed Party cadres and Revolutionary Rebels (the 'worker' successors to the Red Guards) in all provinces. However, whatever the rhetoric about triple alliances, at this stage military control was the first priority to overcome urban disorder and stiffen the administration for the tasks of spring sowing in the countryside. The PLA instructions were very wide:

'In all institutions where seizure of power has become necessary, from above to below, the participation of the PLA and militia-delegates in the temporary organs of power of the revolutionary triple alliance is indispensible. Factories, villages, institutions of finance and commerce, of learning (including colleges, secondary and primary schools), Party organs, administrative and mass organisations, must be led with the participation of the PLA . . .·where there are not enough PLA representatives available, these positions should better be left vacant temporarily' (*Red Flag*, Mar. 10th, 1967).

Press and radio urged the peasants to concentrate on the sowing, and *Red Flag* (Feb. 22nd) even criticised those who launched indiscriminate attacks on all persons in authority – such a policy 'robs the nation of the mature political and organisational skills of experienced men'. On March 6th, it reported that the Central Committee (which had not, apparently, met) urged all rural Party cadres to take the leadership in the spring sowing: 'Those cadres who have made mistakes', it said, 'should redouble their efforts in spring farm work to make amends'.

However, the more the PLA extended itself, the more *it* became the target for criticism rather than the old Party order. In particular, the Rebel group it failed to choose as its partner in a triple alliance sooner or later appealed over its head to Peking for arbitration. Sheer military involvement made the PLA vulnerable politically. In Peking itself, the PLA was midwife to a revolutionary municipal committee (the sixth 'triple alliance' formed to that time; 22 to go) of which Hsieh Fu-chih, Minister of Public Security, was chief; two of the four vice-chairmen and 14 of the 97 committee members were from the PLA.

On April 6th, the Party Military Affairs Committee issued a directive forbidding PLA units to suppress any rebel faction or to use force to secure order. It was to be a free time for all, and through the summer, the maximum violence and disorder of the Cultural Revolution occurred. The scale of the violence is impossible to estimate reliably, for the evidence is fragmentary and from biased sources. One Red Guard source retailed a speech by Hsieh Fu-chih in which he is supposed to have said that production in Peking fell by 7 per cent in April because of 'armed incidents'. However, it is unlikely that the statistical services of Peking were up to any such precise estimate so soon after the event. He is alleged also to have said that between April 30 and May 10, there were 130 armed struggles around the city, involving 63,000 people in all, with 50 to 100 casualties per incident.

Radio and press continuously appealed throughout the summer for an end to violence, to attacks upon soldiers and interference with public property[11]. The PLA was probably at the limit of its tolerance when the Wuhan incident in July dramatically illustrated its vulnerability and the central leadership's dangerous dependence on the PLA. The Wuhan Military Region commander was Chen Tsai-tao, a veteran Party soldier who had commanded the 4th Army in 1934 and become a full general in 1955. In the formation of Wuhan's Revolutionary Committee (the 'triple alliance'), he backed the One Million Heroes Rebel group as his collaborators. A coalition of seven Red Guard groups appealed to Peking against this, saying that the One Million Heroes was just a front for the old 'capitalist roaders' of the provincial party. Hsieh Fu-chih and Wang Li (head of the Party propaganda department) visited Wuhan to plead for the excluded Red Guards, and were promptly arrested by the PLA. Demonstrations against Chen in Peking, furious protests from the centre, rumours of the personal intervention of Chou En-lai, of paratroop drops on Wuhan and gunboats being sent from Shanghai up the Yangtze to Wuhan, finally secured the release of Peking's emissaries. The air force was said to have taken over security functions in Wuhan. Most of the military command acknowledged their errors and returned to the fold, although Chen himself was replaced by an officer from the Peking Garrison.

The details are suspect, but the substance of the incident dramatically revealed the weakness of the PLA as a substitute for a popular revolutionary force. Attacks on the capitalist roaders in the PLA followed (e.g. *Red Flag*, Aug. 17), but briefly, since to turn the attack on the PLA itself was to threaten the only safeguard left to the existing leadership, the sole framework left for holding together the country. Lin Piao is said to have restricted himself to urging patience upon the generals who met in military conference in Peking on August 9th. However, there were contradictory tensions within the national leadership. On the one hand, some leaders sought to protect the PLA; on the other, some of the Cultural Revolution Group were said to be pressing for selected Red Guards to be armed to help safeguard public property. It was perhaps the second group which sponsored or encouraged the attack on the Foreign Ministry in the same month, and the attacks on foreign embassies, culminating in the sack of the British Charge d'Affaires office on August 22nd.

But the violence was not restricted to Peking. 'A wind of armed struggle is developing in several regions', the *People's Daily* noted on August 19th, and the New China News Agency reported opposition to the formation of Revolutionary Committees in eight provinces. Ceaseless adjurations and edicts from the central leadership seemed to have little or no effect. Tougher measures were required to repudiate the wilder men. On August 20th, Wang Li of the Cultural Revolution Group was dismissed, and others immediately around him accused of being Kuomintang agents. The honour of the PLA had received its sacrificial victim. On August 25th, the national press launched a campaign: 'Support the army and love the people', and the PLA was ordered at all costs to restore the tattered urban administration to order. On September 5th, Red Guard sources reported that Chiang Ch'ing had publicly defended the central leadership, the Revolutionary Committees and the PLA against 'a gust of foul wind' on the ultra-Left and the Right among the Red Guards.

In the same month, Mao toured some provinces in order to examine the situation at first-hand. His verdict stressed the need to re-educate the Red Guards and Revolutionary Rebels lest they turn to the extreme Left. They must stop trying to be active in reforming society as a whole, and return to their schools and workplaces to form triple alliances there – where, we might add, the dangers were much less, and in any case, overseen by the PLA. It was clear that the situation had to be stabilised as rapidly as possible, the glaring gaps in ruling class solidarity closed lest it incite outsiders to try and get in. However, the Party administration could not just be restored in its old form or the opponents would redouble their efforts to destroy it and might, in addition, destroy the Peking leadership as well. Revolutionary Committees must be created as rapidly as possible, even if in practice it meant no more than a new name for the civil administration of the PLA or the old Party organisation itself. Revolutionary Committees must be created in the remaining 22 provinces by January, 1968, it was announced. Where disputes occurred, factions should send representatives to Peking for arbitration. As it happened, only seven more provinces received their Revolutionary Committees by the deadline, suggesting how difficult the stalemate had become in many provinces.

One major source of grievance, then, was who was to share in the prizes of new order. In October, Hsieh Fu-chih offered some clarification to the aspirant groups in announcing a new Party Congress in 1968 – in May or June, or just before October 1st[12]. The Congress, he said, must be organised from the top downwards lest the old guard dominate it – 'In this way, it will be possible to ensure that the rebels among the Party members will be in a majority'. And it should be much larger than past Congresses, not 1,000 but 10,000 representatives[13]. This would be a Congress with a vengeance, swamped with Peking nominees and incapable, by reason of its size, of deciding anything of significance. The 8th Congress was held in 1956, and, under the constitution, Congresses were to be held at four-year intervals. Yet the 9th, so long delayed, was not mentioned again in 1968, and one must presume that, with all safeguards, the Peking leadership still could not be sure of a majority.

With the winter, activity tended to fall. The Peking press concentrated on conservative themes, and the joint New Year editorial of the *People's Daily*, *Red Flag* and *Liberation Army Daily* stressed the need to consolidate, to complete the rectification of the Party organisation and strengthen it. In order of precedence, the Party and the Young Communist League (supposed to have been disbanded in 1966) appeared before the Red Guards. This did not mean that there were no dissonant voices at all. In Shanghai, troubles were reported, and in February, the press was once more taking to task 'anarchism', indiscipline and disobedience among workers and students. It was clear also that the events of 1967 had created a subterranean network of contacts and communications in particular areas which defied the Peking attempt to reimpose silence.

A further 12 Revolutionary Committees were set up by April, but many of them were little more than PLA-cadre fronts. Increasingly, criticisms were levelled at over-hasty rehabilitation of those disgraced – the 'mass organisations' were under-represented, and many of the old cadres were sneaking back into the new order, cadres which were "Left" in form but Right in essence'. Mao's current instruction (reported, *People's Daily*, 12th April) described the opposition to the Cultural Revolution as the same as that of the Kuomintang. The hardening of the line was a prelude to further violence. It came with the first intimations of spring, and blossomed in the summer heat. Yet it did not reach the proportions of mid-1967, perhaps because only one faction of the central leadership was supporting a greater role for the Revolutionary Rebels, the others being more concerned with the restoration of order.

The August 1st Army Day editorials unequivocally demanded absolute obedience by all to the PLA. On August 5th, the *People's Daily* denounced domestic polycentrism and demanded absolute obedience to centralised control (the paper said it was merely reiterating instructions contained in orders issued on July 3rd, 24th and 28th). The agency of social change, the leadership of the movement, was the 'working class' (*People's Daily*, August 15th). In practice, this meant the recruitment of teams of workers and peasants to take over detailed execution of policy from the hard-pressed PLA units – to assume control of schools and universities, of factories and urban administration. The PLA remained in command, but its agents now became squads of civilians under military and cadre supervision. In the cities, teams of vigilants were able to fill the gaps created by the erosion of the old public security organs.

Kwantung boldly set the target of one million men to join such teams, and Kweichow announced that up to 10 per cent of the workers in any one factory could participate in the takeover of educational institutions. Mao's instruction on such teams stated that they 'should stay permanently in the schools and colleges, take part in all the tasks of struggle-criticism-transformation there and always lead these institutions'[14]. Either there was a great deal of surplus labour in the factories, or overall production was likely to suffer by cutting the labour force.

At different stages, the leadership had tried to control the Red Guard factions – by placing them under PLA command, by sending them to the Communes for labour, and, even, for a brief despairing moment, on fruitless Long Marches. The shift to 'the leadership of the working class' can similarly be seen as a way of ridding the labour force of Revolutionary Rebels, shunting the worker factions into detailed and isolated work which would permit the restoration of order under PLA control. The Chinese working class has no independent class organisations with which to identify itself, to crystallise its policy. It exists in the Maoist teams by permission of the Party leadership. No doubt De Gaulle, testing the mild temperature of 'participation', would quite like to create teams of 'working-class' youth to bloody student noses, but nobody should be misled into thinking that this is somehow an authentic proletarian act. As will be suggested later in the article, wherever authentic proletarian organisation has in fact appeared, the central leadership has been quick to try and crush it.

On September 5th, it was announced that the last two Revolutionary Committees had been formed. The national press returned to the point from whence the Cultural Revolution began in the spring of 1966 – a critique of journalists and 'some intellectuals'. Liu Shao-chi remained the prime casualty, the scapegoat and warning to all the other cadres now to be rehabilitated. On National Day (Oct. 1st), the Peking press said that the 'handful of capitalist roaders' had now been overthrown and power returned to the proletariat (the same claim was made, somewhat prematurely, by *Red Flag* on July 1st). On October 15th, Peking radio said that China's Krushchev had been deprived of all Party posts, although presumably he still remained President of the Republic, and on November 1st, Liu was the first time publicly named by the radio in a broadcast reporting the decisions of an enlarged (sic) plenary session of the central committee, meeting since October 13th. Liu had been formally deprived of all powers and rank and expelled from the Party.

Is this all it was supposed to be about? For two and a half years, the Party's power had been systematically eroded, for no better reason that 'an extremely small handful' of 'renegades, spies, counter-revolutionaries, and cadres taking the capitalist road', led by Mao's erstwhile hier, now described as 'the main traitor, workers' thief and Kuomintang running dog'. It would strain the imagination too far to think so much had been gambled for so little. While the Red Guards rampaged in Peking streets, Liu and the Party Secretary, Teng Hsiao-p'ing, remained untouched in their Government residences. Liu is still not officially destroyed, since only a full Party Congress can ratify his explusion from the Party, and a National People's Congress, his dismissal as President of the Republic. Such devotion to constitutional niceties suggests how vulnerable the leadership feels itself to be: violence against an important member of the Party can be the precedent for violence against those that inherit.

IV. The Provinces.

The provincial level is the crucial area to observe the Cultural Revolution, and yet it is the area where there is least information. The essential issues have been decided here, rather than in the Peking leadership clique. What follows are some notes on Sinkiang,

Szechuan and Tibet, not at all because they are representative – indeed, they are among the least representative provinces of China – but because they illustrate some features of the opposition.

(i) *Sinkiang* is in the far north-west, with a long common border with the Soviet Union and a large non-Chinese population (Turkic tribes, who inhabit also the adjacent Soviet territory). Since 1955, the head of the administration has been a Hunanese, Wang En-mao, controlling the provincial Party, government and Sinkiang PLA units. The last is particularly important, since there are said to be 600,000 troops in Sinkiang along the Russian border. Lop Nor, the main nuclear testing site, is in Sinkiang, as well as plants of nuclear significance; the main gaseous plant producing enriched uranium is at Lanchow in neighbouring Kansu.

The Red Guards in Peking launched successive poster and press attacks on Wang in 1966, accusing him of ruthless brutality in controlling his fief. He is said to have repressed Red Guard attempts to enter Sinkiang – turning their trains round and despatching them back to Peking, gaoling others, and even driving some to a death by starvation in the Gobi desert. The attacks did not meet their target. Wang is said to have been received amicably at Mao's court in Peking on December 31st, and in February, 1967, the Cultural Revolution was officially suspended in Sinkiang on the grounds that it was a sensitive border region. The suspension coincided with a rumour that Wang had threatened to seize the nuclear installations in the north-west unless he was left in peace.

However, in June there were reports of fighting in Urumchi (Sinkiang's capital), and again in August. In between – in early July – again it was rumoured there had been a settlement between Wang and Peking. The Red Guard verbal attack continued unabated, as did reports of more trouble through 1968. Certainly, Sinkiang was one of the last provinces to establish a Revolutionary Committee. In the Peking announcement of its creation, Wang, the chief leader of the province since 1955, was not included among the list of 'capitalist roaders' ousted during the Cultural Revolution, but he was included as 'third vice-chairman'. However, when an important Albanian delegation recently visited Urumchi, it was Wang who met them on behalf of the province and made the main address of welcome. He was described as vice-chairman of the Revolutionary Committee and Political Commissar of the PLA Sinkiang Military Area Command[15]. Thus, in practice, very little appears to have changed in Sinkiang, whatever the rhetoric.

(ii) *Szechuan* is in the south-west, adjacent to Tibet. It is vital as a key grain producing area. It is also what the Red Guards called the heart of the empire of the south and south-west. The former Party head, Li Ching-chuan, the 'local emperor', came under heavy attack. Kweichow radio (Kweichow is a neighbouring province) permitted a former Party secretary from Ipin in Szechuan, Liu Chieh-t'ing, to broadcast his criticisms of Li (presumably he could not broadcast them in Szechuan itself). He accused Li of seeking to maintain Szechuan's grain capacity as a bargaining counter against Peking; of suppressing Peking's instructions to collectivise agriculture and create Communes; of giving collective agricultural property over to private peasant production; and of gaoling him, Liu, for two years for criticising the way the province was administered.

Liu, like many of the rebels, had his own fortune to think of – regicide is one way of trying to inherit the crown (Liu and his wife were subsequently both named as members of the Szechuan Revolutionary Committee). So that the truth of these accusations cannot be taken for granted. However, there was a fairly violent struggle for power in the province. In May, 1967, fighting was reported in Chengtu (the provincial capital), and also in June. On June 11, Red Guard sources alleged that 300 had been killed on June 7th in Chungking because the PLA political commissar had led 30,000 workers in defence of the old guard and against the attacks of 800 Red Guards (the figures seem very unlikely). Peng Chen, the Peking chief purged in the spring of 1966, is said to have visited Szechuan for talks with Li, to create, as the posters said, 'a stronghold of opposition' for the capitalist roaders. When Marshal Peng (purged in 1959) was re-arrested in 1966, it was in Szechuan.

In early July, a Peking team visited Szechuan, and also Yunnan province in the south; the leadership of Yunnan was said to be in league with Li to control the whole southwest. The visit did not settle the issue, for further fighting was reported in August, and also in the summer of 1968. A Revolutionary Committee was not established until May, 1968, one year after the announcement of a Preparatory Committee. All this, despite the fact that the strong-arm general of Tibet, Chang Kuo-hua, was transferred to Szechuan in late January, 1968 (he became subsequently Chairman of the Revolutionary Committee).

(iii) *Tibet* is certainly the most backward and barren province, geographically isolated from China proper and yet crucial for defence purposes by reason of its long and troubled border with India. Given the border problem and the Tibetan history of sporadic revolt against Chinese rule, the PLA has inevitably played the dominant role in Tibet. Tensions between the immigrant Chinese and the Tibetans are, however, probably less important for the Cultural Revolution than friction between the military rulers and the immigrant workers, exiled from their homes to work impossible hours in impossible conditions.

The conflict in Tibet, according to Red Guard sources, was between the Rebel Headquarters, supported by the mass of Chinese workers in Tibet, and the Great Alliance, sustained by the PLA under General Chang Kuo-hua (appointed in 1951). Very few Tibetans seem to have been involved at all. Chang was accused of suppressing the Red Guards and supporting the local Party leaders. In early February 1967, the old guard was said to be in control of Tibet, and the PLA to have declared martial law. On February 17th, some 120 were said to have been killed in fighting in Lhasa, and on February 18th, Lhasa radio reported that three PLA divisions had been drafted into Tibet. Simultaneously, Red Guard sources said the Cultural Revolution in Tibet – as in Sinkiang – was suspended. The Military Affairs Committees of the Party in Peking issued a statement saying that Chairman Mao fully supported General Chang, and Chang's critics were evil liars.

Some disturbances continued in 1967, and in August, some 500 Tibetan refugees crossed into India (the highest figure since 1962, when the border dispute with India broke into hostilities) with lurid accounts of persecutions. Again, Tibet's Revolutionary Committee did not make its debut until the very last minute. Yet, Peking must have felt moderately confident when it transferred Chang out of Tibet in January, 1968, to become Commander of the Szechuan Military Region; although not so confident that it appointed a successor – Chang remained in *de facto* control of the Tibetan Military Region and head of its Military Control Commission.

Other provinces also had bitter and sustained conflicts, although the exact alignments are not always clear. In Kwantung, for example, there have been persistent reports of violence from Canton, of clashes both between workers and students, and between Rebels and the PLA. Canton's proximity to Hong Kong makes it particularly subject to inflamed rumours, transmitted by excitable travellers. But there are more objective indices of some disturbance – the 90 per cent fall in passenger traffic between

Canton and Hong Kong in August, 1967; the 41 bodies washed up in Hong Kong in June, 1968. On June 8th, the Canton *Southern Daily* said that some 'class enemies' had 'fanned the evil wind of economism on a large scale in order to corrupt the combat spirit of the revolutionary masses. Some have incited the reactionary ideology of anarchism and sabotaged socialist labour discipline'[16]. On the other hand, the Canton international trade fairs have continued on schedule, and food and water supplies to Hong Kong have not been dramatically interrupted.

V. The People's Liberation Army.

The PLA has been an additional casualty in the Cultural Revolution. Spread too thinly over too wide a range of duties, its military capabilities can only have been weakened. The Peking Garrison has provided senior officers wherever needed to fill doubtful provincial gaps – for example, to head the Inner Mongolian Revolutionary Committee or take over Wuhan. It has also been purged, as when the deputy commander, Fu Chung-pi, tangled with a Red Guard faction and was dismissed[17]. The PLA generally has had also to submit to factional onslaughts – as Chiang Ch'ing put it in September, 1967, when she rebuked the Red Guards for attacking the PLA: 'Everywhere we seized their guns, beat them up and reprimanded them. But they did not strike back or argue'[18]. If they did not strike back, then the experience must have been a demoralising one for the troops.

The administrative tasks constantly expanded, and PLA senior officers were expected to take the initiative in setting up and manning the Revolutionary Committees[19]. On the other hand, the supply of officers was pruned by purges[20]. As the PLA seemed almost to be dissolving into a civilian administration, so the US escalated its war in Vietnam, the Russians were said to have installed missile sites along the Chinese border, and Moscow indicated how far it was prepared to go in subjugating critics by invading Czechoslovakia. The pressure within the PLA and the Party leadership to call a halt to the Cultural Revolution so that the army could resume its military role must have grown steadily stronger.

VI. The Workers.

Since the Cultural Revolution was primarily an urban phenomenon, the industrial working class inevitably played an important role. In the older cities, there is now a settled core of urban industrial workers with a relatively long history. It is a group which is highly privileged relative to newcomers to the city, and even more so relative to the peasants. The core of the urban industrial working class still includes men with political experience which long predates Communist rule, and possibly, for a few, stretches back as far as the great general strike of 1927. Such experience is at a premium during the turmoil of the Cultural Revolution, perhaps suggesting what the Party leadership attacks as 'ultra-Leftism'.

Theoretically, the settled core of industrial workers is protected by movement controls from massive dilution with new rural immigrants, but in practice, urban working conditions are so much better than rural that there is constant pressure from peasants trying to get into the city. The municipal authorities through check-points at railway and bus stations, on incoming highways, by use of the ration card, try to prevent illegal entry or the expulsion of illegal immigrants. Any breakdown in the administrative structure permits both new immigrants to enter the city, and those previously exiled to distant provinces (where labour is scarce) to return. Officially enterprises are permitted to recruit labour only through local labour departments, and, where rural labour is concerned, only with the agreement of the city and rural Commune authorities. When the economy is slack, the pressure to recruit labour is weak, and the problem of the authorities is how to expel the unemployed from the city. But every increase in the tempo of industrial activity tends to threaten the control system − enterprises have a strong incentive to evade the regulations in order to employ cheap rural labour. Over a long period, migration raises the urban population well beyond the employment capacity available when the economy is slack. For example, after the disasters of 1960-61, the Government officially sought to cut the urban population from 130 million to 110 million up to 1963, and banned the recruitment of rural labour. The effects of these proposals were probably not dramatic, since it is beyond the capacity of the urban administration to check everyone (despite the organisation of 'Street Committees', District Committees, and so on, designed to check the urban population). In any case, the steady expansion of the economy since 1963 has probably prompted enterprises to recruit rural labour once more. If the urban labour force were not diluted in this way, the labour scarcity would become such that there would be a substantial pressure to raise wages.

If individual enterprises have an incentive to evade the controls on recruitment, the Government itself is also seeking to squeeze industrial costs. It has proposed the 'worker-peasant' system to span the credibility gap. This system is supposed to overcome the distinction between town and country, but in fact it is the revival of a rather nasty capitalist tactic to employ cheap labour on temporary contracts from rural Communes, while sending expensive permanent urban workers out to the Communes. Rural labour is not a charge on the city, receives few fringe benefits (housing, medical services, old age pension), and urban labour is paid by the rural Commune (if the worker is old, the city avoids the cost of his pension while he is retired and therefore unproductive). However, rural labour is suitable only for a limited range of jobs, particularly seasonal and unskilled work (such as loading and unloading on the railways, in ports, mines and lumber plants). The clash between temporary and permanent workers and their mutual attack on the Party officials that sustain the system is one thread in the Cultural Revolution as it affected the cities and key industries, particularly the railways.

At the end of 1966, there were reports of large-scale sackings among temporary and contract workers in Shanghai.[22]. Retrospectively, we might guess this occurred because the Shanghai Party officials feared a purge and sought to appease the grievances of permanent workers and damage production in order to discredit the Cultural Revolution. Peking ordered the reinstatement of such workers, and this, in conjunction with massive immigration of Red Guards into Shanghai, precipitated a wave of industrial disputes, including strikes, demands for increased pay and lower hours. Just before Christmas, a harbour strike had begun, and the railways subsequently went on strike: together, this could have provided the beginning of a general strike. Some Party officials are said to have raided the banks to pay increased wages and year-end bonuses as a means of safeguarding their own position against a purge threat.

In the middle of this, some eleven Revolutionary Rebel organisations combined in the Shanghai Revolutionary Rebel Headquarters to seize the city administration. In retrospect, it seems, this *coup* was executed not so much by workers as by the faction that hoped to replace the existing Party administration (and probably included a good many ambitious cadres) but was frightened by the appearance of a complete collapse in order.

54

For the city was not only flooded with thousands of Red Guards, but also youth returned from exile in the provinces or rural areas, and peasant immigrants. Strikes threatened to paralyse the entire city, different factions were fighting openly for supremacy, and thousands of workers took the pretext of the Cultural Revolution to put down tools and take free trains to visit Peking and complain of their conditions.

The revolt in December and January, according to *Wen Hui Pao* (Jan. 21st, 1967), 'swept over the whole city and quickly spread to the rural areas with temporary crushing success'. In the middle, 'hundreds of thousands' of temporary and contract workers demonstrated against the system of their employment, imposed, according to instant official explanations, by the evil capitalist roaders. Chiang Ch'ing offered the same explanation when she met a delegation of contract workers on December 26th[23]. Yet the new Revolutionary Municipal Committee made no move to rectify the anomaly, and a bold statement of the All China Federation of Trade Unions in mid-January went so far as to say existing policy on contract employment was to remain as it was.

Temporary workers did not give up. Despite a ban on the independent organisation of temporary workers[24], they continued to organise and agitate. Red Guard sources even said that one organisation of temporary workers launched an attack on the Shanghai Revolutionary Municipal Committee, saying that conditions for workers were no better than in Kuomintang days. The unemployed held a rally on February 20th, demanding that they be permitted to keep their jobs in order to help the Cultural Revolution. The Municipal Committee, now firmly in the saddle and protected by the PLA, sternly rejected their demand and ordered them to leave their jobs; it reproved them for 'egotistical ideas' and 'economism'.

The Revolutionary Rebels were clearly not in the main ordinary workers, and, indeed, there was much friction between workers and Rebels. *Wen Hui Pao* (May 3rd, 1967) urged the Rebels not to 'regard all workers as conservatives and to fight "civil wars" against them. We must be aware', it went on, 'that, except for a few diehards, most of the workers misled by conservative groups are our class brothers'. In June, press and radio continued to attack 'economism' and also what appeared to be the formation of embryonic independent trade unions, officially stigmatised as workers' 'guild organisations'. These 'guild organisations' had earlier featured in a *People's Daily* article[25] where it was said that they were extending to cover busmen, cooks and technical school students, and were designed to 'formulate economic demands and raise the egotistical interests of particular groups'. The *People's Daily* would not have attacked such organisations if they had been solely restricted to the Shanghai area[26].

In July, the Shanghai Municipal Committee again denounced a second wave of demands for higher wages, improved welfare facilities and a changed labour system. It accused some of a conspiracy — 'they even put pressure on the new revolutionary order by threatening to slow down work or refuse work assignments'[27]. Again, in December, the Shanghai *Liberation Daily* condemned 'some persons (who) are once again demanding greater benefits and higher wages' and others who were trying to organise temporary workers[28]. Early in the New Year, *Wen Hui Pao*[29] attacked 'civil wars' among 'proletarian revolutionaries' in Kiangsu, Chekiang and Anwhei provinces. These battles, it said, had started in January, 1967, and in some cases, had not yet ceased. In particular, it mentioned a plot to seize the railways — 'These few people (the plotters) were so mad as to make out a plan for first controlling the towns and villages along the Shanghai-Nanking railway lines, occupying south Kiangsu, and advancing to control Shanghai and Chekiang'.

55

Forces, it said, were assembled in south Kiangsu, and included former Party cadres[30].

The railways were a particularly sensitive area throughout 1967 and 1968, a sector most easily sabotaged since there are very few lines and what there are, are crucial for the economy. In addition, the railways must have been very overburdened with traffic, since Red Guards and Revolutionary Rebels had been using them free since mid-1966. The authorities persistently warned railwaymen to stay at work, to prevent sabotage and resist all attempts to stop trains running. In August, 1967, troubles were reported from Canton, and in the following January, a conference of railway workers was called in Peking to discuss the problems of keeping the lines open. In the following months, stoppages, disputes and fighting were reported on the route to Lanchow in the north-west, in Kwantung in the south, and, in particular, in Kwangsi on the route to North Vietnam. On August 9th, Red Guard sources mentioned an instruction issued to railwaymen to end all violence along the Kwangsi route, to dismantle all factional strongholds along the Kwangsi line, return materials stolen from the shipments to Hanoi, and return arms lifted from the PLA (the order was supposed to be dated July 3rd, and to repeat orders issued by the Kwangsi provincial authorities on June 13th). Again, another conference of railwaymen met in Peking in mid-May, and Chou En-lai is said to have pinpointed the place of maximum difficulty on the railways as Liuchow, a point on the line from Nanning in Kwangsi to Hanoi. On August 11th, Peking radio celebrated the victory of its supporters over the faction that had seized the Liuchow line.[30a]

Some of the major oil, coal and steel centres were also said to have been affected by spasms of revolt. It has been estimated that two-thirds of the mining labour force is 'worker-peasant'. In 1967, clashes affected the main steel centre, Anshan, also the industrial city of Wuhan, as well as Paotow, Shanghai and Chungking. The leading role of the 'working class' was embodied in factory reorganisation to set up 'collective control' of production. Again, this was a 'revolution from above', designed almost certainly to inhibit authentic revolt rather than enshrine it, and to prevent wage pressures. It was said collective responsibility had replaced individual responsibility, wages had been made more egalitarian, and the clerical staff heavily pruned[31].

The overall evidence is fragmentary in the extreme, but it does suggest that some workers have been stirred into activity by the Cultural Revolution. The sediment will not settle in the coming years.

VII. Stability

China is a very large country, and thus quite capable of supporting apparently large conflicts in a few isolated places without this affecting the majority of the population or even being seen by visiting foreigners. Thus, there is a grave danger that the impact of the Cultural Revolution will be exaggerated. Probably the mass of the peasantry (excluding those immediately around large cities) has been untouched, and the rural cadres only slightly affected. The 1967 harvest is officially rated as very good, and there is no evidence of real hunger in the accessible parts of the country (although some reports have stressed the increase in the urban black market over the past two years). The middle level cadres in the cities have probably suffered much more, with significant effects in terms of urban administration, the demoralisation of the urban Party, and a probable decline in official initiative. Yet even here one must not exaggerate. Many of the important local cadres have probably learned to swim in the new tide of the Cultural Revolution, and learned to swim on top[32]. Perhaps around the cities, peasants have been affected, and possibly there has been more peasant hoarding of foodgrains (both because the procurement administration is weaker, and because the black market offers high incentives to those prepared to risk trading on it).

The speed with which the last Revolutionary Committees were created suggests that the process·was not much more than the re-baptism of the old order. That order has kept the countryside moving, and kept up the foodgrain output, without which the cities could not have made 'revolution'. The concessions made to the peasants in 1960-61 – for example, the right to cultivate private plots for a private market – have not been withdrawn.

The trade figures show no dramatic variation over the two and a half years of the Cultural Revolution, and the export figures (from non-Chinese sources) are some index of the state of agriculture. In 1966, exports to the West reached a record level for the fifth year in succession. In 1967, exports to the non-Communist world fell by 12 per cent, but imports were roughly the same. Sales to Hong Kong in the first half of 1968 were slightly below the comparable period for 1967; the lowest point in 1967 in sales to Hong Kong was reached in September, and affected textiles and livestock the worst[33]. This is fairly mild stuff beside some of the wilder accounts of the Cultural Revolution. It means that important Communes and factories have kept up output, and transport has shifted the goods.

The Canton trade fairs have continued to attract foreign businessmen, and routine trade negotiations have been sustained (Chinese trade missions visited Bonn and Paris in the spring of 1967, and Sino-German negotiations continued over a 3 million ton steel rolling mill). China's purchases of gold on the London market continued – a routine shipment of £49 million bullion left London for Peking in May, 1967. External assistance also continued – to Nepal, wheat to Egypt (50,000 tons), the promise of £100 million to Zambia for the Zambia-Tanzania railway.

Quite clearly also the nuclear programme continued. Although no scientific publications have been received from China since October, 1966, and the fate of University science departments is unclear, the Government research staff have been excluded from the Cultural Revolution[34]. China's sixth H-bomb test took place on June 17th, 1967, and a seventh was suggested by foreign seismographs on December 24th although not officially confirmed (the Japanese also alleged a further test on July 13th). This does not just mean that the nuclear sites, plants and labour have been free of trouble, but also that the massive inputs of power from the national economy have been available. When US diffusion plants were working full blast to stockpile Uranium 235, they consumed an eighth of national electricity supply. Although China has probably found a cheaper way of doing this, it must still impose a major demand on national energy resources, a demand that must have been met despite any disturbances. In the longer term, the programme might be affected by the decline of the output of appropriately skilled manpower from the institutes of higher education.

Industrial output in 1968 is compared favourably by Peking with 1966, which suggests that possibly 1967 was a poor year. Foreign estimates propose a 15-20 per cent drop in total output last year, but a slow expansion in 1968. Virtually nothing has been said officially about the Third Five Year Plan, of which this is, theoretically, the third year. Other projects have been completed this year – for example, the Yangtze bridge at Nanking was completed in October, some ten years after it was first begun under Soviet guidance.

Thus, although this evidence is indirect and fragmentary, there have been narrow limits to the Cultural Revolution. In particular areas, there have been major changes, but these have been perhaps relatively isolated. In Peking, in the central Party leadership, the limits have been least. One estimate suggests that, of the 11 members and alternate members of the Politburo active in 1965, eight have been dropped; of the 11 active members of the Party Secretariat, three have survived; of the 10 known directors of Central Committee departments, only one seems still to be active; 52 and 40 per cent of the Central Committee membership have been attacked during the Cultural Revolution[35].

VIII

The Cultural Revolution was an attempt by a section of the central Party leadership to re-establish central control over the whole country, perhaps as a prelude to accelerating the rate of overall economic growth. To do this, it had to destroy opposition at every level of the Party. It secured a monopoly of all official propaganda agencies, but it did not secure victory. On the other hand, the opposition remained (so far as one can tell) fragmented.

The national crisis which originally precipitated the Cultural Revolution remains as before. China's rate of economic growth is too slow to give any assurance that it will ever catch up with the advanced powers, that it will ever be able to institute a tempo of growth which will submerge domestic cleavages and integrate the country. What was lacking to institute Mao's order was an agency for social change sufficiently powerful and diffused throughout the country, sufficiently separate from the old Party, to execute his will. The central leadership was forced to rely on the army, and then, to rehabilitate the Party, lest disorder sweep away both sides in the conflict. Yet this retreat has settled none of the important issues, and indeed, it has exacerbated the solution of those issues. The Party administration, bowed but unbeaten, remains the sole effective guarantee of China's unity and continued output. That administration has been itself fragmented by the Cultural Revolution, and perhaps, in part, demoralised, so that although it is the only framework holding the country together, it is now even less likely to take bold initiatives in development.

Outside the Party, the youth and some sections of workers have been involved in action, have seen the local ruling class completely discredited, have read reams of dirt on all the bureaucrats, and have perhaps glimpsed freedom. They cannot all be bought off with places on Revolutionary Committees, for there are too many of them. Subterranean communications survive, and pockets of resistance will continue, probably through to the next explosion. For Mao's defeat is a defeat for Chinese development, and he will once more be forced to take up the same issues again if Peking's power is to survive. Next time he tries, he may find an authentič revolt on his hands.

Thus, as China returns to silence once more, a legacy remains. On the one hand, stalemate within the fragmented ruling class; on the other, a legacy of simmering hostility among the other urban classes.

1. **Red Flag, 23 Feb 1967.**
   Unless specifically stated, the sources for much of the material in this article are: the serious Western press (viz **Sunday Times, The Times, The Observer, The Economist, Le Monde,** etc); **Survey of Mainland China Press** (SCMP), USIS, Hong Kong; **China Quarterly** (CQ), London; **Far Eastern Economic Review** (FEER), Hong Kong; **Peking Review,** Peking.

2. This article will, in the main, take for granted the arguments and material on the Cultural Revolution presented in earlier issues of **IS** — cf.

   The Notebook, **IS 26**, autumn 1966, p 7.

   Nigel Harris, China: What Price Culture? **IS 28**, spring 1967, p 22.

   Tony Cliff, Crisis in China, **IS 29**, summer 1967, p 7.

3. Jan 1968; cf **FEER** 40, Oct 3 1968, p 74.

4. cited Tiewes, F, The Purge of Provincial Leaders, 1957-8, **CQ** 27, July-Sept 1966, p 21.

5. The details can be found in: Audrey Donnithorne, **China's Economic System,** London, 1967. The same author has also discussed the conflict between grain-deficit and grain-surplus provinces in her evidence to the Joint Economic Committee of Congress, **Mainland China in the World Economy, Hearings,** Washington, 1967, pp 46-50.

6. cf Cliff, **op cit.**

7. cf. Donnithorne, **Hearings, op cit.**

8. Harald Munthe-Kaas, Peking correspondent, **Sunday Times,** 25 June 1967.

9. Oct 24 1967, published in the **Cultural Revolution Bulletin,** Dec 11 1967.

10. The mangoes were originally a gift from Pakistan, but immediately deified by their contact with the Chairman. They subsequently circulated China — one, it is said, even being deposited in the strong vault of a bank in Shanghai. Giant models of the mangoes were displayed on the National Day march in Peking, Oct 1st.

11. For example, the June 6 order, signed by the Central Committee, State Council, Military Affairs Committee and Cultural Revolution Group.

12. Cultural Revolution Bulletin, op cit.

13. The Chronicle, **CQ** 33, Oct-Dec 1967, p 153.

14. **Peking Review** 42, Oct 18, 1968, p 5.

15. **Peking Review,** ibid, p 4 and p 29.

16. BBC Summary of World Broadcasts, 111, 2799, cited **CQ** 35, July-Sept. 1968, p 186.

17. SCMP 4169.

18. Quoted Bridgeham, P, Mao's Cultural Revolution in 1967: The Struggle to Seize Power, **CQ** 34, April-June 1968, p 6.

19. Up to August 1967, the Revolutionary Committees (6 in number) were headed by 3 PLA men and 3 Party cadres; the 18 vice-chairmen included 6 from the PLA, 7 Party cadres and 5 'others' (presumably from rebel or Red Guard organisations). Of the 9 Revolutionary Committees created up to February 1968, 7 were headed by PLA men, 2 by Party cadres; and of the 37 vice-chairmen, 23 were from the PLA, 10 from the Party and 4 'others'.

20. On the purge in the PLA, 3 of the 7 vice Ministers of Defence fell; the director and two of the five deputy directors of the PLA General Political Department; the Chief of the General Staff (and the subsequently appointed acting Chief of Staff) and 4 of his 8 deputies; the commanders of the armored force, the artillery and the railway corps; 4 of the 13 military region commanders; 9 of the 13 first political commissars; 13 of the 25 military district commanders; 17 of the 25 military district political commissars; all are said to have been dismissed. Of course, the figures are collated from doubtful sources, and it is quite unclear how many have really been permanently discharged, and how many merely rusticated for a brief period.

21. State Council order, Dec 1957 and Dec 1965.

22. **People's Daily,** Dec 26 1966.

23. MacDougall, Colina, Second Class Workers, **FEER** 19, May 5-11 1968, p 306.

24. Central Committee and State Council order, February 1967.

25. Reported **Le Monde,** 16 March 1967.

26. cf Also **Wen Hui Pao,** Shanghai, March 11 1967.

27. Shanghai radio, July 6, 1967.

28. MacDougall, **op cit.**

29. January 10 1968.

30. BBC Summary of World Broadcasts, III, 2665, cited The Chronicle, **CQ** 34 April-June 1968, p 163; cf also Shanghai radio broadcast, citing report of Security Command Headquarters, PLA Unit 6410, in BBC Summary World Broadcasts, III, 2788. The Chronicle, **CQ** 35, July-September 1968, p 182.

30a. An unofficially published version of a document supposed to have been issued by the Finance and Trade Front of Kung Ko Hui, Canton, contains what is called a transcript of the Peking meeting between Chou En-lai and representatives of Kwangsi factions. The transcript includes charges that in June and July, whole trains intended for Vietnam were highjacked by factions, the Grand Rebel Army of Liuchow and its opponent, Lien-Chih, for the internal power struggle; the loot included 11,800 cases of ammunition and 16,000 rifles (cf **Financial Times** report, Nov 13, 1968, p 9).

31. For a report on the new order in Shanghai No. 3 Iron and Steel Works, **cf Peking Review** 43, October 25 1968, p 16.

32. For example, on an earlier period, cf Hunter, Neale, Three Cadres of Shanghai, **FEER** 231, June 1 1967.

33. cf Jones, P M H, Annual China Issue, **FEER** 40, Sept 29-Oct 5 1968.

34. Point 12 in the Central Committee programme for the Cultural Revolution of August 1966.

35. Neuhauser, C. The Cultural Revolution and the Party, **Asian Survey,** VIII/6. June 1968.

ON

"THE GREAT PROLETARIAN CULTURAL REVOLUTION"

February 1967

By W.F.H.

F.H. Wang is one of the few active Chinese Trotskyists belonging to the older generation. Wang joined the Chinese Communist Party in 1925 and was sent by the Party to study in the Eastern University in Moscow, where he accepted Trotskyism in 1927. When he returned to China in 1929, Wang worked secretly inside the Chinese Communist Party and he was working under Chou En-lai for about one year. Wang at the same time also kept secret contact with those Trotskyists who had returned to China because they had been expelled from the Party in Moscow. In the winter of 1929, the Moscow underground Trotskyist organisation was betrayed and all the Trotskyists were arrested and with the identity of Wang revealed, he was henceforth expelled from the party. Wang then began to work openly for the Trotskyist tendency. At that time, there were four Trotskyist groups in China: Wang's group, Our Voice; Proletariat, the most influential group led by Ch'en Tu-hsiu and Peng Shu-tse, both members of the Central Committee of the Communist Party, who had become Trotskyists after reading documents obtained from Wang's group; October, the group founded by Liu Yen-ching who was one of the twelve members attending the founding congress of the Chinese Communist Party and together with Trotsky, he drew up the first platform of the Left Opposition in China at Prinkipo; and Struggle, a group formed by four Trotskyists on their return to China.

The four groups, due to political and generational differences, were unable to unite until 1st May 1931, and only after the persistent urge by Trotsky himself. But then the Trotskyists were only able to work under a unified leadership for less than a month when all the members of the Central Committee except Ch'en Tu-hsiu were arrested by the Kuomintang.

Wang was also arrested and got a long term imprisonment of seven years. He had to serve only four years and was released at the end of 1934. Returning to Shanghai, Wang together with the few remaining comrades, re-organised a

61

new leading committee and began to publish two papers, one agitational called *Struggle*, the other a theoretical journal called *Spark*. The two monthly journals lasted from 1935 to 1942.

In 1937, Wang was arrested once again by the Kuomintang. He was sent to a secret prison in Nanking where he suffered brutal psychological pressure and torture, and was in solitary confinement. At the end of November 1937, the Japanese were approaching Nanking and Japanese planes were bombing the city days and nights. It was at that time that the second united front between the Kuomintang and the Communist Party was formed and as a result all communist prisoners except Wang were set free. Wang became the only inmate in the prison and on the last day of November the last remaining prison officer said to Wang that he was leaving the prison and that Wang could go too.

Wang went to Wuchang; arrived there at the beginning of December and found Ch'en Tu-hsiu. They planned with a few others to enlist in the army to begin armed struggle. A general named Hu Chi-fong who had come to be disillusioned with the Kuomintang was prepared to take them but when Hu Chi-fong was suddenly dismissed, the Trotskyists' plan fell through.

Ch'en Tu-hsiu then proposed to align with the so called "democratic groups", such as the Salvation Society, the Democratic League and the Workers' and Peasants' Party. Wang disagreed and thought that it would be just another form of popular front and left for Hong Kong and then Shanghai.

Back in Shanghai, Wang again worked on the editorial board of *Struggle*, which was acting as the Central Committee of the organisation.

By 1939, a discussion on the nature of the Sino-Japanese war had begun in the Trotskyist organisation and this was to lead to a split shortly afterwards.

Wang was of the view that if the American Army intervened in the war and became the main opponent of Japanese Imperialism, then the war would change its character and become a war between Japan and the United States, with China as a junior partner on the American side. He believed that if the Americans intervened, the attitude of the revolutionary should be revolutionary defeatism, which Wang meant to be an emphasis on the importance of victory over Japanese imperialism but for the weaker, Chinese side the most powerful potential weapon was revolution. Wang believed that only revolution could achieve a real victory over imperialism. But Peng Shu-tse, an influential member in the leadership, insisted that however much the American Army might dominate its Chinese partner, the war would not change its character and that there would be no question of revolutionary defeatism and the revolutionary attitude should be one of defence.

Peng Shu-tse came out to be supported by the majority, and was soon to stop any further discussion on the issue both in *Struggle* and the internal bulletin of the organisation. Wang and his supporters decided to publish their own mimeographed paper entitled *Internationalist*. There was thus a de facto split.

62

The Japanese Army surrendered and between August 1945 and 1949 when the Red Army arrived, the Kuomintang was unable to establish firm domination in Shanghai and the two Trotskyist groups took advantage of the situation to expand. Peng's group published a theoretical journal *Chu-chang (Truth)* and a youth journal *Youth and Women*, while Wang's group published a journal called *New Banner*. Wang's group had about sixty or seventy members in Shanghai and about two hundred in the country as a whole. Peng's group probably had three hundred members in the whole country.

In 1948, Peng began to organise a new party, the Revolutionary Communist Party. Wang organised a new party a few months later, the Internationalist Communist Party. In May, 1949, the Communist Army arrived at the Yangtze River and approached Shanghai. Peng's group decided to move the leadership of their party to Hong Kong. Most members of Wang's group remained in China although Wang himself also moved to Hong Kong to organise the group there. Even after the Communists took Shanghai, members of Wang's group continued to function until 22-3 December 1952, when all Trotskyists were arrested throughout China.

The few Trotskyists who left China and went to Hong Kong seemed to have been very quiet and their influence almost non-existent. Peng has moved to and worked in Europe. Wang has written a lot, from literary critiques to screenplays; but the most important are probably, *Mao Tse-tung Thought and Sino-Soviet Relationship* (published under alias San Yuen) and *Studies on Mao Tse-tung Thought* (published under alias Shuang Shan).

However, over the past two years, Hong Kong has witnessed a mini-revival of Trotskyism in that two of the existing radical youth groups which developed spontaneously since the late sixties and the seventies have been significantly infuenced by the ideas of Trotskyism. The two groups are *Combat News* (Revolutionary Marxist League) and *Rive Gauche* (International Socialist Youth League).

The article on the Great Proletarian Cultural Revolution printed below is the translation of a long essay by F.H. Wang which has been published in Chinese in the form of a pamphlet. The biographical notes on F.H. Wang have been based on an article entitled "Memoirs of a Chinese Trotskyist" appearing in the summer 1974 issue of "International", the theoretical journal of the International Marxist Group in Great Britain. Peng Shu-tse has also expressed his views on the Cultural Revolution elsewhere. He called for critical support of Liu Shao-chi and his views are therefore very much different from those of F.H. Wang. Readers who are interested in Peng's views should refer to the pamphlet "The Great Proletarian Cultural Revolution" published by the Pathfinder Press, New York.

I. THE VARIOUS CONTENDING FORCES WITHIN THE CHINESE COMMUNIST PARTY

According to Mao Tse-tung and his followers, the various forces and their relationship in the Chinese Communist Party before and during the Cultural Revolution can be described as follows:

(1) Within the top leadership, there exists a "handful of capitalist roaders" who are "ultra-reactionary capitalist rightists, counter-revolutionary revisionists .... anti-party, anti-socialist and anti-Mao Tse-tung thought elements;"

(2) There are four kinds of party cadres: (a) "the good"; (b) "the relatively good"; (c) "those who have committed serious errors, but are not anti-party, anti-socialist rightists"; (d) "a minority of anti-party, anti-socialist rightists".

Of course we are unable to carry out any survey or make use of any statistics to prove or dispute this claim by Mao and his followers on the strength of the four categories of party cadres. However, from the activities during the last few months since the beginning of the Cultural Revolution, there is sufficient reason to refute the Maoist claim as inaccurate.

It should be pointed out that the massive scale and momentum of the Cultural Revolution which Mao initiated do not correspond to what he originally set as his objectives. It is hard to believe that in order to "strike at a handful of capitalist roaders", Mao would have to ask millions of high school and primary school students to quit school for a whole year, to spend massive sums of money and resources in order to transport and feed these "little guards" when they travel all over the country, to upset and interfere with the smooth running of all cultural and educational apparatus as well as the party machinery, to break the myth of unity within the Chinese Communist Party and further, to provide ammunition to the American imperialists and Russian revisionists in their anti-Chinese propagandizing. If the truth were what Mao and his followers claimed then they are paying a very high cost in order to achieve minuscule objectives. Mao would have using atomic bombs against small sampans. This cannot happen and would never happen.

The fact that Mao and his clique had to wage a "great revolution" of such magnitude to strike at "those in power" indicates that the opponents certainly are not a minority. Their numbers are not small, but large. They might even turn out to be very large!

We do not know how large this group is among "those in power" nor do we know whether they are the majority or minority in the Central Committee of the Communist Party. But from every indication, Mao's opponents might be the majority (Maoist documents often reveal the fact that the Maoists are in the minority), and they became the minority during the 11th plenary session of the 8th Central Committee of the C.P.C. mainly due to Mao's exertion of pressure, political or otherwise.

What are described as "good" or "relatively good" cadres, that is, those who have been always submitting to and agreeing with Mao's words and actions, despite the Maoist claims, cannot be a majority. As we all know, personnel of communist parties are always controlled by the General Secretary of the party. Whoever attains the position of General Secretary will have members of his faction appointed to most of the important positions in the party. This was the case with Stalin and it was also the case with Khruschev. The so-called "party chairman" or other supreme title holders are all undoubtedly respected and glorified, but in dealings with the large number of party cadres, the General Secretary's position is more effective. Even Lenin, especially after he had had the stroke, deeply felt the infringement and interference by Stalin. Somehow, Mao Tse-tung also has this feeling. Today Liu Shao-chi and Teng Shiao-ping lead the opposition in the Chinese Communist Party, and it is they who have been General Secretaries – one after the other – for long periods of time and who have placed their connections in important positions in the Party.

The opposition headed by Liu Shao-chi, Peng Chen, and Teng Shiao-ping within the Communist Party have more than just a few in its ranks (numerically much more than the Maoists) and they are extremely influential. They don't have their own organization (or to be more exact, apart from the party bodies already in existence, they have no other special organizations), but their own clique has been tightly formed and efficiently organized. The formation of this clique is not due to unity in thoughts, but based on a long period of association in party work and other activities. Basically they subscribe to the thoughts of Mao Tse-tung and their dis-satisfaction with Mao is due to the failures of Mao's foreign and domestic policies in recent years. The pain brought by these failures has opened their eyes and they realize that Mao is not an infallible divinity; that he is liable to commit mistakes; that because of his old age and ill health he might have illusory and impractical ideas. For these reasons, Liu and his clique would wish that Mao take an honorary role and leave the handling of the country and the party aside.

Within the highest and higher strata of the Party, it is believed that more than a few cherish this thought. The mid-level and lower level party cadres have no opportunities to directly associate with and get to know Mao and thus they may not hold similar views. But surely the painful experience of the "Three Red Banners" is not easily forgotten by these party cadres since their position at the mid-level and lower level provides them with experiences that are more vivid and closer to the truth than those of the high level party cadres. Due to this, it seems that they have lost faith in the "brilliant leadership" of the Thought of Mao Tse-tung. In the eyes of these cadres, Mao and the Central Committee of the Party are inseparable-- they are one and the same thing. These cadres would never have separated Mao from the Party, not to mention a contradiction between the two. Following the "Three Red Banners", however, if there is some member of the Central Committee coming out and criticizing Mao in the name of the Party, they would perhaps listen to him and perhaps even stand by the "Party" in opposing the "Chairman". This is a new phenomenon of great importance, because the existence of this phenomenon among the middle and lower level party cadres implies that the opponents of Mao have a potential mass base, although they may not as yet have a mass following.

Of course there exist, in the party, those genuinely anti-party, anti-socialist opportunistic, easily changeable, bureaucratic, degenerate elements. These people may even exist in far greater numbers than one would think, but they would not be in opposition to Mao; they would not have opposed Mao over principles or policies. However, in order to protect their own already established position, they would be prepared to support anyone who protects them. If today's "revolutionary" spear of Mao is directed towards them, they would be on the side of the "capitalist roaders". However, if the Maoist clique should temporarily wish to use them in order to "expose" and "attack" the "power holders", they would be willing to side with Mao.

The above is what we consider to be an accurate reflection of the opposition in the Chinese Communist Party.

II. WHAT'S BETWEEN MAO AND LIU?

Although there is some information concerning the changing relationship of the membership in the top level of the Chinese Communist Party, it is still very difficult to accurately describe how they come together and separate. Perhaps only the future historians can tell the story approximated to the truth many years later. What we can and must discuss here and now are merely two questions (a) What is the relationship between Mao Tse-tung and Liu Shao-chi? (b) Why has Lin Piao taken the place of Liu Shao-chi to become Mao Tse-tung's "closest comrade in arms"?

In many respects, Mao and Liu represent two opposing or contrasting sets of characters. If Mao tends to be a "revolutionary romanticist", Liu tends to be a "revolutionary realist". Mao has an air of both a Chinese peasant and a classical Chinese scholar. Liu is closer to the worker and more like a typical modern Chinese intellectual. Mao's knowledge and studies were mainly Chinese oriented while Liu is much less conversant with classical Chinese knowledge. Mao took up Marxism-Leninism only after his movement had had some achievement and Liu had received Marxist education overseas before he participated in the revolution. Mao has great potential powers, worships heroism and is imbedded with idea of the divine rights of kings. Liu cares even for the minutest little thing, he is more akin to the common folk and is more convinced of democracy. Mao is bold to initiate and places much emphasis on the subjective initiative. Liu is cool-headed, over-cautious and more realistic in considering the objective conditions. Mao, is impatient and considers the ends justify the means; "dogmas" are no constraint for him. Liu progresses steadily and sees connection between ends and tactics; principles have some hold on him. Mao has, all along, worked with students, peasants, and soldiers and has devoted most of his energies to the building up of the "gun barrels" while Liu has centered most of his work on the labor movement and party affairs, the planning and organizational work of the party machinery .... In sum total, the two person differ very much in their strong and weak points. They do not belong to the same type and in fact they are very much opposites.

And yet, we must ask how in the past they have complemented each other and gone thru a long period of constant co-operation.

Disregarding the less important aspects, the main reasons is that Liu Shao-chi has assisted Mao Tse-tung to defeat the latter's long time enemy Wang Ming. Liu has also, on the ideological level, formulated a framework for "Mao Tse-tung Thought" and engineered its supremacy. He made it possible in 1945 when the party held its Seventh Congress, for the Thought of Mao Tse-tung to be written into the consititution of the Party as the only recognized guide line.

This is the most important reason why, for the past twenty years, Mao Tse-tung's "closest comrade in arms" and the publicly acknowledged successor has been Liu Shao-chi.

Liu Shao-chi held up the Thought of Mao Tse-tung and made Mao's thought "a supreme authority". He helped to establish Mao as the supreme and single leader. Is this part of Liu's tactics? Has he acted against his principles in order to gain

Mao's confidence? Has Liu always been anti-Mao and merely held up this Thought for the purpose of "hoisting the red flag against the red flag"?

We don't think this is the case.

For years, many "China watchers" who claim an understanding of China have said that Liu Shao-chi was the leader of the so-called "International Sect", and that he has always been anti-Mao. The recent open dispute between Mao and Liu, according to them, therefore justifies their belief.

This, however, is contrary to the facts.

The so-called "International Sect" is applied to those who were educated in Moscow and upon their return to China did not participate in actual organizing activities but instead used their overseas qualifications to maintain prominence in the Party. They attached much self-importance to their connections with the Communist International but are seldom independent---merely depending on the orders they receive from Moscow and not developing their own strength or self-reliance. The main representative of this group, of course, is Wang Ming. Liu Shao-chi has never played such a role whether before Wang Wing or after him. Liu does not belong to this "International Sect". Liu has been engaged in communist activities for several decades. In the earlier period, he was engaged in the labor movement, while later in party organizing and administrative work. His attitude towards work has been practical and down to earth. In his relationship with other members inside the party, there has never been a case of Liu using foreign help to develop his own sphere of influence. Thus if there exists a Liu Shao-chi faction within the party, it would have been one formed gradually thru practical work and could not be the outcome of following any "International line".

However, if we are to contrast Mao and Liu, Liu can be described as belonging to an "International Sect" in one sense. As we pointed out earlier, in any comparison between Mao and Liu, Liu is more aptly described as a revolutionary realist. He is a typical new style intellectual who is close to the workers. He has been trained systematically in Marxism-Leninism starting in his early days overseas. He surely has a better understanding of the world as well as the history and present conditions of the international workers' movement and the international socialist movement. He would attach more importance to the internationalist nature and international relationships of the communist movement. To put it quite simply, Liu Shao-chi should be considered to have a greater knowledge of other countries and the world and is more capable of seeing things in an international perspective. Compared to Mao's nationalism and nationalistic perspective, Liu is surely internationalist and belongs to the "International Sect".

However, in the past, Mao's nationalism and Liu's internationalism have not conflicted and, in fact, have complemented each other.

The reason is that Liu's strong points supplemented quite well Mao's weak points. Whether in general party work or in the particular struggle with the "International Sect", Mao's success cannot be separated from Liu's support. Without Mao's "nationalism", Liu's "internationalism" cannot be rooted in the backward soil of China. Without Liu's "Internationalism", however, Mao's "Confucianism" would have been unable to defeat Wang Ming's "Marxism". To have described things in this way is, of course, vague and abstract, but in essence and broadly speaking, it is correct.

If this were the case, then when and how did the contradiction between Mao and Liu rear its head to become more important than the complementary nature of

67

the two? When and how did they become the leaders of the two factions involved in an internal struggle inside the Chinese Communist Party?

From various kinds of evidence, we can say that the serious contradiction between Mao and Liu began in 1957[1], and that the source of the contradiction was the internal policy of the "Three Red Banners" and the "anti-revisionist" foreign policy.

Under the "Three Red Banners, the general line of socialist construction, the Great Leap Foreward and People's Communes" Mao has manifested all his traits in character and thought. There is the innocent equalitarianism of the peasantry; there is the wild imagination and impractical ideals of the old Chinese scholars; there is the idea of Dai Tung which means "world for all", an idea subscribed to by many--from Confucius to Sun Yat Sen; there is the belief in "communism in one country", an idea borrowed from Stalin, but further refined by Mao. The practice and implementation of such ideas also revealed Mao's courage, great abilities, and will to initiate. Under the slogan "Smash all Constraints", Mao was able to negate the scientific "dogmas" of Marx, Engels and Lenin; he did not even attach too much importance to the lessons of Stalin's success or failure.

When the weak and strong points of Mao were so clearly manifested, would the man with such different traits of character and thought, Liu Shao-chi, follow Mao all the way without any opposition? This is impossible.

With the victory of the Chinese communists, Mao has enjoyed tremendous prestige. It is possible that in the beginning for a short period of time, Liu supported the "Three Red Banners", but when the implementation of that policy led to horrifying results even Peng Teh-huai and many others realized that their disastrous dimension was Mao's fault and spoke out. The more cool-headed and clear-thinking Liu Shao-chi who has a firmer grasp of theory and ideology would certainly express disagreement.

How did Liu express his disagreement? Is it like what the Red Guards claim in one of their big character posters, that Liu Shao-chi and his "black gang" forced Mao to abdicate the position of State Chairman of the People's Republic in 1958 during the 6th Plenum of the 8th C.C. of the CCP? Is it true that having dethroned Mao, Liu Shao-chi and Teng Shiao-ping began to run the whole show while on one hand they respected and steered away from Mao and, on the other, pursued the "capitalist and revisionist line"? We do not wish to make guesses. We only want to establish this fact, a fact that can be established, namely that the "Three Red Banners" as a policy of the CCP for "socialist construction" is the basic cause of the confrontation between Mao and Liu.

The disagreement arose firstly out of domestic policies and it was further accentuated by opposing attitudes on foreign affairs, especially on the question of Russia. How they differ in this respect is something which we know even less about. In principle, we believe that both Mao and Liu are against the Russian revisionists. The difference is mostly on the level of tactics. Mao has been a brilliant tactician, he knows how to manipulate artfully and cunningly for self benefits and sometimes he would give up his principles in order to suit his tactical design and to make temporary gains. Yet how did he come to be the most die-hard "dogmatist" in the struggle against revisionists over the years, at the cost of isolating China and the Chinese Communist Party from the sympathies of the people of the world (including the international proletarian revolutionaries)? The main reason is that the personal destiny of Mao Tse-tung is so interwoven with the Sino-Soviet conflict that any important

68

compromise, even tactically, would affect the authority and position of Mao. Ever since the appearance of "Khruschevites without Khruschev", Mao was careful, perhaps too careful, in making sure that "Maoists without Mao" would not exist. For this reason, Mao had to make sure that his win would be complete and total. He would not therefore make concession on compromise even on small tactical points.

But this attitude is harmful to the Chinese Communist Party, to China and to the international anti-imperialist and revolutionary movement. At least to hold such an attitude is unwise. The greatest enemy of the Chinese Communists is American imperialism and to successfully and victoriously repel this arch enemy, China has to compromise with the U.S.S.R. But instead of doing this, Mao is, to a certain degree, promoting American and Russian co-operation. Mao Tse-tung has always mocked Wang Ming's strategy, saying that Wang wanted to "fight with two fists". But today, he is even worse—he is using both of his hands and his feet and is attempting to fight all his enemies at the same time. Foreign Minister Chen Yi has invited both the Americans and the Russians to fight at the same time, the earlier the better. And this ridiculously unsound tactical design of Mao is well displayed. However, not only do the experienced politicians and tacticians in the party, but also ordinary workers consider such policies impractical.

Liu Shao-chi and his friends would of course disagree with Mao, and they did so.

However, the foreign policies which directly caused the public burst of disagreement between Mao and Liu are twofold: first, the question of united action in providing assistance to the Vietnamese people; and secondly, the coup initiated by the Indonesian Communist Party and its subsequent tragic failure. The so-called united action is, of course, in line with the tradition of revolutionary workers' movements and the tradition of the Communist movement. In order to fight against the class enemy in a particular struggle, revolutionary workers and parties should temporarily forget their differences on large matters of principle and unite and act together. This kind of action is appropriate on the question of aiding Vietnam. However, the Chinese communists have reacted to such a proposal with passive negation. This attitude not only provides a good pretext to the Russian communists who actually "unite with the Americans while pretending to aid the Vietnamese," but also separates the once sympathetic Japanese and North Korean communist parties from the Chinese. Liu, Teng, and Peng Chen together with others surely expressed great dissatisfaction with this policy of Mao. We do not have any documents on the real facts but let us take note of this: the General Secretary of the Japanese Communist Party and others visited China in 1966 and had talks with the Chinese delegation headed by Peng Chen. After these talks, Peng Chen had not publicly appeared and the Japanese communists gradually changed their allegiance. This could perhaps be revealing.

How close the coup by the Indonesian Communist Party is connected with Chinese policy is unclear. We do not have actual information which would allow us to know for sure whether there were differences of opinion among the Chinese communist leaders on the policies of the Indonesian communists. However, the coup was obviously under the influence of the armed revolutionary line of the Chinese. It is also obvious that its tragic failure accelerated "the power struggle" inside the Chinese Communist Party. The abortive coup organized by the Indonesian communists took place at the end of September 1965 and the first signal of the "Great Proletarian Cultural Revolution" of the Chinese communists, "Criticising Hai Jui", was given in November the same year. This coincidence in the timing is certainly not accidental.

The tragic failure of the Indonesian communists represents the nadir of the many drawbacks suffered by the Chinese communists on the diplomatic level in Asia, Africa, and Latin America. The situation having reached such a state necessarily gives rise to ample opportunities for those who have ever disagreed with Mao in foreign policies, to "vehemently attack" the "Party" and Mao Tse-tung.

III.   WHY HAS LIN PIAO REPLACED LIU SHAO-CHI?

Why has Mao replaced Liu Shao-chi with Lin Piao? This question is comparatively simple.

First, Mao's control of the military has always been better than his control over the Party, trade unions and other organizations. This is due to two facts: first, Mao has always attached much importance to the gun and therefore paid much attention to the selection of cadres in the army; secondly, the masses in the army and its low level cadres are replaced regularly making the army more susceptible to influence from the top leader's prestige and authority—as opposed to the influence of the leaders of the army.

Second, the submission of "professional soldier" Lin Piao to Mao is much more unconditional in comparison to the "Independent-minded" Liu Shao-chi. Ever since he succeeded Peng Teh-Huai as the Defense Minister, Lin Piao has systematically sought to (strictly speaking he has been following orders) deify Mao and make Mao's thought into a sort of religious bible for the peoples' Liberation Army. Thus he gains the confidence of the heart of the "great leader".

On the one hand, Mao has to rely on the army to purge the opposition in the party and trade unions and other organizations; on the other hand, in order to reward Lin Piao's effort to make him into a god, Mao Tse-tung decided to replace Liu Shao-chi with Lin Piao as his "close comrade in arms".

If Liu Shao-chi had previously been made the second in command as a reward for sanctifying Mao Tse-tung and engineering the supremacy of the thoughts of Mao Tse-tung, then Lin Piao is able to replace him because he has made Mao into a god and has upheld the thoughts of Mao as absolute religious dogmas.

Mao Tse-tung and his thoughts at two different stages require two different people to play the role of high priest.

To establish Mao's thoughts as the supreme guide is indeed utterly ridiculous but it is still a matter of theories, ideologies and thoughts. This is the job of a theorist or at least it requires a politician with some qualities of a theoretician.

To establish Mao's thoughts as religious dogma (or perhaps as the utterings of the occult) enters into the realm of emotions, beliefs, and faiths. This job requires religous fanatics or a conspirator who can pretend to be fervent.

The substitution of Liu by Lin, from the angle of Mao's relationship with them, and their relationship to Mao's thoughts, should be viewed precisely as the relationship described above.

If we want to look at the actual process of the internal power struggle of the Chinese Communist Party to find out how Lin Piao actually became the greatest apostle of Mao Tse-tung and the high priest of the religion of Mao, it tends to be extremely difficult, because that involves innumerable personal relationships. We, as outsiders, of course are not in a position to grasp them; even those inside the party and at the highest level might not understand. There is therefore no need to guess. To make such guessess would have nothing to do with serious Marxist analysis

What can be discussed are merely the following:

Who takes the intiative in the partnership between Mao and Lin? Many people, especially those having just heard of the dramatic promotion of Lin, thought that Mao was either seriously ill or so old that he became the puppet of Lin. They are of the opinion that Lin was using the prestige of Mao and the army to attack Liu Shao-chi and his clique so that he would himself obtain the control of the Party. However, this has been proven wrong. By all indications, Mao is still firmly in control. In "Mao-Lin Co.", Mao is obviously taking the intiative and being decisive.

Of course, this does not exclude in this partnership any initiative by Lin nor do we ignore his importance. To jump from the ninth position (according to the votes Lin received at the election of the 8th Central Committee of the CCP) to number two, to be in special favour with the "great leader", to hold the "great leaders" highest hopes, to have the "great leader" going out of his way to replace his long time successor, Liu Shao-chi, with him, Lin Piao must have done everything to please and co-operate. He might even have used tricks (including "making his way thru the queen") to achieve his aim to be the "closest comrade in arms".

Another question is whether or not the rise to prominence of Lin Piao and the liberation army means to imply that the army is above the party in a state of Napoleonic dictatorship. I personally don't see anything like this taking shape. In making use of various conflicting forces, letting them confront each other, constraining and balancing each other, all in order to maintain one's own ruling position, Mao Tse-tung has always followed Napoleon—Napoleon the third. Mao Tse-tung is a brilliant tactician. When he uses a certain force against another force, he pays no regards to principles. To place the army under the party is a communist principle, but when actual struggle necessitates the use of guns to blast the heads of party bosses, Mao would not be restrained by "dogmas". However, if you think that Mao would replace the party with the army, you are wrong - - - - - when the time comes, when actual struggle gives rise to such needs; when the various contradictions around him require the control of the army by the party, he would use this very principle he tramples on and use the party to control the army. (Unless Mao died and therefore would not have enough time to do it or Mao was unable to do it because of the changing relationships within the party or within the country.)

That people emphasized the possibility of a military dictatorship is due to their belief that the relationship between the Chinese Communist Party and the Liberation Army is analogous to the relationship between the party and the army in the traditional capitalist countries. But the analogy is inappropriate. The relationship between the Chinese Communist Party and the Liberation Army cannot be compared to that between the parties and armies in capitalist countries. It cannot even be compared with the Russian Communist Party and the Red Army. The Red Army was the outcome of the Soviet Government but the Chinese Communist Government was the outcome of the Liberation Army. Since 1927, generally speaking, the Chinese Communist Party has been inseparable from the army—the party is, of course, the political guide and soul of the Army, but at the same time, the Army is often the organizer, propagandist and promoter of the party.

Therefore, the party and the army of the Chinese Communists are not to be absolutely separated. They are not incompatible.

Hence we cannot assume that Lin Piao would become the Chinese Napoleon the 1st because of his rise to power. Nor should we predict that China would have to go thru a period of military dictatorship, because Mao today uses the Army to "liberate" the party.

One more question: What does this process of changing from "sanctified" to "god-like", from "supreme thought" to "the only religious creed", and finally to "the utterances of the occult" which would exorcise all "freaks and monsters" imply?

There is no need to go deeply into this. Obviously, this is an indication that during the seven or eight years, whether in China or overseas, within the party or among the masses, Mao Tse-tung's prestige has reached a low point. It indicates that people are losing faith with the "brilliant leadership" of Mao Tse-tung; that opposition to Mao Tse-tung's policies within the Party are raising their heads; that internal struggle within the Party caused by serious errors in the Mao Tse-tung leadership has intensified. It also indicates the tragic dimension of the results of this erroneous leadership which intensifies the contradictions between the masses of workers and peasants and the rapidly degenerating ruling party and at the same time it also intensifies the contradictions between the existing classes in Chinese society.

All in all, this does not in the least imply that Mao Tse-tung and his thoughts are rising in prestige. In fact, the opposite is true. When one prays to god, kneels in front of the Buddha and makes use of the utterance of the occult it at best only provides an indication of the serious nature of one's illness.

IV. RED GUARDS AND THE GENERATION OF YOUTH

Another accurate indication of the seriousness of the illness is the indiscriminate use of drugs and medicine—and the Red Guards are one of those drugs and medicines which Mao Tse-tung uses indiscriminately.

The question of "Red Guards" is the most perplexing of the many perplexing phenomena arising out of the "Great Proletarian Cultural Revolution". Obviously. among all the leaders of the Communist Party at present, Mao is still the most powerful. The control he holds on the Party, the administrative apparatus, the Army and the Police (open or secret) might not be greater than that held by Stalin in the thirties (I believe it is greater), it would certainly not be less. But then Stalin harnessed his secret police to get rid of his opposition in the party, the army, and the administrative apparatus. Why then does the more respected. more powerful Mao Tse-tung who is also in a firmer position not use similar, simpler methods like organizational techniques, administrative orders or the secret police to deal with Liu-Teng and their followers? Why must he mobilize the masses of young people and authorize them to rebel, resulting in upheavals everywhere in the whole country?

This is the question that has puzzled the so-called "China experts" who call the Red Guards' movement the enigma wrapped in the mystery of the Cultural Revolution. People are unable to solve this mystery and they say that Mao is very sick and has lost the power to make judgements because of brain damage; some say that he is dead and that the person appearing at the Gate of Heavenly Peace is a fake with all ideas originating from Chiang Ching and Lin Piao; some say that he has gone nuts and is having epileptic fits and would not trust anyone but the "Queen", close courtiers and the faithful head of the army ...

The assumptions of these "clever people" are all wrong. No matter how strange this phenonmenon of the Red Guards is, it can be adequately explained, and it is quite in accordance with Mao's thoughts.

We have pointed out that for the Red Guards Movement to be possible, there in an exceedingly important objective foundation which must have been built, namely the spiritual life of the generation of youth under the communist rule. This life is "frustrating, hopeless, earthy and empty". It is of course an inevitable result of the bureaucratic rule of the Chinese communists. It is also a passive protest and a manifestation of extreme discontent with this rule and its accompanying absurd youth policy.

Mao Tse-tung established himself thru leading student movements and he has a thorough understanding of the feelings and characteristics of youths. He is also a superb tactician and is quite good at manipulating various contradicting forces without regard to principles. When he discovers that the party and administrative apparatus have been, to a large degree usurped by his opponents, he would have no hesitation to utilize the young people. He utilizes their deeply felt but passive discontent; mobilizes them; supports them and turns their passive discontent into aggressive actions directed against his opponents--the "capitalist roaders in the party". In Mao's estimation, when such an action is taken, several birds are killed with one stone. Firstly, the anger of the young people which would originally have been directed towards him would now be redirected, purifying his black spots, alleviating him of responsibilities; he became the "Great Helmsman" in an effort to combat bureaucratism, corruption and capitalist degeneration. Secondly, Mao is able to fight against the Liu-Teng clique and totally destroy his opposition while, in the process, he actually strengthens his own absolute rule. Thirdly, in the form of a mass movement, "making revolution" on one hand while "educating" on the other, Mao hopes to train a massive number of new cadres who will be absolutely faithful to the Thoughts of Mao and who will be able to replace those bad, old corrupt cadres and thus preventing the next generation from entering the road to "revisionism".

Having these aims in mind, Mao uses every means to mobilize the young people. The most important being the announcement he made that the long time idea "heroic fathers bear heroic sons and reactionary fathers have bums" is a "reactionary theory of lineage"; he announced that this class line which had been used to suppress young people is "thoroughly historical idealism". ("Carry the Great Proletarian Cultural Revolution Thru to the End"–editorial, Peoples' Daily, Jan. 1, 1967)

We have divided the youths in China into the following three categories: (a) offspring of workers and peasants, they are the majority; (b) offspring of "bad families", their number is smaller; (c) the offspring of "heroes and great men", their number is the least. Among these three categories of people, the most unhappy, the most discontented would be the second. They would be the most willing to see disturbances because they have everything to gain and nothing to lose. In the past they felt frustrated and hopeless because they only saw the absolute control of the Communist Party with few indications of change. Now it is different–Chairman Mao turns out to be on the side of justice, redressing their unjust repression and explaining that their mistreatment is entirely due to the power holders in the party and the apparatus men. Mao calls on them to rise up and "rebel", to "seize power" and to get rid of "the handful". What an awakening spring thunder and what a gigantic impulse! It is no wonder that the youthful generation appeared frantic, their "enthusiasm reaching the sky". They pledged to "defend Chairman Mao to their deaths" and swore to "overthrow those power holders who have taken the capitalist road".

73

Of course very few of those who have had the opportunities to enter school and to become Red Guards belong to the second category. Among the students and the Red Guards, the majority are not the offsprings of "heroes and great men" either. (This third category is, in fact, discriminated against by the Cultural Revolution Group of the Central Committee. They have been specifically advised not to become the leaders of Red Guard organizations.) The majority of the Red Guards belong to the first category—the offsprings of workers and peasants and the ordinary dwellers in the cities. They are unhappy with the status quo; they are anti-bureaucratic and their dissatisfaction is partly caused by their own experience and partly a reflection of the discontent of their parents. Therefore they can also be inflamed and agitated by the tricky "anti-power holder" slogans of Mao Tse-tung.

With Mao Tse-tung's Red Guards, many people are reminded of Hitler's "Youth Corps". Of course there are many fundamental differences between the two. If we equate the two without taking into account the major differences, the analogy will be absurd. There is, however, at least one point on which the two are similar, that is a section of the "power holders" in both cases have harnessed the discontent of the masses of young people to attack the ruling class and the system. They both raise high the specter of revolution and preach high sounding slogans; they mobolize the youth, organize them and attack the opposition within the ruling class as well as the genuine revolutionary elements.

Hitler utilized the discontent of the young people caused by the degeneration of capitalism to "make revolution" in order to defend capitalism. Similarly, Mao Tse-tung utilized the discontent among the young people caused by the bureaucratic rule of the communist party and called on them to "make revolution" in order to protect this bureaucratic rule.

The class nature of Hitler's "revolution" and Mao Tse-tung's "revolution" are different, but they are similar to the extent that the causes and the circumstances under which the masses of young people are used are very similar. The intense contradictions between the ruling class and the people, especially the masses of young people are very much the same.

In the "normal" capitalist countries, if a crisis develops in the existing ruling system, the problem is solved thru parliamentary struggle. But when capitalism develops into an "abnormal" stage, when there exists an "abnormal" crisis in the country, democratic parliamentary struggle becomes useless and so the result is fascism, nazism or some similar "revolutionary" method of dealing with the crisis and thus preserving the capitalist system. Similarly, within the communist parties themselves and in countries ruled by communist parties, when conditions are normal and healthy, all kinds of problems (large and small contradictions) should be solved by methods of democratic centralism. It should be so with the party; it should be so with the government (the soviets). During Lenin's time, there arose continously contradictions and crises which were overcome by using this method. But when the conditions of the party and the country become more and more abnormal, that is more and more degenerated, the traditional means to resolve contradictions becomes inappropriate and other "emergency actions" are used. History has shown us two different kinds of emergency actions: one is Stalinist—the use of secret police and judicial frame-ups to carry out large scale murders and massacres; the other is that of Mao Tse-tung—the mobilization of the masses supplemented by the Stalinist method. The former is a conspiracy of the few which seeks the approval and participation of the masses, but seeks the same goals as the former.

That Stalin and Mao should use different methods in attempts to resolve their contradictions is, of course, partly due to their differences in personalities, but more importantly, the difference arises from the fact that the two are in different positions. Mao has not followed Stalin in this respect[2] which may be attributed to the fact that Mao is confident (maybe even over confident) of his authority and prestige. With such a confidence, Mao seems to be of the opinion that although by using "organizational tactics" or other conspiratorial means, he all the same can get rid of his enemies (they are occupying many positions in the party, the administrative apparatus and elsewhere), it would be inadequate, incomplete, insufficient and furthermore non-educational. So he decided to mobilize thousands and millions, to practice "great democracy", to "struggle, criticize and transform", in order to thoroughly crush the opponents he dislikes and to train a large number of new cadres who are innoculated against "revisionism". He realizes that to do what he is doing would lead to large scale opposition and disturbances, but he believes that every development will follow the line that has been laid down and will not go astray.

V. THREE POSSIBLE OUTCOMES

Will things develop as Mao has wished?

First of all let us point out the three objective possible outcomes of the "Great Proletarian Cultural Revolution": (1) from a state of armed confrontation could develop a state of civil war, even a prolonged state of civil war; (2) "the Great Cultural Revolution" reaps the expected victories and within a short period of time (assuming one or two years) accomplishes its task; (3) from a pseudo-revolution develops a genuine revolt—the revolutionary masses pulled all the "kings and emperors", including the big one—Mao, down from their horses. Then the Chinese socialist revolution would make great strides on the road to proletarian democracy.

Let us examine the first possibility. It is a common occurence today in China for "struggles with words" to be eliminated in favor of "struggles with arms". But will these "armed struggles" turn into a small scale civil war or even a large scale and prolonged civil war? This is possible, but an examination of the present circumstances, reveals that it is unlikely. Certainly, the Liu-Teng faction (if they make up their minds to carry out armed confrontation) are able to find some Liberation Army troops which are loyal to them. However, if these troops were not stationed at the Sino–Russian border and if they did not receive any open or secret assistance from the "Russian Revisionists", under existing conditions, it is incomprehensible that they could resist the Mao-Lin military forces for a long time, not to speak of their victory in a civil war.

Therefore, provided that Mao does not die suddenly (which should come as no surprise to a man of 72), and provided that there exists no serious armed conflict between China and Russia, the possibility of civil war, especially a prolonged and large scale civil war is very small if not nil. To discard this possibility would be equivalent to saying that the Liu-Teng faction would be unable to wage an effective counter-attack in this internal struggle of the Party or gain victory in this struggle. Simply because Mao-Lin and their followers have made arms and weapons the only "argument" in this "debate" and since the opposition cannot hold up any arms or is not resolute at all to hold arms, they would be unable to participate in any "debate" or win in the "debating".

Well then, is the second possibility cited above the only outcome of the Great Proletarian Cultural Revolution? Will Mao Tse-tung achieve his aims as he has wished? Not necessarily.

The Liu-Teng faction, being unable to use arms against arms, to use armed criticism to oppose the armed criticism of Mao and Lin, has revealed their Achilles' heel. However if they are a principled opposition, if they have a political program different from that of Mao and Lin; if they insist on carrying thru their correct line and are willing to wage a resolute struggle, then even without military might to back them up, they are not destined to be vanquished. They may be temporarily beaten but ultimately, after a longer or shorter period of time, they would come out victorious.

History, or the history of the workers' movement, has given us many examples that the truth will follow a zig-zig path to its victory.

Even Mao-Lin and Company have often repeated that the army does not exist in a vacuum but is affected by both the class struggle and political struggle. It may take longer to see the effects on the army when compared to other organizations of the masses and it may be more difficult to see actions arising from such effects, but be it longer or more difficult, it does not mean that it is impossible. As soon as the army is stirred to action, it will be more centralized and more intense and in the end, more decisive.

Therefore, being deprived of military strength momentarily does not mean its deprivation forever. Arms can change hands. The real question is whether you have got a correct political stand which will eventually win you the military strength; whether you have the will to win the military strength with your correct political program.

However, regrettably, the Liu-Teng faction is not an opposition having the principles described above and they are not an opposition which would stand up and fight for the truth. Nor do they have the will and determination to implement their program at the risk of bringing the struggle to the level of civil war. Basically they (at least those among the top leadership) are followers of "Maoism". They have all along shouted "Long Live Chairman Mao" and "Long Live the Thoughts of Chairman Mao". They did not do this purely for tactical motives, but did it with all their hearts. They were actually "loyal to the King"! If they were ever dissatisfied with Mao or disagreed with Mao's policies, they were merely "offering sincere advice" and they certainly had no intention of annoying Mao, not to speak of "conspiring to overthrow" him. Secondly, the anti-Mao faction is not an opposition based on principles and therefore they would not have any systematic program; there is no banner that they can hold upright and defend thru combat. They can only appear as a passive shadow behind the Maoists, and this determines the nature and strength of their struggle and their "counter attack". It also determines the passiveness, pessimism, and weakness of their struggle. In reality, up till now, we can witness only three ways with which the anti-Maoists present themselves in struggle: (a) "The Heavenly King possesses holy understanding and our crimes should be punished by execution" (mostly the top level leaders); (b) promote "economism" and be "generous on behalf of the country" in order to win the hearts of the people (mid-level cadres); (c) "lie down and do nothing" and let whatever be done to them be done (low level cadres) The way they are going is going to get nowhere.

Since the nature of the opposition of the Liu-Teng faction is such that they have used such methods to wage their struggle, it would be save to say that they could hardly resist the forces of Mao, not to speak of defeating them.

In this respect, it can be said that Mao Tse-tung would defeat his opponents and that is to say, he would accomplish the "task of the Cultural Revolution".

But in another respect, the Maoists would not accomplish their task, — or at least would not fulfill the task as they set out to fulfill.

By looking at the actual development of the "Great Cultural Revolution", it can be ascertained that although the "counter-attack" of the "power holders" has not achieved their aims, it has been successful in upsetting the plans of the Maoists. The originally thought to be well controlled mass movement has sidetracked from the line Mao has laid down and obviously Mao has over-estimated his ability to control. Originally the Red Guards' movement and other "revolutionary rebel groups" were formed from the above to below and now they are developing according to their own logic and emanating their independent effects from below to above. They are not to be constrained within the domain of their creators. In order to cope with this unexpected development, the Maoists appeared to be uncertain of their measures— whether to advance or retreat. They continued to shift positions frequently and their friends and enemies constantly replaced each other. What is even worse is that the Maoist constantly discover that they have lost their controlling position and are confined to a passive role. Under these circumstances, Mao had to go back on his promises and tear off his hypocritical mask by using naked military force to suppress his opponents and as a result of this, people have lost faith in Mao and he has lost prestige.

Under these circumstances, two crises have developed: firstly, industrial and agricultural productions came to a halt as did most trades and transportation—another "natural calamity" might arise; secondly, the crisis of a genuine revolution which could endanger the rule of the Chinese Communist Party. The first crisis was caused mainly by the passive resistance of the "power holders". And the second was caused by the mass movement arising from the internal struggle of the CCP.

Facing the threats of these two crises, the Maoists would most likely (they are doing it already) limit their scope of attack and would agree to compromise with more "power holders" in order that the "Great Cultural Revolution" might end as soon as possible.

Such an ending cannot be said to be a victory of the anti-Maoists, but on the other hand, it cannot be said that the Maoists have "victoriously accomplished their tasks".

In summary, we may say this: if we limit our discussion on the Maoists and anti-Maoists and if the mass movement which has been called upon to take .part in the struggle has operated within the framework of the "Thoughts of Mao Tse-tung", then under existing conditions Mao would most likely win in the existing power struggle. He would purge those whom he wanted to purge. But this victory would have been a "degenerating" and compromised one.

But if the matter is not limited to one between the Maoists and the anti-Maoists, and that is to say, if in the process of struggle, the masses which have been stirred up to action have gone over the limits of the Mao-Lin and Liu-Teng cliques and there appears in the movement a current which can genuinely represent the interest of proletarian socialism, then the fundamental nature of the "Great Cultural Revolution" will have been changed. It is no longer an internal struggle between the bureaucrats. It has become a struggle between bureaucrats and anti-bureaucrats. This is what has been described as the third possible outcome of the Cultural Revolution. When this state of affairs eventuates, Mao, in order to suppress those "revolutionary demons" he has released, will assess the magnitude of the need and proceed to compromise with his opposition as soon as he can. And if Mao were purged, those people who would have done this would not be those he wanted to purge, but the genuine revolutionaries.

VI.   WILL MAO TSE-TUNG'S AIMS BE REALIZED?

However, let us temporarily leave the discussion on the third possible outcome and concentrate our discussion now on the "subjective aims" of Mao Tse-tung in mobilizing the Red Guards. Let us then examine and assess whether or not Mao would be able to achieve the aim of "three birds with one stone" which we have touched upon briefly above.

The first aim is that of changing the direction of the discontent among the people. Can the Red Guard Movement relieve the discontent of the masses, especially that of the sensitive young students, accumulated over the years against Mao and the Communist Party? Can they then attack the "handful of power holders who have taken the capitalist road" and at the same time support and promote the prestige of Mao?

This is unlikely. Even if it appeared to be so, it had to have been a fleeting phenomenon which has now passed. Of course Mao has made use of his advantage in this respect. That is he has always been the accuser and never the accused. If he also defeats his opponents, he would have placed all sorts of accusations and responsibilities on to the others and used the vanquished as the scape goats to be sacrificed to God. But as the Chinese communists have always said: "the people's eyes are bright and clear", meaning that any palm of a great dictator is not sufficient to cover all the eyes and ears under the sun! Victory itself of course implies tremendous persuasive powers, but the more important questions are how these victories have been achieved and what kind of victories they are. But if what has brought victories to Mao is blatant suppression by the guns, is shameless lies and un-principled tactics, and if Mao, in order to secure victory, uses the same methods to treat his enemies and supporters and furthermore, if the victory that he has won is not commendable but corrupt, then Mao Tse-tung, following a victory of this kind, would be unable to find his scape goat to sacrifice to the "god of the People".

But right now, Mao is using exactly the same kind of means to secure his victories and winning the kind of victory described in the paragraph above. As a result, the victory of Mao would only bring dissatisfaction to the Great Helmsman. The victory only leads to the concentration of the dissatisfaction, especially those of the disillusioned youths, on Mao himself.

Let us have a look at the other aims that Mao has in mind. Firstly, Mao would wish to organize this mass movement to defeat all of his opponents in the party and in the country so that ideologically the party and the country would be united by the "Thoughts of Mao Tse-tung" and organizationally, the party and the country would be controlled by Mao. Secondly, Mao would wish to train a large group of new cadres who would be immune from "revisionism" and "bureaucratism".

Can these be achieved?

To answer the first point, we have to make clear as to the degree of "unity" and the degree of "control". Up to a certain degree, the ideology of the Chinese communist party during the past twenty years has always been unified under the thoughts of Mao Tse-tung and likewise organizationally, Mao has always been in control. However, Mao was not happy with the extent of unity and the extent of control, especially during the last few years. This "unity" and this "control" have been seriously challenged. Dissatisfied, Mao wanted to strengthen them. Yet how absolute do "unity" and "control" have to become before Mao is satisfied? Obviously he wants them to be more so than Stalinist Russia, even than Hilter's Germany! He wants to become the most absolute Pope during the Medieval dark ages; he wants to become the supreme head of a religion like Muhammed. He wants to make every single word or phrase of his to become "the highest instruction", "the absolute truth"; he wants his selected works to be the Bible and his quotations to be some sort of "magical incantations". He wants this Bible and the "magic incantations" to substitute for the sum total of human knowledge, present and past; to be the encyclopaedia of "proletarian culture". In order to fulfill his objective, he cans all other works "feudalist" and "capitalist" and burns them all. And by calling them "evil dirts", he persecuted all those intellectuals who have attained a certain degree of achievement in literature, history, philosophy or art.

Mao Tse-tung's policies in relation to this respect are totally and ridiculously reactionary and are contrary to Marxism-Leninism. However this will be discussed elsewhere. All that needs to be said is whether it is possible to establish this kind of unity and this kind of absolute control.

Impossible!

It is impossible regardless of what angle we examine it from. Starting from a general feature of human thought, submission to authority and resistance to it almost exist together; considering the present stage of progress in human thoughts, the new collectivism cannot but include the "autheben-ed" individualism; from the development of China's culture, it has reached such a level that the masses have been more or less enlightened and the intellectuals have been baptised by science and democracy; (from the development of culture on a world-wide scale,) no matter how strong the adverse current, socialism will inevitably replace capitalism and democratic communism will take the place of police controlled communism.

Therefore Mao's ambition in this respect which surpasses that of Shih Wang Ti and Stalin will only be proven by history to be a sheer illusion and a ridiculous instance of anarchronism. Granted that Mao succeeds in achieving the absolute unity and control in appearance for a short period of time, this would only mean that history will be punishing him and the system he tries to establish with extra strength at a much higher speed.

Concerning the other question as to whether or not thru the Red Guards movement Mao would be able to train a whole generation of new cadres who would be immune to "revisionism" and "bureaucratism", we would answer this way. The new cadres are being trained and eventually they will become full fledged cadres, but the cadres thus trained would not be immune to degeneration into "revisionism" and "bureaucratism".

Why? We have explained elsewhere and we shall not discuss it in great details again. All in all, if we don't follow the policies of permanent revolution, if we don't thoroughly give up the reactionary policy of "socialism in one country", if we don't regard the success of the Chinese revolution as the spark for socialist revolutions in other parts of the world (including the underdeveloped part and the highly developed capitalist countries) and regard it as a self-sufficient base for "the construction of the prosperous and strong socialist fatherland", if we don't hold up the preliminary socialist construction as an example of the superiority of socialism (even in poor countries) over capitalism, in order to attract the working class and the poor of the old capitalist countries to the side of socialism that they carry out socialist revolutions in their own countries, then in a "poor and empty" country, the leaders of the victorious socialist revolution will find no effective ways to oppose or prevent "revisionism" and "bureaucratism"'

Under Mao's policy of the Stalinist "communism in one country", the great number of cadres to be selected from the Red Guards of today will degenerate into bureaucrats easier and faster than the old cadres (who presently are having their heads bashed, but who once went thru a long period of real struggle) because they seized power" thru a revolutionary dress rehearsal. They completed their "long march" with free train tickets, and they are immature successors who have been artificially raised in the green house of Mao Tse-tung's "Cultural Revolution".

VII. PSEUDO-REVOLUTION AND REAL REVOLUTION

In order that the Chinese Revolution will not go sour, that the future revolutionary cadres will not degenerate into a state of "revisionism" and "bureaucratism". we should make every effort to turn the possibility of the third outcome into a reality, that is, to convert the pseudo-revolution into a genuine revolution.

Let us first talk about the reality of this outcome.

One year ago or even half a year ago nobody, not even Mao Tse-tung, would have believed that the state of "rebellion" would develop into that of today. Now when witnessing the recent disturbances all over the country, anyone who denies the possibility of or the necessity for a revolution under the Chinese communist rule would have to be politically color blind.

One very fine aspect of the "Great Cultural Revolution" is the clear revelation that the "internal contradictions" and the "external contradictions" accumulated during the seventeen years of communist rule have been numerous and deep. They are so profound that they can only be solved by a revolution—one which is not authorized and staged by the ruling clique, but a genuine revolution.

This objective need-predetermines that the "Great Cultural Revolution" initiated by Mao Tse-tung will have to develop into a genuine revolution and that it is possible for it to develop into one. But how would this potential and possible reality manifest itself objectively? And how do we, as revolutionaries, subjectively realize this goal?

Objectively, during the past six months and especially in the last two months, many actions of the "revolt" have actually gone past the official limitations. This is to say that some elements of a genuine revolution have already been incorporated within the pseudo-revolution. When Mao-Lin and company cheered the "January Revolution" of Shanghai, they were also trying desperately to urge the Liberation

Army to be involved in the revolution. They were also frantically calling upon every "dictatorial mechanism" to suppress the "counter-revolutionists". At the same time, the People's Daily republished an old article of Mao entitled "On Correcting Erroneous Ideas in the Party" in an endeavor to oppose what developed in the "revolutionary mass organizations" such as "localism", "small factionalism", "extremely democratic", "non-organizational view point", "subjectivism" and "individualism". This clearly indicates that the mass movement has moved outside the limit which the authorities have set down. Again the third issue of "Red Flag" in 1967 carried an editorial which said: "At this stage when the proletariat and the capitalist class with a handful of its agents in the Party are waging a decisive battle, those who stand fast to reaction, including landlords, rich peasants, capitalist right-wingers, bad elements, counter-revolutionary revisionists, and American-Chiang spys, appeared from every direction. These "freaks and demons" come out to spread rumors and confuse the people and cheat them. And further, they gather people who don't understand the true facts and establish counter-revolutionary organizations and frantically involve themselves in counter-revolutionary activities. For example, the so-called 'Chinese Workers and Peasants Red Flag', 'The Honorable Veteran Army', "the United Action Committee" and other 'revolutionary groups' which have been organized by the revisionists and are actually "Royalist' organizations. These are reactionary organizations. The masses in these organizations have been cheated and we should try and educate them." (see "On the power seizure struggle of the proletarian revolutionary groups").

These words tell us vividly that the masses have risen. Among them are of course the "vermin", the harmful elements, "who would loot during the fire". Apart from that, however, even Chen Po-ta had to agree that there are still the majority of ordinary workers and peasants who "have been cheated". The masses, having suffered tremendously under years of bureaucratic dictatorship, now see the opportunity to effect reforms and changes. They rise resolutely to settle the accounts with the bosses who have sat on their heads. "Economism runs amok" and this forces Mao to cope with it. This is an indisputable indication that the "Great Cultural Revolution" is no longer totally controlled by the authorities. The pseudo-revolution begins to metamorphose into a genuine revolution.

The "Great Cultural Revolution" is changing and developing. Change and development is an inevitable tendency. However, it is hard to predict how it will change and develop, especially hard to predict in clear terms.

What we can predict is this: if there is no vanguard with a clear cut political program in leadership, then even if this revolution develops to an extent greatly surpassing the limitations set down by Mao or Liu, it will be suppressed again sooner or later. It might either serve one of the opposing groups (most likely the Maoists) or be suppressed by a coalition of the two opposing forces. In this case, the social contradictions under the rule of the Chinese communists, which was once brought into the open, would not have been resolved. They will submerge again temporarily, waiting for new eruptions.

Therefore, the present situation in China which promises a genuine revolution should be viewed timely and understood correctly by the internationalist proletarian revolutionaries, who should make further revolutionary intervention in order that the genuine revolutionary leftists now rising in groups might have an alliance and leadership that would lead them to struggle in the correct and definite direction.

In short, the development of the "Cultural Revolution" depends first of all on whether revolutionaries can make the genuine revolutionary potentials realize objectively.

To give revolutionary aid, or to intervene, to provide the revolutionary masses with correct leadership, we have to distinguish the genuine revolutionaries from the pseudo-revolutionaries in the multitudinous and diverse rebel organizations. Since all these rebel groups, on the surface at least, uphold Mao and chant "Long Live Chairman Mao", this is no easy task.

As to exactly what the "revolutionary line of the proletariat" is or what "the capitalist revisionist line" is, neither has publicly announced any concrete program. So ordinary people will be unable to decide who is real and who is fake, who is revolutionary and who is counter-revolutionary. It is just as difficult to judge who is really supporting Mao and who is not. We have seen many important leaders of the Cultural Revolution being classified all of a sudden as members of "black gangs". There is an equal number of people who were regarded as counter-revolutionary only yesterday, have been "rehabilitated". Since not everything done by the "Maoist supporters" is revolutionary nor everything done by the "anti-Maoists" counter-revolutionary, it is extremely difficult to set up standards to distinguish the pseudo-revolutionaries from the genuine, yet these standards need to be set up.

Without setting out these standards, the genuine proletarian revolutionaries will not know what to support and what to fight against; whom to align with and whom to oppose. Nor do they know where to go and what to struggle for.

The following standards which are being proposed are, in my opinion, appropriate for the present conditions in China. We can distinguish whether individuals or organizations are genuinely revolutionary by measuring them against these standards which can also be considered as the tentative program for a genuine Chinese Proletarian Revolutionary Party.

These standards are:

(1)   Whether or not the group or person opposes efforts to deify the great leader;

(2)   Whether or not it opposes bureaucratic privileges, corruption and degeneration;

(3)   Whether or not it supports and really practices the principles of the Paris Commune, i.e. whether the elections of factory committees, peoples communes of the various regions, the committees of peasants, are by secret ballot and whether the peoples communes will replace the "people's committees" of all levels;

(4)   Whether or not in words and deeds, the constitutional rights of the working masses are guaranteed (detailed in the third chapter of the Constitution of the People's Republic of China): freedom of speech, publication, association, demonstration and strike; the freedom of religion; and that person's bodies and residences should not be violated;

(5)   Whether or not it opposes the use of the pretext of "anti-economism" to reduce or deprive the welfare enjoyment and living guarantees of the workers and peasants;

(6)   Whether or not it would allow political opponents ample opportunities to debate and the right of rebuttal;

(7)   Whether or not it would allow and carry out a sufficient and complete evaluation of the internal and external policies since the establishment of New China;

(8)   Whether it would support and allow sufficient freedom in the creation of art and literature and other cultural activities with the single exception of a general clear-cut political standard to be applied;

82

(9)   Whether it recognizes that in opposing Russian "revisionism", it should not prevent us from engaging in a united front with Russia to fight against the chief enemy--American imperialism;

(10)   Whether in theory and in practice, it believes that the interests of Chinese socialist construction should be subordinate to the interests of world revolution.

The genuine revolutionary left are those who reply to the above questions in the affirmative, no matter what flags they hoist or what "king" they "defend". On the other hand, those who answer the question with "no's" should be considered rightists and pseudo revolutionaries whether they support Mao or Liu.

We are opposed to all right wing pseudo-revolutionaries and support all revolutionary leftists and we are willing to participate in united actions with them. We request that all revolutionaries unite under this program.

VIII. THE QUESTION OF REVOLUTIONARY LEADERSHIP

The Transitional Program of the Fourth International began thus: "The world political situation as a whole is chiefly characterized by a historical crisis of the leadership of the proletariat. "The historical crisis of mankind is reduced to the crisis of the revolutionary leadership".

This historical judgement was correct 29 years ago when it was first written and it remains so today. Not only is it correct in relation to countries which have had this kind of revolution. It applies not only to other countries in the world, but also to China, and in a certain sense, it is most applicable to China today.

Since in today's China, under Mao Tse-tung's rule, the objective prerequisites for a political revolution for proletarian democracy have ripened, if have not yet "begun to get somewhat rotten". "The turn is now to the proletariat, i.e., mainly revolutionary vanguard". (See "The Transitional program")

If there exists in China a well-organized proletarian revolutionary party with a large membership and a correct Marxist-Leninist program, then the pseudo-revolution started by Mao Tse-tung himself would certainly be or have already been transformed into an anti-bureaucratic, genuine, revolution for workers' democracy.

Unfortunately, this is not the case.

The genuine left wing of the Chinese communists, the Chinese section of the Fourth International, owing to subjective and objective reasons, ceased to exist today under communist rule--at least, it does not exist as an organized and co-ordinated political group. Therefore they have not and cannot take any impact on the present political struggle. However, their ideas still exist, at least they still have some influence on the proletariat in the big cities. For example, the 19th issue of the "Red Guards Battle News" published in Shanghai this year mentioned the fact that "within the rebel groups, there were detected some Trotyskyist schismatic activities."

When the political climate becomes more and more favorable to the growth and perpetuation of genuine Marxism-Leninism, then the seeds of old thoughts and new ideas will germinate.

The factors favouring the germination of these seeds are the desire of the masses of workers and peasants for democratic rights under the existing bureaucratic totalitarian rule and the demands of all revolutionaries for world socialist revolution under the choking influence of narrow-minded nationalism.

The more Mao Tse-tung's regime becomes a crazy personal dictatorship, the more it deprives the poor masses of their rights, and the more the country becomes isolated, all the more spontaneously and wildly will the seed of revolt breed.

As such, the conditions for a political revolution for proletarian democracy under the rule of Mao Tse-tung are ripe. The only question is how to provide the correct leadership. Speaking of leadership, the first thing that comes to mind is the reconstruction of the Chinese Section of the Fourth International and the intensification and development of its thoughts and ideas.

Without doubt, this is something to be seriously considered and must be put into practice. It is because the programme of the Fourth International represents and has represented during the past forty odd years the first, the most consistent and most stainless banner in the international communist movement to oppose degenerate bureaucratism. It represents the only organization which has upheld the tradition of Marxism-Leninism after Stalinism betrayed and poisoned the ideals and tasks of communism. Therefore, we firmly believe that in order for socialist revolutions in capitalist countries and anti-bureaucratic political revolutions for proletarian democracy in "socialist countries" to be successful, we must follow the correct road and not neglect this flag or forget this tradition.

From an understanding of this, are we to conclude that only under the direct leadership of the Fourth International Parties, organizationally and ideologically, will these revolutions be successful and develop along a correct path? Are we to say that without the direct leadership and control of the Fourth International Parties, these revolutions would not be successful or genuine?

No, of course not. To draw this conclusion would be the worst kind of sectarianism.

Let's take the case of China where we should realize that before the reconstruction and redevelopment of the Chinese Section of the Fourth International, anti-bureaucratic political revolutions will occur, not just once but many times, and that these revolutions will be led mainly by left wing leaders who have left the ranks of the bureaucrats. These leaders could have partly relieved themselves from the hold of Stalin—Maoism, and have objectively taken on various positions of the Chinese Section of the Fourth International although they would not have called themselves Fourth Internationalists and they may even vehemently denounce the Fourth Internationalists. What should be our attitudes towards them? Of course we should support their revolution resolutely and earnestly criticize their short-comings and courageously take part in their combat troops in order that the aims of anti-bureaucratic-politics can at least be partly achieved.

All in all, the most important thing is the essence and the implementation of the political program and as to in whose name, under what flag and whether under our direct control or not, is only of secondary significance.

One of the greatest crimes committed by Stalin in the modern history of revolutionary movements is the fact that he destroyed and negated everything which was not directly controlled by Stalinists. If we are to take a similar attitude (even if only a tiny bit), then the only result would be that history will march in great strides contemptuously, past our tightly closed little door.

However, are we to apply the supporting attitude described above to the Liu-Teng faction in the present struggle in China?

I don't think so—not now at least.

The reasons are as follows: first, judging from the presently available information, the Liu-Teng faction has not "initiated" any revolution, on the contrary, they are the objects of the "revolution" initiated by the Mao-Lin faction. Therefore the barren slogan of "Support the Liu-Teng faction" implies the maintenance of the status quo, an objection to "disturbance" and an objection to "the seizure of power". We are dissatisfied with the status quo; we do not object to disturbance and we do not object to the seizure of power. We are opposed to "the seizure of power for Chairman Mao", but wholeheartedly agree to the "seizure of power" for the interests of the masses of workers and peasants." Secondly, by looking at the facts in the past and their performances today, Liu and Teng and their followers have not basically stepped out of the domain of Stalinism-Maoism and they have been even more deeply rooted in the ruling hierarchy of the Chinese Communist Party. The so-called "revisionist" line which they profess and execute is mainly an effort to stop Mao's over adventurist policies. Basically they are "right to middle". Therefore, the Liu-Teng faction should not be equated to the revolutionary left and their victory cannot be a victory for the revolutionary left. We can even believe that should one day the revolutionary left be winning, the Liu-Teng faction would immediately terminate their weak and passive resistance and kneel in front of the Maoists begging for forgiveness in order to stop the revolutionaries from victory. Therefore we should not create an illusion among the masses—the illusion that the Liu-Teng faction is equivalent to the revolutionary left.

That we do not promote the slogan "support the Liu-Teng faction" does not prevent us from time to time from supporting them (especially their followers) on certain concrete issues and engaging in united actions with them (not only the masses, but the leaders as well). This is because our main attack is obviously against the personal dictatorship of Mao Tse-tung and that owing to circumstances, the Liu-Teng faction may come (either in earnest or on pretence) comparatively close to certain points of our political program.

IX. WHAT CLASS INTERESTS DOES THE CULTURAL REVOLUTION SERVE?

What has been discussed above concerns mainly the political and factual aspects of the "Great Cultural Revolution". We would like to discuss a deeper theoretical question, namely-what class interests does Mao Tse-tung's "Great Cultural Revolution" serve?

The case with Stalin was crystal clear–he represented the interests of conservative bureaucrats of U.S.S.R. and the position of the "centrists" of the bureaucrat caste in particular. He engaged in every kind of manoeuvre, now attacking the left, now the right, savagely and stubbornly, protecting the interests of the bureaucrats and at the same time the social foundations on which the bureaucrats depend for their survival–the system of nationalized and state-owned properties.

What about Mao Tse-tung? Of course he also represents the interests of the bureaucrats. However, his stands are somewhat different from Stalin's. It appears that Mao directly represents the left of the ruling class and the "Great Cultural Revolution" is directed at what was vaguely equivalent to the right in the CP of the Soviet Union those days. Is this indeed the case?

No.

Since the time around 1930 when the Chinese Communist Party made a decisive break with the left opposition, it does not have any more genuine left wing among its ranks (at least not among its leadership). Since then, all internal struggles which have ever happened inside the Chinese Communist Party, be it between Mao Tse-tung and Wang Ming, between Mao Tse-tung and Chang Kuo Tau, Mao Tse-tung and Liu Shao-chi, were all caused by tactical differences or even on account of personal interests. Seldom have they been due to differences in revolutionary principles. If ever the question involves ideologies, at the most, they are differences within the Stalinist School: Stalinist Right and Stalinist Left. Both of them, right and left, if measured by the rule of Marxism-Leninism, are Centrists. It was the case with Stalin himself, during the over twenty years of his absolute rule, he sometimes jumped to the left and sometimes to the right, but all the same, he remained a Centrist.

The Chinese Communist Party, which has long been dominated by Stalinism, was naturally affected by this "jumping back and forth". Every jump would correspond with an internal change in the Chinese Communist Party and to complete this change would often imply some kind of struggle, large or small—a struggle between those supporting the new stand and those supporting the old one. In these struggles, Mao has not always been on the left, although generally speaking he was with the left. Mao would not retreat on the question of seizure of political power by force and on the question of uniting with the bourgeoisie Mao would not bind himself to keep any promise.

Therefore, generally speaking, Mao Tse-tung should be considered as a successor to the Stalinist left wing. He particularly accepted Stalinism of the later thirties, namely, the political and economic adventurism, narrow-minded political sectarianism (clothed in ultra-leftist cliches) personal authoritarian bureaucratism and the Bonarpartism manipulating class contradictions.

The left wing of the Stalinists is, of course, not equivalent to the left wing of Marxist-Leninists. It is the left in the Centrists. It is called the "left" only in comparison with the right in the same group. The Stalinists have only had two kinds of attitudes towards capitalism and capitalists: one is submission, compromising at the expense of principles or even surrendering shamelessly; the other is opposition by adventurous, thoughtless, savage and criminal sectarianism and bureaucratism. The former is "right" and the latter is "left". Its "right" is, of course a betrayal of Marxism-Leninism but this kind of "left" has nothing in common with Marxism-Leninism either. Whether "left" or "right", whether it embraces or attacks the capitalist class, it does nothing beneficial for the proletariat or socialist revolution, and in some cases does more harm than good. Therefore we must not confuse the left and right of Stalinism and the left and right of Marxism-Leninism. It is because the essence of the two belongs to different categories and if we equate the two or take the face value of the radicalism of the Stalinist left turn, we would have deceived ourselves.

We can find examples in the internal struggles of the Soviet Communist Party when Trotsky represented the left. On many occasions, e.g. on the slogan of national congress for China after 1928; on the question of collectivization in the Russian countryside in 1930; and on the question of forming a united front in Germany with the Social Democratic Party, Stalin appeared to be on the "left" but in reality he was very "right", because his policies delayed the revolution, or cost a great deal for the progress of the revolution. All of these rendered objectively immense-service to the bourgeoisie and therefore in essence they were "right" or even "ultra-right".

The alleged "left" nature of Mao Tse-tung and his clique should be viewed similarly. Among those who oppose Mao from the "right", there are, of course, some genuine right-wingers (especially among those leaders who have consistently supported the Stalinist position) who support a line of prolonged co-operation with the capitalists. However, there is another group, a very large group, the masses (including some in the higher level of the hierarchy) who have not been tied down by Stalinism and who may not really be "right". Most likely they just appear to be "right" and, in fact, they are "left". In other words, what they support may well be more in the interests of the proletarian revolution of China and the world. Mao's position would be "left" in relation to the first category of anti-Maoists, but would be "right" in relation to the second category. Like Stalin in his days, Mao's position is that of the "Centrist bureaucrats". Mao's "Great Proletarian Cultural Revolution" is similar to Stalin's "anti-rightist" struggle in the sense that although it has some "anti-capitalist" connotations, it does not serve the interests of the proletariat. Occillating and jumping back and forth, it invariably serves the interests of the most privileged and the most powerful bureaucrats.

"But isn't Mao Tse-tung's Great Cultural Revolution mobilizing thousands and millions of the non-bureaucratic masses to seize power from the bureaucrats and to rebel? Isn't this solidly attacking or even defeating the bureaucrats?"

True enough. This something we have discussed before and this is what makes things different from Stalin. However, we have also explained that this difference is not fundamental. The forms are different but, in essence, both are for the protection of the interests of the bureaucracy, only that it was more obvious with Stalin. With Mao there were some phony phenomena confusing the perspective.

Yet there seems to be a little bit of real difference which arises from the different tendency and nature of the bureaucracy which each of them represents. Stalin represented the more conservative part of the bureaucracy. These bureaucrats in internal affair had incessantly yielded to the pressure of the capitalist elements and only when they found their position in serious danger, did they begin to wage the counter-attack in a panic. Externally, they always submitted to the pressure of the imperialists and so gave up completely the task of world revolution in the end. The bureaucrats that Mao Tse-tung represents, however, seem to be more radical. Their internal or external policies appear to be extremely left and uncompromising. Under hostile pressures from within and without the country, Mao has not shown indications of backing down. On the contrary, his fighting spirit has been heightened. Does this difference in reaction and performance mean that the Maoists at least represent the revolutionary section of the ruling caste of the CCP?

I don't think this can be considered true. Any Centrist can occillate from left to right and from right to left. Let's take the case of Stalin. From the late twenties until his death, his whole tendency was "right" indeed: compromising with the international imperialists and betraying the world revolution, nevertheless, there had been cases when Stalin turned "left". The most famous of them was the period of time known as the "Third Period" (from 1929 to 1933) during which Stalin used savage and terrorist methods to eleminate the rich peasants internally, while externally he resolved to fight alone--blindly, against imperialism. It was this "Leftist" policy of Stalin's, as we all know, that created the opportunity for Hitler's victory in Germany and a reactionary situation throughout the world, which in its turn forced him to jump drastically to the right, adopting the policy of the "people's front".

Mao Tse-tung's present policy, internal and external, roughly speaking is somewhat equivalent to Stalin's "Third Period". It is anti-thesis of the reactionary policy of "people's democracy". New and heavier blows it will receive, and when its head bumps against the wall, it will probably turn to the right again, to a new submission to the international imperialists, especially American imperialism. The ultra-left policy of today is the result of the ultra-right policy of yesterday, and it can become the cause of a new ultra-right line of tommorow.

How can we break this "Centrist" chain of causes and results? There is only one way and that is to make use of the opportunity created by today's ultra-left policy to deepen the pseudo-revolution, turning it into a genuine revolution so that proletarian democracy will prevail in China.

X. A SHORT POSTSCRIPT

A lot can be said and ought to be said about the "Great Proletarian Cultural Revolution" from the point of view of culture in the strict sense of the word. However the so-called "Great Proletarian Cultural Revolution" of Mao Tse-tung has nothing positive or constructive to do with culture. Everyone knows that it is merely an offhand pretext he picked up in order to cover up his real intention of weeding out his opponents in a power struggle. The ridiculousness of the attitudes and actions Mao has concerning culture and the intellectuals in the "Cultural Revolution" is so contradictory to Marxism-Lenism that we don't have to waste space discussing now. The question perhaps will be dealt with in the future. Here we would like to cite two quotations from Lenin and let each individual draw his own conclusions.

(1) "The old school was a school of cramming, it compelled pupils to imbibe a mass of useless, superfluous, barren knowledge, which clogged the brain and transformed the younger generation into officials turned to pattern. But you would be committing a great mistake if you attempted to draw the conclusion that one can become a Communist without acquiring what human knowledge has accumulated. It would be a mistake to think that it is enough to learn communist slogans, the conclusions of Communist science, without acquiring the sum of knowledge of which Communism itself is a consequence." (See "The Task of the Youth Leagues".)

(2) "Proletarian culture is not something that has sprung nobody knows whence, it is not an invention of those who call themselves experts in proletarian culture. That is all nonsense. Proletarian culture must be the result of a natural development of the stores of knowledge which mankind has accumulated under the yoke of capitalist society, landlord society and bureaucratic society." (ibidem.)

Comparing what Lenin said 47 years ago with what we see happening in China during the "Great Proletarian Cultural Revolution" personally led by Mao Tsé-tung and it is easy to see exactly how Mao has truly "developed" the cultural aspects of Marxism-Leninism.

February, 1967.

Footnote 1:

Recently we came across an unconfirmed document titled "the Self-Criticisms of Liu Shao Chi" which traced his errors back to February 1946 admitting that "he had submitted some written propositions to the Central Committee of the Party, believing that the establishment of The Political Consultation Conference would guarantee the progress óf China into a new stage of peace." This could well be the case, since at that time Stalin was urging the C.C.P. to form a coalition government with Chiang Kai Shek. Apart from this, Liu also pointed out a few mistakes he made but which had to a large extent been resolved in practice.

Footnote H:

The Cultural Revolution and the Red Guards Movement of Mao Tse-tung has been charged by a Russian commentator with "Trotskyism". This is of course absolute rubbish but this is also not entirely groundless. Therefore, in order to explain the correct attitude of revolutionary Marxists towards youths and students, it is necessary and appropriate to tell the old story. In 1923, Lenin was extremely ill and the power of the party was vested with Stalin, Zinoviev and Kamenev. The party was rapidly being bureaucratised. Trotsky felt at that time that to overcome this crisis, "there is not and cannot be any other means of triumphing over the corporatism, the caste spirit of the functionaries, than by the realization of democracy." (see p.23, "The New Course".) And to implement democracy, according to Trotsky, "is a question primarily of instituting healthier relations between the old cadres and the majority of the members who came to the party after October", (ibiuem. p.16.) because of "the fact that the party lives on two separate storeys bears within it numerous dangers." (ibidem, p.17) "Trotsky thus discussed the relationship between the elders and the young people and propounded the possible impact the young people could contribute towards the struggle for the democratisation of the party. He wrote thus, "The latter (the student youth), as we have seen reacts in a particularly vigorous way against bureaucratism. Not for nothing did Lenin propose to draw largely upon the students in order to combat bureaucratism. By its social composition and its contacts, the student youth reflects all the social groups of our party as well as their state of mind. Its youthfulness and its sensitivity prompt it to give an active form immediately to this state of mind. As a studying youth, it endeavours to explain and to generalize. This is not to say that all its acts and moods reflect healthy tendencies ...... But by saying that the youth is our barometer, we give its political manifestations not an essential but a symptomatic value. A barometer does not create weather; it is confined to recording it.... As to the student youth, recruited from all the sections and strata of Soviet society, it reflects in its checkered composition all our merits and demerits, and it would be stupid not to accord the greatest attention to its moods.... The youth are our means of checking up on ourselves, our substitutes; the future belongs to them." (ibidem, p. 23-24.)

Trotsky so correctly assessed the functions and capabilities of young people and yet the Stalinists accused him of having ulterior motives and of manipulating "ignorant" youths to oppose the old revolutionaries and the party. As a result, as we all know, because of a series of objective reasons not favourable to the proletarian revolutionaries, the Left Opposition headed by Trotsky was crushed. The younger revolutionaries were also maliciously suppressed by the bureaucrats. The degenerating process of the bureaucratisation of Soviet Russia was thereby accelerated.

The Soviet commentator pointed to this historical fact in an effort to show that Mao Tse-tung is similar to Trotsky in manipulation of the young people to further his interest in the power struggle.

Is this historical comparison appropriate? No, because although the circumstances have some similarities, they have fundamental differences.

The similarities are 1/ They both enjoyed higher prestige than any other Leader (in the case of Trotsky, Lenin was too ill to be counted in) but they did not control the party machinery directly (Trotsky is more so than Mao) and 2/ in order to "seize power", both of them understood the importance of the young people.

But the similarities stop here.

The differences are more pronounced and fundamental. These differences are: firstly, the fact that Trotsky belonged to the minority in the party was not only due to historical reasons of the Bolshevik party, it was also because Trotsky represented the revolutionary position of the anti-bureaucrat proletarian left tendency and Stalin represented the bureaucratic, and conservative stand tending to compromise with capitalist class within and outside the country. Affected by the influence of revolutionary low tide, there were more mass support for the latter stand and the Stalinists had the opportunities to control the party machinery. However, Mao Tse-tung lost his influence on the party because of his fouled policies over the past ten years, internally or externally, especially the former. Mao just squandered his own prestige. Secondly, Trotsky wanted to depend on the youths and students to combat bureaucratism but he did not want to destroy the party nor did he want the older generation be substituted by the young people. He said, "to want to put the old generation in the archives would be madness." (ibidem p.19) However the "Red Guards Rebellion" initiated by Mao Tse-tung was to "shelve" all the old cadres and even, to follow the footsteps of Stalin, to kill them all off.

Thirdly, Trotsky attached much importance to the strength of the young people but never elevated them on to a level above the working class. In the struggle against bureaucratism, he attached the utmost importance to the factory cells. He vested the hope to overcome the crisis in the party on the continuous inflow of manual workers into the party. Needless to say, Trotsky would not make use of his supreme power and authority in the Red Army as Chairman of the Military Committee to use the barrel of the guns to blast the "dog heads" of the bureaucrats. In this respect, Mao Tse-tung was different. He elevated the students to a very high position and made use of them to oppose the workers, the army and the party cadre.

Fourthly, Trotsky saw the importance of the youths and students and treated them genuinely as the "mirror of the party", as the "barometer" of the political climate of the Soviet regime, as "means of checking up on ourselves". To put it in another way, Trotsky was to rely on the sensitive youths to get rid of the bureaucratic atmosphere and ingradients so that genuine democracy could be restored in the party. However, when Mao Tse-tung incited the students to rebel, his main purpose was to sanctify himself and to destroy the very limited democracy existing inside or outside the Chinese Communist Party.

SECTION TWO

MAO'S CHINA

AND

THE "PROLETARIAN CULTURAL REVOLUTION"

(Written for *New Politics*, Dec. 31, 1967)

By Raya Dunayevskaya

Raya Dunayevskaya was secretary to Leon Trotsky during his exile in Mexico, but broke with him at the time of the Hitler — Stalin pact because Trotsky insisted that Russia had to be defended. She, on the contrary, asserted that the Russian Revolution had degenerated into a state capitalist tyranny. Since the 1940s she has been closely associated with American workers' movements and has written on numerous aspects of the class struggle as well as lecturing widely on the subject in the United States, Western Europe and Africa. She is at present chairman of the National Editorial Board of the American publication News and Letters, a Marxist-Humanist group based in Detroit.

Raya Dunayevskya is the author of two books, Marxism and Freedom, and Philosophy and Revolution.

Of Marxist Humanism, Raya Dunayevskaya has written, "Marxist Humanism will remain alive so long as a new world on truly new, human beginnings has not been established. Totalitarian Communism understands this so well that the counter-revolutionary suppression of the Hungarian Revolution went hand-in-hand with the suppression of thought . . . . the great Hungarian Revolution raised the Humanist flag clearly. Because Marxist Humanism, to me, is the only genuine ground from which to oppose Communist totalitarianism, I felt the compulsion to show that Humanism is not something invented by me, but came directly from Marx who fought what he called " 'vulgar Communism,' writing that communism, as such, is not the goal of human development, the form of human society.' "

"Mao's China and the Proletarian Cultural Revolution" originally appeared in New Politics vol. 6, no. 2, Spring 1968 and was subsequently included in the second edition of Marxism and Freedom.

Now that the Cultural Revolution has slowed its pace, there is time to take a closer look at this startling phenomenon.

The Red Guards may appear to have emerged out of nowhere, but on August 18, 1966 they arrived one million strong in para-military formation to hear Defense Minister Lin Piao, Mao's "closest comrade in arms," explain the big-character poster "BOMBARD THE HEADQUARTERS." They learned that the headquarters were those of the Communist Party where they would find "persons in authority taking the road back to capitalism." When these teenagers streamed out of the square they seemed armed with something hardier than "Mao's Thought."

For the next month the bourgeois press had a field day describing the rampage against "all the old" in China, from Confucian texts and priceless art treasures, to many Communist leaders. It was even more bizarre to follow the young Maoists' attacks on Western imperialism, not so much the living, barbarous U.S. imperialism that was raining bombs on a Communist ally, North Vietnam, but against "Hong Kong haircuts" and the bourgeoisie-feudal reactionary music of Bach, Beethoven and Shostakovitch."

Within a couple of months, those teen-age hooligans were doing more than roaming the streets, putting dunce caps on "anti-revolutionaries." By the end of 1966, a proliferation of Red Guard and "Red Rebel" groups had abandoned their forays against foreign embassies to go into formerly forbidden ground, the factories and fields. "Seize control committees" tried to oust established factory managers while imitating them in lording it over the workers and forbidding strikes. Soon not only the Western press but the official Chinese press was talking of "civil war."

But where was this civil war? In Sinkiang, where army units disobeyed the seize control committees? In a "handful" of anti-Maoists within the Communist Party? And if it existed only in Mao's overactive imagination, what was its purpose? What objective conditions impelled the transformation of the Cultural Revolution into what Hegel might have called "a giddy whirl of self-perpetuating disorder?" To what extent was its disorder its order, that is, planned from above? To what extent had its internal dialectic propelled it beyond the boundaries set for it?

The anti-Maoist bourgeois press, the Maoists and their apologists all describe the Cultural Revolution as nothing short of a "second revolution."[1] The bourgeois analysts depict Mao as a man looking back nostalgically to the days of the Long March and slipping into occasional fits of paranoia. The Maoists and their apologists paint a portrait of Mao (there are 840 million actual portraits[2]) which shows him forever young, forever moving forward, forever combatting those Party, State and army bureaucrats who would lead the new generation from the path of "uninterrupted revolution" to the path of revisionism.

Factual information about events in China is hard to find. But the value of this description of a "second revolution" can be assessed. What is necessary is, first, to see China in its world context, especially in the period immediately preceding the Cultural Revolution and, second, to keep one's pre-suppositions aside so that the dialectic of the Cultural Revolution can be followed in and for itself. This is particularly important because the origins of the Cultural Revolution are tangled inextricably with the course of the war in Vietnam.

THE CRUCIAL YEAR: 1965

When Mao came to power in China he saw no need for mass participation in any "uninterrupted revolution." Indeed, it was not until seven years later, in 1956, that he saw a need to convene a Congress of the Chinese Communist Party, which had last met eleven years before, in 1945. The 1956 Congress declared China to be "state capitalist,"[3] a formulation with which this author agrees. Within a month the Hungarian Revolution erupted. It was soon followed by voices of revolt in China,[4] whereupon Mao thought up the Great Leap Forward, which would bring China "directly to Communism," bypassing both capitalism and "socialism." Instead, it brought the country to the edge of famine. Shortly thereafter, Mao stepped down as head of state, while retaining his post as Chairman of the CCP.

The American decision to bomb North Vietnam in February 1965 put the Communist world to the test. China, which had pictured itself as the besieged fortress, had to face the fact that U.S. imperialism had turned North Vietnam into a genuinely besieged fortress. Kosygin's visit to Peking immediately after seemed to bode a closing of Communist ranks, or at least a united front to help Hanoi. But nothing of the sort happened. Mao had quite a different perspective. For him, 1965 was to see the turning point in the struggle for world dominance. Against the U.S.-NATO axis and the Moscow-Warsaw axis, he projected a Peking-Djakarta axis. Nothing, least of all a united front with Russia to help the Vietnamese fight U.S. imperialism could be allowed to interfere with that perspective and the strategy that flowed from it. Where the others were ready to hold world perspectives in abeyance once the strategy of a Peking-Djakarta axis disintegrated, Mao became the more adamant in his single-mindedness of China as the central and sole leader of "world revolution," to which Vietnam must be subordinated.

In September 1965, an attempted coup against military leaders in Indonesia failed. On October 1, the military started a bloodbath against Communists and other oppositionists which resulted in the slaughter of hundreds of thousands. Any perspective of a Peking-Djakarta axis was quashed for the foreseeable future. Despite more recent[5] attempts to rewrite the history of the Indonesian Communist Party (KPI), in October 1965 not even Mao could think of a way to lay the blame for the greatest disaster in Communist history at the door of "Russian Revisionism." Aidit, the KPI leader, had aligned his party with China as soon as Mao came to power. Peng Chen acknowledged that Aidit's ascendency dated from his acceptance of Maoism.[6] If the KPI's line was characterized by class collaboration rather than class struggle[7], if "peaceful coexistence" underlay all the KPI's actions, it was at the direction of the Chinese Communist Party. In short, the collapse of the Peking-Djakarta axis was the result not only of counter-revolutionary terror in Indonesia but of the class collaborationist line of the KPI which prepared the way for it. And that line was laid down in Peking.

For Mao, the Indonesian crisis was a test of the ability of his Central Committee to draw "the correct conclusions." Apparently, many of the members failed this test. Not only was pressure for a united front with Russia exerted by outside Communist parties, including the North Korean, but reports leaked from the Japanese CP indicate that Liu Shao-sh'i was not the only Chinese leader who pressed for such a united front. For Mao this was the last straw. His own cadres had not properly understood the tale of "sitting on the mount and watching the fight of the tigers." The Russians did understand the tale: "From all this it becomes clear that the Chinese leaders need a lengthy Vietnam war to maintain international tensions . . . There is every reason to assert that it is one of the goals of the policy of the Chinese leadership in the Vietnam question to originate a military confrontation between the USSR and the United States."[8] The Chinese Central Committee, however, still had to learn who the main enemy was.[9]

No wonder the Cultural Revolution had been limping along, restricted to the arts. The leadership would have to be shaken up, hardened or discarded. Mao decided to "disappear."

The Chinese press and the wall posters now reveal that during the critical period from November 1965 to May 1966, when Mao dropped out of sight and the speculations in the Western press ranged from "ill health" to "perhaps even death," he had left the "oppressive atmosphere" of Peking to prepare the Proletarian Cultural Revolution. When he returned he was ready to take on not only the foreign parties but his own Central Committee as well as readying the so-called Red Guards. He summoned a Party Plenum, the first in four years, to meet on August 1. The resolution of this body gave a categorical answer to those who had called for a united front with Russia on the Vietnam war: "The Plenary sessions maintain that to oppose imperialism it is imperative to oppose modern revisionism. There is no middle road whatsoever . . . . It is imperative resolutely to expose their (Russian Communists') true features as scabs. It is impossible to have 'united action' with them."[10]

"Russian revisionism" was not alone in being rejected. The other CPs around the world were rebuffed; any that did not acknowledge the CCP, as the sole leader of world Communism were denigrated.* Internally, the title of "Chairman Mao's closest comrade-in-arms," passed from Liu to Lin Piao. All motions were carried unanimously.

Now Mao was ready to transform the Cultural Revolution. He announced the means of this transformation, not at the Plenum, but at a mass rally in Peking. It was a "new force," divorced not only from the legal structures of Mao's Single Party-State-Army but from production itself. All schools were to be closed for an entire year. Rootless teenagers, who owed loyalty to none but Mao, who know no world outside of Mao's China, for whom both history and revolution existed only as they "made" them, would carry through the Great Proletarian Cultural Revoltuion.

THE RED GUARDS

> . . . pure Insight . . . completes the stage of culture. It takes nothing but the self . . . it comprehends everything, extinguishes all objectiveness.
>
> – Hegel, *Phenomenology of Mind*

"Shoot Brezhnev!" "Burn Kosygin!" These were some of the posters carried by the Red Guards who surrounded the Russian Embassy in Peking, marching, singing, shouting and harassing anyone who ventured out for food. But this was not exclusively an anti-Russian act, it was part of the process of "hardening" the Chinese and some self-created havoc in China was not viewed as too high a price to pay for achieving this objective.

When the Sino-Soviet conflict first burst into the open in 1960, the Chinese masses were confused and dismayed. As one refugee told me:

---

*China was not about to forget that Cuba had dared to make a public statement about Chinese methods and procedures being "exactly the same as the ones used by the United States Embassy in our country . . . our country had liberated itself from the imperialism 90 miles from our shores and it was not willing to permit another powerful state to come 20,000 kilometers to impose similar practices on us."

We had no specific love for the Russians; there had actually been very little contact between Russians and Chinese. But the regime itself had always played up the Russians as our greatest friends and Stalin's *History of the Communist Party* had been studied as much as any work by Mao. And now all we heard about them was that they were "revisionists." Somehow, instead of hatred against the Russians, a feeling of utter isolation descended upon all of us.

No feeling of isolation ever bothered Mao. He is forever ready to make a "great Leap Forward" over objective conditions, confident that will and hard work, especially hard work by 700 million souls, can achieve miracles, "Make one day equal twenty years." Far from leaving the miraculous work by itself, however, the CCP spelled it out as follows: "Each person must work ten hours and engage in ideological studies for two hours a day. They are entitled to one day of rest every ten days . . . "

The voices of revolt heard during the brief period of the "One Hundred Flowers" campaign and again during the disastrous "Great Leap Forward", which brought the country to near famine, were silent during the development of the Sino-Soviet conflict. Despite the absence of similar manifestations of opposition, Mao nevertheless insisted on the creation of Red Guards for his new Great Leap Forward.

While in 1960 the Chinese masses were dismayed at their isolation, in 1966 it was the Russians who were dismayed. For the Red Guards, the enemy was not only "Russian revisionism" but Russia itself. Mao's favorite statement remained: "You learn to make revolutions by making them just as you learn to swim by swimming." The Red Guards were told daily that they were, indeed, "making revolution." So satisfied was Mao with the work of the Red Guards in the months of August and September that he was thinking of institutionalizing them. As the *Peking Review* was to express it later: "When Chairman Mao, the red sun which shines most brightly in our hearts and our most respected and beloved supreme commander, received in Peking a million young Red Guards, not only had a "new day dawned" but no holds were barred against anti-Maoists.

This new leap, like its capitalized predecessor, tripped over the objective conditions it scorned. In the course of the Maoist terror mass opposition surfaced. Somehow the "handful" of anti-Maoists had managed to "dupe" so many that the ruling clique admitted that "perhaps we are temporarily in a minority." Even more important, the opposition had roots directly in production, in the factories and the fields. They were, in fact, the proletarian and peasant masses. They wore no red armbands, waved no books of quotations from Mao but they went out on unprecedented strikes and fought pitched battles with the Red Guard "seize control committee" that invaded their factories.

Mao, like other rulers, capitalist and Communist, is so convinced of the backwardness of the masses that he was taken by surprise. At first he said that the masses had been "duped by the economists, the revisionists." Considering that the Red Guards were his invention and that he had been so satisfied with their vicious vandalism against the "old culture" and "persons in authority taking the road back to capitalism" during the months of August and September, he had now to make a decision: whether to follow the Red Guards as they shifted from these attacks into those on "management" of production. He allowed criticism to appear on the wall posters against Chou En-lai who had asked the Red Guards to keep out of production and away from the agricultural communes. Then the *Red Flag* began to write against "phoney" Red Guards who "wave the red flag to attack the red flag." Finally, however, both the *People's Daily* and the *Red Flag* printed editorial warnings to "industry" that it was not sacrosanct.

Of all the myths created by the "Cultural Revolution", none is a greater hoax than

Mao's dependence on, and confidence in, the youth. His readiness to turn away from his old "comrades-in-arms" was not for purposes of leaving the fate of "the world revolution", Sino-centered, in the hands of the youth. As Mao himself had told Snow in 1965, "the youth could negate the revolution."[11] The Army alone had always enjoyed his confidence, became the crux of his original contributions to "Marxism," was incorporated into the Constitution. On the other hand, he at no time trusted the youth, in or out of power. This distrust rose to fever pitch in 1958 when it became clear that they were in the forefront of the opposition both to his Thought in the 100 Flowers Campaign and to his Great Leap Forward. He sent them to build the dams, not to become the "ruling cadres".

There is no country on earth where the leadership is kept in such old hands. The Politburo members average close to 70 years; even the alternate members average 63. For a brief moment in 1964 it looked as if Mao might entrust some serious responsibilities to the Communist youth organization as he spoke to it about "successor generations." However, even that brief moment in the sun was surrounded by the slogan "Learn from the Army". And, indeed, the whole of 1965, it was the Army that was to be emulated, especially as it "studies Mao's Thought." Then not only was the plan jettisoned but so was the whole youth organization, when, seemingly, the Red Guards were created.

Far from proving Mao's unshakeable confidence in the youth, the creation of the Red Guards is a manifestation of his belief that the country, including the youth, had to be "shaken up", had to be made to live by and sleep by (literally, with the "little red book" at their sides) Mao's Thought. It is true that, in the New Year editorials, it seemed as if Mao was following the Red Guards' demands to have a say in management of production. No one knows how many have been arrested or taken to prison and tortured or actually beaten ·to death; estimates run as high as 60,000 prisoners and thousands beaten to death[12] but the talk now of the "indiscipline"[13] of Red Guards does not augur well for them either. In any case, the masses, workers and peasants, did rise up against the new badgering, and the dissolution of the trade unions did nothing to stop the anger of the masses against the regime: The bitter and bloody struggles had begun. Nothing helped much. The point of no return had been reached. The deluge came. Soon the press in the West and in China itself was talking of "civil war."

In reality, what followed can best be called a "preventive civil war," deliberately provoked by Mao. But in provoking it he sealed the fate of his regime. The immediate outcome of the current struggle cannot affect that fate. In unleashing this struggle he has laid bare not only the divisions in the ruling stratum but the *class* divisions between rulers and ruled. Mao is caught by the objective conditions of a world divided between two and only two giant industrial powers. He does not have the advantage Stalin had, the use of world CPs as outposts of his foreign policy. He has no confidence in the world proletariat, and the Chinese proletariat has no confidence in him. They are finished with "Great Leaps Forward" that throw them backward. In this situation, to take the rootless elements and transform them into the tools of the ruling clique is the only answer, and it is no answer. Mao, his heirs and his "cultural revolutionaries" cannot escape the non-viability of the state capitalist system they have created, the end product of which is "Mao's Thought."

REVOLUTION OR RETROGRESSION?

Some self-styled revolutionaries are ready to forgive Mao every crime in the book and leave a few blank pages for those he might invent later, on the ground that he is the foe of U.S. imperialism which is the chief enemy of world revolution. They are ignorant of fundamental class divisions within each country, China included, and illogically link those opposites, war and revolution.

Fighting wars is Mao's specialty. He knows the problems far more intimately than he knows Marxism, and on guerrilla warfare he is a genius. But the problems he now faces at home, on his Russian borders[14], and in the struggle against "Russian revisionism" cannot be solved by guerrilla warfare. Neither at home nor abroad is he leading a fight against hated enemies – the ruling class he, himself, represents, or an imperialist occupying power. Rather, Mao's fight is directed against the Chinese masses at home and Russia abroad.

The world hadn't learned of the Sino-Soviet conflict until 1960, but, in fact, Mao's price for helping Russia crush the Hungarian Revolution and resist Poland's challenge to Russia's leadership of the Communist world was the 1957 nuclear pact. It was only when "in the spirit of Camp David" Khrushchev reneged on sharing Russia's nuclear know-how with China that Mao turned against the policies of "peaceful co-existence" he had devised at Bandung. Mao's substitute for the policies of "peaceful co-existence" was the declaration that the under-developed countries were the "storm centers of world revolution".

Throughout the period of 1960-64, while these ideological battles were splitting the Communist parties, what China was, in fact, concentrating on was the creation of its own *force de frappe*. China's first atomic explosion in 1964 came on the eve of Khrushchev's fall. The following year his answer to those who wanted to enter into common action with Russia when the United States began to rain bombs on North Vietnam was to devise "a spontaneous, new type of organization" (the Red Guards) that would teach his leadership just how Sino-centered "world revolution" is.

For some Western students of China, Mao's aim in the formation of the Red Guards was to create "an organization of a new type with built-in safeguards against bureaucracy,"[15] as if a new type of organization can be created by ukase. Those who mix erudition with apologetics tell us – in the words of one apologist – that Mao "has always been fearful of controlled bureaucratic power." It is a little difficult to believe that a man who heads a vast totalitarian state and who whipped out a para-military organization overnight is so revolted by bureaucratic power. It is no less difficult to believe the writer who sees "something profoundly anti-organizational" in the formation of Mao's Red Guards. But then, Prof. Schurmann thought that the bloody Russian purges in the 1930's were for the purpose of bringing "the sons of workers into cadre positions at all levels of the organizational system." And now he likewise sees that the "sons and daughters of the poor are coming into leadership positions in China."[16]

Contrast this to the testimony of a young refugee from Mao's China who told me that living conditions had become so bad that the African students who had come to China looked rich by comparison: "We were very interested in these new arrivals, their countries, their revolution, but we were not permitted to fraternize with them. They were ghettoized both as to living quarters and any socializing. We also wanted to ask them for things we were short of, and we were stopped from doing that. We all felt very frustrated. I felt more strongly than ever that things were reeling backwards."

In this state capitalist age, revolution and counter-revolution are so interlocked that even those who understand the relationship of thought to objective conditions speak of Mao's "revolutionary fervor" and "revolutionary voluntarism." Hegel, instead of praising Stoicism saw it as "a general form of the world's spirit only in a time of univeral fear and bondage."[17] Marx saw the need to listen to impulses from a new, objective revolutionary force, the proletariat, and to transcend the ideas of others, whether bourgeois idealists, radical putschists or anarchist voluntarists, before a truly revolutionary philosophy of liberation could be elaborated. Lenin saw the need to show that, although "the petty bourgeois in a frenzy may also wish to smash up the state," what distinguished Bolshevik violence was that "we recognize only one road, changes from below – we wanted workers themselves to draw up, from below, the new principles of economic conditions."[18] As against these discoverers of the dialectic of thought and the dialectics of liberation, men who could not conceive of the shaping of history without a "Subject," today's self-styled revolutionaries think it enough for "the supreme commander and great helmsman" to order social change for it to be realized. But is that revolution? Or liberation?

They see the enemy as "Russian revisionism." Russian Communism has, of course, not only revised Marxism but transformed it into its opposite. But that opposite is the very foundation of "Mao's Thought." In his recent, most basic[19] and most revolutionary-sounding challenge to "Russian revisionism," *A Proposal Concerning the General Line of the International Communist Movement* Mao says:

> For a very long historical period after the proletariat takes power, class struggle continues as an objective law independent of man's will .... For decades or even longer ... for an entire historical period ... there are classes and class struggles in all socialist countries without exception.

He repeats this theme over and over, concluding that it may remain true "perhaps for even a century."

But if classes and class struggles continue under "socialism", what is the point of overthrowing capitalism? Surely no more deadly deviation has ever been proclaimed as "a principle of Marxism-Leninism." This is not a theory of revolution. It is a theory of retrogression, all the more serious since it is proclaimed not in the name of fascism but of Marxism-Leninism.

Mao has always propounded "protracted struggle," raising it to the level of theory. But to the masses this is not theory, it is the weight of exploitation they have had to endure in all class societies, except that it was not called "socialism." One Communist refugee, after telling about work during the "Great Leap Forward" – "the most primitive labor imaginable, as if we were to build a whole dam by hand. We lacked even such simple devices as a block and tackle to lift heavy rocks. These had to be pushed into place by sheer brute force" – insisted that the worst was not the work but the discussion meetings that followed:

> We didn't know which was the hardest to bear – the labor, the food, or the meetings. We had to describe what we did that day, and we had to speak about our attitude to what we did. Although I had volunteered for the job – the Great Leap Forward sounded great to me at Peita (Peking University) – I now began to feel as if all our labor was forced labor. I kept my tongue, but you couldn't always keep quiet, since if you kept silent your team leader would see you afterwards and ask what was the matter. I felt like I was nothing more than an ant, not only because of the unthinking labor but because you so often said yes when you meant no .... Moreover, my own experience kept intruding into the study of "Mao's Thought" they didn't jibe either theoretically or practically. But I didn't dare say so, out loud or even to myself.

A spectre is haunting Mao, the spectre of the Hungarian Revolution. To this day he boasts that he urged Khrushchev to send the tanks into Budapest. To this day Mao's China has consistently fought the humanism of Marx:[20] "The modern revisionists and some bourgeois scholars describe Marxism as humanism and call Marx a humanist .... In particular they make use of certain views on 'alienation' expressed by Marx in his early *Economic-Philosophic Manuscripts*, 1844 .... In the early stage of development of their thought Marx and Engels were indeed somewhat influenced by humanist ideas .... But when they formulated the materialist conception of history and discovered the class struggle as the motive force of social development, they immediately got rid of this influence."

A basic document of the Cultural Revolution, "Raise High the Great Banner of Mao Tse-tung's Thought and Carry the Great Proletarian Cultural Revolution Through to the End," openly admits: "If serious steps were not taken to remold them (the intellectuals) they were bound at some future date to become groups like the Hungarian Petofi Club."[21]

The Red Guards were intended to be the agents of that "remolding." They were built outside the structure of the CCP, not so much to fight "the bureaucracy" as to force those on top and those on the bottom to face the realities of China's position in a world divided between two industrially advanced lands. In such a world, a technologically backward country like China that has no perspective of world revolution "in our time" feels compelled to drive the masses all the harder. Under private capitalism this was known as primitive accumulation; under state capitalism, calling itself Communism, it is called, internally, "fighting self-interest"[22], and, externally, "Mao Tse-tung's Thought Lights Up the Whole World."[23] The country it now lights has already sunk to the barbarity and depravity of televised public executions. The "self-interest" it now fights is not so much that of "the main person in authority taking the road back to capitalism" as the interests of the Chinese masses, including those they now call "phoney" Red Guards: "large scale struggles of masses with masses, work stoppages ... armed struggle against real Red Guards." As we enter 1968, the issue has not been decided; despite the command of the Army, that permanent restorer of class order, not all of the rival Red Guard groups in factories and communes have joined "a single organ based on systems." While Mao, on his 74th birthday, holds to his "theory of revolution", that the success of socialism "requires from one to several centuries", The masses see only retrogression down that road. As one refugee from Mao's China expressed it:

"Retrogression, that's it; that really is it. Mao is a retrogressionist. That's the word that escaped me when I said everything seemed to be reeling backwards. That word hadn't come into my consciousness because I was afraid to face its consequences. But retrogression does really sum up Mao's Thought ... Humanist tendencies are very strong among the Chinese. It can raise their spirits once more. I believe the youth stands ready to make a new revolution."

Whether or not the Peking University student is right or wrong in her analysis of the present situation, it is clear that the forces unleashed by the "Cultural Revolution" have by no means been stilled. And Mao's latest campaign against the "ultra-leftist" concept of "doubting all and overthrowing all" is proof of the fact that the "Cultural Revolution" has escaped the confines set for it.

FOOTNOTES

1. "Mao's Second Revolution", by K.S. Karol, *New Statesman,* Sept. 1966. Mr. Karol has since outdone himself by explaining that the deification of Mao's Thought is needed to preserve "the legitimacy of the Chinese Revolution and the socialist

perspective that it has opened before the country." See the Introduction to his book on China, reprinted as "Why the Cultural Revolution?" *Monthly Review,* Sept. 1967.

2. *Peking Review* #31, July 28, 1967: "More than 840 million copies of portraits of Chairman Mao, or over five times the number produced in the preceding 16 years, were printed in the eleven months from July 1966 to the end of May 1967 . . . There are 33 different portraits of the great leader of the world's people."

3. *Documents of the First Session of the First National People's Congress of the People's Republic of China.* Foreign Language Press, Peking, 1955. Repeated in *Eighth National Congress of the CCP.* Vol. 1 (Documents), Peking, 1956.

4. The best work is *The Hundred Flowers Campaign and the Chinese Intellectuals,* by Roderick Macfarquhar (New York: Praeger, 1960). See also *Communist China: the Politics of the Student Opposition* by Dennis Doolin (Stanford Univ. Press, 1964).

5. *Peking Review* #30, July 21. 1967

6. *Peking Review,* June 4, 1965. Also reprints Aidit's and Sukarno's speeches

7. For further discussion of the KPI, see my three articles, "Indonesian Communism: A Case of World Communism's Decomposition" in *News & Letters* (Detroit), October and November 1965.

8. From a "secret" letter of the CPSU to other CPs, published by *Die Welt* (Hamburg) and reprinted in the *New York Times,* March 14, 1966.

9. It is interesting to contrast what *Peking Review* (No. 35, August 25, 1967) writes now, "Peng Teh-huai and His Behind-the-Scenes Boss Cannot Shirk Responsibility for Their Crimes", with what was the official story even as late as 1965, which Edgar Snow *(The Other Side of the River,* p. 641) reports as follows: "Peng also became keenly aware of China's dependence on Soviet material and technical aid . . . P'eng neither led any 'conspiracy' against Mao, as reported abroad, nor was 'arrested.' The Chinese party leadership does not work that way. P'eng still holds his seat in the Politburo."

10. The Plenum Resolution, excerpted, was printed in *The New York Times,* August 14, 1966. Naturally it has been reproduced in full in *Peking Review.*

11. The interview granted Edgar Snow in January, 1965, was published in *The New Republic,* February 27, 1965.

12. Stuart Schram, in the revised 1967 edition of his Mao Tse-tung, who has been an analyst quite sympathetic to China, and stressed the great achievements of Mao, has made this estimate. The official broadcasts and statements speak only of "masses" never reporting actual figures of the total number arrested, beaten and humiliated much less those actually killed.

13. When Mrs. Mao Tse-tung made her first attack on the Red Guards in September 26, 1967, she told them: "It's a mistake to go running around the streets. Last year was the time to kindle the flames of revolution. To go into the streets now is precisely the wrong thing to do." By December 1967 Lin Piao reminded the Red Guards that they must remember the Red Army "cherishes" them and they must therefore obey and reveal their own "selfish" shortcomings.

14. *Look,* October 3, 1967, carries an article by A. Doak Barnett, "Tensions on the China-Soviet Border", with a map which details the disputed borders which China now says were gotten as a result of "unequal treaties."

15. *Mao Tse-tung* by Stuart Schram (Penguin, Baltimore, 1967). The most perceptive as well as scholarly analysis of the national streak in Chinese Communism, including

that of Mao Tse-tung, is not, however, in a study of Mao, but in a study of a founder of Chinese Marxism, *Li Ta-Chao and the Origins of Chinese Marxism* by Maurice Meisner (Harvard Univ. Press, Cambridge, 1967)

16. A strange admixture of apologetics and erudition characterizes Professor Franz Schurmann's major work, *Ideology and Organization in Communist China,* which he had modestly introduced with these words: "The writing of this book has been like the Chinese Revolution, a long process climaxed by an act", which, however, despite the seven years of research (1957-65) in Chinese, Japanese and Malayan languages, did not result in any analysis of the army. As the work went to press, Lin Piao made his famous speech on "People's War", where he likened the industrial countries of the world to "the city", and all the technologically underdeveloped countries to "the country" which would surround the city and win, just as Mao had done in China. Whereupon Prof. Schurmann rushes into print as if the speech, rather than the Army Lin now heads, accounts for the Army's importance; "After I had completed this book, I realized that I had omitted an important area of organization: the army." By the time he made that admission still another "area of organization arose: the Red Guards." Professor Schurmann was prepared with analysis of that too (*New York Review of Books* October 20, 1966). It seems that "thousands of young students swarmed into the streets and *formed* the red defense guards." And, after testifying to the spontaneity of this "mass movement," he has since written very nearly everywhere (See especially *Diplomat,* September 1966 and his answer to Professor Levenson's critique of his piece in the *New York Review of Books*) on the thesis that "Mao Tse-tung has always been fearful of concentrated bureaucratic power and the present purge may be said to conform to his general approach to politics."

17. G.W.F. Hegel, *Phenomenology of Mind,* p. 245. The work is finally available in paperback.

18. *Selected Works,* Vol. VII, p. 377

19. The Plenum Resolution in August 1966 reiterates this to be "the programmatic document" that must continue to be studied as it gives a "scientific Marxist-Leninist analysis of a series of important questions concerning the world revolution of our time . . . "

20. The Fourth Enlarged Session of the Committee of the Department of Philosophy and Social Science of the Chinese Academy of Sciences held on October 26, 1963, was specially devoted to that problem. See *The Fighting Tasks Confront Workers in Philosophy and the Social Sciences* (Peking, 1963).

21. This quotation from the *Peking Review* is used by Ellis Joffe in his important article "Cultural Revolution or Struggle for Power" in *China Quarterly,* July-September 1966 which has a special section on "China Mid-1966." Especially important on the cultural aspects is "The Fall of Chou Yang" by Merle Goldman who has just published an excellent work not limited to the present "Cultural Revolution."

22. New York Times, Dec. 31, 1967. On Dec. 26, 1967, Mao's 74th birthday, the official Chinese news agency announced that no less than one-half a billion copies of Mao's works have been published in 23 languages. They pointed out that before the Cultural Revolution there were only 13 plants publishing his works but now there are 180 plants, and they publish them in foreign languages as well.

23. The *Peking Review* has established a new section with this title.

THE   EXPLOSION POINT

OF IDEOLOGY

IN CHINA

The Situationist International was founded in 1957, the year following the workers councils in Hungary. It was not a body of workers nor one of the disillusioned communists, anarchists or others from the political left. The first situationists were poets, painters, architects and urbanists whose programme was based on what they called "the construction of situations". In the first place this meant the bringing together and fusion of separated art forms in the creation of a single unified environment. Nor was this process restricted to a new focusing of contemporary artistic activity. All the great artistic visions and masterpieces of the past should be pillaged and their contents made real: "subverted" as the situationists called it, as part of a real script. All scientific knowledge and technical skill could be brought into play in the same way. For the first time art and technology could become one: put on the same practical footing with reality. Working out the widest possible unified field of such "situations" would reveal the true dynamic and shape of the city. Most utopian visionaries since Fourier paled before the situationists: Everyone will live in his own cathedral. There will be rooms awakening more vivid fantasies than any drug. There will be houses where it will be impossible not to fall in love. Other houses will prove irresistibly attractive to the benighted traveller . . . . (Formulas for a New City) The situationists pointed out that "A new form of mental illness has swept the planet: banalisation. Everyone is hypnotised by work and by comfort: by the garbage disposal unit, by the lift, by the bathroom, by the washing machine. This state of affairs, born of a rebellion against the harshness of nature, has far overshot its goals — the liberation of man from material cares — and become a life-destroying obsession. Young people everywhere have been allowed to choose between love and a garbage disposal unit. Everywhere they have chosen the garbage disposal unit. A totally different spiritual attitude has become essential — it can only be brought into being by making our unconscious desires conscious, and by creating entirely new ones. And by a massive propaganda campaign to publicise these desires. (Gilles Ivain, Formula for a New City, International Situationiste NO. 1, 1958)

In the 60s, members of the International Situationist published several important books (e.g. Society of the Spectacle, by G. Debard) which were articulate and damning critiques of modern society. In 1966, an essay by a member of the International Situationist was published by a few students of the University of Strasbourg who had been elected to the student union, with university funds. The pamphlet, known as "Of Student Poverty; Considered in its economic, political, psychological, sexual and, particularly intellectual aspects, and a modest proposal for its remedy", poured shits on student life and loves (and a few other things) and was distributed at the official ceremony marking the beginning of the academic year, and on the occasion, only de Gaulle was seemingly unaffected. That was a preliminary shirmish between modern capitalism and the new revolutionary forces which it is beginning to engender. Subsequently thousands of copies of the pamphlet were reproduced, preparing the French youths ideologically for the May Revolution in 1968, in which the Situationists actively participated. The infamous pamphlet has been translated into English, Swedish, Italian, Dutch, German, Spanish and Chinese.

Christopher Gray, one time member of the International Situationist wrote of the relevance of Situationist ideas for today, "Above all, I think, its iconoclasm, its destructivity. What the S.I. did was to redefine the nature of exploitation and poverty. Ten years ago people were still demonstrating against the state of affairs in Vietnam — while remaining completely oblivious to the terrible state they were in themselves. The S.I. showed exactly how loneliness and anxiety and aimlessness have replaced the nineteenth century struggle for material survival, though they are still generated by the same class society. They focused on immediate experience, everyday life as the area people most desperately wanted to transform.

Rediscovering poverty cannot be separated from rediscovering what wealth really means. The S.I. rediscovered the vast importance of visionary politics, of the Utopian tradition — and included art, in all its positive aspects, in this tradition. People today will never break out of their stasis for the sake of a minor rearrangement. There have been too many already. Only the hope of a total change will inflame anybody. Who the hell is going to exert themselves to get another frozen chicken, another pokey room? But the possibilities of living in one's own cathedral . . . . "

"Explosion Point of Ideology in China" originally appeared in number 11 (October 1967) of the Internationale Situationiste.

The dissolution of the international association of totalitarian bureaucracies is in its final hour. To use the terms of the "Address to the revolutionaries of Algeria and of all countries", published by the situationists in Algiers in July, 1965, the irreversible "crumbling of the revolutionary image" that the bureaucratic lie opposed to the whole of capitalist society has become obvious as a pseudo-negation and as an actual support. The dissolution took place, first of all, where official capitalism had the greatest interest in supporting the imposture of its adversary: at the level of the global confrontation between the bourgeoisie with the so-called "socialist camp". In spite of all attempts to patch it up, that which already had never been socialist ceased to be a camp. The disintegration of the Stalinist monolith is from now on manifest in the co-existence of some twenty independent lines, from Rumania to Cuba, from Italy to the block of Vietnamese-Korean-Japanese parties. Russia has become incapable of even holding a common conference of European parties, preferring to forget the time when Moscow reigned over the Comintern. The Izvestia of September 1966 blamed the Chinese leaders for throwing 'unprecedented' discredit on 'Marxist-Leninist ideas'; and virtuously deplored a style of confrontation "where insults are substituted for an exchange of opinions and revolutionary experience". Those who choose this method confer absolute value on their own experience and reveal, through their interpretation of Marxist--Leninist theory, their dogmatic and sectarian mentality. Such an attitude is necessarily linked to interference in the internal affairs of brother parties..." The Sino-Russian polemic, in which each power is led to impute to its adversary every conceivable anti-proletarian crime, being only obliged not to mention the real fault (the class power of bureaucracy), includes for both sides the sobering vision that what had only been an unexplainable revolutionary mirage has fallen back to its old point of departure. The simplicity of this return to sources was perfectly exposed in February in New Delhi, when the Chinese embassy described Brezhnev and Kosygin as the "new tsars of the Kremlin", while the Indian government, anti-Chinese ally to this Muscovy, simultaneously discovered that "the present masters of China have donned themselves with the imperial cape of the Manchus". This argument against the new dynasty of the Middle Kingdom was refined even more the following month in Moscow by Voznezhsenski, the modernist state poet, who, envisioning Koutchoum and its hordes, counts on "eternal Russia" to build a rampart against the Mongols who threaten to bivouac among "the Egyptian treasures" of the Louvre. The accelerated decomposition of bureaucratic ideology, as evident in the countries where Stalinism has seized power, as in the others where it has lost every chance of seizing it, should naturally begin at the chapter on internationalism. But this is only the beginning of a general and irreversible dissolution. Internationalism could only belong to the bureaucracy as an *illusory proclamation* at the service of its real interests, as one ideological justification among others, since bureaucratic society is precisely the world of proletarian community turned upside down. The bureaucracy is essentially a power established on national State possession, and it is the logic of this reality, which it must finally obey, according to the particular interests imposed by the level of development of the country in its possession. Its heroic age passed with the happy ideological times of "socialism in one country" that Stalin had been wise to maintain by destroying the revolution in China and Spain, from 1927 to 1937. The autonomous bureaucratic revolution in China-as in Yugoslavia a short while before-introduced into the unity of the bureaucratic world a dissolutive germ which has dislocated the whole business in less than twenty years. The general process of decomposition of bureaucratic ideology presently reaches its supreme stage in the very

107

country where that ideology was most necessary, due to the general backwardness of the economy, where the subsisting revolutionary ideological pretention had to be pushed to its summit: in China.

The crisis that has deepened in China since the spring of 1966 constitutes an unprecedented phenomenon in bureaucratic society. No doubt the ruling class of bureaucratic state capitalism, habitually exercising terror as a matter of course, over its exploited majority, has often found itself in Russia or Eastern Europe torn internally by rivalries and by the need to settle accounts that stem from the objective difficulties it encounters, as well as from the subjectively delirious style a totally hidden power is forced to adopt. But the bureaucracy, which must be centralised due to its mode of appropriation of the economy, always made its purges *from the top down*, since it must draw from itself the hierarchical guarantee to every participation in the appropriation of the social surplus-production. The summit of bureaucracy has to remain stationary because the legitimacy of the system resides there. It must keep its dissensions to itself (which it always did from the time of Lenin and Trotsky); and if men must be slain or changed, this must always have the same indisputable majesty. Unexplained and mute repression can then descend to each level of the apparatus as complement to what has been instantaneously decided at the summit. Beria must first be killed, then judged (after which his faction or anyone else can be hunted down), because power that liquidates defines in liquidation the faction to be destroyed at will and by the same act redefines itself as the supreme power. That is what has not worked in China; despite the fantastic raising of the bid in the struggle for the totality of power, the permanence of the proclaimed foes *shows clearly that the ruling class has split in two.*

A social crisis of such amplitude obviously cannot be explained in the anecdotal style of bourgeois observers. (who see the cause as being dissensions over foreign strategy). It is already notorious that the Chinese bureaucracy quietly bears the insult of the crushing of Vietnam on its own door-step. Neither could personal quarrels over succession to power put so much at stake. When certain leaders are reproached with having "kept Mao Tse-Tung from power" since the 1950's, everything leads one to believe that this is a case of one of those retrospective crimes commonly fabricated by bureaucratic purges- Trotsky conducting the Civil War on orders from the Mikado, Zinoviev being Lenin's second to please the British Empire, etc. The man who could have taken power from a man so powerful as Mao would not have slept as long as Mao was around to come back. Mao therefore would have died that day, and nothing could have presented his faithful successors from attributing his death to-say Khrushchev. If the rulers and polemicists of the bureaucratic states have a better understanding of the Chinese crisis, their statements cannot for that matter be more correct because in talking about China, they must dread revealing too much about themselves.

In the end the greatest mistake of all is made, by the leftist debris of Western countries, who are always the willing dupes of mouldy sub-leninist propoganda. They evaluate very seriously the role in Chinese society of the continuation of allowances to the capitalists who rallied the cause, or otherwise are researching the skirmish to find out which leader would represent ultra-leftism or workers' autonomy. The most stupid among them thought there was something "cultural" about this business, up until January, when the Maoist press pulled the bad trick on them in admitting that it had been "from the start, a struggle for power". The only serious debate would be to examine why and how the ruling class could have fractioned into two hostile camps; and any research into this is of course denied to those who do not admit that the bureaucracy is a ruling class, or who ignore the specificity of this class, and reduce it to the classical conditions of bourgeois power.

Concerning the *why* of the rupture within the bureaucracy, it can only be said with certainty that it is the kind of question that puts the very domination of the ruling class at stake, *since, in order to forcibly resolve this question, neither side hesitated to risk immediately the common basis of their class-power*, by endangering all the existing conditions of their administration of society.

The ruling class must then have known it could no longer rule as before. There is no doubt that this was a conflict over the management of the *Economy*, it's certain that the collapse of the successive economic policies of the bureaucracy was the cause of the acuity of the conflict. The failure of the policy of the so-called "Great Leap Forward"-principally due to the resistance of the peasants- not only closed the perspective for an ultravoluntarist take-off of industrial production, but even led to a disastrous disorganization that made itself felt for several years. Even the increase in agricultural production since 1958 seems very scant, as the population growth remains superior to the growth of food. It is less easy to say over what precise economic option the ruling class split. Probably one side, consisting of the majority of the party apparatus, trade union cadres, and economists wanted to continue or increase more or less considerably the production of consumer goods, and to sustain the effort of the workers with economic incentives. This policy, while making at the same time certain concessions to the peasants and above all to the workers, implied an increase of consumption, be it hierarchically differentiated for a good part of the lower-bureaucracy. The other side, consisting of Mao and a large part of the high-ranking officers of the army, wanted no doubt to resume at any price the effort to industrialize the country, an even more extreme use of *ideological energy* and terror, a limitless over-exploitation of the workers, and perhaps an "egalitarian" sacrifice in consumption, for a considerable part of the lower bureaucracy. Both positions are equally oriented toward maintaining the absolute domination of bureaucracy, calculated in function of the need to erect barriers to the class struggles that menace this domination. At any rate, the urgency and the vital character of this choice was so evident to everyone that both camps preferred to run the risk of immediately aggravating the whole of the conditions, in which they found themselves, with the disorder of their very schism. It is very possible that the obstinacy on both sides is justified by the fact that there is no right solution to the insurmountable problems of the Chinese bureaucracy, that therefore the two options facing one another were equally inapplicable; and yet a choice had to be made.

In order to know *how* a division at the top of the bureaucracy could descend from point to point to lower levels, recreating at every stage rivalries remote-controlled in reverse order throughout the party and state, and finally in the masses, one should bear in mind the surviving remnants of the ancient model of administering China with provinces that enjoyed semi-autonomy. The denunciation by Pekinese Maoists in January 1967 of "independent fiefs" clearly evokes this, and the development of the troubles in the past few months clearly confirms it. It is quite possible that the phenomenon of regional autonomy of bureaucratic power, which only manifested itself weakly and sporadically around the organization of Leningrad during the Russian counter-revolution, found in bureaucratic China firm and multiple bases, emerging out of the possibility of a co-existence with the central government of clans and clienteles that held whole regions of bureaucratic power as direct property, and on this basis made compromises among themselves. Bureaucratic power in China was not born from a workers' movement, but from the military regimentation of peasants during a twenty-two year war. The army has remained tightly knit to the party (every ruler has also been a military chief) and remained the principle school where the party selects its cadres from the peasant masses it trains. It seems, furthermore that the local administration installed in 1949 was greatly dependent on the zones through which the various army corps moved, descending from the north towards the south, leaving in their wake each time, men who were linked to them by geographical origin (or family ties- a factor in the consolidation of bureaucratic cliques, which was revealed in full view by the propaganda directed against Liu-Shao-Chi and others). Such local bases of semi-autonomous power in the bureaucratic administration could thus have been formed in China by a combination of the organizational structures of the conquering army, and the productive forces it found to control in the conquered regions.

When the Mao faction began its public offensive against the solid positions of its adversaries, by putting students and children of regimented schools on the march, it had in no way the immediate purpose of a "cultural" or "civilizing" remolding of the working masses, already pressed as much as possible into the ideological straight-jacket of the regime. The nonsense against Beethoven or Ming art, in the same way as the invectives against the positions still occupied or already reconquered by a Chinese bourgeoisie, that was ostensibly annihilated as such, were played out only for the amusement of the peanut-gallery-not without calculating that this primitive ultra-leftism could find a certain echo among the oppressed, who have, after all, reasons to believe that there are still obstacles in their country, to the emergence of a classless society.

The principle aim of the operation was to have appeared in the street, at the service of this tendency, the *ideology of the regime* which is, by definition, Maoist. The adversaries who could really only be Maoist found themselves already in a bad light by the start of the quarrel which was why their insufficient 'self-critique' expressed in fact their resolution to keep the positions they controlled. The first phase of the struggle can then be qualified as a confrontation of the official *owners of the ideology* against the majority of the *owners of the machinery of the economy and the State.* However, the bureaucracy, in order to maintain its collective appropriation of society, needs as much the ideology as the administrative and repressive machinery, so that the adventure into such a separation was extremely dangerous if it did not come quickly to an end. It is known that the majority of the apparatus, and Liu Shao-chi, himself, despite his poor position in Peking, resisted obstinately. After their first attempt to block Maoist agitation at the university level, where "working groups" had taken a stand, the agitation swept into the streets of all large cities, and began to attack everywhere-by means of wall-newspapers and direct action, the officials whom they had been told were responsible. This didn't exclude errors and excesses of zealousness.

These officials organized resistance wherever they could. It is likely that the first blows between workers and 'Red Guards' were led by party 'activists' in the factories at the disposition of local officials of the apparatus. Soon the workers, exasperated by the excesses of the Red Guard, began to intervene on their own. In every case where the Maoists talked of 'extending the cultural revolution' to the factories, then to the countryside, they gave themselves the air of having *decided* upon a decline which, in fact during the whole of autumn 1966, had escaped them and had already in fact come about despite their plans. The decline of industrial production, the disorganization of transportation, irrigation, of state administration up to the ministerial level (despite the efforts of Chou En-Lai); the menace which weighed on the autumn and spring harvest; the total halt of education-particularly serious in an underdeveloped country-for more than a year, all of this was only the inevitable result of a struggle whose extension is solely due to the resistance from that part of the bureaucracy in power, which the Maoists found they had to kick out.

The Maoists, whose political experience is hardly linked to struggle in an urban environment, will have had a good occasion to verify the Machiavellian precept: "Be careful not to incite sedition in a city while flattering yourself to be able to stop or direct it at will." (Florentine Chronicles). After a few months of pseudo-cultural pseudo-revolution, it was the real class struggle that appeared in China, the workers and the peasants beginning to act for themselves. The world couldn't ignore what the Maoist perspective meant for them; the peasants, who saw a menace to their individual plots of land had in several provinces begun to divide among themselves the land and tools of the 'popular communes' (these being only the ideologically-dressed pre-existing administrative units generally duplicating the old cantons). The railroad strike, the general strike of Shanghai (officially viewed, like in Budapest, as the favored weapon of the capitalists); the strikes in the big industrial agglomeration of Wuhan, Canton, Hupeh, the steel and textile workers in Chungking, the attacks by the Szechwan and Fukien peasants, ended around January and brought China to the brink of chaos. At the same time, following the lead of workers who had organized themselves as the 'Purple Guard' in Kwangsi to fight the Red Guard in September, 1966, and after the anti-Maoist riots in Nanking, 'armies' sprang up in various provinces such as the 'Army of August lst' in Kwantung. The national army had to intervene everywhere in February-March to subdue the workers, to direct production through the 'military control' of factories, and helped by the militia, to even control work in the countryside. The workers' struggle to maintain or raise their salaries, the famous tendency to 'economism', (economic incentives similar to the Liebermann doctrine and cursed by the masters of Peking), could be accepted even encouraged, by certain local cadres of the apparatus in their resistance to the rival centralist Maoist bureaucrats. But it is certain that this struggle was led by an irresistible tide from the working base: the authoritarian dissolution in March of 'professional associations' which had formed after the first dissolution of the regime's trade unions whose bureaucracy was escaping the Maoist line, shows it very well. Thus *Jiefang Ribao* condemned in Shanghai around March 1967: "the feudal tendencies of those associations formed not on a class basis (incidentally the quality that defines this class-basis is the pure monopoly of Maoist power), but on a basis of trades whose objectives are the partial and immediate interests of the workers within those trades". This defense of the true owners of the permanent, general interests of the collectivity was equally expressed on February ll, in a joint directive from the Council of State and the Military Commission of the Central Committee: 'All elements who have seized or stolen arms must be arrested'.

When the solution to this conflict- which obviously cost tens of thousands of lives in the struggle between large fully equipped units, even involving warships – was handed over to the Chinese army, we find that the army itself was divided. It had to assure the pursuit and intensification of production at a time when it was no longer capable of assuring the unity of power in China—besides, its direct intervention against the peasantry, given that the army was recruited largely from the peasants, presented the gravest risks. The truce sought during March-April by the Maoists, declaring that all party personnel were redeemable with the exception of a "handful" of traitors, and that the principle menace was 'anarchism', revealed more than just a worry over the difficulty of putting a stop to the outburst of youth, brought about as a result of the experience of the Red Guard- *it revealed the essential anxiety of the ruling class that had come to the brink of its own dissolution.* The party, the central and provincial administration, was decomposing. The question was to re-establish labor discipline 'The idea of exclusion and overthrow of all cadres must be unconditionally condemned' said *The Red Flag*, in March. And already in February, *New China* declared: 'You crush everyone with responsibilities... but after you have taken over an administration, what do you have on your hands besides an empty room and official stamps?' Rehabilitations and compromises follow one another at random. The very survival of the bureaucracy is the supreme cause, which has to move its different political options to the back-ground as simple means.

Beginning with the spring of 1967 it was possible to say that the 'Cultural Revolution' movement had come to a disastrous failure, and which was certainly the biggest ever in the long series of failures of bureaucratic power in China. In spite of the extraordinary cost of the operation, none of its goals were reached. The bureaucracy was more divided than ever and every new power installed in the regions held by the Maoists was divided in turn: the 'Triple Revolutionary Alliance'- of army, red guard, and party-didn't stop decomposing, as much due to the antagonisms among these three forces (the party, above all, kept out of the way, only getting involved in order to sabotage), as to the continually aggravated antagonisms within each one. It seemed to be as hard to put the machinery back together as it would have been to build a new one. To say, the least, two-thirds of China was in no way controlled by the power of Peking.

Next to the governmental committees of the partisans of Liu-Shao-chi, and the movements of workers-struggles which continued to affirm themselves, the War Lords reappeared under the uniforms of the independent "communist" generals, treating directly with the central power, and conducting their own politics, particularly in the peripheral regions. General Chang Kuo-hua, master of Tibet in February, after street fighting in Lhasa, used armour against the Maoists. Three Maoists divisions were sent to 'crush the revisionists'. But they only met with moderate success; Chang Kuo-hua was still in control of the region in April. On May 1st he was received in Peking with negotiations ending in compromise: Peking's mandate was that he form a revolutionary committee to govern Szechwan, where in April a 'revolutionary alliance' influenced by a certain General Hung, had already taken power and jailed the Maoists. Since then, in June, members of a people's commune had seized arms and attacked the military. In Inner Mongolia, the army took a stand against Mao in February, under the leadership of Liu Chiang, deputy political commissar. The same thing happened in Hopeh, Honan, and Manchuria. In Kansu, General Chao Yung-shih succeeded in an anti-Maoist putsch in May. Sinking, where the atomic installations are located, was neutralized by common consent in March, under the authority of General Wang En-mao; yet he was reputed to have attacked 'Maoist revolutionaries' in June. Hupeh, in July, was in the hands of General Chan Tsai-tao, commander of the Wuhan district- one of the oldest industrial centers of China. In the old style of the 'Sian incident', he had two of the principle leaders of Peking, who had come to negotiate, arrested. The Prime Minister had to make the trip, and the restitution of his emissaries was announced as a 'victory'. At the same time 2400 factories and mines were paralyzed in the province, as a result of the armed uprising of 50,000 workers and peasants. As a matter of fact, at the beginning of the summer it turned out that the conflict was continuing everywhere. In June 'conservative workers' of Honan attacked a textile mill with incendiary bombs. In July, the coal miners of Fushun and the oil workers of Tahsing were on strike, the miners of Kiangsi were hunting down the Maoists and there were calls for struggle against the 'industrial army of Chekiang', described as a 'terrorist anti-marxist organization'. The peasants threatened to march on Nanking and Shanghai. There was fighting in the streets of Canton and Chungking. The students of Kweiyang attacked the army and seized the Maoist leaders. And the government, which decided to forbid violence "in the regions controlled by the central authorities," seemed to have a hard time of it even there. Incapable of stopping the trouble, information was cut off through the expulsion of most of the already rare foreigners in residence.

But it was at the beginning of August, the breaks in the army having become so dangerous, that the official Peking publications themselves revealed that the partisans of Liu wanted to 'set up an independent reactionary bourgeois kingdom in the midst of the army', and the *People's Daily* of August 5th said that 'the attacks against the dictatorship of the proletariat in China have not only come from the higher echelons, but also from the lower'. Peking came around to admit clearly that at least one third of the army had taken a stand against the central government, and that even a large part of the old China of 18 provinces, had escaped its grasp. The immediate consequences of the Wuhan incident seemed to have been very serious; an intervention by Peking paratroopers assisted by six gunboats going up the Yangste from Shanghai was repulsed after a pitched battle; and it seems that arms from the Wuhan arsenal may have been sent to the Chunking anti-Maoists. Furthermore, it should be noted that the Wuhan troops belonged to the army group under the direct authority of Lin Piao, the only one considered loyal. About the middle of August, armed struggles became generalized to such a degree that the Maoist government officially condemned this continuation of politics which had turned against itself, and affirmed that it would win if the struggle were kept to a 'struggle with pen and ink'. It announced the distribution of arms to the masses in 'loyal zones'. But where were such zones? There was fighting again in Shanghai, presented over the preceding months as citadel of Maoism. Soldiers in Shantung incited the peasants to revolt. The leadership of the air force was accused of being an enemy of the regime. And, as in the days of Sun Yat-sen while the 41st army moved to re-establish order, Canton broke into open revolt; the railroad and urban transit workers in the forefront: political prisioners were set free, arms destined for Vietnam were seized from cargos in port, and an undetermined number of people were hanged in the streets. Thus, China sank slowly into a confused civil war, which at the same time was the confrontation between various regions of the bureaucratic state power-by then in shreds-and the confrontation of workers' and peasants' demands against the conditions of exploitation which the torn bureaucratic leadership had to maintain everywhere.

Since the Maoists have shown themselves to be--and we have seen how successfully--the champions of absolute ideology, they have met up to now with the most fantastique degree of respect and approbation among the Western intellectuals, who never fail to salivate to such stimuli. K.S. Karol reminds the Maoists that they forget the fact that "the real Stalinists are not potential allies of China, but its most irreducible enemies: for them, the cultural revolution, with its anti-bureaucratic tendencies, evokes Trotskyism..." Moreover. a lot of Troskyites recognized themselves there--doing themselves perfect justice! *Le Monde*, the most Maoist newspaper appearing outside of China, announced day after day the imminent success of Mr. Mao Tse-tung, finally taking the power it was generally believed to have been his for the past eighteen years. The sinologists, almost all Stalino-Christian--the mixture is everywhere, but heavily present in that newspaper--dragged out the Chinese soul again to bear witness to the legitimacy of the new Confucius. The element of burlesque that has always existed in the attitude of leftist bourgeois intellectuals who are moderately Stalinophile, found the best occasion to blossom before the great Chinese achievements, such as: this "Cultural Revolution" might perhaps last one thousand or ten thousand years; the *Little Red Book* has finally succeeded in "making Marxism Chinese"; "the sound of men reciting passages with a strong and clear voice can be heard in every army unit"; "Drought has nothing frightening, the thought of Mao Tse-tung is our fecundating rain"; "the Chief of State was judged responsible...for not having foreseen the about-face of General Chiang Kai-shek when he led his army against the Communist troops" (*Le Monde*, 4/4/67; this refers to the 1927 coup, which had been foreseen by everybody in China, but which had to be waited for passively in order to obey Stalin's orders); a chorale comes to sing the hymn entitled *A Hundred Million People Take up Arms to Criticize the Sinister Book. "The Perfection of Oneself"* (formerly, the official small work by Liu Shao-chi). The list has no end; we can conclude our listing with this statement from the *People's Daily* of July 31st: "The situation of the Proletarian Cultural Revolution in China is excellent, but the class struggle is becoming more difficult."

After so much noise, the historical conclusions to draw from this period are simple. No matter where China may go now, the image of the last bureaucratic--revolutionary power has shattered. The internal collapse is added to the incessant failures of its foreign policy: the annihilation of Indonesian Stalinism, the rupture with Japanese Stalinism, the destruction of Vietnam by the United States, and, finally, the proclamation by Peking in July that the Naxalhari "insurrection", a few days before it was dispersed by the first police operation, was the beginning of the Maoist-peasant revolution in India. By maintaining this extravagance, Peking broke with the majority of its Indian partisans, that is to say, with the last large bureaucratic party that had remained on its side. What is marked now in the internal crisis in China is its failure to industrialize the country, and to offer itself as a model to the underdeveloped countries.

Ideology, carried to its absolute extreme, shatters. Its absolute use is also its absolute zero. It is the night in which all the ideological cows are black. At a time when, in the most total confusion, the bureaucrats fight one another in the name of the same dogma, and denounce everywhere "the bourgeois hiding behind the red flag", the double-think has itself split in two. It is the joyous end of ideological lies, dying in ridicule. We said, in the issue of *Internationale situationniste* which appeared in August, 1961, that our world would become "at all levels, more and more painfully ridiculous, up to the moment of its complete revolutionary reconstruction". We can see where we are. The new period of the proletarian critique can no longer spare anything that does not belong to it; every existing ideological comfort must be torn away from it in shame and horror. By discovering that it is dispossessed of the false goods of its world of falsehood, it must understand that it is the necessary negation of the whole of world-wide society. And it will know this also in China. It is the global dislocation of the *Bureaucratic International* which is being reproduced now at the Chinese level, in the fragmentation of power in independant provinces. Thus, China finds its past again, which represents the real revolutionary tasks of the movement that was defeated before. The moment where, it seems, "Mao is starting again in 1967 what he was doing in 1927" (*Le Monde* 2/17/67) is also the moment where, for the first time since 1927, the intervention of the masses of workers and peasants has spread over the country. No matter how difficult it will be to become conscious, and to put into practice their autonomous objectives, something is dead in the total domination to which the Chinese workers were subject. The "Mandate from Proletarian Heaven" is exhausted.

intervention of the masses of workers and peasants has spread over the country. No matter how difficult it will be to become conscious, and to put into practice their autonomous objectives, something is dead in the total domination to which the Chinese workers were subject. The "Mandate from Proletarian Heaven" is exhausted.

THESES ON THE CHINESE REVOLUTION

CAJO BRENDEL

> *The Theses on the Chinese Revolution were written during the spring and summer of 1967, when China was in the throes of the "Cultural Revolution". The Theses on the Chinese Revolution were first published in Dutch in the monthly Daad en Gedachte (Act and Thought). In the spring of 1969 they were published in France in Cahiers du Communisme de Conseils. In 1971 the first English edition appeared as an Aberdeen Solidarity pamphlet. In 1973 an Italian edition was published in Caserta. The Theses appearing in this book are exactly the same as the second English edition (which is the same as the first) published by Solidarity.*

> *Solidarity is a libertarian communist group in the United Kingdom. Its organisation consists of a number of autonomous groups based in various industrial cities in the United Kingdom. A glimpse of the political outlook of Solidarity may be obtained by scrutinising the following document entitled "As We See It":*

> *1. Throughout the world, the vast majority of people have no control whatsoever over the decisions that most deeply and directly affect their lives. They sell their labour power while others who own or control the means of production accumulate wealth, make the laws and use the whole machinery of the State to perpetuate and reinforce their privileged positions.*

> *2. During the past century the living standards of working people have improved. But neither these improved living standards, nor the nationalisation of the means of prodcution, nor the coming to power of parties claiming to represent the working class have basically altered the status of the worker as worker. Nor have they given the bulk of mankind much freedom outside of production. East and West, capitalism remains an inhuman type of society*

117

where the vast majority are bossed at work, and manipulated in consumption and leisure. Propaganda and policemen, prisons and schools, traditional values and traditional morality all serve to reinforce the power of the few and to convince or coerce the many into acceptance of a brutal, degrading and irrational system. The 'Communist' world is not communist and the 'Free' world is not free.

3. The trade unions and the traditional parties of the left started in business to change all this. But they have come to terms with the existing patterns of exploitation. In fact they are now essential if exploiting society is to continue working smoothly. The unions act as middlemen in the labour market. The political parties use the struggles and aspirations of the working class for their own ends. The degeneration of working class organisations, itself the result of the failure of the revolutionary movement, has been a major factor in creating working class apathy, which in turn has led to the further degeneration of both parties and unions.

4. The trade unions and political parties cannot be reformed, 'captured', or converted into instruments of working class emancipation. We don't call however for the proclamation of new unions, which in the conditions of today would suffer a similar fate to the old ones. Nor do we call for militants to tear up their union cards. Our aims are simply that the workers themselves should decide on the objectives of their struggles and that the control and organisation of these struggles should remain firmly in their own hands. The forms which this self-activity of the working class may take will vary considerably from country to country and from industry to industry. Its basic content will not.

5. Socialism is not just the common ownership and control of the means of production and distribution. It means equality, real freedom, reciprocal recognition and a radical transformation in all human relations. It is 'man's positive self-consciousness'. It is man's understanding of his environment and of himself, his domination over his work and over such social institutions as he may need to create. These are not secondary aspects, which will automatically follow the expropriation of the old ruling class. On the contrary they are essential parts of the whole process of social transformation, for without them no genuine social transformation will have taken place.

6. A socialist society can therefore only be built from below. Decisions concerning production and work will be taken by workers' councils composed of elected and revocable delegates. Decisions in other areas will be taken on the basis of the widest possible discussion and consultation among the people as a whole. The democratisation of society down to its very roots is what we mean by 'workers' power'.

7. Meaningful action, for revolutionaries, is whatever increases the confidence, the autonomy, the initiative, the participation, the solidarity, the equalitarian tendencies and the self-activity of the masses and whatever assists their demystification. Sterile and harmful action is whatever reinforces the passivity of the masses, their apathy, their cynicism, their differentiation through hierarchy, their alienation, their reliance on others to do things for them and the degree to which they can therefore be manipulated by others — even by those allegedly acting on their behalf.

8. No ruling class in history has ever relinquished its power without a struggle and our present rulers are unlikely to be an exception. Power will only be taken from them through the conscious, autonomous action of the vast majority of the people themselves. The building of socialism will require mass understanding and mass participation. By their rigid hierarchical structure, by their ideas and by their activities, both social-democratic and bolshevik types of organisations discourage this kind of understanding and prevent this kind of participation. The idea that socialism can somehow be achieved by an elite party (however 'revolutionary') acting 'on behalf of the working class is both absurd and reactionary.

9. We do not accept the view that by itself the working class can only achieve a trade union consciousness. On the contrary we believe that its conditions of life and its experiences in production constantly drive the working class to adopt priorities and values and to find methods of organisation which challenge the established social order and established pattern of thought. These responses are implicitly socialist. On the other hand, the working class is fragmented, dispossessed of the means of communication, and its various sections are at different levels of awareness and consciousness. The task of the revolutionary organisation is to help give proletarian consciousness an explicitly socialist content, to give practical assistance to workers in struggle and to help those in different areas to exchange experiences and link up with one another.

10. We do not see ourselves as yet another leadership, but merely as an instrument of working class action. The function of **Solidarity** *is to help all those who are in conflict with the present authoritarian social structure, both in industry and in society at large, to generalise their experience, to make a total critique of their condition and of its causes, and to develop the mass revolutionary consciousness necessary if society is to be totally transformed.*

Cajo Brendel, author of the theses, is a member of the Dutch libertarian communist group, Act and Thought.

1.   When the armies of Mao Tse Tung and of General Chu Teh crossed the Yangtse river in April 1949, the seal of defeat was almost set on the forces of Chiang Kai Shek. His power had collapsed and before the autumn the Kuo Min Tang was to be driven from the mainland. The world started talking of a 'victory for communism' in China.

The Kung Tsiang Tang (the KTT or the Chinese Communist Party) was however to characterise its military victory over the Kuo Min Tang as the 'victory of the national bourgeois democratic revolution' which had begun 38 years earlier. What the KTT proposed – and what Mao Tse Tung considered his first task -- was the 'stimulation of the revolutionary process'. The bourgeois revolution, according to their beliefs, would be followed by the proletarian socialist revolution. At a later stage the 'transition to communism' would be on the agenda. There is a striking resemblance between the ideas of Mao and the KTT on the development of the Chinese revolution, and those of Lenin and the Bolsheviks on the development of the Russian revolution.

2.   This similarity is not coincidental. In both countries the revolutions resulted from similar factors and conditions. Both countries were backward at the beginning of this century. Their relations of production and their patterns of exploitation were semi-feudal (or related to feudalism) and were predominantly based on agriculture. Their populations were largely peasant. Religious beliefs permeated both societies, reflecting the social conditions: in China Confucianism, and in Russia Greek Orthodoxy. The social reality in each country formed the basis of similarly oppressive regimes: the Tsars in Russia and the Manchu Emperors in China.

3.   In both Russia and China the revolutions had to solve the same political and economic tasks. They had to destroy feudalism and to free the productive forces in agriculture from the fetters in which existing relations bound them. They also had to prepare a basis for industrial development. They had to destroy absolutism and replace it by a form of government and by a state machine that would allow solutions to the existing economic problems. The economic and political problems were those of a bourgeois revolution; that is, of a revolution that was to make capitalism the dominant mode of production.

4.   The Development Plan issued by the KTT in the autumn of 1949 confirmed all this. It challenged Chinese social traditions, based on family ties and on local and regional government. It advocated agrarian reform through the introduction of more modern methods of production and by the extension of the area under cultivation. The KTT wanted to harness China's immense resources of human labour power and by extending and improving the educational system, to prepare the population for the role assigned to them in a society undergoing industrialisation. China's new rulers wanted a modern road network to bring the areas producing materials into closer contact with the urban industrial centres. According to the KTT the primary task was the creation of modern industry. Mao's programme for the period to follow the 'taking of power' was essentially the programme of triumphant capitalism.

5.   The economic and political problems of the bourgeois revolution were, generally speaking, ready to be tackled in France in 1789. There were, however, enormous differences between the bourgeois revolutions in China and Russia, on the one hand, and that in France on the other. And it is precisely in those areas where the Russian and Chinese revolutions of this century differ from the French revolution that they resemble one another. In France, the bourgeois revolution of 1789 took a classical form – the form of a struggle of the bourgeoisie against the ruling classes of a pre-bourgeois period. But

neither in China nor in Russia was there a bourgeoisie capable of understanding or conducting such a struggle. The characteristic feature of the revolutions in both countries is that they were bourgeois revolutions in which classes other than the bourgeoisie occupied the role played, in the eighteenth century, by the bourgeoisie in France.

These fairly unusual class relationships were to form the basis of Bolshevism in both Russia and China. Bolshevism did not occur in China because Mao Tse Tung and his co-thinkers were Bolsheviks but because conditions in China were similar to those in Russia which originally created Bolshevism. In neither Russia nor China could capitalism triumph except in its Bolshevik form.

6. In both China and Russia feudalism (or its equivalent) had persisted until fairly recent times as a result of the stagnation of agrarian development. In both countries capitalism arose out of what might be called external needs. With it an embryonic bourgeoisie and an embryonic proletariat developed. In Russia capitalism arose as a result of the economic needs of Tsarist militarism. Industrialisation began in Petrograd, in Moscow, in the coal-bearing Donetz basin and around the oilfields of Baku. In China the same process occurred in the major ports of Shanghai, Canton and Nanking. In China, however, the proletariat formed an even smaller percentage of the population than in Russia. Despite the many similarities, this fact was to result in great differences between the revolutions in the two countries.

7. The 'bourgeoisie' which, in China and Russia, developed alongside the process of industrialisation, in no way resembled the 'Third Estate' which, at the onset of the French bourgeois revolution, had proudly proclaimed its right to power. The bourgeoisie in China and Russia arose as a class without any firm economic base of its own. It was supported by foreign capitalism and developed in the shadow of an absolutism which had itself made concessions to foreign capitalism.

8. In Russia, although the working class was small, the conditions of Tsarism ensured that it was very militant. Such militancy, combined with its concentration in certain areas, allowed the Russian proletariat significantly to influence events. It played an important role in both 1905 and 1917 just as the peasants did as a result of their sheer numerical force. Russia also had an intelligentsia for whom history had reserved a special role. From the ranks of the intellectuals came the cadres of professional revolutionaries of the Bolshevik Party. Lenin once said of such professional revolutionaries (and it was far truer than he realised) that they were 'Jacobins bound to the masses', i.e. revolutionaries of a distinctly bourgeois type, advocating a typically bourgeois method (or form) of organisation.

These Jacobin Bolsheviks left their imprint on the Russian revolution just as — conversely — they were themselves to be influenced by the Russian events. They used the word 'smytschka' to describe the needs of the revolution. The 'smytschka' was class alliance between workers and peasants, classes with completely different interests but who, each by itself, could not achieve their own aims in any permanent way. In practice (and as a historical result), this came to mean that the Party occupied a position of authority above the two classes. This situation continued until, as a result of social development, a new class appeared, a class engendered by the post-revolutionary mode of production.

9. In China history repeated itself but in a somewhat different form. Although the Chinese revolution in general resembled the Russian, it differed from it utterly in some respects. There was, firstly, an enormous difference in tempo. Although the Chinese

revolution began in 1911, in the beginning (apart from some important events in 1913, 1915 and 1916) it only marked time. At its onset, in contrast to what happened in Russia in 1917, the mass of the population did not enter the scene. The fall – or rather the abdication – of the Manchus was a belated echo of mass movements of bygone years such as the Tai Ping revolt and the Boxer Rebellion. The abdication was not the sequel to an uprising. The 'Imperial Son of Heaven' offered China the republic on a tray. Imperial authority was not destroyed as French royalty or Russian Tsarism had been but was bequeathed by imperial decree to Yuan Shih Kai. Yuan has been nicknamed the 'Chinese Napoleon' for his unsuccessful attempt at replacing the Empire by a military dictatorship. But this is an inaccurate designation. Napoleon was the executor of the will of the bourgeois revolution whereas Yuan Shih Kai was only the executor of the will of a bankrupt imperial household. As such, Yuan Shih Kai proved an obstacle to the development of the revolution.

Yuan cannot be compared to Bonaparte but is perhaps more like Kornilov, the Russian general who at the end of the summer of 1917 prepared a counter-revolutionary coup. When faced with this danger the Bolsheviks called for resistance and the Petrograd workers intervened on the side of the revolution. Nothing similar could have occured in China where the working class, small as it was, was too weak even to contemplate such action. The progress of the Chinese bourgeois revolution was therefore slowed down.

10. In China historical necessity had thrown up no Jacobins to oppose Yuan Shih Kai; what did exist was a petty bourgeois intelligentsia – radical and republican. Their radicalism was, however, relative in the extreme and only discernible in relation to the reactionary Chinese bourgeoisie who flirted with both Yuan Shih Kai and the empire. This petty bourgeoisie was represented by Sun Yat Sen, who followed in the footsteps of Confucius in advocating class reconciliation. Sun Yat Sen sought a compromise between ancient China and a modern (i.e. bourgeois) republic.

Such illusions certainly could not stimulate revolutionary attitudes. They explain why Sun Yat Sen capitulated without resistance to Yuan Shih Kai when for a short time after 1911 he found himself in the foreground of events. Yuan Shih Kai's lack of success was due primarily to the forces of separatism and decentralisation which had rendered impossible the continued existence of the Manchu monarchy and had seriously impeded the maintenance of the former power structures even under a modified form.

11. China in 1911 did not become a national bourgeois state as France, Germany or Italy had become after their respective bourgeois revolutions. Consequently China fell prey to a handful of generals such as Sun Chuan Fang and Feng Yu Hsiang who fought each other for over a decade, whereas in Russia generals such as Denikin, Kolchak and Wrangel only entered the scene after the revolution of 1917. In Russia the generals fought the peasants, the workers and the Bolsheviks; in China the generals fought to prevent events like those that had taken place in Russia in 1917 before there was any chance of their occurrence. They attempted not to erase events but to preclude them by extending their power over the greater part of China. But all of them failed. It was not until the late twenties that Chiang Kai Shek succeeded; at a time when the revolution had entered a new phase.

Chiang Kai Shek was unlike the other generals; he was not a feudal war-lord nor did he represent the well-to-do peasants. He was the general of the Chinese 'Girondins', the general of the Kuo Min Tang. His party had been forced into revolutionary activity for a short period by the pressure of the masses, now beginning to play an active part in events.

After marking time for a quarter of a century, the Chinese revolution had reached the stage which the Russian revolution had reached in February 1917, despite the still very different social conditions in the two countries.

12. The Kuo Min Tang (the National Party of China) is the oldest party to have played a role in the Chinese revolution. It was the heir of the Tung Min Wuo ('United Front of Revolutionaries') which itself continued the traditions of the 'China Awakes' secret society. This was formed outside China by Sun Yat Sen in 1894 with the support of emigre petty traders. The petty bourgeois base of this group remained tradesmen and intellectuals but it also comprised many soldiers and officials with careerist notions. It also gained support from the ranks of the Chinese bourgeoisie, still in its infancy.

13. The outlook of the KMT was as vague as its heterogeneous composition might lead one to expect. It failed to realise that, as in all bourgeois revolutions, the development of China's economy depended on an agrarian reform and on the freeing of the peasantry from feudal forms of ownership. The confusion was inevitable for this freeing of the peasantry was inseparably connected with the breakdown of traditional Chinese family relationships. These relationships were an integral part of the future China envisaged by Sun Yat Sen and the KMT.

The KMT were republican nationalists and the logical consequence of nationalism was a struggle against imperialism. But this was impossible for a party whose bourgeois supporters were so strongly linked to that very imperialism. So confused were Sun Yat Sen's ideas that he seriously believed that China could be unified and strong under a central power supported by foreign capital. He failed to realise that such foreign capital benefited most from China's weakness. The main feature of the ideas of Sun Yat Sen and the KMT was, however, their notion of a general reconciliation between classes. This unrealistic ideal incontestably corresponded to the fact that the KMT was the political expression of basically antagonistic interests.

14. It was only in the early twenties, when the Chinese people took action to defend themselves against an oppressive imperialism, that the KMT moved to the left. The party was reorganised and Sun Yat Sen drew up a programme for it which for the first time recognised the agrarian problem as basic to the development of Chinese society. The programme was however so obscured by Confucian terms that hampered its revolutionary interpretation that the left and right wings of the party could interpret it as they chose.

Despite this, the KMT was driven by events for a while to fight imperialism and the forces of reaction which had remained as strong as they had been in 1911. For a time it seemed as if a form of 'Jacobin democracy' would appear within the nationalist party. The revolution gained momentum but this only exacerbated the contradictions between the various social groups which composed the KMT. As the revolution moved forward, all that was reactionary within China arose against it.

15. The Kung Tsiang Tang (the Chinese Bolshevik party) emerged in the years 1920-21 for much the same reasons as the Russian Bolshevik Party had been formed twenty years before. As the Chinese bourgeoisie was failing in its own mission, the workers and the peasants became the fighting force of the revolution. Because it was a bourgeois revolution and not a proletarian revolution that was the order of the day, the organisation formed in the struggle – in the wake of the shortcomings of the KMT – proved to be of bourgeois type: a party. The party was created on Leninist lines because conditions were similar to those which had given rise to the Bolshevik Party in Russia. Its internal structure and its social and political ideas corresponded to these material circumstances.

16. The Chinese scholar Chen Tu Hsiu who founded the KTT made of it a faithful copy of the Russian Bolshevik Party. This was confirmed by Mao Tse Tung himself when, in a speech on the occasion of the 28th anniversary of the KTT in June 1949, he said: 'It was through the practices of the Russians that the Chinese discovered Marxism. Before the October Revolution the Chinese were not only ignorant of Lenin but also of Marx and Engels. The salvoes of the guns of the October Revolution brought us Marxism-Leninism.' The Chinese concluded from this that 'it was necessary for us to follow the way of the Russians.'

This conclusion was correct, but only because 'Marxism-Leninism' has nothing in common with Marxism other than terminology. Marxism was the theoretical expression of class relationships *within capitalism*. Leninism is a transformation of social-democratic ideas to fit particular Russian conditions. And these conditions were to shape Bolshevism more than did the social-democratic ideas. If Leninism had been Marxism, the Chinese would have had nothing to do with it, and what Mao said of other western theories could have been applied to Leninism itself, namely: 'the Chinese have learned much from the West but nothing of any practical use.'

17. Although the KTT could borrow its structure from the Russian Bolshevik Party as a result of the similarity between conditions in the two countries, these conditions were not identical. It was therefore necessary to modify Leninism to fit Chinese conditions just as Lenin had previously changed western ideas to fit the Russian situation. As the situation in China resembled that in Russia more closely than Russian conditions resembled those of western Europe, the alterations made were less drastic.

Undoubted changes were made, however, and Chinese Bolshevism while remaining Bolshevism was to reflect a much stronger peasant influence than did the Russian variety. This adaption to more primitive conditions was not consciously undertaken but occurred under the pressure of reality. The visible influence of this pressure was the total renewal of the party around 1927. As long as it had remained a faithful copy of the Russian model, the KTT had been completely impotent in the maelstrom of the Chinese revolution, but once it identified more closely with the peasant masses, it became an important factor. This explains why Chen Tu Hsiu was expelled in 1927 at the time of the 'renewal of the cadres'. The 'rebels in the countryside' were joining in large numbers. Chen Tu Hsiu, the Marxist scholar, was replaced by Mao Tse Tung, the peasant's son from Hunan.

18. A third party to appear in the Chinese revolution was the Democratic League. Founded in 1941, the League sought from the beginning to act as a buffer between the KMT and the KTT. In the newspaper *Ta Kun Pao* (January 21, 1947), close contacts of the League defined its activities as 'conducting propaganda for democracy and acting as intermediaries between the KMT and the Bolsheviks with a view to achieving national unity'. Elsewhere the League defines itself as being directed towards the end of civil war and towards peace.

The League sought to reconcile the irreconcilable. The compromise put forward (the League themselves used the word 'compromise') was an attempt similar to the one made by Sun Yat Sen in 1912 when he gave way to Yuan Shih Kai 'to avert a civil war'. But in 1912, the revolution once begun, civil war was inevitable. All attempts to compromise at that stage or later in history only had one result: an intensification of the civil war.

19. It has been said of the Democratic League, founded by the coalition of various groups and small parties, that most of its supporters were academics or students and that they used the word 'democracy' much as it is used in the West, namely to mean the rule of the bourgeoisie. What is true in this characterisation is that these scholars were the heirs to the Mandarins who had ruled China for over 3,000 years but what they had learnt from western bourgeois democrats was but a thin veneer over their basic Confucian philosophy. The basic feature of this philosophy is its concern for 'peace' and the avoidance of class struggle. The Mandarins of the League maintained close economic and family ties with the uppermost stratum of Chinese society. This social layer had one foot in bourgeois society but also maintained feudal interests.

This social background was eloquently expressed in the politics of the League; despite its outwardly severe critique of the KMT, its practical actions were confined to attempts at reforming the KMT. Such attempts were fruitless. The 'faults' of the KMT could not have been eliminated without eliminating the social circumstances which had given rise to both the KMT and the Democratic League.

20. The end of the civil war in China could not have been achieved by the compromises suggested by the League but only by pursuing the civil war to its conclusion. The League never abandoned its pacific policies but reality forced it eventually to modify them. Hesitatingly, reluctantly and too late in the day, even on their own admission, the League declared war on Chiang Kai-shek, whom they (politically short sighted as they were) had always taken for a moderate man. At that very moment Chiang Kai-shek returned to his policy of destroying the advocates of policies of compromise and moderation, which he had temporarily interrupted during the war with Japan. The Democratic League, caught between the left and the right, was crushed by the unfurling of events and disappeared. That was in the autumn of 1947.

21. In the years 1927 to 1947 the Chinese revolution under-went a second period of stagnation. During this period the KMT was in power, having separated itself from its youth and its own Jacobin wing. This was the Girondin period which had begun with the defeat of Sun Yat Sen and of the left.

In the spring of 1927 social antagonisms brought about a political crisis and a subsequent split in the party. In the April of that year there were two KMT governments; a left wing one at Wu Han and a right wing one at Nanking. The differences between them were not great for the Wu Han regime itself was to keep its distance from the peasantry, now becoming active. The Nanking regime reacted in the same way. There was no difference between the agrarian policies of the two regimes.

When the peasant movement in Hunan took on the appearance of a mass revolt, Tan Ping San, the Minister of Agriculture at Wu Han, travelled to the province to 'prevent excesses' . . . (in other words to suppress the revolt). Tan Ping San was a Bolshevik and a member of the KTT (then working in close collaboration with the KMT). Chen Tu Hsiu, then still Party Leader, reasoned as follows: 'An agrarian policy which is too radical would create a contradiction between the army and the government in which the KTT is participating. The majority of army officers come from a background of small landowners who would be the first people to suffer in an agrarian reform.'

This is yet another example of why it proved necessary to renew the ranks of the Bolshevik Party with peasants. It was clear, moreover, that the Wu Han administration stood between the peasant revolts and the Nanking government and that, because of its petit-bourgeois base, it did not take its flirtation with radical Jacobinism too seriously. As a result it was forced to surrender to Nanking at the beginning of 1928, leaving Chiang Kai-shek master of the situation.

125

22. As the Nanking government of Chiang proved victorious in the critical year of 1927, great working class uprisings had to be put down in Shanghai and Canton. It is claimed by some that these uprisings were attempts by the Chinese proletariat to influence events in a revolutionary direction. This could not have been the case. Twenty-two years after the massacres in these two towns the Chinese Ministry of Social Affairs announced that in China there were fourteen industrial towns and just over a million industrial workers in a population of between four and five hundred millions — i.e. industrial workers comprised less than 0.25% of the population. In 1927 this figure must have been still lower.

With the proletariat insignificant as a class in 1949, it seems unlikely that they could have engaged in revolutionary class activity twenty-two years earlier. The Shanghai uprising of March 1927 was a popular uprising whose aim was to support Chiang Kai-shek's Northern Expedition. The workers only played a significant role in it because Shanghai was China's most industrialised town, where one-third of the Chinese proletariat happened to live. The uprising was 'radical-democratic' rather than proletarian in nature and was bloodily quelled by Chiang Kai-shek because he scorned Jacobinism, not because he feared the proletariat. The so-called 'Canton Commune' was no more than an adventure provoked by the Chinese Bolsheviks in an attempt to bring off what they had already failed to achieve in Wu Han.

The Canton uprising of December 1927 had no political perspective and expressed proletarian resistance no more than the KTT expressed proletarian aspirations. Borodin, the Government's Russian adviser, said that he had come to China to fight for an idea; it was for similar political ideas that the KTT sacrificed the workers of Canton. These workers never seriously challenged Chiang Kai-shek and the right-wing of the KMT; the only serious, systematic and sustained challenge came from the peasantry.

23. After his victory Chiang Kai-shek found himself master of a country in which the insoluble contradictions of the traditional social system had produced social chaos. The Nanking government saw before it the task of re-organising China, but it was impossible to turn the clock back.

Chiang Kai-shek was obliged to embark on new roads and was ready to do so. He dreamt of being, if not the Jacobin, at least the Girondin reformer of China, just as Kerensky had dreamt of being the great reformer in the Russian revolution. Kerensky, like a comic opera hero, had strutted across the Russian political scene between February and October 1917, believing he could dominate events, whereas in fact it was events that were carrying him forward.

Chiang Kai-shek can be compared to Kerensky in several ways: neither had much criticism to make of imperialism; both were faced with agrarian problems which resulted in the basic instability of their regimes; both became puppets of reaction as a result of their own ideals. Kerensky's 'socialist' beliefs (the word can be interpreted in many ways!) led him to become the ally and friend of many of the most reactionary elements in Russia. Chiang Kai-shek who, as a cadet in the military academy, had dreamt of 'renewing China with his sword' in his own lifetime, eventually became a member of a clique of whom T.V. Soong*was the most typical member. But the wealth of Soong* and other large financiers presupposes both a form of commercial imperialism and the mass poverty of the Chinese peasantry. Kerensky's policies were similarly dictated by the social position of his friends, such as Nekressov, a position based on the poverty of the Russian peasantry. While

*In fact Chiang's father-in-law.

126

Kerensky's government in Russia lasted only a few months, the Chinese 'Kerensky' period of the KMT lasted until World War II.

24. Although the accession to power of Chiang Kai-shek impeded the progress of the bourgeois revolution, the revolution had already begun and the main revolutionary force, the mass of the peasantry, continued to press forward. In the early thirties, scarcely three years after the country had been 'pacified', there was a series of peasant insurrections. Thus the KMT armies were fighting against the revolutionaries – the peasantry – who had been continually oppressed and cheated and were now being driven to extremes of desperation.

Wherever the masses took action they undertook a general partition of the land. This partition was so radical in the province of Kiangsi that the KMT were forced to legitimate it when they 'pacified' the rebellious area in 1934, although such land reform was scarcely in accord with their general policy. Chiang Kai-shek had declared, it is true, that he intended to regulate land ownership so that each could have his share, but outside Kiangsi where the partition was imposed by peasants themselves no such reforms took place.

The KMT claimed that co-operatives would improve the living standards of their participants and, although the number of such co-operatives rose from 5,000 to 15,000 between 1933 and 1936, they only in fact served the interests of the landowners. The Swedish anthropologist Jan Myrdal, who lived for a time in a country village in Shansi, recorded that the peasants themselves had told him that the credit system brought them further into poverty. Their debts to the landlords increased and the troops of the KMT enforced payment. Such conditions, as recorded by Myrdal, lend weight to the assertion that the revolution which smouldered throughout the thirties to explode in the forties was overwhelmingly a peasant revolution.

25. The Nanking government under Chiang Kai-shek completely failed to resolve China's most urgent problem, that was the agrarian problem. Their incapacity in this field stemmed from the close links between the KMT and those sections of Chinese society whose interests most favoured the maintenance of the traditional system. The overt and direct oppression of the peasantry under this system was of a distinctly pre-bourgeois nature and showed that remnants of feudalism were still in existence.

Here can be found the source of the increasing corruption within the KMT: such corruption was not the result of personal characteristics of the KMT leaders but of the social system itself. The KMT was not corrupted because it sought support from the propertied classes but by the fact that it was based on such classes. This corruption greatly exacerbated the social problems of China. The Nanking government and the parasitical classes which it represented held back development and tended to destroy China's economy.

But once this economy was challenged the government itself was doomed. After twenty years of tentative attempts, the peasant masses at last discovered how to unite in a revolutionary force. It was not the working class, still very weak, which brought about the downfall of Chiang Kai-shek but the peasant masses, organised under primitive democracy into guerilla armies. This demonstrates another fundamental difference between the Chinese and Russian revolutions. In the latter the workers were at the head of events at Petrograd, Moscow and Kronstadt, and the revolution progressed outward from the towns into the countryside. In China the opposite was the case. The revolution moved from rural to urban areas. When Kerensky called upon the army to help him against revolutionary

Petrograd, his soldiers fraternised with the Bolsheviks. But when the armies of Mao Tse Tung and Lin Piao approached the Yangtse river, the peasant soldiers of the KMT deserted en masse. There was no question of a defence of Nanking or of the China of Chiang Kai-shek. The spectre of feudalism was driven out of China and capitalism was bloodily born there, the result of a social caesarean section carried out with the bayonets of peasant armies.

26. As a peasant revolution, the Chinese revolution showed its bourgeois character as clearly as did the Russian revolution. When the peasants began to move, Lenin and his colleagues were forced by events to abandon their ideas on the 'agrarian question'. They adopted the Narodnik policy based on the so-called 'black partition' under the slogan of 'the land to the peasants'. In China the KTT used a similar slogan, also borrowed from others (notably from Sun Yat Sen) and which, as in Russia, had been similarly forced upon them by reality itself.

27. In 1926 the two childhood friends from the province of Hunan Mao Tse Tung and Liu Shao Chi, both strictly followed the Party doctrine. The former wrote in a study of the old class structure in China that 'the industrial proletariat is the motive force of our revolution'. The latter wrote in a pamphlet that 'the social and democratic revolution can only succeed under the leadership of the workers' unions'.

The ink was scarcely dry, however, when the peasants of Hunan challenged such opinions with an irresistible force. Deeply impressed by what he had seen during a short visit to his native province, Mao Tse Tung came to believe that it was not the workers but the peasants who would be at the fore-front of the revolution. He wrote in a report that, 'without the poor peasants there can be no question of a revolution'. Whoever acted against the peasants attacked the revolution; their revolutionary tactics were beyond reproach.

28. Mao Tse Tung depicted in great detail the revolutionary tactics of the peasants of Hunan in a report on the revolutionary movement in that province. These tactics were used throughout China as much during the long 'Kerensky period' as in 1949 and 1953. The houses of village tyrants were invaded by crowds, their corn confiscated and their pigs slaughtered. Landowners were dressed up as clowns and paraded through the villages as prisoners; meetings were held at which the poor expressed their grievances against the rich, and tribunals were set up to try exploiters. These were the methods of struggle spontaneously developed by the Chinese peasants. In China, just as in Russia, it was not the party which showed the way to the peasants — the peasants showed the way to the party.

29. The social changes which occurred in the Chinese countryside between 1949 and 1953 were characterised by partition of the land, the dispossession of the landowners, the breaking up of the social groups connected with them and, finally, by the destruction of the patriarchal family which was the basic production unit of traditional Chinese society. The social significance of this process was that it put an end to the old system which was in decline and seriously hindered the development towards private ownership of land (the most important means of production in China).

The result was the same in China as it had been in Russia. Those who had been landless peasants became small landowners. After four years of agrarian revolution, there were between 120 and 130 million independent peasants in China.

30. Of the development of Russia after 1917, Karl Radek had written, 'the Russian peasants have made the feudal land on which they worked until now their own

property'. This remains the basic fact although it can be partly concealed by various juridical fictions. The Bolshevik economist, Vargas, wrote in 1921, 'the land is worked by peasants who produce almost as private owners'. Radek and Vargas were absolutely correct.

The first phase of the Russian revolution produced capitalist private ownership in the countryside, which naturally led to new social differentiations. A new class of agricultural labourers developed alongside a class of well-to-do peasants. Of similar developments in China, Mao Tse Tung was to write in 1955: 'in recent years the spontaneous forces of *capitalism** have expanded day by day in the countryside; *new rich peasants** have appeared everywhere and a large number of well-to-do peasants are trying desperately to become rich. On the other hand, a large number of poor peasants still live in misery and poverty because the means of production are insufficient. Some of these poor peasants are in debt while others are selling or letting their land.' Later, in the same article, Mao writes of 'a group of well-to-do peasants who are developing towards *capitalism**'.

31. Partition of the land created, both in Russia and China, the conditions under which agriculture could enter the sphere of modern commodity production.

Such a system of commodity production arose in Western Europe under the form of classical capitalism. In such a system there no longer exist the closed units in which needs are fulfilled by local labour alone and in which production is geared to local consumption. A peasant no longer consumed all his own production nor produced for the satisfaction of all his own needs. Specialisation developed and the peasant began to work for the market just as industry did.

The peasant supplied industry with primary products and the non-agrarian industrial workers with food. In return, industry supplied the peasant with the machinery to improve and increase production. This specialisation led to an increasing interdependence between agriculture and industry.

In Russia and China this type of development also took place, but not along classical lines. Both these countries lacked a modern bourgeoisie which is the historical agent of this type of social change. Its historical role had been taken over by the party and the state. The development towards capitalism in these two countries was also the development towards state capitalism. At first it might appear as if this development was the product of a supposedly 'socialist' ideology. On closer inspection, however, it appears that state capitalism was not the result of such an ideology but rather that this 'socialist' ideology was the consequence of the new inevitability of state capitalism.

32. Because state capitalism implies a restriction of 'free' market mechanisms and of the traditional 'freedoms' of the producer, it encountered both in China and in Russia the resistance of peasants who had just established themselves as free producers. The historical need to overcome this resistance inevitably resulted in a Party dictatorship.

The climate of resistance among the Chinese peasantry is clearly demonstrated in an episode described in the Party's theoretical journal in 1951 as follows: 'The young Liu Shao-chi had worked as a farm labourer for more than ten years. During this time he had suffered from bitter poverty. It was not until the victory of the revolution that he was able to marry and start a family. During the campaign for agricultural reform he was very active and was elected secretary of his village youth league. Once he had received land however he refused to continue working for the Party. When reproached, he replied: "All my life

*Brendel's emphasis

129

I've been poor. I owned no land. Now I own land, I'm content. There is no need for further revolution".' The Party replied that the revolution had not yet ended. The revolution could not be ended until a modern, stable economy had been established without which, despite the land partition, agriculture would once again stagnate.

33. In 1953, when the agrarian revolution was under way – that is to say, after the partition of land had taken place, China saw the onset of a violent struggle between the peasants and the KTT. The object of this was the building of a state capitalist economy. Alongside this development there arose also increasing tensions between the workers and the government.

In these two respects, events in China in the fifties resembled events in Russia in the twenties. But events in the two countries were by no means identical. China witnessed nothing like the development of workers' councils or the growth of these tendencies of self-management in the Russian factories which had forced Lenin to adopt the slogan of 'All Power to the Soviets', despite this being in its essence, in opposition to Bolshevik ideology. Nevertheless, similarities can be seen underlying, on the one hand, the decision of the First All-Russian Congress of Councils of National Economy (in May 1918) to the effect that eventual nationalisation of the factories could only be undertaken with the consent of the Supreme Council of National Economy*, or the decree of the 10th Party Congress of March 1921 which forbade the further confiscation of enterprises†, and, on the other hand, the Chinese measures introduced in September 1949 forbidding even workers in the private sector from striking.

While the Russian proletariat were developing new methods of struggle, the Chinese proletariat were resorting to the classical strike weapon. But in both countries legislation was directed at the self-activity of the workers. Behind the thin facade of the so-called 'dictatorship of the proletariat' could be found, in both countries, the features of capitalism.

34. In both China and Russia there was a contradiction between the claims of the Bolshevik Party and social reality. In relation to the trade unions, this led to a 'discussion' in which the truth was meticulously avoided even when the facts were fairly clear.

In 1952 the Chinese unions were purged of officials who, it was stated, 'allowed themselves to be led too much by the workers', i.e. who 'showed too much concern over the workers' living standards', or who 'proved overzealous in ensuring workers' rights'. Meetings were called at which attacks were made on those who 'failed to understand that, while strikes are necessary in a capitalist country, they are superfluous in a socialist state'. A campaign was launched against 'laxity in labour discipline', in much the same tone as Trotsky had used in Russia. General Hou Chi Chen, who had elaborated the new trade union laws, declared: 'It is no longer necessary, as it once was, to struggle for the downfall of capitalism.'

In 1953, at the 7th Congress of Chinese Trade Unions, it was stated that 'the direct and selfish interests of the working class must be subordinated to those of the state'.

Although in China too debate clouded reality, at the 1953 Congress of Trade Unions the truth was stated far more bluntly than it had ever been in Russia.

35. That the Chinese Party could express itself more openly than its Russian counterpart was a direct result of the different situations existing in the two countries. In Russia the realities of Bolshevik ideology had to be more carefully hidden as a result of

*See *The Bolsheviks and Workers Control* p. 43.
**ibid pp 77 et seq.

the more important role played by the working class in the country. After all, the Bolshevik regime in Russia had known a 'Workers' Opposition' based on the trade union of metalworkers and an armed proletarian insurrection at Kronstadt.

No such pressures had been put upon the Chinese Bolshevik Party. As a result it had fewer compunctions in dealing with the working class and could consequently allow itself a freer hand in coping with the peasantry. Until the early thirties the Russian Party vacillated between the workers and the peasants, at times acting against one section while giving way to the other. From the beginning of the revolution the Chinese Party could follow a straight line. As a result, it could develop a stronger state capitalist policy in relation to agriculture, and moreover do so at an earlier date.

36. From the moment of the Bolshevik victory in China the working class was weaker than that in Russia. Agriculture was more primitive and therefore more dependent on industry. As a result the Party had more elbow room and met with more success in its agrarian policy. In October 1953 the Party began to fight against the private capitalist tendencies which had resulted from the partition of the land. Three and a half years later, in 1957, ninety per cent of Chinese agriculture had been organised into co-operatives. This first period of collectivisation was followed, in August 1959, by a second phase: the introduction of the Peoples' Communes. This second phase of collectivisation had only been going a few months when it encountered a massive and menacing resistance from the peasantry. In Russia the Bolsheviks had met this resistance earlier.

37. In China the struggle between the peasantry and the state party reached its peak later than its corresponding struggle in Russia. As a result of China's larger number of peasants, the struggle proved more deeply rooted and more dangerous to the new state. In Russia the ideological repercussions of this conflict did not occur until long after the peasant uprisings had been suppressed: it was not until 1925 that Bukharin issued his famous appeal to the peasants, 'Enrich yourselves!' In China the order of events proved quite different. The peasant uprisings occured in December 1958 in Hunan Hopeh, Kansu, Kiangsi and Kuangtung provinces but the ideological struggle had taken place two and a half years before in the period between the two periods of agrarian collectivisation known as the 'Hundred Flowers' period.

38. It is quite wrong to see the resistance against the Mao regime during the 'Hundred Flowers' period as a preliminary to the events of the Red Guards period of the Cultural Revolution. During the 'Hundred Flowers' period it was the Party which found itself the accused, denounced for suppressing individual liberty and creating a division between itself and the people, in short of 'behaving like a new dynasty', as a spokesman of the opposition put it. The Party was being accused by people who, consciously or not, reflected the aspirations of the small agricultural producers. During the Cultural Revolution, instead of being the accused, the Party was then the prosecutor and the accusations it levelled were not the suppression of individual liberties but an over-indulgence in personal liberty. While the 'Hundred Flowers' period was a struggle against the Party's state capitalist attitudes, the Cultural Revolution — as will be shown — was a conflict between the Party and the 'new class'.

In China this 'new class' developed more quickly than in Russia. One of the main reasons for this was the ability of the KTT to move more quickly and more strongly towards state capitalism in the first years that followed its victory. In China many of the most profound social changes occurred sooner after the revolution than in Russia. As is often the case in history, what was initially a brake became a stimulus to further development.

39. In the middle of January 1956 the Chinese Bolshevik Party held a conference during which it decided to change its policy with regard to scientists and writers. Chou En-lai, the Prime Minister, promised the intellectuals better treatment, admitted that a gap had developed between the Party and the intellectuals, and conceded that this could partly be blamed on Party officials. On 21 March 1956 the 'People's Daily' wrote that the Party should make greater attempts than ever to rally the intellectuals back to its ranks. By 'intellectuals' they were referring to the new intellectuals rather than to the old political idealists who formed the Party cadre and who belonged to the intelligentsia. At the same time open attempts were made to persuade Chinese intellectuals abroad to return home. On 2 May 1956 Mao Tse Tung made his famous speech in which he said 'Let a Hundred Flowers bloom and a Hundred Schools of Thought contend'. Thus began the 'Hundred Flowers' period. It was pure coincidence that it began at the same time as the 'thaw' in Russia or as the Polish 'spring in autumn'. This coincidence was to lead to a misconception that these were similar phenomena.

40. Misunderstandings were heightened by the fact that in China too people used the word 'spring'. If however a comparison with this Chinese 'spring' is to be sought, it will not be found in the European developments of the fifties but rather in the Russian events of early 1918. In March of that year Lenin proclaimed the need to attract people from the professions. In 1921 and in the following years of the NEP relations between the Bolsheviks and the scientists and specialists steadily improved until they once more came under attack from Stalin.

In 1928 the first famous trial took place in Russia against certain engineers. The event in some ways resembled the purges of the thirties but was in essence different. Trials also took place in China, for example that against the author Hou Fu, widely read in this period. That cases such as this occurred before even the beginning of the 'Hundred Flowers' period only demonstrates how complex reality is and how, beyond all the analogies, there remain profound differences between the Chinese events and those of Russia.

41. Despite these differences, the 'Hundred Flowers' period in China can be compared to the NEP in Russia. Changes in economic policy took place in China during this period – namely, a pause between the two periods of collectivisation. In Russia this period lasted ten years if dated from Lenin's change of policy towards the intellectuals, or seven years if dated from the formal adoption of the NEP on 21 March 1921. As a result of her backwardness, China's corresponding phase was to prove much shorter, but did not occur until six and a half years after the Bolshevik victory. The systematic building of state capitalism, for which both countries needed intellectuals, began later in China, which was a more backward country; but, once begun, the process continued at a faster tempo as the Chinese did not need to make the detours that were forced on Lenin (see thesis 35).

42. The period of the 'Hundred Flowers' lasted only a year. While the hundred flowers were flowering and the hundred schools of thought were contending, comments of the following kind could be read in China: 'When the Communists entered the town in 1949 they were welcomed by the people with food and drink and they were regarded as liberators; now the people keep clear of the Communist Party as if its members were gods or devils. Party members behave as police agents in civilian clothing and spy on the people.' Or: 'The unions have lost the support of the masses because they side with the Government at decisive moments.'

To dissatisfaction such as this must be added that caused by a low standard of living and by widespread hunger. One cannot help recalling that Kollontai had said in Russia in the early twenties that the bars of the prison cells were the sole remaining symbols of soviet power − or how the Workers' Opposition had criticised the economic situation. But in China the working class was still weak. No workers' opposition had appeared. The reality of the situation, namely the defence of the liberty of peasant entrepreneurs against the state capitalist tendencies of the Party, was better expressed in the literary critiques of the 'Hundred Flowers' period than it had been by pamphleteers during the NEP. In Russia this had been mixed up with a primitive proletarian critique − something which did not occur in China.

43. The 'Hundred Flowers' period was in no way related to the events in Russia or Poland after the death of Stalin. Nor was it related to the critique which began in China in the early sixties, despite the fact that in a number of instances the Party was the common object of these criticisms. In the 'Hundred Flowers' period the Party was criticised *because* it was state capitalist; in the sixties it was criticised *despite* its state capitalist position. Whereas in the 'Hundred Flowers' period the critics were against both state capitalism and the Party, in the sixties the critics were against Mao Tse Tung but not in the least against state capitalism. Behind these apparent subtleties there lay important differences.

44. In 1957 while the seed of the 'Hundred Flowers' was germinating in the fertile soil of the existing social relations, the Party replied to criticism by a sharp campaign against 'right-wing deviationists' which lasted until April 1958. Then in the summer of that year, the Party announced its policy of the 'Three Red Flags' which it had been preparing for some months.

− The first 'red flag' was the 'general policy of socialist construction: the joint development of industry and agriculture by the simultaneous utilisation of modern and traditional productive methods.

− The second 'red flag' was the 'great leap forward': the attempt vastly to increase the production of steel and power.

− The third 'red flag' was the formation of 'peoples' communes' throughout the countryside as the second phase of agrarian collectivisation.

From this it can be seen that after the short 'Hundred Flowers' period the Party continues on its state capitalist course more decisively than ever. China was now at the stage that Stalin's Russia had reached in 1928, eleven years after the Bolshevik revolution. China had taken nine years to reach this stage. Her development had been more rapid and the methods used more radical.

Such 'progress' however was not achieved without trouble. When towards the end of 1958 the 'weapon of critique' of the 'Hundred Flowers' period was discarded and the peasants took the road of a 'critique by weapons', the Party had to back-pedal. In December 1958, April 1959, and on several subsequent occasions, the Party had to modify its 'Communes' programme before eventually abandoning it in 1962. A similar fate met the other two 'red flags'. In the spring of 1962 the policy of the 'Three Red Flags' was completely abandoned.

45. History repeats itself, but in ever new forms. In Russia there was a fairly strong peasant resistance at the beginning of 1921. The Party took a step back and announced the NEP, only to renew its fight against this resistance in 1928. In China phenomena similar to the NEP were witnessed in 1956-7, after which the Party began a struggle against the peasants which resulted in uprisings similar to those seen in Russia in 1921. The Chinese Party then back-pedalled as Lenin had in 1921. What resembled the NEP in China therefore took place in two distinct periods, the 'Hundred Flowers' period and the period between 1962 and 1964 when a new 'radical' course was again set. But the Chinese events of 1964 no longer resembled what happened in Russia at the end of the NEP. At best they resembled the second phase of a delayed NEP. A new conflict was then beginning, not between the Party and the peasantry but between the Party and a 'new class'.

46. In the mid-sixties China entered a new phase which the Party called the 'Great Socialist Cultural Revolution'. In a three-volume work published in the autumn of 1966 it was stated that, 'The victory of the socialist revolution does not mean the end to a class society or to the class struggle'. The authors went on to say that after the proletariat had established its power through a political victory, there were other struggles to be fought in the fields of culture, literature, art, philosophy, life-style and everyday conduct. It was because of this that China had been involved in inter-class struggle on the cultural front since 1949.

This is a typical example of Bolshevik mystification: there had not been a socialist revolution and power was not in the hands of the proletariat. Instead there had been a bourgeois revolution which, as a result of specific historical circumstances, had been carried out by the peasantry. It had taken the form of state capitalism and had subsequently evolved a very unusual ideology. This ideology required a presentation of the facts in such a manner as to imply that, from the outset, the capitalist nature of the revolution had rapidly become socialist. This sleight of hand boils down to the fact in China, as in Russia, state capitalism is presented as 'socialism' and the power of the Party as 'the dictatorship of the proletariat'.

The new ideology also develops the false idea that, after its allegedly political victory, the working class has yet other victories to win. But the real power of the working class, as of any other class, does not lie in political institutions but is of a social nature. It implies above all a revolution in the relations of production, associated with a revolution in all other relationships. In China the relations of production changed. Feudalism was replaced by capitalism. As earlier in Europe, one system of exploitation was replaced by another. As long as revolutions in relations of production only result in one form of exploitation replacing another, they will result in the emergence of institutionalised political power. When a change in the relations of production does away with exploitation, political power will cease to exist. One cannot speak of political domination by the proletariat where the proletariat is still exploited. Once the proletariat frees itself, all forms of exploitation and of class domination will cease.

The concept according to which the 'political power of the proletariat must be used to win victory in the cultural field' is based on a fundamental misunderstanding of the link between relations of production on the one hand and political and cultural relations on the other. These wrong ideas arose from the fact that the respective roles of the social and economic infrastructure of society and of its political and cultural superstructure were reversed.

Cultural and economic changes are not brought about by the instrument of politics but come about when the economic foundations of society are being transformed. The opposite is learnt if – as is the case of Russia and China – reality too is violated and wage-slavery is presented as the opposite of what it really is. The 'Great Socialist Cultural Revolution', we would stress, had nothing to do with socialism. Nor was it in any real sense a revolution.

47. What the KTT labelled as a 'cultural revolution' led, in late 1966 and in early 1967, to violence on such a wide scale that the world spoke of a 'civil war'. It should not

134

be thought however that these are mutually contradictory categories. Cultural developments, historically, have often been violent. In our opinion there is a direct link between the conflicts expressed in art and literature in the early sixties and the violence which broke out in later years. The Chinese scholars and literary critics fought for essentially the same things as were later to be fought for physically. As so often in history, and as has previously been seen in Chinese history itself (see Thesis 44), an ideological struggle preceded an armed struggle.

It was no coincidence that the work already mentioned on the 'cultural revolution' dealt only with literature. The KTT were not wrong in emphasising the relationship between the struggle of the Red Guards and the earlier literary struggle. They were wrong, however, in their distorted view of that relationship. The struggle of the Red Guards did not have a cultural objective. The opposite was the case. The cultural struggle expressed conflicting social interests. The Chinese Bolsheviks failed to appreciate the opposing social interests precisely because they were Bolsheviks and limited by Bolshevik ideology. They described the conflicts of 1966-67 as 'cultural' instead of explaining these conflicts in the field of culture as stemming from antagonistic social interests.

48. The French journal *Le Contrat Social* (edited by the Institute of Social History in Paris), called the 'Great Socialist Cultural Revolution' a 'pseudo-cultural pseudo-revolution'. This might appear to coincide with our viewpoint. We have said it was wrong to explain social conflicts through cultural mechanisms. We have said that there was no 'revolution' at this period. This is true, but the writer in the French journal meant something else. By 'pseudo-cultural', the French journal meant anti-cultural, and by 'pseudo-revolution' it meant counter-revolution. But in China during the sixties there was neither a revolution nor a counter-revolution, neither physical nor literary. What happened was a conflict between the 'new class' and the Party, just as occurred in Russia after Stalin's death.

But there is an important and specific difference between the parallel developments in China and in Russia. In Russia there was the same upheaval but the defenders of the traditional type of Party were labelled 'anti-party', and the 'new class' won its victory easily and almost without violence. In China, where the Party was much stronger for historical reasons (see Theses 35 and 41), the 'new class' experienced more resistance and violence erupted. If in the fifties Molotov and those around him had succeeded in mobilising the Army against the Mikoyan faction, developments in Russia might have shown more resemblance to those in China.

49. The agitation of the Red Guards was no more than a reaction against an earlier action by the 'new class'. To grasp this one need only study the literary conflict that took place in the early sixties. Despite the fact that it was couched in literary terms, the true social nature of this conflict became clearly visible in January 1961 after the author Wu Han had published his novel *Hai Jui Dismissed from Office* (Peking *Arts* and *Literature* edition).

Although this dramatic story was to be severely criticised by the Party's official press several years later, the same author in 1961 published *Three Family Village* in collaboration with Teng To and Liao Mo Sha. Between January and August Teng To began a regular column entitled *Evening Tales from Jenchan* in a Chinese paper. These were short contemplations in the classical Chinese style and apparently dealt with former periods of Chinese cultural prosperity. The allegorical nature of these articles is, however, transparently obvious and within the framework of depicting the Ming dynasty or old

135

time's Chinese culture he was referring to the contemporary People's Republic of Mao Tse Tung and the KTT and aiming his blows against the Party dictatorship.

Teng To was undoubtedly the most brilliant of Mao's critics and his works contain constant attacks on political fanaticism and persecution because of the disastrous effects they have on harmonious social and economic development. In his column *Evening Tales of Jenchan* dated 30 April 1961 Teng To further clarifies his position. The article is on 'the theory of the precious nature of labour power' and Teng To makes it clear that he considers the wasteful use of so 'precious' a commodity to be harmful to production. By such criticism Teng To distinguishes himself from the critics of the 'Hundred Flowers' period. He appears as something which previous critics were not, namely as the spokesman for a group with an undoubted interest in production. When in his *Evening Tale* of 22 April 1962 Teng To asks if one can base oneself on theory alone and tells the Party bureaucrats that 'people can't do things all alone', one must see it in the light of the 'new class' staking a claim to being heard and listened to.

50. The Party's tame critics claimed that writers such as Wu Han, Liao Mo Sha, and Teng To 'wanted to restore capitalism' in China. Such an accusation slots into the jargon of Bolshevik ideology but is patently absurd. Capitalism being the existing economic system, there was no need to 'restore' it. What was at most possible was that some Chinese preferred traditional liberal capitalism to the state capitalism variant which existed in China.

Who then were the critics? Classical capitalism had made little headway in China and the embryonic classical bourgeoisie had been destroyed or exiled in the late forties. Its residual representatives are today to be found in Formosa or elsewhere. In the unlikely event that there are people in China who favour a return to the social relations of classical private capitalism, Teng To, Liao Mo Sha and Wu Han are not amongst them. While their enemies within the Party constantly publish long attacks on the works of these writers to prove their hostility to the current regime, nowhere in the quotes does any hostility appear towards the system of state capitalism. It is true that *Three Family Village* (the joint work of these three pilloried authors) contains a semi-overt attack on the 'people's communes', but these criticisms are neither of state capitalism nor of the Party, which was in fact itself now abandoning the 'communes' policy.

In *Three Family Village* Teng To criticises Mao's famous phrase, 'the east wind is stronger than the west wind' and Mao's characteristation of imperialism as a 'paper tiger'. Teng To's criticisms spring from his standpoint as a realist. When, in his *Evening Tales*, he attacks the KTT's general policy as being based on illusions, he is echoing his criticisms of the people's communes. In both instances he is expressing his preference for efficiency. Teng To does not treat history daintily and he attacks political idealists like Mao who try to channel the process of social development according to their own political wishes. In other words, Teng To and his fellow writers are not opposed to state capitalism, they are only opposed to the Party.

51. The story of Wu Han's novel *Hai Jui Dismissed from Office* concerns a party official who, despite his honesty, is sacked from his post because of divergent ideas. It is probable, as suggested by the author's critics within the Party, that the novel alludes to those who were expelled from, and persecuted by, the Party after the Lushan conference in 1959. The conclusion drawn by the critics was however that Wu Han was defending 'right-wing opportunists'. This relapse into the traditional jargon tells us nothing either about Hai Jui or about those expelled from the Party. The Party pen-pushers could only

monotonously reiterate that the writers wanted to 'restore capitalism'.

If, however, nothing can be learned about Hai Jui, or about his creator Wu Han, from the criticisms of his detractors, much can be learned from the author's articles and letters which appeared after the publication of his book. Wu Han therein declares that he himself was among those who did practical work and kept in close touch with reality. Teng To expressed a similar preference for reality when he wrote in his *Evening Tales* column that 'those who believed that they could learn without a teacher would learn nothing'. The 'teacher' referred to by Teng To throughout his work is historical reality, the actual development of the productive process. It is precisely this type of criticism that identifies Wu Han and Teng To as spokesmen of the 'new class'.

52. In China the 'Great Socialist Cultural Revolution' was nothing more than an attempted self-defence by the Party against the increasing pressure of the 'new class'. Against the literary attacks of Teng To, Liao Mo Sha, Wu Han and others, the Party at first used purely literary weapons. The 'Thoughts of Chairman Mao' were published in the famous 'little red book' in which are contained Mao's pronouncements on art and literature uttered at Yenan in May 1942. When Mao said, in the forties, that 'writers must place themselves on the Party platform and must conform to Party policies', he meant something rather different than the use that was to be made of this phrase some twenty years later.

When the 'new class' changed its weapons the Party followed suit. The literary conflict between the 'new class' and the Party developed into a physical struggle. The stake in this struggle was just as obvious as in the previous literary phase. But there was a difference. Reality could be ignored on paper; in real life it could not. The 'new class' in China was a product of social development, just as it had been in Russia, and as such the Party felt obliged to defend it. This explains why, at a certain stage, Lin Piao had to hold back the Red Guards and why Mao Tse Tung himself had to call a halt to the 'Cultural Revolution'. What was at stake then was neither literature nor cultural affairs but production and the Chinese economy.

53. Information, both official and semi-official, on recent events in China is vague, contradictory, politically distorted and incomplete. Any attempt to build a social image of Mao's opponents, against whom the violence of the 'Cultural Revolution' was directed, confronts great difficulty. It is rather like the task the police undertake when it seeks to build up an 'identikit' picture from a mass of partial or incomplete testimonies. Doubtful and uncertain details must be discarded in favour of the features common to the many partial or inadequate reports. From these features can be built up a composite mental image which, while lacking specificity, nevertheless demonstrates all the *general,* i.e. *essential* features. Such features provide a distinct and immediately recognisable framework. Applying this method, Mao's adversaries are found:

- to be living in large and middle sized industrial towns (Chou En-lai said at a dinner in Peking on 14 January 1967, that it was in such towns that the Party first felt obliged to move against its opponents);
- to comprise, within their ranks, high Party officials and well-known men (speech by Chou En-lai and articles in the Peking *People's Daily*); and people in official positions (leader in the theoretical review *Red Flag*);
- to have fortified themselves in powerful positions (leader in *People's Daily* and *Red Flag*);
- to have some of their number in the management of the railways (articles in

People's Paper and *Red Flag*);

- to be attempting to gain the workers' support by wage increases and the bestowing of social benefits and through the distribution of food and other goods (the *People's Daily* and the *Red Flag*);
- to have interests closely tied to production (statement of a pro-Maoist group in Shanghai);
- to distinguish themselves from the masses through their dress and life-style, neither proletarian nor peasant (numerous street witnesses);
- expressing opinions characterised by the Maoists as 'economistic'; these opinions reflect the atmosphere of industrial life and come into head-on collision with the Maoist conception that 'political work forms the basis of economic work' (the *People's Daily* and the *Red Flag*);
- to favour a policy which would, according to the Maoists, drive a wedge between the 'dictatorship of the proletariat' (i.e. the dictatorship of the Party) and the 'socialist system' (i.e. state capitalism) (the *People's Daily* and the *Red Flag*).

From all that precedes, Mao's opponents give the impression of being a group with roots in industrial life and including many Party officials. They have financial influence and are in a position to allocate the products of industry (both food and other commodities). They have the power to grant wage increases and other social advantages. They can therefore be characterised as managers.

54. The clearer the picture of Mao's opponents becomes, the more readily are they identifiable as the 'new class'. The real social differences between them and the Party correspond exactly to the theoretical differences between Wu Han and Teng To on the one hand and the Party on the other. It is no coincidence that in the early sixties Wu Han was not only an author but also assistant mayor of the large industrial town of Shanghai. Neither is it a coincidence that in the mid-sixties the mayor of Shanghai was one of those fighting the Party with more than a pen. Their so-called 'economism' was the atmosphere they encountered every day in the industrial climate of Shanghai.

The intervention of the Chinese 'new class' (or managers) does as much to clarify the attitudes of their literary predecessors as a study of the latters' writing does to clarify the practical activities of the Chinese managers. The charge that the managers wanted to sever the links between the Party and the economic system shows that the managers – just like the writers – were not directing their blows against state capitalism as such but against the power of the Party. They did not consider the two as inseparable. They wished to destroy the stifling influence of the Party, not to abolish state capitalism. In fact, they believed that state capitalism could only prosper once freed of the political fetters of the doctrines of Mao Tse Tung and of the KTT.

55. What the 'new class' is proposing in China is a different conception of the Party, in other words an entirely different kind of Party from that conceived of by Mao Tse Tung.

During his visit to London, Kosygin, the Russian Premier, said that the Russian government sympathised with Mao's adversaries in China. This declaration fits in perfectly with our analysis of Chinese events. It was not the 'ideological conflict' with which the Russian leaders sympathised. What they identified with was the struggle of the managers of the 'new class' against the traditional Party. Their sympathy for the 'new class' stemmed from the fact that such a class had already proved victorious in Russia, personified by such manager-administrator types as Kosygin and Mikoyan.

In Russia the old style Bolshevik Party had been replaced by a Party of a new type. This gives us an insight into the objectives of the anti-Maoists in China. However, despite similarities, one must constantly stress that events had developed differently and at different tempos in the two countries.

56. In Russia the traditional, old style Party and the 'new class' were natural enemies. This was not the case in China where, because the proletariat had always been weak, the Party had not been forced to pay as much heed to the workers as had its Russian counterpart. As a result the Chinese Party had a freer hand. Its policies were more drastic and direct (see Thesis 35). It moved faster and more confidently towards state capitalism. This is why the Chinese Party differed from its Russian counter-part and why in China the borderlines between the Party and the 'new class' are less easy to discern.

Mao's opponents are so strong, even within the Party itself, that at an Executive Conference held early in 1967 only six of the eleven present supported Mao. In Russia the 'new class' came to power imperceptibly, the traditional Party having proved an anachronism. In China the rise of the 'new class' has been associated with struggle for control of the Party.

57. This struggle for the Party in China makes the situation more complex. Definitions such as 'old-style Party' and 'new-style Party' mean different things in the Chinese and in the Russian contexts. While the 'new class' in China is seeking to escape from the stranglehold of the Party, the Party is seeking to reform itself to ensure its continued domination over the managers. This gives rise to the totally erroneous impression that the 'Cultural Revolution' was directed against the Party, whereas in reality it was directed against the 'new class'. Such misunderstanding is heightened by the fact that it was Mao himself who first used the term 'new-style Party'.

What Mao meant by this phrase is the very opposite of what is represented by the 'new-style Party' in Russia, correctly seen by Mao as the instrument of the 'new class'. Mao sought to make the 'new-style Party' a barrier to the advance of the 'new class'. In Russia the 'new class' rebelled against the power of the traditional Party; in China the Maoists rose up against a Party structure in which they found their own power too circumscribed. Whereas in Russia the development of the 'new class' was compared to the 'thaw', in China Mao wanted to prevent the occurrence of such a 'thaw'. To this end he used the Red Guards, who threw China into turmoil. Yet despite this result of their intervention, its real purpose was to 'freeze' the social relations.

58. We have sought to analyse the social characteristics of Mao's opponents, but we hope it will be realised that every detail cannot be fitted into this analytical framework. Information leaking out of China concerning battles between Red Guards and workers for the control of several factories in Manchuria confirms no doubt that the 'Proletarian Cultural Revolution' was neither proletarian nor a revoluton. But no one will assert, we hope, that the workers who fought Mao's Red Guards were managers or members of the 'new class'.

One does not think of the managers either when one looks at the 1967 uprising against Mao Tse Tung in the capital city of Kiangsi province. The movement took the name 'The First of August Movement' in reference to the time, forty years earlier, when organisations were briefly formed in that part of China on the model of workers' councils, these had played a part in the conflict between the left and right wings of the Kuo Min Tang.

Still more difficult to place is the Chinese head of state, Liu Shao Chi who, even within the Party, had always held an independent position. The Maoists of the 'cultural revolution' call him their enemy, but Liu himself takes care to distinguish himself from all other opponents of Mao. It is obvious that many different developments are occurring simultaneously in China. But although reality is more complex than any abstract schema, the exceptions do not contradict the rule. Whatever the forces may have been against which the Red Guards and the 'cultural revolution' were unleashed, the situation can only be understood by the appearance on the scene of the 'new class', with its own indisputable claims.

59. The 'new class' in China did not appear from nowhere. It was the product of the development of specific social relationships in that country, just as previously it had developed in Russia from similar social relations. This explains two facts: firstly the endurance and obstinacy of the struggle against Mao which is continually breaking out in new places; secondly the repeated calls to order made to the Red Guards for moderate action without too much violence. These phenomena are related to one another and are both connected with the economy. Millions of Red Guards cannot be withdrawn from industry and education (i.e. from the preparation for future industrial knowledge, and therefore the preparation of the industry of the future) and be mobilised against the 'new class' without severely disorganising industrial development. As soon as the Red Guards are directed anew into production, industrial development is stimulated. Likewise the 'new class' is also stimulated.

60. From the preceding Theses one can conclude that the so-called 'cultural revolution' is not another step towards state capitalism as has been claimed. On the contrary: the struggle of the KTT is directed against the very requirements of state capitalism in full development. The Chinese 'cultural revolution' was a struggle by the Party to defend itself, a struggle against the 'new class' produced by state capitalism, a struggle against attempts to adapt the political apparatus to the reality of social conditions. It cannot be predicted what forces either the Party or the 'new class' will be able to mobilise. Even in China no one can prognosticate on this matter. But in the final analysis, this is not the issue. How many times the Party can still win is not fundamental. What is important is whether it will be the managers or the political bureaucrats who will wield power in the conditions of state capitalism. This can be predicted without the pressures and balances of the moment. In the social, historical and economic framework of state capitalism, the ultimate victory of the 'new class' is the only logical perspective.

'EVERYTHING REMAINS THE SAME

AFTER

SO

MUCH

ADO."

K.C. KWOK

This essay originally appeared in the 29th issue of the 70s Biweekly in Hong Kong and the Activist, a political magazine of New Left students at Oberlin College, Ohio U.S.A. K.C. Kwok was the psuedonym of an American student activist who spent a certain period of time with the 70s Biweekly group in Hong Kong. K.C. Kwok was originally Maoist oriented. When in America in the late sixties, 70 and 71, he was an active member of the SDS and participated in the War Council of the Weatherman. Although he did not go underground with the others, he was sympathetic to Weatherman politics. He developed his views on the Cultural Revolution expressed in this essay when he was in Hong Kong working and discussing with members of the 70s Biweekly and with ex-Red Guards whom he came into contact with through the 70s Biweekly.

1.   As a result of the practice of struggle having gained rich experience and having entered a higher stage, the maturity of the political thinking of the revolutionary people of China has also entered a higher stage. A new stream of ideas, reviled by the enemy as the "Ultra-Left thought trend" (i.e., "overthrow the new bureaucratic bourgeoisie," "abolish bureaucratic organs," "thoroughly smash the state machinery" and similar truths), wanders among the revolutionary people like a "spectre" before the eyes of the enemy.

The political-ideological weapon of the revolutionary people for winning the complete victory in the proletarian socialist great revolution has begun to appear in a new form in the Ultra-Left faction.[1]

2. Facts revealed by the masses, and the indignation which they brought forth, first told the people that this class of "red" capitalists had entirely become a decaying class that hindered the progress of history. The relations between them and the people in general had changed from relations between leaders and the led, to those between rulers and the ruled and between exploiters and the exploited. From the relations between revolutionaries of equal standing, it had become a relationship between oppressors and the oppressed. The special privileges and high salaries of the class of "red" capitalists were built upon the foundation of oppression and exploitation of the broad masses of the people ... With relation to the facts of the January Storm, the overthrown class is none other than the class of "bureaucratism" formed in China in the last 17 years ... There is no place for reformism – combining two into one – or peaceful transition. The old state machinery must be utterly smashed. "Completely smash the old exploitative system, the revisionist system, and the bureaucratic organs."[2]

3. Chairman Mao, with his great all-embracing proletarian feelings, announced to the world that China's first Marxist big-character poster "is the manifesto of the Peking Peoples Commune in the 1960's." It was these words that announced the official beginning of the vehement development among the masses of the Great Proletarian Cultural Revolution. These words also showed that Chairman Mao "wisely and with genius foresaw the emergence of a brand new situation in our state organs,"[3] that is, political organs of the Paris Commune type. In the January Revolution, Chairman Mao once again proposed the name "Peoples Commune of China." That meant that, as an ultimate result of the first Great Cultural Revolution, China would advance in the direction of a "Peoples Commune of China."[4]

4. Even before the Cultural Revolution officially began, Chairman Mao, in his famous May 7 directive, had already depicted the contents of this new type of political structure – the "Peoples Commune of China." But people in general regarded the sketch in the May 7 directive as an idealistic "communist utopia." Everyone thought that it was not practical to take the May 7 directive as the immediate goal of our recent struggle. At present it is only part of the educated youth that keep reciting the May 7 directive, and loudly declare that they want to fight for realization of the May 7 directive. They realize that only the new society sketched in the May 7 directive, which is different from the existing society, is the society in which they will gain liberation.[5]

5. Recently, a so-called "new trend of thought" prevails in society. Its principal content is to distort the major contradictions of socialist society into one between the so-called "power holders," i.e., the "privileged persons" who hold "property and power" and the masses of the people. It demands an incessant "redistribution" of the social property and political power under the proletarian dictatorship. The new trend of thought equated the current GPCR with a conflict for wealth and power "within a reactionary ruling class." It has equated the headquarters of Mao-Lin with that of Liu-Teng-T'ao. It has branded all leading cadres as privileged persons and thrust them all into positions of objects of revolution.[6]

6. The quintessence of the crisis in China known as the Great Proletarian Cultural Revolution (GPCR) which gave birth (and a painful one at that) to the above, Maoists notwithstanding, lies in the following: the whole brouhaha started as a conflict between

the official owners of the ideology and the majority of the owners of the machinery of the economy and the state, but developed into a power struggle between the true owners of the general interests of the collectivity and the developing Ultra-Left (and this is *not* ironic) which started out having a role in the first conflict but ended up diametrically opposed to, not just Liu Shao-ch'i, but to the bureaucracy. The Ultra-Left developed unevenly and confusedly during the GPCR and is an inherent reaction to the historical process which led to the rise of a bureaucracy-state which installed itself after the revolution for national liberation was believed to be victorious. The GPCR gave rise to the particular historical moment when, in China, the conditions and advances made during the first 17 years of CCP rule created the ripe moment for the development of new demands, spawned by those conditions but negating the mechanism which created them.

7. The struggle then revolves around the utopia (colored by the democracy-centralism dichotomy): the self-justifying tendency of the utopia once it becomes an ideology, and the nature of the utopia itself. The historical role of the utopia must remain clear. Leszek Kolakowski has pointed out that: "The desire for revolution cannot be born only when the situation is ripe, because among the conditions for this ripeness are the revolutionary demands made of an unripe reality." These demands form a utopia which is the negation of the existing reality, a desire to transform it. The existence of such a utopia is the prerequisite for reaching it. This negation cannot be viewed as the opposite of construction because it is not; it is the opposite of affirming existing conditions. Utopia becomes "a tool of action upon reality and of planning social activity." Kolakowski writes: "It [the revolutionary movement] is a total negation of the existing system and, therefore, also a total program. A total program is, in fact, a utopia. A utopia is a necessary component of the revolutionary Left, and the latter is a necessary product of the Social Left as a whole."[7]

8. Revolution in underdeveloped countries presents a particular problem simply because of the very development of history: "In these countries the economic backwardness fostered by colonial domination and the social strata that support it, the underdevelopment of productive forces, impeded the development of socio-economic formations which should have made immediately feasible the revolutionary theory elaborated in the advanced capitalist countries for more than a century. All of these countries at the same time they enter the struggle don't have heavy industry, and the industrial proletariat is far from being the majority class. It is the poor peasantry that assumes that function."[8]

9. In China the peasants' struggle was against American, European, and Japanese imperialism as well as the local reactionary elements, namely the Kuomintang. The Chinese national liberation movement appeared after the rout of the workers movement, a direct consequence of the defeat of the Russian revolution that, right from its victory, was transformed into counter-revolution, serving the bureaucracy that pretended to be communist. With the defeat of the Chinese workers' movement as early as 1925-27 combined with only Stalin's advice, China had to fight colonialism and imperialism by itself and relying on the peasants. Such conditions gave rise to, as shall be seen, a partial utopia.

10. The situation in China created a utopia which negated the reality of foreign oppression, as well as the debris of a colonial, semi-colonial and semi-feudal China. In short, it led to the New Democracy period. Mao: "If we know nothing about production and do not master it quickly, if we cannot restore and develop production as speedily as

possible and achieve solid successes so that the livelihood of the workers, first of all, and that of the people in general is improved, we shall be unable to sustain our political power, we shall be unable to stand on our feet, we shall fail ... In this period all capitalist elements in the cities and countryside which are not harmful but beneficial to the national economy should be allowed to exist and expand. But the existence and expansion of capitalism in China will be restricted from several directions ... Restriction versus opposition to restriction will be the main form of class struggle in the new democratic state."[9] Thus, the result: because they fought imperialism by themselves and on only a part of the total revolutionary terrain during a given point with its particular conditions, they developed, in response (and there were other alternatives) a partial utopia – in practice, a bureaucracy.

11. The justification is capital accumulation. The bureaucracy seeks to realize what the bourgeoisie merely conceived. What the bourgeoisie has done for centuries, "through blood and slime," the bureaucracy wants to achieve consciously and "rationally" in a few decades. But bureaucracy cannot accumulate capital without accumulating lies: what made up the original sin of capitalistic wealth is sinisterly baptized "social primitive accumulation." The New Democracy result, "the bourgeois state without the bourgeoisie" (Lenin), cannot emancipate the mass of workers because improving their social condition depends not only upon the productive forces but also upon their appropriation by the producers. The bureaucracy can create the material conditions to realize emancipation of the workers and substantially improve their social conditions. The utopia, however, has become bureaucratized: the conditions that the bureaucracy creates give rise to new demands which negate the existing bureaucratic state. Such is the case with the Ultra-Left.

12. In the case of China, this utopia has been transformed into the state ideology. The introductory sentence of the General Outline of Party Rules reads: "The Chinese Communist Party is the vanguard of the Chinese working class. It is the highest form of class organization of the Chinese working class. Its goals are to realize socialism and communism in China." This places the utopia in a strange contradictory situation of being the continuous negation of the existing society, while at the same time functioning as that society's official ideology. The most salient feature of this contradiction is the possibility that the leadership's treatment of the utopia merely serves to protect and justify the established regime by eliminating or minimizing all historical elements of the utopia which would indicate progress of socio-historical development beyond that regime.

13. In peasant-bureaucratic revolutions, only the bureaucracy aims consciously and lucidly at power. The seizure of power corresponds to the historical moment when the bureaucracy lays hold of the State and declares its independence towards the revolutionary masses, even before eliminating the colonial residues and before achieving effective independence from abroad. Exclusive owner of the entire society, it then declares itself exclusive representative of its superior interests. In doing so, the bureaucratic state is the Hegelian State realized. Its separation from society sanctions at the same time the separation into antagonistic classes: the momentary union of bureaucracy and peasantry is only the fantastic illusion through which both achieve the immense historical tasks of the absent bourgeoisie. Bureaucratic power built on the ruins of pre-capitalist colonial society is not the abolition of class oppression: it merely substitutes new classes, new conditions of oppression and new forms of struggle, for the old ones.[10]

14. The bureaucracy is essentially a power established on national State possession, and it is the logic of this reality which it must finally obey, according to the particular interests imposed by the level of development of the country in its possession.

The utopia, partial from the beginning – being a reaction to and negation of the under-developed, colonial situation – becomes the ideology of the bureaucracy. Given the authoritarian notion that the bureaucracy is essential for capital accumulation, it then utilizes the utopian ideology to invoke the martyrdom of such curiously neo-religious slogans as "sacrifice Now for Future Generations" which was the driving logic behind the Great Leap Forward. "Here we have an obvious contradiction. If their State is going to be a genuine people's State, why should it then dissolve itself – and if its rule is necessary for the real emancipation of the people, how dare it call itself a people's State." (Bakunin)

15. Mao realizes that these contradictions exist, and, unlike the Russians goes so far as to not only admit them but list them. The Chinese have taken the Leninist concept of democratic centralism as the chief bureaucratic mechanism for reaching the utopia, which is now a matter of state policy. Separating the concept into its two mutually contradictory parts, the Chinese then formulated the slogan: "From top to bottom; from bottom to top." This mechanism, essentially the decision making mechanism, should function to give substance to the utopia. In fact, the bureaucracy must be centralized due to its mode of appropriation of the economy, leaving the division of the concept to make clear the dichotomy existing between top and bottom. Mao, again, is aware of the problem and, in part, risks all to destroy Liu *et al* because of it.

16. The Great Proletarian Cultural Revolution has undergone a good deal of retrospective romanticization, forgetting that (and this is crucial) Mao could not (and did not) foresee exactly what was going to happen. The Liu-Mao struggle was the product of the first 17 years of Communist rule which increasingly raised problems of the bureaucracy (for example, the red vs. expert problem) and reached a high point during and following the Great Leap Forward debacle which saw Mao's powers considerably decreased. In December 1958 Mao resigned the State Chairmanship, though he retained the chairmanship of the party. "I was extremely discontented with that decision, but I could do nothing about it." Maoists emphasize that the differences between Mao and Liu are significant and that the policies Liu sought to pursue were disastrous. True. The whole affair takes on an air of revolutionary purity when Mao seeks the help of the people to prevent Liu and his revisionists from taking over the bureaucracy. Liu Shao-ch'i, of course, wanted to keep the entire struggle within the party and in the beginning circulated a letter "stressing that these debates should be restricted to the academic level and should not be discussed in public on a political level." Even the mumbo-jumbo about "future generations" essentially amounted to somehow training young cadres to be so pure that even though they may be bureaucrats they won't forget to ditch the bureaucracy when the time comes – even though they'll decide when that time has come. Mao was fighting the increasing bureaucratization of the bureaucracy. He never foresaw the development of a force which was opposed to the bureaucracy itself.

17. When the Mao faction began its public offensive against the solid positions of its adversaries, by putting students and children of regimented schools on the march, it had in no way the immediate purpose of a "cultural" or "civilizing" remolding of the working masses, already pressed as much as possible into the ideological straight jacket of the regime. The nonsense against Beethoven or Ming art, in the same way as the invectives against the positions still occupied by a Chinese bourgeoisie (that was already annihilated as such) were played out only for the amusement of the peanut gallery – not without calculating that this primitive ultra-leftism could find a certain echo among the oppressed who have, after all, reasons to believe that there are still obstacles in their country to the

emergence of a classless society. The principal aim of the operation was to have appeared in the street, at the service of this tendency, the ideology of the regime which is, by definition, Maoist. The adversaries who could really only be Maoist found themselves in a bad light by the start of the quarrel which was why their insufficient "self-criticisms" expressed in fact their resolution to keep the positions they controlled.[11]

18. The streets of Peking were turned into battle-fields overnight by the Red Guards who criticized the work teams in the universities, insulted the leaders of Government and national institutions and dragged out whoever seemed to be a bad element. The bureaucracy, in order to maintain its collective appropriation of society, needs the ideology as much as the administrative and repressive machinery, so the adventure into such a separation was extremely dangerous and quickly came to an end. Soon after a few months of the pseudo-cultural pseudo-revolution, it was the real class struggle which appeared in China. The Red Guards started in August, 1966, and by January, 1967, Liu and four top members of his faction had made self-criticisms at mass, open trials. By this time the struggle had become increasingly violent and the development of the mass organizations formed to struggle against the "handful of capitalist roaders" took on a new role.

19. The nature of the Ultra-Left is very confusing and information fragmentary. Three factors confuse the situation: (1) Mao's position was unclear from the beginning which confused the Ultra-Left; (2) there was an Ultra-Left force which developed at the top, including members of the Cultural Revolution Central Committee; (3) the uneven development of various groups created a confused situation and acted to disunite the Ultra-Left. The Ultra-Left was not a small sectarian group but a large – though non-unified – number of mass organizations which gradually shifted positions. Numbers such as 30-40 million have been bantered about – but it is unclear except to say that these were significant organizations with significant numbers of total members.

20. The goal of the Ultra-Left was clearly stated: "to overthrow the new bourgeoisie and build a new society without bureaucrats similar to the Paris Commune – the Peoples Commune of China." To the official view of the CCP under Mao that "95% of the cadres are good" the Ultra-Left posited the view that "90% of the cadres must step aside." This view was clarified by Sheng Wu-lien, an Ultra-Left organization in Hunan province, to mean that 90% of the cadres are part of a useless bureaucracy which should be eliminated. The question of whether these cadres have correct or incorrect consciousness is irrelevant – the point is that they are bureaucrats. Sheng Wu-lien concludes that they are indeed unnecessary because during the brief period of January 1967 when their power was reduced to nothing the situation was vastly improved.

21. As everybody knows, the greatest fact of the January Revolution was that 90% of the senior cadres were made to stand aside. In Hunan, Chang P'ing-hua, Chang Po-shen, Hua Kuo-feng and the like had their power reduced to zero. At the Center (Peking), power seizures took place in the Ministry of Finance, the Radio Broadcasting Administration Bureau and other departments; and the power of people like Li Hsien-nien, Ch'en Yi, T'an Chen-lin, as well as that of Chou En-lai who represented them, was greatly diminished. Into whose hands did the assets go at that time? They went into the hands of the people, who were full of boundless enthusiasm, and who were organized to take over the urban administrations and the Party: government, financial and cultural powers in industry, commerce, communications, and so forth. What the editorial called for was truly realized, i.e. that "the masses should rise and take hold of the destiny of their socialist

country and themselves administer the cities, industry, communications, and finance."[12]

22. The storm of the January Revolution turned all this within a very short time from the hands of the bureaucrats into the hands of the enthusiastic working class. Society suddenly found, in the absence of bureaucrats, that they could not only go on living, but could live better and develop quicker and with greater freedom. It was not at all like the intimidation of the bureaucrats who, before the revolution, had said: "Without us; production would collapse, and the society would fall into a state of hopeless confusion." As a matter of fact, without the bureaucrats and bureaucratic organs, productivity was greatly liberated. After the Ministry of the Coal Industry fell, production of coal went on as usual. The Ministry of Railways fell, but transportation was carried on as usual. All departments of the provincial Party committees fell, but the various branches of their work went on as usual.[13]

23. Sheng Wu-lien was formed on October 11, 1967 in Hunan province and was a coalition of twenty Red Guard and rebel-worker groups, numbering a total of between two and three million followers. The only three documents (including *Whither China?*) written by the Ultra-Left to reach outside China were produced by this group. Sheng Wu-lien took as its goal the Paris Commune, believing that Mao had laid the basis for the struggle towards this goal. In June, 1966, there was Mao's statement, during the first stage of the GPCR, describing the big character poster at Peking University as "the manifesto of the Peking Peoples Commune of the sixties in the 20th century." In addition, there was the Cultural Revolution's first official document which specifically named the Paris Commune as a model for the new China. Lastly, there was the short-lived "Shanghai Peoples Commune" in January 1967. The goal was Mao's or so it seemed.

24. Chairman Mao stated: "This is one class overthrowing another. This is a great revolution." This shows that the Cultural Revolution is not a revolution of dismissing officials or a movement of dragging out people, nor a purely cultural revolution, but is "a revolution in which one class overthrows another."[14]

25. What is the reality? "Peaceful transition" is only another name of "peaceful evolution." It can only cause China to drift farther and farther away from the "Commune" depicted in the May 7 directive, and nearer and nearer to the existing society of the Soviet Union. What Chairman Mao puts forward, i.e. "revolution in which one class overthrows another" and "a great alliance of proletarian revolutionaries to seize power from the capitalist roaders," solves the question of practical transition toward the commune. The rule of the new bureaucratic bourgeoisie must be overthrown by force in order to solve the problem of political power. Empty shouting about realization of the May 7 directive without any reference to power seizure and complete smashing of the old state machinery, will truly be the "utopian" dream.[15]

26. The "August Revolution" of 1967 saw the creation of another aspect of the Paris Commune which was in line with the analysis of armed struggle: no standing army, the people are armed. Following Chiang Ch'ing (Ms. Mao) who, in July, stated that arms should be used for the defense of the Cultural Revolution, "arms grabbing" became a national pastime creating a "movement" that turned the whole nation into soldiers.

27. To seize the fruits of victory won by the proletariat in August, and turn the mass dictatorship again into bureaucratic rule, the bourgeoisie in the revolutionary committees must first disarm the working class. The guns in the hands of the workers have infinitely strengthened the power of the working class. This fact is a mortal threat to the bourgeoisie, who fear workers holding guns. Out of spontaneous hatred for the

,bureaucrats who tried to snatch the fruit of victory, the revolutionary people shouted a resounding revolutionary slogan: "Giving up our arms amounts to suicide." Moreover, they formed a spontaneous nationwide mass "arms concealment movement" for the armed overthrow of the new bureaucratic bourgeoisie.[16]

28: The August gun-seizing movement was great. It was not only unprecedented in capitalist countries, but also, for the first time in a socialist country, it accomplished the fact of turning the whole nation into soldiers. Before the Culutral Revolution, the bureaucrats did not actually dare to hand over arms to the people. The militia is merely a facade behind which the bureaucrats control the armed strength of the people. It is certainly not an armed force of the working class, but rather a docile tool in the hands of the bureaucrats. In the gun-seizing movement, the masses, instead of receiving arms from the hands of the bureaucrats like favors from above, for the first time seized arms from the hands of the bureaucrats by relying on the violent force of the revolutionary people themselves. For the first time, the workers held their "own" arms. Chairman Mao's inspiring call, "Arm the Left," was the intensive focus of the courage of the working class. But the issuance of the September 5 directive (to return the weapons to the Army) completely nullified the call to "Arm the Left." The working class was disarmed. The bureaucrats again came back to power.[17]

29. The struggle was violent and protracted. The necessity for arms was crucial, so crucial that shipments of arms to Vietnam were stopped and arms stolen in order to fight the army, the PLA, which was used as a stabilizing force – in other words, to combat the Left.

30. It is now seen that the present army is different from the people's army of before the Liberation. Before Liberation, the army and the people fought together to overthrow imperialism, bureaucratic capitalism, and feudalism. The relationship between army and people was like that of fish and water. After Liberation, as the target of revolution changed from imperialism, bureaucratic capitalism and feudalism to capitalist-roaders, and as these capitalist-roaders are power-holders in the army, some of the armed forces in the revolution have not only changed their blood-and-flesh relationship with the people that existed before Liberation, but have even become tools for suppressing the revolution. Therefore, if the first GPCR is to succeed, it is necessary to bring about a basic change in the army.[18]

31. It is now seen that a revolutionary war in the coûntry is necessary before the revolutionary people can overcome the armed Red capitalist class. The large-scale armed struggle in August between the poletariat and the Red capitalist class, and the local revolutionary war, proved this prediction. The experience created by the local revolutionary wars in August is moreover unparalleled in history and very great. Contrary to the expectations of the mass of mediocre people, history advanced in the direction predicted by the "heretics." Hitherto unimaginable, large-scale gun-seizing incidents occurred regularly in accordance with the pace of historical development. Local wars of varying magnitude broke out in the country in which armed forces were directly involved. The creative spirit and revolutionary fervor displayed by the people in August were extremely impressive. Gun-seizing became a "movement." Its magnitude, and the power and heroism of the revolutionary war, were so great that in that moment people were deeply impressed that "the people, and the people alone, are the motive force of historical development."[19]

32. Sheng Wu-lien described themselves as "soviets" fighting for the realization of a "Peoples Commune of China" against the "Kerenskys" in the Revolutionary Committees. Sheng Wu-lien is in agreement with Chiang Ch'ing who splits the history of

Communist China into three negative phases: the "seventeen years" from 1949 to 1966; the "fifty days" of early summer 1966 when Mao was absent from Peking; and the present period (which was since September 1967). Sheng Wu-lien goes one step farther and names the person responsible: it is Chou En-lai, the "chief representative of China's Red capitalist class." Chou En-lai is particularly dangerous because there is "control of the army by the bureaucrats."

33. Other mass organizations throughout the country were also Ultra-Left, but repression was so strong against Sheng Wu-lien that other organizations were hesitant to declare themselves Ultra-Leftist. In actuality, only two organizations, Sheng Wu-lien and the May 16th Corps, were declared by the top-level leaders to be ultra-left counter-revolutionary groups: Sheng Wu-lien because it had published its analysis and the May 16th Corps because it was a top-level Blanquist conspiracy. A large number of other organizations can be ascertained to have been Ultra-Leftist on the basis of their actions but in the confusion of the GPCR a strange series of situations ensued. A typical example would be the April 22 Rebel Grand Army in Kwangsi province which had been engaging in arms grabbing from shipments bound for Vietnam and fighting with the local forces of the bureaucracy. The April 22 group was declared "ultra-leftist" on the local level and its leaders were called to Peking to meet with Chou En-lai and other leaders. It seems that in the confusion only three things were clear: first, Chou En-lai couldn't declare all the Ultra-Left organizations counter-revolutionary because that would unify them and show clearly their strength; second, the April 22 Rebel Grand Army was under the impression that they were supported by Mao; and third, the April 22 group was unsure of its strength and the strength of the Ultra-Left. The result was that after the Peking meeting, the April 22 Rebel Grand Army was absolved of all charges, pacified, and Kwangsi stabilized in favor of the bureaucracy. This scenario was repeated with other mass organizations like the Canton province August 1 Combat Corps and others who in the confusion were partially pacified and then were destroyed.

34. Not to be confused with these mass organizations is the conspiratorial May 16th Corps which operated at the top level of the bureaucracy. A secret organization, the May 16th Corps consisted of high-level CCP intellectuals and bureaucrats. This organization is still shrouded in mystery. Exactly who was involved is unclear. The May 16th Corps centered its activities on the army and Chou En-lai. In part, the May 16th Corps was contrived in order to purge high-ranking leftists and thus absolve the CCP leadership of responsibility for policies which led to ultra-left excesses. The affair resulted in not only the purging of some high-ranking officials, but was left open-ended with the declaration that there might even be top party persons higher than those already exposed who were involved. The future will probably bring the news that Lin Piao was the leader.

35. The May 16th Corps is only important insofar as it affected the bottom level Ultra-Left organizations. The argument of the CCP and Maoists generally is that the May 16th Corps was the prime mover behind *all* Ultra-Leftist organizations and that the members of these organizations were "hoodwinked." The degree of influence, and the connections between the May 16th Corps and other organizations is unclear, but also largely irrelevant. The connection is only important for the "hoodwinked" argument: that somehow 30-40 million people were manipulated and fooled into believing that the bureaucracy should be destroyed in favor of a structure similar to the Paris Commune. The absurdity of that argument lies in its incredible arrogance.

36. The Ultra-Left was ultimately crushed, though underground organizations

exist according to news from refugees in Hong Kong. The Hsia-fang system, sending people to the countryside, was effectively used at the end of the GPCR to separate and decimate the remnants of the Ultra-Left, but their future has not yet been decided.

37. As of today, are these basic contradictions of Chinese society resolved? Has the objective of the first Great Proletarian Cultural Revolution been attained? As stated above, the form of political power has superficially been changed. The old Provincial Party Committee and old Military District Committee have become the "Revolutionary" Committee" or "Revolutionary Committee Preparatory Group." The old bureaucrats continue, however, to play the leading role in the "new political power." The contradiction between the old Provincial Party Committee and old Military District Command on one side, and the people on the other, and the contradiction between the capitalist-roaders of the 47th Army and the people, remain basically unresolved. The contradiction between the new bureaucratic bourgeoisie and the mass of the people is also basically unresolved; it appears in the new form of contradiction between Sheng Wu-lien and the "new political power." All the basic changes which must be carried out by the first GPCR, such as overthrow of the new bureaucratic bourgeoisie, changes in the armed forces and the establishing of the commune, have not been carried out. Of course, such "redistribution of property and power" was partially and temporarily realized during the January Revolution and August Storm. But the fruits of victory of both the January Revolution and August Storm were basically usurped by the Red Bourgeoisie. Social reforms were aborted. Social changes were not consolidated and fully realized. And the "end" of the first Great Proletarian Cultural Revolution was not attained. As the masses have said: "Everything remains the same after so much ado."[20]

This article makes heavy use of *Whither China?*, a document written in early 1968 by an ultra-left group in Hunan province. It has been printed in many places, including *PL Magazine* (Vol. 8, No. 5, August 1972) and *Survey of the China Mainland Press* (no. 4190). Footnotes refer to the *PL Magazine* edition.

1. *Whither China?*, p. 81
2. *Ibid.*, p. 72.
3. *Red Flag*, Nov. 3, 1967, editorial.
4. *Whither China?*, p. 70.
5. *Ibid.*, p. 70.
6. *Shanghai* magazine, *China News Service*, no. 188.
7. Kolakowski, *Towards a Marxist Humanism*.
8. Mustapha Khayati, "The Poor and the Superpoor," *International Situationiste*, No. 11, October 1967.
9. Mao Tse-tung, *Report to the 2nd Plenum of the 7th Central Committee*.
10. Khayati, *op. cit.*
11. International Situationists, *The Explosion Point of Ideology in China*.
12. *Whither China?*, p. 71.
13. *Ibid.*, p. 72. As a matter of fact, coal production and transportation (along with the economy as a whole) suffered greatly during this time. Whether the cause of this suffering was ultra-left anarchism, revisionist sabotage, or the time devoted to political struggle is a matter of dispute.
14. *Ibid.*, p. 71.
15. *Ibid.*, p. 71.
16. *Ibid.*, p. 79.
17. *Ibid.*, p. 79.
18. *Ibid.*, p. 76.
19. *Ibid.*, p. 76.
20. *Ibid.*, p. 84.

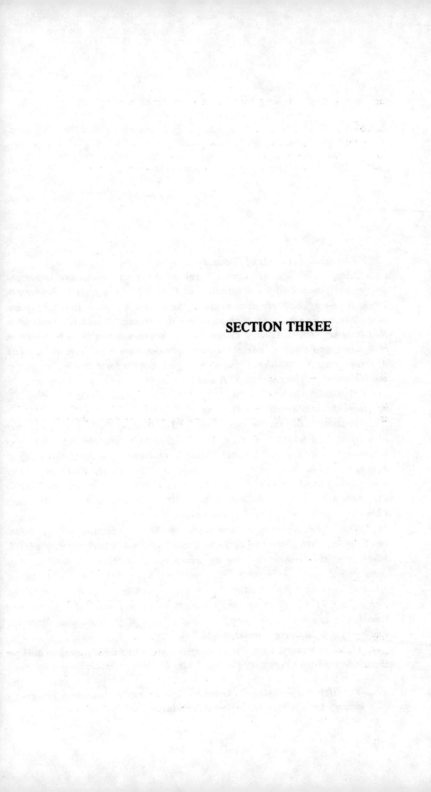

SECTION THREE

This section consists of five essays.

The first is "Whither China?", one of the most famous and important documents produced by the ultra-left in China. The essay, dated January 6, 1968, is one of the three documents of the ultra-left organisation, Sheng-wu-lien. The full name of Sheng-wu-lien is "Hunan Provincial Proletarian Revolutionary Great Alliance Committee." Sheng-wu-lien is literally province, proletariat, and alliance. The other two documents are a program and a group of resolutions. In "Whither China?", Sheng-wu-lien set forth its aims, as well as the methods of their realization. It also named the enemy: Chou En-lai and the other "capitalist roaders" in the Party. However, it seemed that the group still had some illusions about Mao Tse-tung.

In the second essay in this section, "The Dusk of Rationality", a former ultra-leftist Red Guard in Canton, Yu Shuet, further developed the views and sentiments expressed in "Whither China?". Yu Shuet completed this essay in February, 1974, one year after her escape to Hong Kong. There were three others who joined her in the escape. Two were believed to be drowned during the marathon swim in the cold winter. Ms Yu is writing a book on Mao's China.

The third essay is a translation of the introduction of the book, "Revelations that Move the Earth to Tears", which is a collection of poetry, letters, and short stories written by young people of China today. Some of these young people have taken refuge in Hong Kong. Some are still in China. Some of the works published in the book have been smuggled out from China. The author of the introduction, Wu Man, is also a former ultra-leftist Red Guard who swam to Hong Kong in early 1973. "Revelations that Move the Earth to Tears" is being translated into English.

The fourth essay is an interview of Wu Man conducted by the editors of the Undergrad, the paper of the Students' Union of the University of Hong Kong.

The fifth essay is the Li I-che poster which became available in Hongkong only in early 1976. There is a separate introduction to the essay.

WHITHER CHINA?

Note: This draft solicits your opinions on the following questions. Is it appropriate to announce it publicly at present? May it serve as the "Inaugural Declaration of the 'Ultra-Left' Commune?" How should it be further revised? Please write your opinions on the right-hand margin of each page and return this draft to the issuing source before the 20th.

A soldier of the Steel 319 Corps,
"Seize Military Power" of Sheng-wu-lien,
First Middle School, Red Rebel Committee.
January 12, 1968

When the counteroffensive in the struggle against the adverse current reached July, August and September [of 1967], the people of the whole country had a sense of vigorous growth, believing that there was hope of the Great Proletarian Cultural Revolution being "carried through to the end," and that all traditional ideas that fettered the mind of the people would be cast aside. However, an adverse current of counter-revolutionary reformism appeared after October at the upper levels and descended below. An atmosphere of class compromise [in place of class struggle], calling for "an end to the first cultural revolution," suddenly became intense. Again, the people of the whole country were bewildered. The educated youth and students in particular, being extra sensitive, were the first to feel it. Again, questions were asked. What shall we do? Whither China? The establishment of the "Ultra-Left" Commune was for the sake, first of all, of answering this solemn question.

To answer this question correctly, it is necessary earnestly to sum up the very rich experience and lessons brought forth since 1967 by the greatest revolution in history, principally the experience of great significance created by the "January Storm" and the "August partial domestic revolutionary war" [in later sections of this essay, this is usually referred to as the "August Storm"; for convenience, this shorter term will be used in this translation].

(1)   The Scientific Prediction

Contemporary China is the focus of world contradictions, and the center of the storm of world revolution. As regards this crucially important subject of where China is going, the great teacher of the world proletariat, Comrade Mao Tse-tung, has outwardly made only an abstract prediction.

Just before the world-shaking Great Proletarian Cultural Revolution was to rise from the east with the force of a thunderbolt, Chairman Mao, with his great all-embracing proletarian feelings, announced to the world that China's first Marxist big-character poster "is the manifesto of the Peking Peoples Commune in the 1960's" [PR, No. 6 (February 3, 1967), p. 13]. It was these words that announced the official beginning of the vehement development among the masses of the Great Proletarian Cultural Revolution. These words also showed that Chairman Mao "wisely and with genius fore-saw the emergence of a brand-new situation in our state organs" (Red Flag, No. 3, 1967, editorial), that is, political organs of the Paris Commune type. In the January Revolution, Chairman Mao again proposed the name "Peoples Commune of China." That meant that, as an ultimate result of the first Great Cultural Revolution, China would advance in the direction of a "Peoples Commune of China."

However, because the revolution had developed at the time only to a very low level, historical limitations enabled almost no one to understand the ultimate goal of the first Cultural Revolution as pointed out by Chairman Mao. People regarded this statement of Chairman Mao as words of general praise and gradually forgot it.

Even before the Cultural Revolution officially began, Chairman Mao, in his famous May 7 Directive [1966, in PR, No. 32 (August 5, 1966). pp. 6–7: sections in bold type], had already depicted the contents of this new type of political structure—the "Peoples Commune of China." But people in general regarded the sketch in the May 7 Directive as an idealistic "communist utopia." Everyone thought that it was not practical to take the May 7 directive as the immediate goal of our recent struggle. At present it is only part of the educated youth that keep reciting the May 7 Directive, and loudly declare that they want to fight for realization of the May 7 Directive. They realize that only the new society sketched in the May 7 Directive, which is different from the existing society, is the society in which they will gain liberation. But even among the educated youth, there are many who think it impractical to realize in the near future the kind of society described in the May 7 Directive. It is truer to say that their energetic publicity about the May 7 Directive is self-consolation for their dis-satisfaction with reality, than it is to say that they are striving with full faith for the realization of the May 7 Directive.

Chairman Mao's scientific prediction has left a utopian impression in people's minds. This is in accord with the fact that class struggle has not yet developed to an acute and high stage. The development of new productive forces in China today has brought into conflict the class that represents the new productive forces [presumably the proletariat, the representative of which Sheng-wu-lien claims to be] and the decaying class that represents [old] production relations which impede the progress of history. [Probable meaning: the present Red bourgeoisie, which still represents the old (i.e., capitalist) production relations, prevents the proletariat from exercising its self-govern-ment which would correspond to the new (i.e., socialist) production relations.] Moreover, it will lead inevitably to a great social revolution, and a new society will inevitably be born amid the fierce flames. This objective law is the solid basis for

154

Chairman Mao's scientific—not utopian—prediction. At present, people do not yet understand this law. It is natural, therefore, that this scientific prediction has left people with the impression of being purely a utopian dream of the beautiful future? People believe that China will pass peacefully into the society depicted in the May 7 Directive.

What is the reality? "Peaceful transition" is only another name for "peaceful evolution." It can only cause China to drift farther and farther away from the "Commune" depicted in the May 7 Directive, and nearer and nearer to the existing society of the Soviet Union [which Sheng-wu-lien abhors]. What Chairman Mao puts forward, i.e., "revolution in which one class overthrows another" and "a great alliance of proletarian revolutionaries to seize power from the capitalist-roaders," solves the question of practical transition toward the commune. The rule of the new bureaucratic bourgeoisie must be overthrown by force in order to solve the problem of political power. Empty shouting about realization of the May 7 Directive, without any reference to power seizure and complete smashing of the old state machinery, will truly be the "utopian" dream.

(2)   The January Revolutionary Storm

Lenin once made this famous statement: "Any revolution, as long as it is a true revolution, is, in the final analysis, a change of class. Therefore, the best means of heightening the awareness of the masses and exposing the deception of the masses with revolutionary vows, is to analyze the class changes that have taken place or are taking place in the revolution." Let us follow this teaching and make an analysis of the class changes which took place in the January Revolution, so as to expose the deception of the masses with revolutionary promises.

As everybody knows, the greatest fact of the January Revolution was that 90 per cent of the senior cadres [of the Party] were made to stand aside. In Hunan, Chang P'ing-hua, Chang Po-shen, Hua Kuo-feng and the like had their power reduced to zero. At the Center [Peking], power seizure [by representatives of the Cultural Revolution] took place in the Ministry of Finance, the Radio Broadcasting Administration Bureau and other departments; and the power of people like Li Hsien-nien, Ch'en Yi, T'an Chen-lin, as well as that of Chou En-lai who represented them, was greatly diminished. Into whose hands did the assets go at that time? They went into the hands of the people, who were full of boundless enthusiasm, and who were organized to take over the urban administrations and the Party, government, financial and cultural powers in industry, commerce, communications, and so forth. What the editorial had called for was truly realized, i.e., that "the masses should rise and take hold of the destiny of their socialist country and themselves administer the cities, industry, communications, and finance."

The storm of the January Revolution turned all this within a very short time from the hands of the bureaucrats into the hands of the enthusiastic working class. Society suddenly found, in the absence of bureaucrats, that they could not only go on living, but could live better and develop quicker and with greater freedom. It was not at all like the intimidation of the bureaucrats who, before the revolution, had said: "Without us, production would collapse, and the society would fall into a state of hopeless confusion."

As a matter of fact, without the bureaucrats and bureaucratic organs, productivity was greatly liberated. After the Ministry of the Coal Industry fell, production of coal went

155

on as usual. The Ministry of Railways fell, but transportation was carried on as usual. All departments of the provincial Party committees fell, but the various branches of their work went on as usual. Moreover, the working class were greatly liberated in their enthusiasm and initiative for production. The management of industrial plants by the workers themselves after January was impressive. For the first time, the workers had the feeling that "it is not the state which manages us; but we who manage the state." For the first time, they felt that they were producing for themselves. Their enthusiasm had never been so high, and their sense of responsibility as masters of the house had never been so strong. Changsha Weaving and Spinning Mill and other factories also created rebel working-groups and countless other new things. [According to information reaching the outside world from Shanghai, the situation there was far from happy at this time and was reflected in workers' criticisms of changes enforced by the Red Guards.]

This was the true content of the class changes in the January Revolution. As a matter of fact, in this short period some places realized, though not very thoroughly, the content of the "Peoples Commune of China." The Society found itself in a state of "mass dictatorship" similar to that of the Paris Commune. The January Storm told people that China would go toward a society which had no bureaucrats, and that 90 per cent of the senior cadres had already formed a privileged class. The objective law of the development of class struggle caused the majority of them to stand aside in January. The fact that 90 per cent of the senior cadres had to stand aside in the storm of the January Revolution was certainly not an error by the "masses." "The masses are the real heroes." Those who committed the most serious crimes were duly punished: "very few received undue punishment."

Facts as revealed by the masses, and the indignation which they brought forth, first told the people that this class of "Red" capitalists had entirely become a decaying class that hindered the progress of history. The relations between them and the people in general had changed from relations between leaders and the led, to those between rulers and the ruled and between exploiters and the exploited. From the relations between revolutionaries of equal standing, it had become a relationship between oppressors and the oppressed. The special privileges and high salaries of the class of "Red" capitalists were built upon the foundation of oppression and exploitation of the broad masses of the people. In order to realize the "Peoples Commune of China," it was necessary to overthrow this class.

The January Revolutionary Storm was a great attempt by the revolutionary people, under the leadership of Chairman Mao, to topple the old world and build a new world. The program of the first great proletarian political [sic!] revolution was formulated at that great moment. Chairman Mao stated: "This is one class overthrowing another. This is a great revolution." This shows that the Cultural Revolution is not a revolution of dismissing officials or a movement of dragging out people, nor a purely cultural revolution, but is "a revolution in which one class overthrows another." With relation to the facts of the January Revolutionary Storm, the overthrown class is none other than the class of "bureaucratism" formed in China in the last 17 years. . . .

There is no place here for reformism—combining two into one—or peaceful transition. The old state machinery must be utterly smashed. "Completely smash the old exploitative system, the revisionist system, and the bureaucratic organs." . . .

The problems of system, policy, and guideline touched upon in the January Revolution mainly concerned such capitalist systems of labor employment as contracted labor and temporary labor, as well as the revisionist movement of going to the mountainous areas and the countryside.

At present, the "Ultra-Left" must organize people to sum up and to study properly the multitude of things created by the January Revolutionary Storm. These new things are the embryonic form of a new society of the Paris Commune type.

(3) The Revolutionary Committees

Why did Chairman Mao, who strongly advocated the "commune," suddenly oppose the establishment of the "Shanghai Peoples Commune" in January? This is something which the revolutionary people find hard to understand.

Chairman Mao, who foresaw the "commune" as the political structure which must be realized by the first Cultural Revolution, suddenly proposed: "Revolutionary committees are fine!"

Revolution must progress along a zigzag course. It must go through a prolonged course of "struggle–failure–struggle again–failure again–struggle again–until final victory."

Why cannot communes be established immediately?

This is the first time the revolutionary people tried to overthrow their powerful enemy. How shallow their knowledge of this revolution was! Not only did they fail consciously to understand the necessity to completely smash the old state machinery and to overhaul some of the social systems, they also did not even recognize the fact that their enemy formed a class. The revolutionary ranks were dominated by ideas of "revolution to dismiss officials" and "revolution to drag out people." The wisdom of the masses had not yet developed to the degree at which it was possible to reform society. Therefore, in the final analysis, the fruit of the revolution was taken away by the capitalist class [of the China of 1967].

Any revolution must naturally involve the army. Since a Red capitalist class is already formed in China, the army of course cannot detach itself from this reality. Yet the January Storm did not in any way touch on this vital problem of all revolutions–the problem of the army. Thus it may be seen that the [January] Revolution lacked depth and remained at a low stage of development. The degree of maturity of the political thought of the revolutionary people also was in conformity with this low level revolution–it, too, remained at a very immature stage.

At this kind of time when complete victory is impossible, to try to achieve real victory is Left adventurism. In light of the inevitability that the capitalist class will seize the fruits of the revolution, the correct strategic policy is to enable the people to forge their political and ideological weapon in struggle at a higher stage and, through the ebb and flow of the revolution, to prepare their strength for winning the final victory. Otherwise, if "communes" are established while the masses have not yet fully understood that their interest lies in the realization of "communes" in China, the "communes" will be communes in name only, and in reality they will be sham "communes," essentially the same as the present revolutionary committees in which power is usurped by the [Red] bourgeoisie.

Therefore, Comrade Mao Tse-tung, the great supreme commander of the proletariat, did not hesitate in the least to go against the dream, cherished by immature revolutionaries, for the immediate establishment of communes. He adopted the correct strategic policy, and at the same time called upon the army to "Support the Left"

[January 23, 1967]. "Support the Left" is, in fact, Chairman Mao's ingenious means of carrying out cultural revolution in the armed forces. . . .

The three-in-one combination is the concrete content of the Revolutionary Committees. [What is meant is the informal alliance between Army, cadres, and mass organizations which preceded the official formation of Revolutionary Committees.] Proposing the three-in-one combination is tantamount to helping the reinstatement of the bureaucrats already toppled in the January Revolution. Moreover, the three-in-one combination will inevitably be a type of regime for the [Red] bourgeoisie to usurp power, in which the army and local bureaucrats will play a leading role. Chairman Mao also called the revolutionary committee of the three-in-one combination a "provisional organ of power." It is only a transitional form, and not the ultimate product of the first Cultural Revolution. The ultimate product of the first Cultural Revolution will be the "commune" and not the revolutionary committee . . . . However, the aforementioned transitional form is necessary. To deny the transitional form is Leftist empty talk.

(4)   The February Adverse Current

The force and intensity of the January Revolution caused the bureaucrats to carry out a hurried usurpation of power. Contrary to their usual attitude, they adopted the most urgent and savage means of suppression. This proves negatively the intensity of the "redistribution of property (of means of production) and power" resulting when 90 per cent of the senior cadres stood aside in the January Revolution. The tragic consequences of the February Adverse Current also prove the correctness of Comrade Mao Tse-tung's prediction that "there can be no immediate victory."

The "Red" capitalist class gained an almost overwhelming ascendancy in February and March [1967]. The property (of means of production) and power were wrested away from the hands of the revolutionary people and returned to the bureaucrats. In early spring, in February, Lung Shu-chin, Liu Tzu-yun, Chang Po-shen, Hua Kuo-feng, and bureaucrats throughout the country and their agents at the Center, wielded unlimited power. It was their heyday, while the power of the revolutionary people dropped to zero. Moreover, large numbers of revolutionary people were thrown into prison by the state organs—public security, procuracy, and judicial organs—controlled by the capitalist class.

Intoxicated by his victory of February-March, Chou-En-lai—at present the chief representative of China's "Red" capitalist class—hurriedly tried to set up revolutionary committees in all parts of the country. If this bourgeois plan had been achieved, the proletariat would have retreated to its grave. Therefore, without waiting for the establishment of all the revolutionary committees, the Central Cultural Revolution Group [of Chiang Ch'ing, etc.] gave orders at the end of March to launch a counteroffensive. From then on, the great August Storm began to brew.

In the struggle to hit back at the February Adverse Current, the important sign that the revolution had entered into a higher stage was that the problem of the army really began to be touched upon. During the January Revolution, the revolutionary people had very childish ideas on the problem of the army. They thought that as soon as the local capitalist-roaders were overthrown, the armed forces would unite with the revolutionary people in accordance with Chairman Mao's order for union from the upper to the lower levels. The bloody facts of the February Adverse Current made the people aware that the upper-to-lower order alone could not bring about an implementation of Chairman Mao's intentions in the armed forces. The common interests of capitalist-roaders in the armed forces and those of local capitalist-roaders would make it impossible for the army to carry out Chairman Mao's revolutionary line. It was necessary to carry out cultural revolution from the lower level upward in the army, and to rely on the people's revolution—the locomotive of progress in history—in order to change the antagonism between the army and the people brought about by the control of the army by the bureaucrats.

The struggle since February has placed the grave problem of the army before the broad masses (previously it had been discussed only before Chairman Mao and a few others). This is gradually providing the conditions for solution of the problem through the strength of the broad masses of the people. It has been scientifically foreseen that in the new society of the "commune," the military force will be very different from the present-day army. The struggle since February has enabled this idea of Chairman Mao gradually to take hold of the masses.

(5)   The August Local Civil Revolutionary War

Since the end of January [1967], the rebels have written many articles on the problem of the armed forces.... Many articles discussing the problem of the army are very immature and have great shortcomings. These writings, however, constitute a new thing which history will prove to be of significance.

How well Engels spoke when he commented on utopian socialism:"Let the pedlars of the circle of authors solemnly find fault with the imaginations which at present can only make people laugh. Let them gratify themselves with the thought that their strict way of thinking is superior to such mad ideas. What makes us glad is the gifted ideological buds and gifted ideas that show themselves everywhere by breaking through the outer shell of imagination. These things the mediocre people cannot see."

There are two essential points in the articles about the army.

1.   It is now seen that the present army is different from the people's army of before the Liberation [i.e., before 1949]. Before Liberation, the army and the people fought together to overthrow imperialism, bureaucratic capitalism, and feudalism. The relationship between army and people was like that of fish and water [Mao's favourite picture for describing the ideal relationship between guerrillas and the masses]. After Liberation, as the target of revolution has changed from imperialism, bureaucratic capitalism and feudalism to capitalist-roaders, and as these capitalist-roaders are power-holders in the army, some of the armed forces in the revolution have not only changed their blood-and-flesh relationship with the people that existed before Liberation, but have even become tools for suppressing the revolution. Therefore, if the first Great Proletarian Cultural Revolution is to succeed, it is necessary to bring about a basic change in the army. The "Ultra-Left faction" has found the basis for its thinking in *Quotations from Chairman Mao*. Chairman Mao ... has also pointed out that after the troops were kept in barracks, they became separated from the people.

2.   It is now seen that a revolutionary war in the country is necessary before the revolutionary people can overcome the armed Red capitalist class. The large-scale armed struggle in August between the proletariat and the Red capitalist class, and the local revolutionary war, proved this prediction. The experience created by the local revolutionary wars in August is moreover unparalleled in history and very great. Contrary to the expectations of the mass of mediocre people, history advanced in the

direction predicted by the "heretics." Hitherto unimaginable, large-scale gun-seizing incidents occured regularly in accordance with the pace of historical development. Local wars of varying magnitude broke out in the country in which the armed forces were directly involved (in some places, including Kiangsi and Hangchow, the army fought directly). The creative spirit and revolutionary fervor displayed by the people in August were extremely impressive. Gun-seizing became a "movement". Its magnitude, and the power and heroism of the revolutionary war, were so great that in that moment people were deeply impressed that "the people, and the people alone, are the motive force of historical development."

For a short time, the cities were in a state of "armed mass dictatorship." The power in most of the industries, commerce, communications, and urban administration was again taken away from Chang Po-shen, Hua Kuo-feng, Lung Shu-chin, Liu Tzu-yun and their like and put into the hands of the revolutionary people. Never before had the revolutionary people appeared on the stage of history in the role of masters of world history as they did in August. Primary students voluntarily did the work of communications and security. Their brave gestures in directing traffic, and the pride with which "Storm Over Hsiang River," "Red Middle Committee" [See Document 5] and other mass organizations directly exercised some of the financial- economic powers, left an unforgettable impression with the people.

August was the time when the power of the revolutionary mass organizations rapidly grew, while that of the bureaucrats again dropped to zero. For the second time, a temporary and unstable redistribution of property and power took place. Once more, society tried to realize the great "People's Commune of China." Once more, people tried to solve the problem raised in the May 7 Directive, namely, that "the army should be a great school" and "workers, peasants, and students should all study military affairs." This attempt had not been made in the January Revolution. Before Liberation, the army actually was a great school which maintained excellent relations with the masses, and which combined the roles of soldiers, students, civilians, peasants, and workers. This was summed up by Chairman Mao just before the victory of the Democratic Revolution. Why then, more than ten years after Liberation, should the question again be raised of improving army-civilian relations, and "the army should be a great school"? As said in the preceding paragraph, it is because after the Liberation the army has undergone changes and, to greater or lesser degree, has separated itself from the masses. As a result, the question is again put on the agenda.

The great pioneering act of the August Storm was the emergence of an armed force [in addition to the Army] organized by the revolutionary people themselves. This force becomes the actual force of the proletarian dictatorship (or dictatorship over the capitalist-roaders). They and the people are in accord, and fight together to overthrow the "Red" capitalist class. The people, instead of lamenting the fall of the Military Region command—a bureaucratic organ—rejoice at it. Yet formerly they used to think they could not get along without it. This fact has enabled the proletariat to foresee more realistically where China's army is going, and to envisage the armed strength of the new society—the "Peoples Commune of China." It may be said with certainty that China will be a society in which the army is the people, the people are the army, the people and the army are united as one, and the army has shaken off the control of the bureaucrats. . . .

(6) The September Setback

While people were rejoicing, boldly forging ahead, and loudly talking about a "thorough victory," the great teacher of the proletariat saw a new danger on the horizon. Let us look at the content of this new danger!

On the one hand even the "Red" capitalist class, owing to the nakedness of its "February suppression of rebellion," keenly perceived the inevitability of its own defeat. After May, China's "Red" capitalists changed their tactics. In many places there appeared a trend of cadres "making appearances." One after another, Red capitalists like Sung Jen-ch'iung in the Northeast and Chang po-shen in Hunan–bloodsucking vampires who used to ride roughshod over the people–suddenly displayed "fervor" for the revolutionary struggle of the slaves. Individually they declared support for the revolutionary masses in their bombardment of the power-holders in the military region or district commands. As at that time the revolutionary people had not yet tried to overthrow the capitalist-roaders as a class, and as the proletariat and the broad masses of revolutionary people were still under the influence of the doctrine of "revolution through dragging out people" and "revolution by dismissal of officials," people believed that the purpose of the Cultural Revolution was the purging of individual capitalist-roaders and that it was proper to use some of the revolutionary leading cadres (who were also bureaucrats) for attacking other bureaucrats. As a result, this tactic of big and small Chang Po-shens easily deceived the people. This determined the objective inevitability that the [Red] bourgeoisie would wrest the fruits of victory of the August Storm. Meanwhile, owing to the hurried suppression by the bourgeoisie and the immediate counteroffensive by the proletariat after February, dictatorship by the revolutionary committees–a power organ during the transition to the 'Commune'– had not yet begun. There was no [protracted] period of transition in which the "Red" capitalists could fraudulently win the trust of the people and suppress the people. The people therefore could not learn from bloody facts that the capitalist-roaders were a class; and did not accept the program of the first Cultural Revolution–a revolution of one class overthrowing another. Thorough social revolution could not be carried out.

On the other hand, to realize the demand in the May 7 Directive for changes in the army, it was necessary to carry through to the end the Cultural Revolution in the field armies. It was also necessary to cause the field armies to "support the Left." As a matter of fact, without first launching an all-out campaign of "supporting the Left" among the field armies, it would be Leftist adventurism to carry out the Great Proletarian Cultural Revolution among the field armies and try to win an immediate victory.

There was also the problem of the Great Proletarian Cultural Revolution in the rural areas. If no revolutionary storm took place in the countryside, no power-seizure of any kind would represent the true interests of the peasants. The May 7 Directive called for factories to set up and operate farms, and for rural villages to set up and operate workshops. It indicated that in the new commune, the differences between industry and farming, and between urban and rural areas, will be much smaller than at present. This reduction of the gap should be brought about by launching a peasant movement–a locomotive of historical progress–guided by the Thought of Mao Tse-tung. Before the peasant movement is launched, it is empty talk to try to win a complete victory of the first Great Proletarian Cultural Revolution. While complete victory is unrealistic, the task of the Marxists-Leninists is to show the hypocrisy of the clamor for "thorough victory."

161

Should the [Ultra-Left] Marxist-Leninists have power, they should exercise it in banning the cry to "immediately overthrow the revolutionary committee and establish the commune" as well as any agitation for this purpose, so that the splendid name of "commune" may not be tarnished by false practice.

Meanwhile, the capitalist bureaucratic class in the Party and army began to carry out sabotage against the Central Cultural Revolution Group in August and September. They deliberately created confusion in the army, and caused stagnation in economic and other spheres. [As a matter of fact, this "stagnation" was largely brought about by the disorders during the "August Revolution."] A senior army cadre openly and arrogantly assailed the Central Cultural Revolution Group. This was their general policy in August and September. "Does the Central Cultural Revolution Group still want the Peoples Liberation Army? If it doesn't, then we will pack up and go home. The Central Cultural Revolution Group has so shifted the veteran army cadres that they are separated from their wives and children, their homes broken up, and their kin lost!"

In view of this series of developments . . . the wise supreme commander, Comrade Mao Tse-tung, once again disregarded the unrealistic demands of impatient revolutionaries for victory and made a broad retreat after September [1967] . . . The extent of this retreat was unprecedented. The unlimited relaxation of the cadre policy after September was in fact an extensive concession to the capitalist-roaders, who were allowed to remount the stage . . . .

But because the revolutionary forces of the proletariat have been greatly strengthened, the retreat has not ended in a "rout" as it did in February. This time the bourgeoisie has not been able, as in March, to devour the revolution in one gulp. In Hunan, the revolutionary forces bombarding Chou En-lai were not annihilated. On the contrary, they established Sheng-wu-lien and have made progress in certain respects. This is proof that the revolutionary force has grown up and become strong.

To seize the fruits of victory won by the proletariat in August, and turn the mass dictatorship again into bureaucratic rule, the bourgeoisie in the revolutionary committees must first disarm the working class. The guns in the hands of workers have infinitely strengthened the power of the working class. This fact is a mortal threat to the bourgeoisie, who fear workers holding guns. Out of spontaneous hatred for the bureaucrats who tried to snatch the fruit of victory, the revolutionary people shouted a resounding revolutionary slogan: "Giving up our guns amounts to suicide." Moreover, they formed a spontaneous, nationwide mass "arms concealment movement" for the armed overthrow of the new bureaucratic bourgeoisie.

The August gun-seizing movement was great. It was not only unprecedented in capitalist countries, but also, for the first time in a socialist country, it accomplished the fact of turning the whole nation into soldiers. Before the Cultural Revolution, the bureaucrats did not dare actually to hand over arms to the people. The militia is merely a facade behind which the bureaucrats control the armed strength of the people. It is certainly not an armed force of the working class, but rather a docile tool in the hands of the bureaucrats. In the gun-seizing movement, the masses, instead of receiving arms like favors from above, for the first time seized arms from the hands of the bureaucrats by relying on the violent force of the revolutionary people themselves. For the first time, the workers held their "own" arms. Chairman Mao's inspiring call, "Arm the Left" [no such direct statement by Mao has been found], was the intensive focus of the courage of the working class. But the issuance of the September 5 Directive [to return the weapons

162

to the Army] completely nullified the call to "Arm the Left." The working class was disarmed. The bureaucrats again came back to power.

(7) The Political Enlightenment of the Proletariat

The editorial of July 1, 1967 [in PD, taken from RF, No. 11] raised the question of Party building. During the violent class struggle in July and August, a very small number of "Ultra-Leftists" put forward the demand that the "Ultra-Left should have its own political party." It was felt necessary to have the basic level organizations of a revolutionary party in order to realize Comrade Mao Tse-tung's leadership in the Communist Party, to actuate the people to overthrow the new bourgeoisie, and to fulfill the task of the first Cultural Revolution. In this way, the dream of a few intellectuals in Peking in the initial stage of the movement to rebuild a Marxist-Leninist Group became, for the first time, a practical and steadily growing demand of the fighting proletariat: "To make revolution, it is necessary to have a revolutionary party!" [It would seem that the authors of the essay advocate the formation of "Marxist-Leninist" cells at the "basic levels" of the existing Party. The paragraph, however, is not entirely clear.]

During the past several months, the class struggle has entered a higher stage. What sort of stage is it? In this stage, the revolutionary people have already accumulated the rich experience of "redistribution of property and power" on two occasions (the January and August Revolutions). This experience is the program of the first Cultural Revolution, which was produced by the January Revolution, for a great revolution in China in which one class overthrows another. It is to "overthrow the new bourgeoisie and build a new society without bureaucrats similar to the Paris Commune—the Peoples Commune of China." There is also the method, suggested in the August Storm, of gradually bringing about revolutionary changes in the Army and of armed seizure of power.

The reverses and the higher-stage struggle after September [1967] also tell the revolutionary people why neither the January Revolution nor the August Revolution ended in thorough victory; why, after such prolonged struggle, the fruits of victory were snatched away by the bourgeois bureaucrats; why the bourgeoisie was able to recapture the assets and power which they had lost in August; and why the courage and pioneering spirit displayed by the proletariat in the January Revolution and August Storm was almost completely extinguished and submerged. The appearance of a large-scale adverse current tells people that all illusions about bourgeois bureaucrats, and all distrust in the people's own strength, must be completely abandoned; and that the revolution of one class overthrowing another must be carried out.

However, the Revolutionary Committee is a product of the "revolution of dismissing officials." In Hunan, Chang P'ing-hua and Liu Tzu-yun were dismissed from office, but that did not remove the acute antagonism between the new bourgeoisie and the masses of the people. Moreover, a new situation of acute antagonism has emerged between the Revolutionary Committee Preparatory Group and the people, represented by Sheng-wu-lien. A new bourgeois reactionary line, and a new adverse current of capitalist restoration, have again appeared. A complete and stable "distribution of property and power" has not been realized. The revolution of dismissing officials is only bourgeois reformism which, in a zigzag manner, changes the new bureaucratic bourgeois rule prior to the Cultural Revolution into another type of bourgeois rule by bourgeois

163

bureaucrats and a few representatives from several attendant mass organizations. The Revolutionary Committee is a product of bourgeois reformism.

Problems cannot be solved by merely dismissing a few officials. Bourgeois reformism will not work. The result of reformism—the Revolutionary Committee or its Preparatory Group—again brings about a new bourgeois dictatorship, which arouses even more violent opposition from the people. Events in Heilungkiang, Shantung, Shanghai, Kweichow, Hunan, and other places where revolutionary committees or preparatory groups for such committees have been established, have proved, or are proving that China cannot move in the direction of bourgeois reformism through revolutionary committees, because that means capitalist restoration. China can only go in the direction of the thoroughly revolutionary socialism of the "Peoples Commune of China" as proclaimed by the "Peoples Commune of Peking" of the 1960's [see Mao's statement of June 1, 1966, mentioned in Chapter I] The people should be brought to understand this truth and to form their own resolution to carry it out, instead of our determining it for the people. . . .

It is only when all panaceas are proved useless that the revolutionary people will resolve to follow the most painful and most destructive, but also thorough, road of true revolution. The struggle in the transitional period of the revolutionary committees will inevitably disillusion the masses regarding their cherished panacea of bourgeois reformism. . . .

The stage of struggle since last September has been educating the people in this regard about the new phase.

As a result of the practice of struggle having gained rich experience and having . entered a higher stage, the maturity of the political thinking of the revolutionary people of China has also entered a higher stage. A new stream of ideas, reviled by the enemy as the "Ultra-Left thought trend" (i.e., "overthrow the new bureaucratic bourgeoisie," "abolish bureaucratic organs," thoroughly smash the state machinery" and similar truths), wanders among the revolutionary people like a "spectre" before the eyes of the enemy. The political-ideological weapon of the revolutionary people for winning the complete victory in the proletarian socialist [sic!] great revolution has begun to appear in a new form in the "Ultra-Left faction." The Thought of Mao Tse-tung, which is carrying out a new social revolution in China, will gradually cause the masses to awake from all contradictions of the past. The revolutionary people are beginning gradually to understand in practice why revolution is necessary, against whom they make the revolution, and how revolution is to be carried out. Revolutionary struggle begins to change from the stage of spontaneity to that of consciousness, from necessity to freedom.

In the higher stage of the struggle since September, a higher stage of the fiery movement of educated youth has also appeared, as well as a higher struggle by contract workers and temporary workers. This plays a great stimulative effect in this stage of enlightening muddled thinking. . . .

When the revolutionary people enter from blindness into the stage of enlightenment of political thinking, when Mao Tse-tung-ism forms an independent, positive, political current of thought among the masses, and its political influence begins gradually to become a fact, the organization and establishment of basic level organizations of the Chinese Communist Party—a political party of Mao Tse-tung-ism—is put on the agenda by Comrade Mao Tse-tung, the revolutionary teacher of the proletariat. Comrade Mao Tse-tung puts forward the principle of rebuilding the Party and reorganizing the class ranks under new historical conditions, i.e., "The Party organization should be formed of advanced elements of the proletariat. It should be a youthful and vigorous vanguard organization capable of leading the proletariat and the revolutionary masses to wage struggles against the class enemy."

The putting forward of this principle for the building of a revolutionary political party—the Mao Tse-tung-ism party (Chinese Communist Party)—that will lead the people to overthrow today's class enemy—the new Red bourgeoisie—proves that in order to fulfill the first true proletarian socialist revolution, and to build in China the "Commune" delineated in the May 7 Directive, the existing Communist Party of China must undergo revolutionary changes. The convening of the 9th National Congress of the Party is not expected to settle completely the question of whither the Communist Party is going [the Congress convened on April 1, 1969]. The political party that will emerge [in the 9th Party Congress?] in accordance with the provisions promulgated by the present Central Committee for rehabilitation, regulation, and rebuilding of the Party (if such a party can be formed) will necessarily be a party of bourgeois reformism that serves the bourgeois usurpers in the revolutionary committees. The convening of the 9th Party Congress will be only a reflection of local "revolutionary committees" in the Central Committee during the transitional period. This determines the fact that the "9th Congress" can never thoroughly settle the question of whither China is going (the core problem of which is whither the Chinese Communist Party and whither the Peoples Liberation Army).

When a truly stable victory gradually becomes possible, the following several questions will become salient.

1. The unevenness of the revolution will assume prominence. The possibility of first winning true, thorough victory in one or several provinces, overthrowing the product of bourgeois reformism—the rule of revolutionary committees—and reestablishing political power of the Paris Commune type, will become a crucial problem if the revolution is to be able to develop in depth with rapidity. This is unlike the previous period, which was a blind and spontaneous stage in which the unbalanced character of the revolution played a decisive role in the development of the revolution.

2. To truly overthrow the rule of the new aristocracy and completely smash the old state machinery, it will be necessary to go into the question of how to evaluate the past 17 years. This is also a major problem of fundamentally teaching the people why it is necessary to carry out the Cultural Revolution, and what its final objective is.

3. To make the revolution really victorious, it will be necessary to settle the question: "Who are our enemies, who are our friends?" This "paramount question of the revolution" requires that we make a new analysis of China's society, where "a new situation has arisen as a result of great class changes," so as to revise the class standings, rally our friends, and topple our enemies.

This series of new questions was raised by Comrade Chiang Ch'ing in her speech on November 12, 1967 [full text in *CCP Documents*, pp. 596–601]. This speech of Comrade Chiang Ch'ing announced the beginning of a new stage, unparalleled in history, into which the Great Proletarian Cultural Revolution has entered. Though this important speech dealt only with the literary and art circles, "the revolution of literature and art is the vanguard of political revolution." The joyous reviving and burgeoning struggle among Chinese literary and art circles shows the direction which China's revolution will take. Actually, Comrade Chiang Ch'ing's speech tells us that the revolution in the previous period . . . was basically dealing with problems in the Cultural Revolution, and with the problem of the 50 days that shielded the past 17 years. It merely touched upon the charm that protects the bourgeoisie. It tells us that the real revolution, the revolution to negate the past 17 years, has basically not yet begun. . . .

The genesis and development of Hunan's Sheng-wu-lien represents prominently the growth in strength of the proletariat since September. Sheng-wu-lien was in fact born of the experience of the Attack With Words, Defend With Arms Headquarters (run by the people)—a form of dictatorship of the January Revolution. It is a power organ of mass dictatorship of a higher grade than those of January and August. It may be compared to the soviets of the January [and February, 1917] revolution in the Soviet Union [at that time still Russia], when power was usurped by the bourgeoisie. The Provincial Revolutionary Committee Preparatory Group also is comparable to the bourgeois Provisional Government in Russia of that time. The contradiction between Sheng-wu-lien and the Preparatory Group is a new situation in which "power organs of two systems co-exist" as the soviets and the Provisional Government co-existed in the Russia of 1917. However, the actual power is in the hands of the Provincial Revolutionary Committee Preparatory Group—the bourgeois Provisional Government.

Sheng-wu-lien is a newborn sprout comparable to the soviets of 1917. It is an embryo form of a more mature "commune." . . . This correct newborn Red political power of Sheng-wu-lien will certainly mature and gather strength continuously amid big winds and waves.

(8) Refute the Reactionary "Second Revolution Doctrine"

The current answer to the serious question of where China is going, an answer which dominates the ideological field, is the reactionary "doctrine of second revolution." People's minds are greatly confused. Almost unanimously they say: "The first Great Cultural Revolution can do only so much. There is nothing we can do except wait for the second revolution." After the failure of the Great Revolution [1924–1927], the admitted division of the country under the warlords became the rule of "Commanders-in-chief of the Kuomintang Revolutionary Army." To maintain and prop up the rule of Chiang Kai-shek, Ch'en Tu-hsiu's reactionary "second revolution" was opportunely brought forth. [Ch'en was the first leader of the Chinese Communist Party, who was expelled in 1927.] The "doctrine of second revolution" used the superficial change in political power to deceive the people. It declared that imperialism, bureaucratic capitalism, and feudalism had been overthrown, that China's bourgeoisie had gained the political power, that the democratic revolution was accomplished, and that we had only to wait for the [second, i.e.,] socialist revolution. This reactionary trend of thought not only dominated intellectual circles in the country generally, but also enjoyed considerable popularity even within the Communist Party.

However, the task of China's bourgeois democratic revolution as determined by the basic contradictions in Chinese society—the contradiction between imperialism, bureaucratic capitalism, and feudalism on the side, and the broad masses of the people, on the other—was not yet fulfilled. Therefore, despite the prevalence for a time of the seemingly strong second revolution, the more vigorous and intensive development of the anti-imperialist, anti-feudal people's revolution was still governed by an objective law that does not change according to man's wish.

Similarly, the task that has to be accomplished at the "end" of the first Great Cultural Revolution is determined by the social contradictions that led to this revolution. Unless the program of the first Great Cultural Revolution, prescribed by these social contradictions, is carried out, the first Great Cultural Revolution can never be brought to an end.

As said in the preceding paragraphs, the basic social contradictions that gave rise to the Great Proletarian Cultural Revolution are contradictions between the rule of the new bureaucratic bourgeoisie and the mass of the people. The growth and intensification of these contradictions determine the need for more thorough changes in the society. This means overthrow of the rule of the new bureaucratic bourgeoisie, complete smashing of the old state machinery, realization of social revolution, carrying out the redistribution of property and power, and the establishment of a new society—the "Peoples Commune of China." This is the basic program and final goal of the first Great Cultural Revolution.

As of today, are these basic contradictions of Chinese society resolved? Has the objective of the first Great Cultural Revolution been attained?

As stated above, the form of political power has superficially been changed. The old Provincial Party Committee and old Military District Command have become the "Revolutionary Committee" or "Revolutionary Committee Preparatory Group." The old bureaucrats continue, however, to play the leading role in the "new political power." The contradiction between the old Provincial Party Committee and old Military District Command on the side, and the people on the other, and the contradiction between the capitalist-roaders of the 47th Army and the people, remain basically unresolved. The contradiction between the new bureaucratic bourgeoisie and the mass of the people is also basically unresolved; it appears in the new form of contradiction between Sheng-wu-lien and the "new political power" [i.e., the Preparatory Group]. All the basic social changes which must be carried out by the first Great Cultural Revolution, such as overthrow of the new bureaucratic bourgeoisie, changes in the armed forces, and the establishing of communes, have not been carried out. Of course, such "redistribution of property and power" was partially and temporarily realized during the January Revolution and August Storm. But the fruits of victory of both the January Revolution and August Storm were basically usurped by the [Red] bourgeoisie. Social reforms were aborted. Social changes were not consolidated and fully realized. And the "end" of the first Great Cultural Revolution was not attained. As the masses have said: "Everything remains the same after so much ado."

Since the basic social contradictions that led to the eruption of the first Great Cultural Revolution have not been resolved but but are becoming more and more acute in new forms, the Great Proletarian Cultural Revolution is developing more intensively and vigorously, in spite of the seemingly powerful reactionary "second revolution doctrine" which dominates intellectual circles and deceives the masses with a superficial change in the form of political power. This development of the Cultural Revolution is in accordance with objective law and independent of the wishes of men. The usurping [Red] bourgeoisie hope to corrode the resistance of the revolutionary people with the doctrine of second revolution. But whoever supports their rule and sinister scheme will certainly go bankrupt, just as Ch'en Tu-hsiu's "doctrine of second revolution" was unable to save the Chiang family dynasty, and as the powerful controls of religious thought failed to stop the disintegration and collapse of the economic basis of feudalism. The new trend of thought (the Ultra-Left trend of thought) is still weak and somewhat immature. But its overcoming of apparently powerful traditional ideas, and the rotten, mummified doctrine of second revolution, will be the inevitable trend of historical development.

The bourgeoisie [in general] always describe the political form of their rule as most perfect and flawless in the service of the whole people. The new bureaucratic bourgeoisie, and the Rightist pig-dogs of the petty bourgeoisie who depend on them, are at present doing [in China] exactly that. They ignore the provisional character of the "Revolutionary Committee" while praising it nauseatingly. Marxist-Leninists must relectlessly expose the suppression of the revolutionary people by the Revolutionary Committee, must energetically declare that the Peoples Commune of China is the society which we proletarian and revolutionary people must bring about in the Cultural Revolution, and must energetically make known the inevitable doom of the Revolutionary Committee. . . .

Some people criticize us for wanting to reach communism in one step by immediately eliminating classes and the three major differences. They say that a regime of the Paris Commune type, as envisaged by Chairman Mao, is a dream; and that all this is unrealistic before the realization of communism. These people deliberately distort our views. We certainly do not wish to do away immediately with classes, with the legal rights of the [remaining] bourgeoisie, or the three major differences. This is indeed impossible before realization of communism. They are taken only as our highest program, not our lowest. Our minimum program calls for the overthrow of the rule of the bureaucratic bourgeoisie and the narrowing of the three major differences. It is of course not [yet] possible to destroy the exploiting classes. After the victory of the first Great Proletarian Cultural Revolution, there will inevitably be new class changes. It is these new class changes that will again lead to new social reform, and so push history forward. . . .

People who criticize us in this way actually are saying that all our efforts will be in vain, that society cannot take a new leap, and that property and power cannot be "redistributed" but can only be somewhat altered. Forgetful gentlemen! The January Revolution and the August Storm already did bring about (although only temporarily and locally) a "redistribution of property and power" and a qualitative leap of the whole society. Has that not already shattered the gloomy liquidationist views you spread?

Cadres of the proletariat have not yet matured politically, and the revolutionary people have not yet produced cadres with true proletarian authority. Hence, we are almost unanimously condemned by people saying that we have no use for cadres and want to make them all stand aside. . . .

We really believe that 90 per cent of the senior cadres should stand aside; and that at best they can only be subjects for education and uniting. This is because they have already come to form a decaying class with its own particular "interests." Their relation with the people has changed from that, in the past, between leaders and the led to that between exploiters and the exploited, between oppressors and the oppressed. Most of them, consciously or unconciously, yearn for the capitalist road, and cherish and nurture capitalist things. Rule by their class has completely blocked the development of history.

Is it possible, instead of overthrowing this class, that they can be persuaded to give up the vested interests derived from their bourgeois legal rights, such as high salaries, and follow the socialist instead of the capitalist road? The proletariat truly has made steady efforts in that direction. Chairman Mao's extensive concessions to the bourgeoisie are the pure expression of these efforts. However, the bureaucrats have once again launched a counterattack, and reverse accounts with increasing frenzy, pushing themselves closer and closer to the guillotine. All this proves that no decaying class has ever been willing voluntarily to exit from the stage of history.

In the new society of the Paris Commune type, this class will be overthrown. This was demonstrated by the iron-clad facts, so surprising to mediocre people, of the great changes in the January Revolution and the August Storm. Those who will rise and take their place will be cadres with true proletarian authority who will be produced naturally by the revolutionary people in the struggle to overthrow this decaying class [of the Red bureaucrats]. These cadres will be members of the commune. They will have no special privileges. Economically, they will receive the same treatment as the masses in general. They may be dismissed or replaced at any time at the request of the masses. Such new cadres with [true] authority have not yet emerged.

However, such cadres will be produced spontaneously as the political thinking of the revolutionary people grows in maturity. This is a natural result of the political ideological maturity of the proletariat.

(9)　Refute the "Leftist" Doctrine of One Revolution

Some infantile revolutionaries of the revolutionary ranks suggest that there is no first or second Cultural Revolution; and that the revolution should proceed until communism is realized. This is the "Leftist" doctrine of one revolution. People who hold this idea are very few in number and they have a low political level. Chairman Mao's theory that the transitional period will be divided into different historical stages is the best enlightenment for them. The revolution must necessarily be in stages. We are for permanent revolution, and also for revolution by stages. . . .

Where China goes also determines where the world goes. China will inevitably go toward the new society of the "Peoples Commune of China."

If dictatorship by the Revolutionary Committee is taken as the final goal of the first Great Cultural Revolution, then China will inevitably go the way already taken by the Soviet Union, and the people will again be returned to the bloody fascist rule of capitalism. The Revolutionary Committee's road of bourgeois reformism is a dead-end.

This is because the present is the age of the great banner of Mao Tse-tung-ism; a great age in which imperialism is going downhill toward its debacle, while socialism goes uphill toward world victory. Today's world is one in which capitalism is definitely dying, and socialism is definitely flourishing. In this great revolutionary period of unprecedented significance, in this era of rapid changes, "miracles—at present not yet thought of but completely conformable to the law of historical development—are bound to happen in the history of mankind." (Ch'en Po-ta, March 24)

Both the victory of the Chinese proletariat and the broad masses of revolutionary people, and the extermination of the new bureaucratic bourgeoisie, are likewise inevitable. The world-shaking great festival of the revolutionary people—the overthrow of the Revolutionary Committee and birth of the "Peoples Commune of China"—will surely come.

The commune of the "Ultra-Left faction" does not conceal its views and intentions. We publicly declare that our objective of establishing the "Peoples Commune of China" can only be achieved by forceful overthrow of the bourgeois dictatorship and the revisionist system of the Revolutionary Committee. Let the new bureaucratic bourgeoisie tremble before the true socialist revolution that shakes the world! What the proletariat can lose in this revolution is only their chains, what they gain will be the whole world!

The China of tomorrow will be the world of the "Commune."

Long live Mao Tse-tung-ism!

THE DUSK OF RATIONALITY

YU SHUET

1). The New Current

There are two distinct currents in the world today.

The "religious socialism" of the orient carries the stagnant muddy water of "selflessness" and "authoritarianism" to joining up with the stream of the "modern society" of the occident. This is a force of life negation.

The other new-born current is that of socialism. We have witnessed the "Sheng-wu-lien" in China and the "May Revolution" in France . . . . . .

Organisation of advanced elements of the masses appear and they reject all the "parties" and "sects" which seek to monopolise revolution. Men have been forced to accept the life-style of existing society, to be kept in a general state of alienation and emptiness as a result of being dominated by material things. Man is alienated from production; alienated from the goods that he has produced; alienated from his own self and alienated from other men. Men seek to relate to the world either through the power to dominate or through passivity or subservience. Now the masses have risen and sought to establish a new relatedness to the world in which man will truly be man, and this new relatedness is achieved through the spontaneity and creativity of love. In the new relatedness, man rediscovers his own existence.

To recognise and assert the value of the self: this is the coming revolution.

The materialistic civilization of capitalism will inevitably result in the elevation of the level of the culture of society as a whole. Before this, the cultural level of the exploited class was low; the oppressed were incapable of being conscious of their own existence. History has perpetuated this contradiction: the exploited class is the fundamental agent of social change. Yet this is the class which is most backward culturally. The class cannot grasp the process of social change to turn it into a revolution for itself. Scarcity has chained the development of human history. All history hitherto is but the history of economic changes, the history of one exploitative relationship substituting for another and the history of the sacrifices of the oppressed in this process of substitution.

The contradiction between the new social consciousness of the value of the individual and the law of value in capitalist society has become more and more intense and irreconcilable. This contradiction lies below the volcano within the capitalist structure.

171

Capital has been utilising its own expansion to soften the contradiction between socialisation of production and private ownership but the expansion of capital, in whatever form, will be unable to save the capitalist economic system from destruction. The more capital expands, the more complete is the deprivation of the value of the individual. A human revolution to destroy capital will soon come.

The socialist revolution, (a revolution that destroys capital, that restores man to his true self, that changes the relationship between man and things from that of man being dominated by things to man controlling things), has shown itself for the first time in the disturbances of the automated era.

All kinds of grandiose "religious socialism" will disappear in this new born socialist revolution.

2). A Critique of Theory:

Looking from an ideological standpoint, one witnesses the sunset of rationalism. The age has surpassed the old revolutions and the ideas of our age will have to go through a new revolutionary critique.

As an ideal of mankind, socialism is the crystallization of human development. Historically, many great thinkers have considered socialist ideas as eternally rational, motivating them to seek the establishment of a rational country and a rational society. However when some of them sought to utilise collective strength to turn socialist ideals into reality, inevitably they have distorted and ultimately betrayed socialism. The poverty of mankind has turned utopian experimentation with socialism into a history of tragedies and the leaders of socialism into leaders of these tragedies.

The Marxist-Leninist socialist movement has experienced the same fate.

Marxist philosophy has not been able to separate itself from the rationalist structure of traditional philosophy. In rationalist philosophy, man had been assigned a very insignificant role and was just a "rational animal". This coincided with the reduction of man to the slave of material forces in the economic history of exploitative societies.

In so far as dialectics is concerned, it is sound only when it is considered as a method of thinking in order to comprehend the world. Yet Marxist philosophy has made dialectics the internal law of nature, society and history. It substitutes argumentative logic for the laws of the world. This is in fact the philosophical foundation of an authoritarian dictatorial society.

In so far as freedom is concerned, Marxist philosophy asserts that "freedom is the understanding of necessity".

What is "necessity"? Necessity to history is a law, to reality is a religion, and to the future, an abstraction.

The society in which man lives will always be longer than individual existence. Man's response to society is usually adaptation and not transformation. Where the character structure of man is dominated and repressed by external forces, the "theory of necessity" is the spiritual factor leading to the formation of the slave psychology.

It is not difficult to understand that the Marxist-Leninist movement guided by "the theory of necessity" is a "rationalist movement". The ends guide and control this movement, which seeks to guide and control human behaviour. This is a movement of the negation of life. The internal reasonableness of life and the world is that there can only be "evolving aims" and there can be no "evolution with predetermined aims."

Freedom as defined in the statement "freedom is necessity", is actually the fear of freedom.

"Freedom is a characteristic of human existence." (E. Fromm) This is a revolution in philosophy.

Human philosophy is what signifies the rise of socialist consciousness.

Inherent in human thought is a rich imaginative and reasoning power. Man's search for life surpasses the limitations of time and space. The development of human thoughts reaches a level much higher than the social economy and social consciousness of an era. However, in the historical context, the cultural level of the exploited class is low and only a few thinkers represent the advances of human thought.

Revolutions in the past yielded results contradictory to beliefs. In the past, the leadership of revolutions ignored the value of the individual in their negation of the old society. When they had attained social power and were elevated to the role of the ruling class, they used all their might to consolidate the social structure and repressed at all cost the value of the individual. During and after the revolution, the masses were agitated by temporary benefits or wishful thinking.

On the one hand is the sublimation of human thoughts. On the other hand is the deprecation of the value of the individual in economic and social changes. The development of human thoughts then runs into direct contradiction to social practice in human society in connection with the consolidation of the value of the individual. To this day, human history has not been able to liberate itself from this negation.

Marxist socialism does include elements of humanism. Marx pointed out that socialist revolution is the destruction of classes. He also elaborated on the labour theory of value. Here Marx propounded a new concept of value – and that is to restore the value of the self. Marx was the first to look for humanism through social economic movements. Prior to Marx, humanism and socialism had been limited to utopian speculation.

However the political practice of Marxism, especially the social movements based on Leninism, has been contemptuous towards the instincts of life and the value of the individual. Therefore it is a struggle between old values and traditional morality in a cage.

The theoretical foundation which guides the political movements of Marxism-Leninism is the theory of classes and class struggle.

From an historical point of view, the society of the slave system was polarised into two contradictory classes, the slaves and the slave-owners. The upheavals of the slaves were the main force of the class struggle. However, taking advantage of the class struggle and attaining ruling power for itself, was the rising class of feudal landlords. In the feudalist society, society was divided into the contradictory classes of the peasants and the landlords. Peasant movements and wars were the main force of class struggle but the rising capitalist class won ruling power from the class struggle. In modern days, capitalist society consists of two contradictory classes. The workers' movement is the main force of the class struggle. Benefitting from the class struggle and attaining political power as a result of the struggle is the new rising party – never has it happened before that the party has become the ruling class itself and stands above society. The proletariat has not attained its own liberation through the class struggle.

In the last analysis, the theory of classes and class struggle is in the realm of knowledge within the history of an exploitative society.

The theory of classes is based on a narrow materialistic perspective. It has solidified the alienation of man. And we must ask, "Can the socialist revolution be guided by this narrow theory of classes?"

In political practice, Marx has degraded the theory of socialism into a theory of classes and substituted the narrow materialistic interests of one class for the noble values of humanism. Because of this, we have seen that Marx's predictions about socialism have not eventuated.

The theory of increasing poverty of the proletariat does not correspond to reality. In countries like Soviet Russia, the workers' movements have been manipulated for the cause of totalitarianism and such historical facts have hinted that only when the proletariat has broken the constraint of economic poverty and cultural backwardness would it attain the necessary preconditions to become a revolutionary force of socialism.

Marx believed that the contradictions between socialisation of production and private ownership would lead to the destruction of productive forces and that this would be the economic dynamic of the inevitable socialist revolution. Here again Marx's predictions have not been realised.

The ability of modern capital to expand has surprisingly shown the adaptability of the capitalist mode of production. Capital has progressively abandoned the earlier form of free competition and the contradictions between socialisation of production and private ownership have been muffled by monopolistic capital and state capital. It has become more and more obvious that the death agony of the capitalist mode of production hinges on capital and the reification of man. The destruction of productive forces would only lead to dubious class resistance.

Marx defined the mission of socialism in the "Communist Manifesto": The theory of the Communists may be summed up in the single sentence: Abolition of private property.

"The abolition of private property" undoubtedly in Marx's time was an epochal battle cry. Now, it represents the narrowness of materialism. Capitalistic private ownership is only one form of property ownership under the capitalist mode of production. It is not the essence of the capitalist mode of production. The essence of the capitalist mode of production is the accumulation of capital itself in the process of exploitation of labour. We would rather say, to sum up socialist revolution in one sentence, "the destruction of capital."

The doctrine of the dictatorship of the proletariat is a hypothesis on socialist revolutionary tactics in Marxism.

Political rule by the proletariat undoubtedly appeals to the proletariat. However it is understood that the so called class rule or class dictatorship can only be realised if the special property rights of the ruling class are firmly protected. The proletariat does not have special property rights of its own class and therefore there needs to be no class rule or dictatorship of the proletariat. The process of the expropriation of the capital of the capitalists should be a revolution of mankind. If in the process of expropriating the capitalists, a dictatorship of the party is established with this party dictatorship monopolising capital then no matter how thoroughly has private capital been expropriated, this dictatorship or political rule will invariably still rule and oppress the proletariat and the masses.

Lenin's "theory of the socialist state" inherits Marx's theories of "destruction of private ownership" and "the dictatorship of the proletariat." But in Soviet Russia and similar countries which have been set up according to the principles of Leninism, what we find is totalitarian rule of the party.

In the Communist Manifesto, what Marx proposed as the policies for the exercise of the dictatorship of the proletariat for the most advanced countries are in the nature of furthering and maintaining state capital and state rule. Such policies do not guarantee the destruction of classes, the destruction of capital or the liberation of man.

174

Such policies are as follows:

1) Abolition of property in land and application of all rents of land to public purposes.

2) A heavy progressive or graduated income tax.

3) Abolition of all right of inheritance.

4) Confiscation of the property of all emigrants and rebels.

5) Centralization of credit in the hands of the State, by means of a national bank with State capital and an exclusive monopoly.

6) Centralization of the means of communication and transport in the hands of the State.

7) Extension of factories and instruments of production owned by the State; the bringing into cultivation of wastelands, and the improvement of the soil generally in accordance with a common plan.

8) Equal liability of all to labour. Establishment of industrial armies, especially for agriculture.

9) Combination of agriculture with manufacturing industries; gradual abolition of the distinction between town and country, by a more equal distribution of the population over the country.

10) Free education for all children in public schools. Abolition of children's factory labour in its present form. Combination of education with industrial production, & c., & c.

The policies mentioned above do not include any which really shake the foundation of the capitalist mode of production. From such policies, we can not discover the seed of socialist mode of production.

After the Paris Commune uprising, Marx injected a new content into proletarian dictatorship:

Firstly, all old state bureaucrats would be rooted out. There would be popular elections and the elected officials would be subject to recall, in order that the employees of the government would be the true servants of the people.

Secondly, the regular army was to be abolished and replaced by the people's militia.

Thirdly, people's management was to be introduced.

The principles of proletarian dictatorship derived from the experiences of the Paris Commune are undoubtedly closer to the spirit of socialism. With the three principles: elimination of bureaucrats, abolition of the regular army and the implementation of people's management, class dictatorship is no longer implied. To this day, no country which calls itself a dictatorship of the proletariat can adhere to these three principles.

Undoubtedly, socialist revolution demands drastic and strong measures. But such measures should evolve from the domain of socialist experiences and from the life of human activities. They should not be the dogmas of any party.

Necessity only presents abstractions for the future. In so far as socialist revolution is concerned, necessity only recognises that the ultimate role of socialist revolution is the destruction of capital, and that is the abolition of the law of value. But people may consider the above to be anti-working class.

Most people however could not accept such critiques of the theory of classes.

Undoubtedly, the worker's movements for economic gains result in the theories of class polarisation and class struggle being in line with the activities of the workers and their psychological conditions. For this reason, Marxism has managed to become the leading force of workers' movements. But people are unaware that the psychology which the theory of classes represents is counter-revolutionary. The theory of classes is not a theory for the liberation of the proletariat.

Workers' struggles are social realities. All struggles in opposition to oppression are naturally right and just. What we oppose is the fact that workers' struggles are being used by parties. The people in the lower strata have always been the worshippers and victims of religions and this is the tragedy of human kind. We earnestly look forward to the time of the arrival of the great self-consciousness of the masses.

The workers' movement is not an inherent part of the socialist revolution; not until the workers converge into unity as a result of the demands on them made by the ruling class, not until they do not have to protect any special class interests apart from opposing the ruling class, and in other words, not until they demand the destruction of capital will the workers' movement be integrated into the socialist revolution.

From the very beginning, the socialist revolution is necessarily a revolution of mankind.

3). The Emergence of Totalitarian State Capital

The expansion of the capitalist mode of production has passed through three different forms, viz., free competitive capital, monopoly capital and state capital.

State capital is the last stage of the capitalist mode of production before it abandons itself. The characteristic of production relations at this stage is that the capital of the important sectors of society is state-owned. Nationalisation of capital is a means to resolve the contradiction between socialisation of production and private ownership. Its emergence corresponds to the automation of national economic life.

In the context of modern capitalist economy, the economic structure of a country may be a mixture of capital in various forms.

The first type consists of some emerging nationalist countries which are at the stage of free competitive capitalism.

The second type consists of those developed capitalist countries, the characteristics of the economic structure of which are the co-existence of free capital, monopolistic capital and state capital. The nationalisation of capital has come about through the internal self-negation of capital step by step. State capital continues to increase its significance as the expansion of automation occurs in the national economy.

The third type consists of the economic structures found in the USSR, China and other similar countries. In these countries, a party has made use of proletarian uprisings or civil war to realise nationalisation of capital. The supreme authority of the party controls and directs state capital. The private ownership of the means of production is eliminated by law. In place is state monopoly. Profit, prices and wages all come under the control of the state.

Because of economic backwardness, in such countries, large numbers of collectives and a small number of free trading entities are found.

The totalitarian state economy of USSR and China belongs to the domain of capitalist economy. From the beginning, state totalitarian economy has never been an independent mode of production. It could have evolved from practically any kind of mode of production, eg. the Caesarism in slave society, the centralised dictatorship of Shi Huang Ti in feudal China, the Bonapartism of the internal crisis of capitalism. All such state totalitarian economies have not modified the essence of the mode of production from which they are derived.

State totalitarian economies are usually the outcome of internal strife in society, crisis in reformation, violence and terror. It is a reaction of the totalitarian spirit to economic order. Historically, it helps to terminate socio-economic confusion and this is the reason for it having the power to unify temporarily. But in the last analysis, it represents a reactionary move against humanity.

The state totalitarian economies of the Russian and Chinese type have been generated in historical circumstances in which the contradictions in the world capitalism system were becoming obvious and where the political system in the countries concerned was going through crisis.

At the time of the "October Revolution", capitalism in the west was approaching the form of monopolistic capital. The capitalist class became aware of the contradiction between socialisation of production and private ownership. And capital began to take the form of monopolistic ownership and state ownership in an endeavour to dampen the economic crisis generated by such contradictions.

On the one hand, the process of competition in capitalism has begun to dispossess individual capitalists. The ruling party which has attained political power will of course not be dependent on the capitalists, nor will it seek to protect the interests of the capitalists. On the other hand the preconditions for implementing a socialist mode of production have not yet been fulfilled. The ruling party has destroyed the individual capitalists and yet it is unable to set up a socialist society which eliminates capital. As a result, class rule becomes highly concentrated. The ruling party itself becomes the ruling class and is above the masses.

It is inevitable for a Leninist party which attains political power in a country through the revolutionary strength of workers and peasants to follow totalitarian state capitalism.

The nature of the economy of the USSR and similar countries has been a very controversial subject. The ruling parties of these countries have declared that theirs is a socialistic economy.

Continued state ownership has been equated with socialism. The Stalinists have taken such views. The Trotskyists who have intense hatred for the Stalinists see eye to eye with the latter on this point.

"The Principles of Communism" (Engels, Oct. 1847) and the "Communist Manifesto" (Marx & Engels Dec, 1847) propounded policies related to nationalisation and state ownership which were mistaken as stepping stones to socialism. Later, Engels made a very good correction. Here we may conveniently quote a paragraph from "Anti-Duhring":

"But the transformation, either into joint-stock companies [and trusts], or into state ownership, does not do away with the capitalistic nature of the productive forces. In the joint-stock companies [and trusts] this is obvious. And the modern state, again, is only the organisation that bourgeois society takes on in order to support the general external conditions of the capitalist mode of production against the encroachments as well of the workers as of individual capitalists. The modern state, no matter what its form, is essentially a capitalist machine, the state of the capitalists, the ideal personification of the total national capital. The more it proceeds to the taking over the productive forces, the more does it actually become the national capitalist, the more citizens does it exploit. The workers remain wage-workers – proletarians. The capitalist relation is not done away with. It is rather brought to a head."

Stalin, Trotsky and their fellow travellers all claimed that the expropriation of the capitalists is the overthrow of capitalism.

However in modern capitalist society, the capitalists themselves are expropriated by capital.

As we judge the nature of the economy of a country, we do not judge by the criterion of who owns the productive forces. We judge by the nature of its mode of production.

What is the essence of the capitalist mode of production? It is not the existence of individual capitalists. It is not the form of private ownership. It is the accumulation of capital and the accumulation of capital is realised through the law of value and the law of profit.

What then is the economy of countries like Russia?

The economy of countries like Russia is governed by capital.

Capital is the production relations of capitalist society. Exchange value becomes capital because, "by maintaining and multiplying itself as an independent social power, that is, as the power of a portion of society, by means of its exchange for direct, living labour power. The existence of a class which possesses nothing but its capacity to labour is a necessary prerequisite of capital." [Wage Labour and Capital: MARX]

In a few words, capital is built on the law of value of labour power.

In countries like the USSR, proletariat have become larger and larger in member. The members of the proletariat represent living labour. And this living labour is a means for state monopolistic capital to accumulate. The proletariat have nothing but their ability to work.

It is therefore not difficult to understand that in these self-proclaimed "socialist" countries, the wage system of capitalist societies has been inherited. The wage system is in essence a manifestation of the law of value. And the law of value is the foundation of the operation of the capitalist mode of production.

In national economies like that of USSR, the so called wages are the same as the wages in capitalist society. They are the value of the labour power and not the value produced by the worker. The workers' wages are average living costs of the workers in money terms. Here the exploitation of the proletariat by state capital has gone unnoticed because of the form in which the wages are paid. Wages have confused the distinction between necessary labour and surplus labour, and generated the false impression of "from each according to his ability" and "to each according to his work".

The only difference between the wage system in Russian style and that of the traditional system in capitalism is that it may be affected by social and economic fluctuations under capitalism. Under the Russian system, the wage system is strictly planned and regulated. But this distinction cannot separate the Russian wage system from the domain of capitalism. On the contrary, this only indicates that the exploitation of labour under Russian state capital is unlimited.

On the other hand, in the national economies like that of USSR the national economic plan is based on the maximization of profits. The personal search for profits in traditional capitalism is necessarily restricted by social competition. But in countries like Russia, the rate of profit is determined by the small handful of leaders of the ruling clique. The control of the rate of profit by the state has become the greatest and cruellest search for profits. State capital exploits the workers most nakedly and endlessly. The low wages, the rationing of consumer goods and the preference for industry and discrimation against agriculture (which is a cruel exploitation of the peasants) are indications of exploitation by state capital, in the USSR, China and similar countries. Such squeezing of necessary labour to increase surplus labour by force for high rates of profit cannot be achieved in any traditional capitalist societies.

In the USSR, China and similar countries, capital has not been destroyed. Capital has simply been artificially brought to a stage of monopoly by the state. And this is totalitarian state capitalism.

Stalin and the Stalinist rulers wished to equate the state ownership of the means of production with ownership by the whole people in order to cover up the exploitation of the working people by state capital.

However ownership by the whole people is more than constitutional recognition. Ownership by the whole people is fundamentally different from all kinds of private ownership, oligarchic monopolistic ownership or state monopolistic ownership in the past. The latter forms manifested themselves in concrete possession and domination. Ownership by the whole people eliminates all concrete possession or domination. Ownership of the means of production by the whole people could only be realised after total changes in the old modes of production.

Such changes include:

1) Elimination of the traditional division of labour. This division of labour has in the past turned workers into the slaves of the means of production.

In USSR, China and similar countries, the old division of labour — division of industry and agriculture, division of mental and physical labour, division of managers and producers and division of production departments — has not been abolished. In fact, through the exercise of state power, such divisions are consolidated. The rulers of the state become the controllers of all the means of production and the workers are but slaves of the means of production. Worse than traditional capitalism, in these countries, the workers have even been deprived of their right to choose their means of production. Workers in their whole lives become certain "economically mutated species" of some special deformed development.

2) Elimination of money, commodities and exchange-value of commodities.

Under the capitalist system, the contradiction between the exchange value of a commodity and its use value is the materialisation of the contradiction between labour and labour power. It is the law of value that has made the workers the slaves of the products.

In USSR, China and similar countries, all fruits of production belong to the state. The price mechanism of traditional capitalism has been substituted by a state controlled price system. But still, the products are regarded as commodity exchange value and the use of money a further manifestation of state capital.

Money, commodities and commodity exchange value are still kept with their functions. Only the running dogs of the totalitarian capitalist can smell socialist fragrance in state ownership of the means of production.

3) Abolition of the wage system.

4) Social production determined by people's consumption needs and a planned economy in which supply is determined by real demand.

State controlled economies like that of USSR do not represent the planned economy of socialism. Such economies are constrained by the aims of the power of the state. Social production, economic needs and state investment are all determined by the ruling party and not the consumption requirements of the people. This is an economic system in which arbitrariness rules. This is a controlled economy, not a planned economy.

Undoubtedly, the existing world is as yet a capitalist world.

4). In China — A Movement Which Seeks to Transform Mankind

The "socialist transformation movement" implemented by Mao Tse-tung in China is a movement to reform human behaviour according to a specific model. It is a movement to dominate the social and economic form according to the design by one man. He has ignored the operational laws of society and no matter how much power he can grasp, or how breath-taking his spirit is, history has deemed that he should fail.

Mao is the first person to turn "socialism" consciously into a religion. He has distorted the communist man's character into a religious character in the endeavour to change society. This separates Mao from other Marxist leaders. To Mao Tse-tung, socialism is the manifestation of absolute rationality. It is an extraction of some dogmas from Marxism. Such absolute rationality in its own specific form is determined by his subjective understanding, living conditions, level of knowledge and the development of his thinking.

Division of labour confines a man to a state of impotence. The religion of Mao Tse Tung has managed to become a social force because of the sense of dependency and the psychology of withrawal of the weak caused by individual impotence within the masses. Here the psychology of withdrawal means the fear of affirming the healthy life instinct.

Religion helps to elevate the imperfect instincts of man into "godlike" qualities, and dogmas are set down the regulate the activities of man.

Socialism is the crystallisation of the development of humanity. Its essence is to regain the instincts of life. Humanistic socialism has rejected the old values which negate life. The new value system is based on life affirmation. It destroys traditional morality. The only truth is life's instincts.

All religions are opposed to humanistic socialism.

Since the purges of 1957, Mao Tse-tung has never stopped organising different "socialist thought" reform movements. The "role of spirit" is the foundation of all religious thoughts and the control of thoughts. "The supreme importance of spirit" is the principle of Mao Tse Tung.

In the economic relation of totalitarian capital, man is thoroughly impotent. The sense of impotence of man has led to dependence and the psychology of worship. This is the socio-psychological foundation of religion. Mao Tse-tung's thoughts have been able to become the dominating religion of China because such thoughts have developed at a very opportune time. At the same time, he has grasped two essentials in controlling the masses. The first is the so called "the viewpoint of the masses" which levels all values to the same plane, shaping man into something without individuality. The other is the "cult of the idol" and this is the religious feeling towards the supreme leader. This has made Mao Tse-tung the focus of all passions and the desires and hopes of the people are sublimated into the worship of Mao. This in effect gives Mao the power to dominate people's thoughts and behaviour.

In order to transform Chinese society, Mao Tse-tung has established the social cultural model through organising various movements. And this model is the "spirit of Lei Feng" praised by Mao Tse-tung. The spirit of Lei Feng is an entirely religious personality. It implies the prevailing of the spirit and mind over the body. The content of this personality is "being like screws" whereby the personal existence of man is negated; "selflessness" whereby the personal worth of man and freedom of human personality are abandoned: a nihilistic will of life-negation; "being able to suffer a lot" where by the material needs of human are despised; and "faithfulness to the thoughts of Mao Tse-tung" whereby free thoughts are crushed. The consciousness of the people is unified by religious thoughts.

The model that Mao Tse-tung uses to reform human thoughts is contrary to the humanism of socialism. It is a mixture of religious thoughts and feudal ideas.

The intellectuals and cadres belong to a caste which has not yet lost the ability to think. Mao Tse-tung has designed a whole set of policies to deal with these dangerous elements. He resorts to sending the cadres and the intellectuals to labour. However, in a society where labour is still regarded by people as an obligation, such labour does not have any socialistic content. Rather, it is a kind of forced labour. The policy of sending cadres and intellectuals down to the countryside and up the mountains has bred sentiments of discontent among them.

Spiritual critique may be used to establish social and cultural models but it cannot change actual social consciousness. The contradiction between actual social consciousness and the social cultural model leads to people wearing masks. And people do not recognise their own existence. Such is the result of Mao Tse-tung's movement to transform man. At the same time, Mao's movements have generated the psychology of religious worship and hostility against aliens. Such undesirable psychological reactions are repeated in the never-ending movements and have been solidified as part of the character structure of society.

On the other hand, Mao Tse-tung seeks to change the totalitarian state capitalist economy and to establish a religious "socialist commune". In 1958, Mao Tse-tung laid down the grand plan of the "People Commune Movement" in the countryside and the cities.

In this movement, the masses shew unheard-of creativity and spirit which surpassed the design of Mao Tse-tung and everywhere great experiments of socialism were carried out. The communes created by the people in 1958 consisted of elements of primitive communes although they were not socialist in essence. But still, it was something new.

The principle of the people's commune is that agriculture is carried on in the cities and industry is developed in the countryside. This is a precondition for the economic self-sufficiency of the commune.

In the cities, the communes took the place of the administrative districts. The commune was not only the basic unit of administrative organisation, it was also a basic unit of economic organisation. The communes in the cities have the economy of a commune — including factories organised on a street community basis, communal dining halls, childcare centres, cultural propaganda units, schools, clinics and farms.

Most of these however had only the form. And as the "People's Commune Movement" failed, they vanished.

In the countryside, the scale of communization was even bigger. Mao Tse-tung's policies on the communes were carried through within a short time. At the same time, the widespread creativity of the masses helped to push the "commune movement" to greater depths.

Agricultural economic organisations in the form of co-operatives and production brigades were elevated to that of communal ownership. The old workpoint system was abolished and the commune supply system was established: free canteens were set up, free childcare centres, free medical services and free education. Undoubtedly, the Chinese people created the first attempt at socialism in history.

But the rural communes survived for less than a year as a result of the disharmony of the national economy. The deep economic and social contradictions and Mao's substitution policies had brought failures for the Chinese people.

After this, China experienced three years of economic difficulties. An opposition was formed within the ruling clique. Even the bureaucrats were expressing extreme unhappiness and the sentiments of the masses were at the bottom Mao Tse-tung was forced to withdraw to the second line and Liu Shao Chi took on the line "three privates and one contract", which was a liberal capitalist road, to salvage the situation.

The failure of the commune movement did not make Mao Tse-tung abandon his subjective design. In a letter he sent to Lin Piao in 1965, he pointed out that the "May Seventh" directives were the blueprints for a new commune. Its spirit was the same as the commune movement in 1958.

The party's internal conditions in 1965 were different from those of 1958. Within the ruling clique, there had appeared opposition forces headed by Liu Shao Chi. They had learnt their lessons in the commune movement of 1958 ie. the idea that except for those reinforcing the totalitarian state capitalist economy, all economic structural changes would weaken the personal power of the rulers and harm the economic development of the national economy. Such opposition forces were directly threatening the position of Mao Tse-tung.

The purpose of Mao Tse-tung in initiating the Cultural Revolution was to eliminate the opposition forces inside the party, so that he might continue the "socialist trans- formation movement" which is well entrenched in his mind, through his own subjectivity.

What has to be pointed out is that the spontaneous revolution of the masses surpassed the line of Mao Tse-tung at every point. Within the rebel forces, there appeared a whole host of advanced elements. For the first time, the history of socialist revolution in China had begun.

In the upheavals of 1966 to 1968, the various struggles — between different sects in the party, the transformation movement designed by Mao Tse-tung, the struggle between the democratic movement of the masses and the conservative forces, and the socialist revolution of the advanced elements — interacted with one another and the whole situation was in a state of confusion. Mao Tse-tung could not keep the movement in his own hands.

Mao Tse-tung ignited the revolution but he could not control it.

Work-teams had been traditional tools with which Mao Tse-tung sought to change society. But under the circumstances of 1966, Mao finally changed his strategy. He tried to use a mass movement controlled by himself to fulfil his aims, viz. to purge the opposition forces of the party, and to carry out a complete surgical operation on society. The "16 points" is a fair indication of this development.

The rebel forces wanted "to liberate oneself by oneself". They had long opposed the constraints of the work teams. "The 16 points" presented them with a convenient weapon in their struggle against such teams. They were not to be restrained in making revolution. They did not want to organise "movements of strikes" and "movements to grab the freaks and monsters" under the control of the work teams. They wanted to put all the bureaucrats on trial. In fact they wanted to try the bureaucratic system itself. The advanced elements of the rebel forces were a very small minority in society. Yet they were the real starters of the Cultural Revolution. From the beginning, they had the fighting spirit of socialist revolution.

Those who do not understand China may doubt the possibility of spontaneous development of socialist revolutionary forces within a totalitarian society. The answer is that the personality found in Chinese society is not simply just a totalitarian one. It is a religious personality coloured by "socialism". Therefore there is a group of advanced thinking elements in the masses, who received "socialist religious" education with critical minds and idealism and then grasped the ultimate ideals of socialism. And with this set of ultimate ideals, they examine existing society and unlike the rest of the masses, they do not regard socialism as a religion for blind worship. They surpass the society in which they live.

Such revolutionary forces had appeared in the "rectification campaigns" in the early fifties but were suppressed quickly during the "Anti-rightist struggles".

In opposition to the "rebel forces" were the "conservative forces".

The elements of the "conservative forces" were usually members of the privileged sections of society. They stubbornly protected the bureaucrats and the bureaucratic system. They viewed the "rebel forces" as "anti-party elements", "elements seeking class revenge" etc. In the period of stability, under totalitarian rule, the individual loses his ability to survive independently. In face of disturbances, individual impotence manifests itself in the lust for power and sadism. The "conservative forces" created "the white terror" in the whole country in the period of fermentation in order to project themselves. And they did so by using their superior positions. The terrorist methods of the "conservative forces" were to attack and take revenge on the revolutionary advanced elements. On the other hand, these were also manifestations of their extreme lust for power and sadism.

Totalitarian rule had generated widespread feelings of personal impotence among the masses. All of a sudden the movement was no longer directly led. And the ordinary masses could not understand. During the early disturbances, they were at a loss and did not know their course.

That was the condition of the period of fermentation.

Mass organisations were formed spontaneously. They were at the beginning the collective formations of the rebel forces in opposition to the bureaucratic system.

Then Mao Tse-tung discovered the strength of the revolutionary mass organisations. Undoubtedly the development of this strength would paralyse the forces of Liu Shao-chi. Mao supported a Red Guard organisation at a middle school affiliated to the Peking University in an appropriate time. At the same time, he told the whole country, "I support you all." What followed was that the mass organisations became sectarian organisations of the masses.

Basing themselves on the "theory of blood heredity" (If the old man was a hero, his son would be a good man. If the old man was a reactionary, his son would be a rotten egg.), some Red Guards became formations of conservative forces or the united action committees of the offsprings of party cadres. The slavish habit of the conservative forces to worship authority deemed them to be very close to Mao Tse-tung. Although the protection of bureaucrats and the old system by the conservative forces were contrary to the line of Mao Tse-tung and presented obstructions to the subjective movements of Mao Tse-tung, ultimately the conservative forces were the only ones that Mao Tse-tung could rely upon.

"White terror" appeared with "the theory of blood heredity". What being struck at were not just the small numbers of rebel forces but the ordinary masses as well. Uncountable numbers of ordinary people died from savage tortures. These expressions of spontaneous fascist behaviour were the by product of the totalitarian personality. It was a great exposure of how totalitarian society deprived man of his human nature.

The White Terror of November ended. White Terror now aimed at the masses. This was to the disadvantage of Mao Tse-tung. Following the end of White Terror, the revolutionary torrent liberated the masses from their inferiority complex.

The persecuted masses thought that they had been liberated by the line of Mao Tse-tung. They then formed organisations of Red Guards defending the "line of Mao Tse-tung". They represented the majority of the people. Their oppressed position made them adopt democratic ideas and they became the forces of democratic movements. But they could not shake away their worship of Mao Tse-tung. On the other hand, part of the masses joined the organisations of the rebel forces. And the slogan "point the spearhead at the capitalist roaders" proposed by Mao Tse-tung corresponded to the revolutionary demands of the rebel forces. As a result, in a certain period the pseudo-revolution of Mao Tse-tung forced the advanced elements of the rebel forces to identify with the line of Mao Tse-tung. However, as the movement intensified, they became the opposition to the Mao Tse-tung line.

"Red Guards" is a term which signifies no special characteristics. All youth organisations, whatever they represented, made use of this term. There was no one single unified "Red Guards Movement". To analyse "the Red Guard Movement" in a loose and simplified way is a misunderstanding of the "Cultural Revolution" by foreign correspondents.

The "Cultural Revolution" revealed the contradictions between the people and the bureaucratic system. But even more meaningful was the fact that the contradictions in Chinese society, including political and economic ones, were exposed through the "Cultural Revolution". If we say that questions were raised about the bureaucratic system as a result of the rectification campaign in 1958, then questions were raised about the socio-economic nature of the whole state as a result of the "Cultural Revolution".

From the democratic consciousness opposing bureaucracy to the questioning of the nature of Chinese society, there has been of course a "leap". Such a "leap" could only be realised through great upheavals like the "Cultural Revolution". "The Cultural Revolution" raised the will of the people to attain the ultimate ideals of socialism and at the same time, inevitably, the pseudo-revolution of Mao Tse-tung was exposed.

During the "Cultural Revolution", Mao Tse-tung several times suppressed the mass movement which was moving forward. This made inevitable the eventual bankruptcy of the "socialist religion" of Mao Tse-tung. The suppression of the mass movement by Mao Tse-tung was not a personal and accidental mistake. It was the result of the fundamental contradiction between Mao Tse-tung's subjective "socialist transformation movement" and the people's socialist revolution.

In January 1967, the masses seized power from the economic, industrial and transportation establishments in the cities and the provinces all over China. It must be admitted that the majority of the masses had not understood the struggle for the seizure of power. Prior to this, the party and the state were such holy religious symbols. The change was too drastic. The masses participating in the seizure of power were unprepared for reconstructing the society. In the "January Revolution", the target of struggle for the seizure of power was limited to the various levels of government departments. The people had not reached such a level of consciousness that they would overthrow the whole "ruling class". Socialism was such a new thing to the masses. Over the years, the ideas of socialism propagated by the ruling party were so distorted. What was to be done after the seizure of power? — the masses paused and were puzzled. While the people were still not equipped in constructing new social organisations and a new economic order, the counter-revolutionary forces of the ruling clique were waiting for them.

The revolution of the people by the people ran into direct confrontation with Mao's conception of the "Chinese People's Commune". The idea of Mao Tse-tung to turn China into a commune was such that its backbone was to be provided by the bureaucrats, and that social reforms in China would be carried out according to his will. On the other hand, the internal strife within the ruling party had not been settled. How could Mao really care about the "May Seventh" blueprint? Mao had supported the revolutionary seizure of power which occurred all over the country. His wish was that with the help of the mass movements this would create a situation where all bureaucrats would stand aside. Such a situation was necessary if Mao was to reconstruct his bureaucratic machine.

Now Mao Tse-tung's design had been accomplished. Naturally he would not allow the spontaneous revolution of the people to deepen. He ordered the implementation of military control in the whole country. The revolutionary power of the people all over the country was to be transferred to the bureaucrats of the military. After the military bureaucrats had taken over, they carried out a counter-revolutionary purge. A large number of fighters within the ranks of the rebel forces were sent to jail and the revolutionary mass organisations were disbanded and suppressed.

That was the notorious "Adverse Current of February and March".

The "Adverse Current of February" was also at the same time a counter-attack at the forces of Mao Tse-tung by the opposition forces in the military. After the adverse current, an illusion was created that Mao Tse-tung and his forces were, together with the people, in trouble. The betrayal of the "January Revolution" by Mao Tse-tung was considered to be a necessary retreat by the rebels. It can be seen how deeply personality may be influenced by a religious character. This is the socio-psychological foundation of the domination of the whole country by Mao Tse-tung who was the personification of truth.

Full scale and total military control represented the beginning of the suppression of the mass movement by Mao Tse-tung.

After the "February Adverse Current", under the direction and control of Mao Tse-tung, preparatory groups of revolutionary committees were set up in the provinces and in the cities, to replace the dictatorship of the bureaucrats of the military. The "preparatory groups" were no revolution in social organisations. It was a means used by Mao Tse-tung to cleanse the bureaucratic organisations. The cleansing could not have been peaceful. Sectarian clashes between local bureaucrats and bureaucrats in the military occurred all over the place. In Honan, Szechuan, Kweichow, Kiangsi and Kwangsi, sectarian clashes turned into armed skirmishes and fighting. There was even a military uprising in Hopei. The setting up of the preparatory groups of the revolutionary committees took a whole six months.

During this time, the people, with their innocent fervour and supreme passion for life, had written for the first time the history of "the armed people" and "dictatorship of the masses". The blood shed in February had not been in vain. The revolutionary thought of "the armed people" had been born. The slogans of the rebel forces now included calls for seizing the arms of the military bureaucrats and the creation of people's own armed forces. Immediately, the people and the bureaucrats were running separate operations for themselves all over the country.

The trend of "arming the whole people" shocked the ruling clique. Mao Tse-tung announced the "September Fifth" directive and ordered that the masses submit and return all arms and ammunition. In face of the huge regular army, the military strength of the people was extremely weak. The people soon had their weapons confiscated by the ruling class. Immediately following this, Mao Tse-tung ordered the dissolution of the mass organisations throughout the whole country. Mao Tse-tung could sense that he could no longer control the tendency of the movement of the masses.

In reality, the mass movement had turned its back on the headquarters of Mao Tse-tung. The rebel forces were against the confiscation and surrendering of arms. They were against the dissolution of the mass organisations. Their opposition to Mao's directive was manifested in their actions. They hid their guns and ammunition and they linked up provincial organisations of the rebel forces and began to prepare for the new struggle.

The resistance of the rebel forces lasted for more than 6 months. Eventually, in July, 1968, Mao Tse-tung made the "July 3rd" and "July 24th" pronouncements. By then, heavily armed military forces were engaged in massive killings of the members of the masses' organisations.

The people were suppressed. Mao Tse-tung was directly controlling the whole situation. He proposed to set up "revolutionary committees". Political power was completely returned to the hands of the bureaucrats of the military and the government. The representatives of the masses were only decorative in function. "Centralised" leadership weakened the power of the local forces. China's political order was becoming more totalitarian. The bureaucratic rule which had been temporarily paralysed was completely restored.

The people walked through the corpses of revolution and continued to move forward. The revolutionary committees ignited a spontaneous anti-restoration movement.

The first "anti-restoration" flag was hoisted by "Sheng-wu-lien" of Hunan. They wanted to overthrow the new bureaucratic ruling machine – the revolutionary committees. They formulated pointed critiques of Chinese society. The system of contracted labour, temporary labour, the treatment of youth (the movement of going to the countryside) . . . . . and other economic systems, policies and directives, all came under their scrutiny and critque. They raised the question "Whither China?", undoubtedly the first query about the nature of Chinese society as a whole. In May, 1969, the Kiangsi rebel forces also organised the anti-restoration movements. Workers went on strike. Students went on strike and the peasants went into towns. Mass assemblies and rallies were held to oppose the revolutionary committees. They declared that the revolutionary committee was the bureaucratic machine of the old capitalist class. They wanted to crush the revolutionary committee and to establish real power for the people. In September the same year, the biggest anti-restoration movement of the rebel forces broke out in Hupeh. A big character poster (When Mankind is liberated, I am liberated) shocked the whole city of Wuhan. The people held up torches and swarmed the streets like a rising tide. The red arm bands of the organisations were worn again. The big flags of the rebel forces were once more waving in the streets. The red flags, red arm bands, seas of faces and the mass processions and demonstrations stirred the whole country. This sudden rising tide was not initiated by anyone; it was organised by no one. And the movement quickly and freely spread like a flood. The size of the movement and the breadth of it made the bureaucrats, big or small tremble. At that time, the bureaucrats even lost their courage to suppress it. The rebel forces set up a province-wide organisation. "The Revolutionary Group Which Resolves to Carry the Great Proletarian Cultural Revolution Through to the End". They had their own theoretical research group (the North Star Study Group); their own papers (Yangtzekiang Review), and their own program – overthrowing the bureaucratic class and realising the socialist revolution. The rebel forces in Hupeh had set up the best model

186

of the integration of the movement of intellectuals, workers and peasants. Even more memorable were the revolutionary actions of the peasants at Ji Shui in Hupeh. What could be said is this: there had never before been any peasant movement which is so socialist and revolutionary in its meaning. The peasants set up their own communal economy managed by themselves and were armed. The revolution of the Ji Shui peasants was epoch-making.

The spontaneous anti-resortation movement of the masses undoubtedly was diametrically opposite to the rule of Mao Tse-tung, although the masses had not attacked Mao Tse-tung. The anti-restoration movement embraced more than a few germinating elements of socialist revolution. The masses began to come into contact with genuine socialism. A group of advanced elements which held the new ideas of socialism was maturing in the ranks of the rebel forces.

The mass movement reached a climax. Mao Tse-tung began a slogans suppression of the rebel forces. Prior to this, Mao Tse-tung made use of the bureaucrats in the military to suppress the masses. This time, Mao Tse-tung himself directly suppressed the revolution. As the chief representative of the ruling class, Mao Tse-tung could not be the leader of the socialist revolution. When the mass movement spontaneously changed into a socialist revolution, this hero of the Yeh Kung style, Mao Tse-tung, suppressed the revolution by the most ruthless means.

Mao Tse-tung authorised a whole series of announcements declaring that "Sheng-wu-lien", "the North Star study Group", "The Revolutionary Group Which Resolves to Carry the Great Proletarian Cultural Revolution Through to The End" and other organisations of the rebel forces as counter-revolutionary. The advanced elements of the rebel forces all over the country were arrested under the pretext of suppressing the "May 16th" group. Mao Tse-tung's pseudo-revolution was completely exposed.

The "Cultural Revolution" showed the total failure of Mao Tse-tung's "socialist transformation movement". Mao Tse-tung's forces were encircled by enemies and difficulties: recognisable or unrecognisable opposition forces had developed inside the ruling clique, opposing Mao Tse-tung's line of "social reconstruction". From their own existing vested interests, they wished to strengthen the rule of totalitarian state capital. The bureaucrats found Mao Tse-tung less and less trustworthy, because the line of Mao Tse-tung weakened the power of the bureaucrats, and as a result, the bureaucrats lacked a sense of security. In relation to the masses, the religious personality had been destroyed by the revolution. There were no more people who would follow Mao Tse-tung's line blindly. What was even more important is that new ideas of socialism had become a social force. The genuine revolution was born from the pseudo-revolution.

The Socialist movement was strangled, but the socialist revolution moved forward.

5). Don't Put the World on Your Shoulder

Socialism is the result of economic movement and cultural progress. The economy, culture, social structure of socialism and the tactics of socialist revolution should be derived from the life force of existing society and the creativity of the masses. The socialist revolution should be a revolution of mankind.

It is realised through the autonomous action of the masses. The proletariat as an oppressed class which holds no special class interests can only seek its own liberation if it integrates its own struggle into the revolution for the liberation of mankind.

All groups, parties or classes, which declare themselves to be the representatives of the lower classes of society, in their endeavour to attain political power, will gain the most. And the most forceful theory would undoubtedly be that corresponds to the psychological conditions of the lower classes. But the proletariat must learn their lessons from history that the proletarians need no "saviour", no religion; they have to elevate themselves through struggles. They can be liberated through the liberation of mankind .

Are you a real supporter of the liberation of the proletariat?

Do you really support the socialist revolution?

If so, then take part in the revolution of the masses and seek the future through the struggles of the masses.

When the "socialism" of Stalin and Mao Tse-tung had become so stale and notorious, the "Fourth International" jumped out to save the "revolution". They wanted to take up the leadership of the workers' movement. According to Trotskyism, this is a task which should be accepted without hesitation. So the programs and flags of the Fourth International were appointed by its adherents as the unchangeable directives for the liberation of the proletariat. Without the guidance and directives of Trotsky, the proletariat would be facing a leadership crisis, and man would come to the verge of degeneration. After Stalin, Trotsky had become another "saviour" who was to "reform mankind". What is pitiable is that when the thoughts and actions of the Trotskyists are examined, the blood connection between them and the Stalinists is so obvious in so many places. Trotskyism holds fast to Leninism (part of which originated from Marxism), a kind of forced and unnatural "socialism". It also is founded on the old domain of the theory of class struggle. Such old theories have been proved by the history of Stalinism to have nothing to do with the liberation of the proletariat.

Firstly, the traditional Trotskyists did not have an objective understanding of the "October Revolution" in Russia.

Trotsky had written in the book "Revolution Betrayed" that "Russia took the road of proletarian revolution, not because her economy was the first to become ripe for a socialist change, but because she could not develop further on a capitalist basis." How ignorant was he of the economy and operation of Russia!? (This may be an ignorance caused by subjective positions.) The reality was not that the Russian economy could not develop further on the basis of capitalism. Rather, it was the opposite and Russian capitalism must eliminate all obstructions in order to march forward.

Why then it was not for the traditional capitalist parties to lead and complete the task of eliminating all the obstructions for the development of capitalism? "The Revolution Betrayed" considered the reason to be "the weakness and lack of strength of the Russian capitalist class". Yes, this may be considered to be a secondary reason. The fundamental reason should be looked for in the conditions in which the "October Revolution" developed. These were the conditions at that time: imperialist wars had caused stagnation in the economy of Russia and people were facing death and starvation. The underdevelopment of the Russian capitalist revolution meant that the theories of the Russian capitalist class could not appeal to the emotions of the Russian people. At the same time, the Russian capitalist class had become subservient to the international capitalist class. It was obvious that the Russian capitalist class could not control and manipulate the upheavals of the peasants and workers. On the other hand a new political party – the Bolsheviks, had been set up. Its ultimate ideal was humanism. Its solgans echoed the psychological conditions of the proletarians. The true nature of this party had not been revealed by any records of history. Undoubtedly this party could understand and control the strength of the peasants and workers. The Bolshevik party used the October uprising of the peasants and workers to grasp political power, and inevitably became the leading force in getting rid of all the obstructions to the development of capitalism in Russia.

The "October Revolution" in Russia changed the history of the development of traditional capitalism and the capitalist class. The democratic task of the Russian bourgeoisie had not been fulfilled by the traditional capitalist class or its parties. Rather, it was fulfilled by a new party – under the leadership of the Leninist party. Capitalism did not develop according to the traditional stages but leaped into the mode of totalitarian state capital. China's conditions and history were similar to those of Russia.

Is dictatorship of the new party "dictatorship of the proletariat"? The bureaucratic standpoint of "Revolution Betrayed" makes Trotskyists the same kind of fish as the Stalinists. It concluded that the democratic tasks of Russia had been "accomplished through the dictatorship of the proletariat." This is a distortion of history. A party and the nature of its dictatorship cannot be judged from an examination of the party's program or its declarations, but rather from the nature of the revolution that it leads and the nature of the mode of production set up after it attains power.

State ownership of land and the means of production in the cities only represent the fully-fledged bourgeois democratic revolution. Lenin himself had agreed on this point on the eve of the revolution. Until now, the mode of production in Russia and similar countries has never been elevated from this. Also, totalitarian state capital has solidified as the economic structure of the country. The "October Revolution" led by the Bolshevik party (not to speak of the 1949 revolution in China) has not surpassed the limits of the bourgeois revolution.

The proletariat does not have a special property interest of its own, hence there can be no dictatorship of the proletariat. If the "dictatorship of the proletariat" is taken as a prognostication, it may be considered as a kind-hearted political myth; if it is equated with the dictatorship of a party, it is a big insult and big lie to the proletariat. (We have already criticised the theory of the dictatorship of the proletariat above.)

Talking about political fairy tales, one thinks of the "theory of permanent revolution." This theory is articulated thus: "changing the bourgeois democratic revolution into a proletarian socialist revolution", "vest the leadership directly with the proletariat". These are undoubtedly most pleasing and revolutionary words. The tragedy is that, socialism is no man-made artificial movement and it could occur only inside the mode of production of a capitalism which is ripe. Furthermore the leadership of the proletariat should not be equated with leadership of the party. "The Theory of Permanent Revolution" has accuracy and truth in its logic but it has been constructed upon a conception of an economic model which was further based on blind calculation. Therefore, there could be no trace of its implementation in society. Quite the opposite, it has helped the ruling party to fool the proletariat.

Trotsky understood the "October Revolution" from the view of the ruling party. Therefore, he made a wrong judgement on the nature of countries like Russia.

There is a weak argument in "the Revolution Betrayed": because the fruits of the workers' revolution ie. the state ownership of the means of production, were still continued in Russia, then Russia is still a worker's state. We understand that the feudal nobles took advantage of the uprisings of the slaves to set up a feudal economy and this may be considered to be in the very broad sense the fruits of the uprisings of the slaves. But we would never recognise the state of the feudal landlord as the state of the slaves. Similarly, the state ownership of the means of production is the manifestation of the utilisation of the people's revolutionary forces by a political party. But such fruits represent the interest of the new rising ruling clique. They are obtained by the ruling party by betraying the interests of the workers. That people find it difficult to accept the Trotskyist conception of a workers' state which does not represent the interests of the workers is nothing of great surprise.

"The state assumes directly and from the very beginning a dual character: socialistic, insofar as it defends social property in the means of production; bourgeois, insofar as the distribution of life's goods is carried out with a capitalist measure of value and all the consequences ensuing therefrom." So says "the Revolution Betrayed".

We have discussed in Section Three that socialist ownership "or ownership by the whole people" is manifested by the mode of production in every way. To summarize: socialist ownership must be based on the elimination of capital – ie to destroy the law of value of labour power. How can we have socialist ownership with the mode of distribution of capitalism? This can be believed only by people who habitually believe in political fairy tales. Without question, this is an indication of a daring betrayal of Marx's views on history.

On the other hand, how vague a concept is "public ownership by society"? "Public ownership by society" in what kind of society? Surely we understand, that Trotsky used the term "public ownership by society" to cover up the "state ownership of the means of production". On this crucial point, the Trotskyists and the Stalinists shook hands. And we have already formulated our critique in the section on "Totalitarian State Capital".

Of course, when Trotsky discussed the nature of countries like Russia, he was embarrassed by the capitalist laws and authorities. At the same time, he quoted the predictions by Lenin and Marx that at the early stages of communism, bourgeois laws, legal institutions and the bourgeois state could not be avoided.

When predictions could not explain realities, we take note of realities and drop the predictions. The people would not accept a communism with bourgeois rule.

It is widely known that countries like the USSR have set up a complete economic and social structure – totalitarian state capitalism. The state organises a very tight bureaucratic machine and a huge regular army, for the purpose of strengthening the totalitarian rule. (On this question of reality, Stalinism, Maoism, and Soviet Revisionism are all the same.) If Trotsky considered that such totalitarian states were preparatory stages towards communism, was he not preaching "peaceful transition"? It seems difficult, but it is Trotsky against himself.

On the class relationship in the USSR and similar countries, the analysis in "Revolution Betrayed" is very unclear.

The Leninist ruling party had eliminated individual capitalists and it was unable to establish a society which represented the interests of the whole people. As a result, class rule became highly concentrated and the ruling clique became the ruling class and was above the whole people. The bureaucrats were attachments to the ruling clique and were like the managerial class of the advanced capitalist states.

"The Revolution Betrayed" confuses the bureaucratic caste with the ruling clique. And on the question of class interests, it makes the wrong analysis and conclusion. It believes, "of all the strata of Soviet society the bureaucracy has best solved its own social problem . . . . . It continues to preserve state property only to the extent that it fears the proletariat."

What is the truth? The bureaucratic caste is the tool with which the ruling clique maintains its rule. It is the ruling clique that controls the veins of society. In a state where politics and capital are highly monopolised, the maintenance of state ownership would be the best way to serve the interests of the small number of rulers. Any dispersion of property will weaken their power. The bureaucrats themselves would wish to cut up and share the properties and power but they were also helplessly controlled and ruled by the highest ruling clique. In Trotsky's conceptual framework, the system of state ownership is identified with the interests of the proletariat. The bureaucrats maintain state ownership merely because of their fear of the proletariat! We cannot but sigh at the ignorance of the interests of the proletariat whom the Trotskyists claim to represent.

Finally, in discussing the perspective of future revolutions in Russia and countries like Russia, "The Revolution Betrayed" completely betrays socialist revolution and stands on the side of the ruling class. It suggests that there would be a revolutionary party overthrowing the bureaucratic system of USSR and this revolution would only a political one and not a social revolution! "It does not destroy the economic base of society. It only peels away the old skin on the top."

In other words, the economic base of totalitarian state capital which has turned workers into the slaves of capital, must be preserved. What is required is simply the replacement of Stalinist "authoritarian bureaucrats" by Trotskyist "democratic bureaucrats". Such is the "revolutionary" platform of the Trotskyists; the "socialist revolutionary" program laid down by the Fourth Internationals!

To the heroes who want to dominate and control the socialist revolution, the people have this to advise them, "Don't put the world on your shoulders."

6). **Beyond Darkness**

Certain "revolutionaries" are found in this era. They tailor "ideals" in their own ways in order to fit into the "practical politics" of specific interests. This of course is not something which has been started off by them, but rather the legacy of tradition. These "revolutionaries" will tolerate and accept all the different new thoughts but they had to kneel down before such legacies. They have raped the ideals and they seek purification with the sense of dilemma and historical tragedies. They have debased the noble sense of historical tragedies. Naturally, they would talk about the progress of history as if social movements and mass struggles which have taken place exist only because of the vested interests. But I believe that if vested interests had not existed, every thing would have progressed in better ways. The ruling cliques of the ages always seize the most opportune movement in history to make use of the struggles of the masses and distort the self movement of society. Yet, such vested interests existed and are still found – this is the tragedy of history.

The world has been submerged in Machiavellian politics and outdated "ideals". The real meaning of life has become difficult to grasp and perplexing to man. Life has also become less real.

Give us ideals! Give us aims! Show us the practical way! – People have become too cowardly. They thirst for dependence and worship. They need the support of a tailored ideal. Or they need to grab power to balance their sense of impotence. They would rather admit defeat than to believe that they can achieve anything by their own efforts. And so as a result, man continues to be enslaved. But the time will come when mankind achieves self consciousness in the grand way, then we should not tolerate the impotence of ourselves and mankind. In our continuing struggles, we do not seek domination or power but rather to just move closer to the only ideal which is – the equality of mankind and the self-consciousness of life.

Ideals, aims and practical struggles are all present in our life, in our commitment.

I witness the growth of new lives on this planet. Gladly I greet them, "Friends, may be we are still too young and weak, but let us not be scared by the lofty "ideals" and "isms". We belong to the realm of life itself."

No, I have not been "preaching". Not that I do not understand it. Perhaps, I am too familiar with it. All along, people are used to detailed information and to tight inferences. But I doubt whether the systems of "truths" we find in history have really convinced people. People were simply scared or terrorised into submission. Modern art is becoming a wide and spreading movement towards the destruction of form. Thoughts are no longer the special privileges of a small group of thinkers. Therefore, our discourse requires no resemblance to the eight-legged style. At the outset, I treated my readers as thinking people and my words are to excite their imagination, to seek vibration on the same wavelength so that this vibration achieves a resonance. I have not endeavoured to convince my readers nor to create a religion. If his heart and soul are close to mine, the words in these pages are enough for us to communicate. If his heart and soul were on a distant planet, he should still be able to see my little spark. If he has not yet struggled out of the grey hard shell, then who is brave enough to break the shell from the outside? What point is there in preaching?

Everyone is equal, you and he or she. Man can think and search. Let's not abandon our own selves; let's not diminish others.

The dusk of rationality has now sunken deeper into darkness. Friends, can you hear that the spring of life is bursting through darkness!

First Draft completed in Feburary 1974.

INTRODUCTION TO   REVELATIONS

THAT MOVE THE EARTH TO TEARS

WU MAN

We are publishing this collection of poems and essays to enable our readers to trace the development of the thoughts of the new generation of youth in Mainland China. In the future it will be a precious momento of the present day.

THE SILENT CHINA

China for many years for most of the time was a silent country. One need not consult ancient Chinese history to find out that the Chinese, reserved, face-saving and ceremonious as they are, should see fit to remain silent. It was the consequence of centuries of physical and cultural domination.

It is said that however, before the Ming Dynasty things were not too bad: what had to be said could sometimes be said. But when the Manchus became alien rulers of China, the mental climate became suffocating and discussion of history or current affairs was barred. By the time of Chien Lung's reign, people would not even talk with their brushes (according to The Silent China by Lu Hsun). Such conditions continued until the twentieth century when the revengeful call "Our China!" exploded, a call which asserted that this nation still existed, that this ancient people had not lost its will to survive, thus promising a glorious future. This event came to be known as the May Fourth Movement. With the question of "Whither China?", there naturally arose much debate and confusion, large and small. But that was a tumultuous moment for China and it awakened many, puzzling some but encouraging others.

A whole generation of youth sought the answer to "Whither China?". Some men spent their whole life without reaching a conclusion. Perhaps they believed that "knowledge is greater than action" and so they stayed in their studies to scrutinise a hundred theses. They analysed the mood and temperament of the nation before they worked out a perfect programme, only ending in more confusion. The more impatient had already hoisted their flags of different colours and prescribed various medicines. Among them were plenty of rash but sincere fighters. The irresponsible trouble-makers who were there merely to prove themselves were few. To the dedicated searcher for truth, it was as if they were facing the monstrous Sphinx who would devour all those unable to answer correctly. Of course, they were not worried about their own lives. But if they were to be devoured by this monster, it would become more mysterious and its appetite more insatiable, and China would further drift into hopelessness.

The situation was desperate and there seemed to be no way out. Then from neighbouring Russia came the gun fire of the October Revolution, heralding the birth of a new world. Marxist communist ideology arrived from Europe and very much inspired the idealistic youths. To disseminate Marxism, a party and a party programme were set up and after thirty harsh and cruel years, they established the "ideal kingdom". "Only socialism can save China." (Quotation of Mao Tse-tung) Mao Tse-tung settled the case which had been undecided for half a century. There was music from all over China and the poets sang their praises and it appeared that even the phoenix came to join the festivities.

However, the fact is that it did not take long for China to return to silence.

THE DESTINY OF LITERATURE

It would be inaccurate to say that Mao Tse-tung only knew how to burn books and bury intellectuals. It would be equally inaccurate to say that Shih Huang-ti only knew how to burn books and bury intellectuals. However, Mao's psychology is very similar to the first Great Emperor of the Middle Kingdom i.e. to impose his own concept of Great Unity. Mao's criticism of Confucianism is not revolutionary but is an attempt to substitute Confucius with himself. Mao is an intellectual. With a wealth of knowledge in Chinese history, he understands well the significance of "rites and music". China is so large and the population so considerable that it would be strange and frightening to enforce total silence. So he could only take one road which is to suppress free art and literature and to establish a unified art and literature. And for that, he would have to burn books and bury intellectuals. As early as 1942 when he had not yet seized power in China, he was already making such preparations and this shows how much importance he attached to this problem. It is no easy task to give a name to this "art and literature of great unity" because there is no ready-made one, certainly not from the history of art and literature. Some call it "realist literature" out of a superficial impression because in the 1930s most writers were left-wing and preached realism, but it is far from the realism of that time. From the policies related to art and literature propounded and carried out by the Chinese communists over the years, we must conclude that realist literature and art have not been tolerated and have been considered freaks and monsters. Just on the eve of the Cultural Revolution, "the theory of the person in the middle" propounded by Shao Chuen Luen was severely criticised. This "theory of the person in the middle" is but a minor aspect of realist literature. It recognises that in whatever kind of society, the radically progressive or stubbornly reactionary elements are always in the minority and the majority of the masses are found in "the middle". The "little men" who are in the majority, accordingly, should be viewed with interest by writers. This theory is only a very ordinary and common-place idea worded in an unclear and inarticulate way. However, it resulted in immediate and vicious attacks from the academic lords of the Party, who used as dynamite a theory which was full of contradictions and vagueness to the point of ignoring the common knowledge of historical materialism of their founding fathers. That the whole thing had become confusing and laughable was unimportant to them as the foremost thing was to destroy and eliminate such ordinary but harmful thoughts. This indeed is a fair indication of the fear and utmost hatred of a literary concept kindred to realism.

When the "theory of the person in the middle" was besieged and hammered, the historical view of "the masses being the heroes" was reiterated and re-emphasized. Under this flag which has been hoisted to the sky, the ruling class of China today has used the name of the people to accomplish the task of an emperor. The people and the masses have been deified verbally in order that they may be fooled. Indeed today's ruling class has in this respect surpassed previous generations. It is clearly and obviously prosaic and a whole pack of lies. Yet there are even educated people who are impressed. They surely are simple and gullible.

No one really knows what kind of literature Mao advocates. It is only known that the so called "proletarian literature" bears no resemblance to realist or similar literature. If it were to be named as "new religious literature", "regal eight-legged literature" or "propaganda literature", none is too appropriate or clear. Further, this would put the authors in a somewhat undignified position. There seems to be a fairly good term and that is "the literature of ideal heroism" which however may be confused with the ancient kind of ideal heroism. And so we add the word "neo" and call it "neo ideal heroism" and the authors would perhaps be prepared to accept this term.

We do not wish to say anything too authoritative on the future of "the literature of neo ideal heroism" but the present facts of life have helped to judge it — that its function is really limited.

Ideal and reality: ideal is always threadbare, empty and hackneyed but reality is rich, alive and full.

Heroes and the masses: the hero is bloodless and rationalistic but the masses are emotional, impulsive and unrestrained.

Personality of the Party and personality of the individual: the personality of the party is obedient, oppressive and passionless but the personality of the individual is eruptive and inexhaustible.

Literature is not just a tool for propaganda. Living literature will not be threadbare, empty or dogmatic but is rich, full and alive; it will not be bloodless and rationalistic, and should be emotional and impulsive; it will not be disciplined and oppressive but is eruptive and inexhaustible. From the standpoint that human history is a process of men attaining greater individuality and freedom and that human civilisation has evolved through a long period of time until today, this is not the first time that literature has heard the knell of impending doom.

The latest tolling of the bell has come from an existentialist thinker: "Before such a failure, the simplest thing to do would be to admit that the so called socialist realism has little to do with the great art . . . indeed, socialist realism should avow its kinship and that it is the twin brother of political realism. It sacrifices art for an end alien to art but which, in the matter of value, may appear to be superior to the latter. In a nut shell, it suppresses art temporarily in order to establish first justice. When justice takes its course, in a still indefinite future, art will in its turn resurrect. People thus apply to the matter of art this golden rule of today's wisdom (that teaches that one should not make an omelette without breaking eggs . . . But breaking more eggs does not mean a better omelette) . . . What the artistic cooks of our time should fear is overthrowing more baskets of eggs than they would have wanted and that, henceforth, the omelette of civilisation will never get done and that art will not resurrect at the end." (Camus, December, 1957, speech made at University of Uppsalla, Sweden)

Thus, with "realism in politics", China has returned to silence. And the "literature of neo ideal heroism" (or what is better known as "socialist realism") must be nothing but blank.

195

THE CULTURAL REVOLUTION AND LITERATURE

Whilst an economic and political system has been established, a social psychology which runs into contradiction with the system has also been shaped.

Such phenonmena have become the order of the day since the social structure of the Middle Ages was demolished with the dawn of the individual in the modern sense. Even in the "socialist" countries like Russia which claim to be on the road to making the dreams of mankind come true, similar occurrences are unavoidable. In fact, we have found even more dramatic manifestations of such conflicts. e.g. the Kronstadt Uprisings and the Hungarian Revolt. This has caused some Marxists to reflect. Over the last twenty odd years, there have been numerous movements to "transform men" in China, especially the Great Cultural Revolution between 1966 and 1969 and the so called "Anti-Lin, Anti-Confucius" campaigns which were both the results of Maoist reflections. Mao knew that if he could not mould a new "social character" according to an ideal plan, his "ideals" could never be fulfilled: this in fact was the crux of the Cultural Revolution. The Great Cultural Revolution was one of the greatest episodes of the political life of the last years of Mao Tse-tung who did not want to see it end so tragically. Mao had been careless and had forgotten that he was in the modern world (he paid too much attention to the influence of tradition in China). He thought that in this era, he could still transform mankind and create the "new man" according to his own will. Obviously, this was not a logical error. Mao Tse-tung had a tragic prescience of his failure but, like a medieval king, he did not lose his self-confidence.

However, the Great Cultural Revolution had burnt its marks in the memories of people more permanently than any other upheavals. Three things have been felt to have developed during and immediately after these three years. They are:

1) The beginning of the end of the Mao Tse-tung era (the collapse of the myth of Mao Tse-tung).
2) The question of "Whither China?" has been asked once again.
3) The appearance of a generation with a new outlook.

People will always remember the Great Cultural Revolution; it was like a festive display of selfless fervour, scenes of great spectacles, the bitterness of struggles, the redness of the blood of fallen comrades; the closeness and flirtation with death; the ever-changing situation, the intensity of self-repression and release, the length of the duration and deepness of despair . . . The new generation of youth and children who have confronted all these will remember some vivid sequences of this whole spectrum of experiences which have become the 'curses" of their lives. They dream of a way to recreate such unforgettable experiences of their lives and the easiest way is naturally literature.

The Great Cultural Revolution has faded out and yet countless spectres are roaming on the Continent of China.

REVELATIONS WHICH MOVE THE EARTH TO TEARS

With the background which we have described above, we shall try to trace the development of the thoughts of this generation of youth in China through this collection of somewhat disorderly poems, essays (letters) and novelettes.

Owing to the political climate of China, the authors of these poems and prose writings did not expect them to appear in print. They were written to be read by the authors themselves or a few people at the most. Even so, the writers tried to be very subtle. So, they did not write easily, but when they wrote, they threw in their body and soul.

196

Naturally, more often than not, they were dissecting and opening up themselves, giving evidence to their existence and pain. On their bodies and in their souls were incurable wounds, sustained during the Great Cultural Revolution. And they trembled at the reality they faced:

> The sun shines above!
> The poisoned river, its sluggish muddy water
> Glistened,
> Rolled on heavily.
>
> *(Self-revelation at the Poisoned River and Old Track)*

A picture that chills: up and above is the bright warm sun (signifying ideal); below is sluggish water reflecting the light of the sun (the ugly reality), which is a description of the China of today. Those who suffer indescribable pain are not in the minority:

> Oh, yes, many boats on the water
> Are rocking aimlessly,
> Soaked and muddied, in bedraggled confusion.
>
> *(Self-revelation at the Poisoned River and Old Track)*

But the author rejects their aimlessness and confusion and points out a road for himself:

> But my little boat,
> A boat on the poisoned river, its that –
> Its sole mast of thought,
> Perpetually pointing skywards!
> Forever after the radiant fiery sun.
>
> *(Self-revelation at the Poisoned River and Old Track)*

This is a loud but sad tune of the idealist, a portrayal of the thoughts of many an educated youth.

Some young thinkers had begun to doubt the beliefs which they held. Not only were they doubting, they were so miserable that they wondered whether there could be an ideal which they could hold fast. For example, in the poem "The Search":

> But the whiteness that I dream after,
> Spread wide and endless;
> I wish I could rest
> My heavy spirit,
> How peaceful!
> Only that it is ruined.
>
> *(The Search)*

So what is too perfect cannot be believed, because it cannot hold the "colours of the soul" – it is a kind of over-anxiety about perfection, because purity does scare people off. Why then the continued search? Well, the search itself is beauty, life and purpose!

> Wandering goes my restless spirit;
> Thinking about this kind of whiteness –
> That time it may grow thin, lose colour,

197

A faded, loyal spirit;
Like white marble, is better.

(The Search)

Life and the search is endless. And purity derives from the search. Yet roaming around day and night leads to exhaustion and illusion. Inside his heart is a desire to attain a certain "state" – a reality! This is the first thing he lacks in his daily life.

That was just about a year after they had painted on the road "The revolution is dead. Long live the revolution!" and pasted on the walls "When there's flint, fire will not be extinct." Experiencing destruction, frustration, and reflection, their disappointment at Mao Tse-tung was becoming more and more intense. This of course was not a light-hearted thing. For a long period of time, Mao Tse-tung had been in the eyes of many youths the embodiment of truth. This collapse had created an intolerable vacuum in their spiritual world, and so they were extremely careful and would think thrice in taking every step. Their works during this period could be found to have this quality, such as in "I Fear what I Love is Only the Beauty in My Heart". But they had seen the real China and this forced them to push their understanding further, resulting in the near completion of their reflections on the Great Cultural Revolution. In the novel "The Ages and the Poems", the first thing that Hsia Yen was saying to Lu Meng whom he had not seen for a long time was: 'If you want the ultimate meaning of the whole thing, it is this: that the question of 'Whither China?' is raised once again. To the thinking people of China, this is a spectacular sunrise.

The real revolution was born from the pseudo-revolution and was immediately terminated, followed by darkness and silent pogroms. They have betrayed themselves. We have betrayed ourselves. The revolution has betrayed the revolution. The flags of ideals have been discarded, being picked up by others and thrown away again . . . and the new generation has walked past the corpse of the revolution, silently forward. Idealistic demands have been increasingly tormenting this generation of youth. They have witnessed and participated in history and their fate leads them to face a future trial.

Is this regrettable? Or fortunate?"

(Chapter Five, The Ages and The Poems)

After a prolonged period of confused identity, they recognised their position which was to become a new generation committed to new ideals. This self-confidence and sense of mission enabled them to shake off the depression and decadence which were becoming more and more prevalent among the youth of their age.

However, in the process of searching for identity, they felt extremely lonely. "The road was long and distant and I shall search everywhere." Chu Yuan could still keep company with a high hat and his long sword, or could befriend the sweet grass and gracious orchids. What they had was a lost faith.

I have been
feeding my life's loneliness
on the blazing fire!
The green flames,
leapt endlessly.
Then it froze,
and turned into three feet of ice!

I still throw the flowers of my life,
Into the graveyards of the future,
Scatter, wilt and wither without regret.
I use Love as groundwork,
Built a hut and guarded myself,
Fighting the cold of the nine worlds,
Never did I know that my loving heart had already turned to ice.

(The Song for Man)

The pseudo-revolution had frozen the poet's heart and the future which existed in hope had died and been buried. This bitter affection had been eroded and later when he met "her", another searcher on the road (it was lucky that he had not willed to die), he could not at the beginning believe what he saw:

I roam the four corners of earth,
To seek the land of beauty,
Instead I read an epitaph;
"The road to beauty: the form — the heart."
Oh! Plato's beauty of the intellect!
But my heart has been frozen,
Now shall it bring forth icy blossoms of love?

(The Song for Man)

This is an ecstatic discovery of a companion of mutual ideals on the same road. They reached out, awaiting the appearance of the "new man". They were scattered in every corner of the country, stubborn and tired, aspiring to return to the "new generation":

With many witty and gay flowers in my hand,
I still look up, waiting,
I am sucking yellow and golden florets,
Wandering endlessly on the boundless land.

(Thank you! The Sparks of Life of the New Generation)

From the snow-bound north to Hainan with its howling baboons and soaring mountains, from the picturesque delta of the Pearl River to the icy lake of Shenyen, from the urbanised cities to the dense forests of Shih Shan, with hundreds and thousands of miles in between, the young people took advantage of "hsia-fang" (sent to the countryside) to establish secret connections, to discuss and to persuade. They read a thousand scrolls and travelled a thousand miles and they cared about the fate of China with the feeling of being at cross-roads. When it was discovered that standing face to face was a group of beautiful and zealous lives, their gratitude burst into acclaims for the new generation:

A golden haze before my eyes,
And I have come before the altar of high ideals:—
The fire of new life is sparkling with white heat on the altar,
My spirit has been consummated by the white flame into pure white!
Oh!

Unending joy.
This white flame wipes out my doubts
And erases my weariness,
Gave my tenacity
The glow of a new life.
Long live! Majestic altar! Great work will be done on earth.
Salute! Sparks of fire! Godly flames that has been born in the Garden of Eden.

(Thank you! The Sparks of Life of the New Generation)

Spectacular and fabulous! Similar acclamation can be seen from "Blossoms! The White Cherry Has Blossomed." This also tells us that the new generation are new idealists. The old idealists who were born during the May Fourth Movement have become decadent, following the path of "political realism". Their ideals have become "the utopia for reaction", and are oppressing and generating this "new generation". However, if the new generation were asked to be more concrete about the content of their "altar of high ideals", it seems that the whole generation would remain uncertain. As described above, it is not in the nature of man to endure a vacuum in the spiritual dimension. Therefore the "altar" is something which they have created to take temporary shelter. The high ideals would of course be perfect and limitless harmony and wonder. Even a person as calm and suspicious as Lu Hsun wrote "Good Story" (written on 14th February 1925) to soothe himself, and we can imagine that state of mind.

As for the coming together of this generation of youths after the Great Cultural Revolution, the readers will have to discover and understand them by reading the documentation and description in the section of short essays in this book:

"What kind of worker and singer, what kind of searcher and sufferer, what kind of sacrifice, awakening, sudden change, running, striding forward, and singing!"

(Dialogue and Subtitles in the Deserted Land)

In this section is their correspondence selected with the addition of titles by the editor. Yet these words in print are the most precious. Writers and historians have always placed great importance on letters and correspondence and this is not hard to understand. It is because correspondence can reflect the mentality of the writer, the relationship between man and man, man and society, in the most truthful and sensitive way. "The letters of Lu Hsun" have so far not been published in Mainland China (with the exception of those found in his "Complete" Works, which have been very strictly selected with added distorted footnotes and interpretations) and the reason for this is that in the hundreds of letters of Lu Hsun, the manifestation of the great soul is total and expresses itself in contempt and scorn for a number of party lords.

In this collection of essays extracted from letters, a very melancholy atmosphere prevails. It is because their own lives are melancholy:

"After tasting all the green fruits of man's wisdom and passions, I, who am twenty-six, have naturally bitter memories. But I still think of beauty and endeavour to imagine the construction of it in its greatest intensity. Inside the huge quantity of bitter juice is a little minute nourishing matter. With chilled heart, saddened white hair, hate since childhood, I do not know what is love. Since a very early age, I have been lonely."

(Untitled)

There is even ruthless surgery upon oneself – (e.g. in "Tortuous Road"), the reader will see vividly and breathe the agony of the age, and be conscious of approaching disaster.

200

"How many impressions have been forgotten? What has happened is like a perfect dream. This to me will have great meaning. The roads which have been passed, I will not tread again. Let green grass and little flowers grow on the roads behind, with fragrance and freedom everywhere! But then I turn my head, those green and white, those little red, golden yellow and light purple, are so lovely, so close to me! My mind is disturbed and I let tears drop. I want to open my arms and embrace them, kissing them. I cannot bear to have another look . . .

I think I am writing to you. There is no doubt about this, and yet, I am also writing for myself to read! Only to give myself a piece of evidence as something to chew on in the future, to remember when I said good-bye to you and to raise the heavy curtain of memories: people's faces are like dreams, the mountains and the rivers are like dreams!"

(To Say Farewell)

Here the lover says farewell to his loved one who has experienced with him great pains in the past and expresses the agony of their separation. Have you ever read such painful and resolute words before? He who has been tormented by ideal desires, wants to widen his horizon, to seek the way and has decided to take an adventurous road. Not long before, he has received a farewell gift, the book "Chai Wen Je" and the friend who sent it has disappeared, drowned. Now he is leaving the book behind for others and is on his way. His friends could not bear to sing the farewell song which Ni An sang for his brother Ni Ching.

The authoress of "the Song of Man" devotes all of her energy to writing. She has completed her plans and is ready to entrust them to her comrades. She wants to devote the little she has. To her, it would be the fulfilment of her life and she would accept calmly the final destruction — the end of a political prisoner! Yet cruel reality reveals to her that even this may not be achieved. She cannot trust anyone and at the same time, she becomes aware of her own childishness. And her pain is so great that she throws the crystallization of her life into the stove fire. She breaks down from the mental strain and falls sick.

"Very few people have the opportunity to face almost certain death which makes them aware of the true history of their whole life . . . and still continue to live . . . after a scrutiny of life, supposing life is still possible!"

(Song of Man)

She finally lives. She has no regrets. Soon she is on the tortuous road once more, where she remains struggling.

Then, there is torturing young love, solemn tenderness and thorough bitterness: "I open my wide and tearless eyes and swear to heaven and earth: that I shall not kill my personality, I shall not twist my nature. I shall love with the greatest love and hate with the most intense hate. I shall keep the warmth of my lover on my lips and take revenge on barbarity!"

("Love" Standing Beside the Waters of the Black Sea)

It is a howl that shakes the iron gates. It is a loud shout of the lover's name and a declaration of war on the world of decadence. In "The Story of a Cup of Water", the two authors discovered through misunderstanding the real meaning of life and love and together they resist the strange attacks from outside with a bitter smile. On reading these works, we should be aware of the fact that in twentieth century China, the oldest and most hackneyed concepts are still being kept alive to the detriment of the youthful sons and daughters. More tragically, sometimes the destruction has not come from outside but is contained in one's own mind. The serious sense of guilt is part of the law of morality in such a society and is an important part of the "social character". And the Party should be "thanked" for endowing society with it. The novel "Shen Ping" utilises this as its subject matter and it tells of a sad, shameful, pitiful but true story with very light and charming diction.

According to the Chou Ju Jen, "To discuss other's ideas is to preach a message, and to preach one's own message is self-expression of one's will." Following this distinction between "self-expression" (spontaneous literature) and "message preaching" (the literature of discourse), the short essays collected in this book should be grouped under the category of "self-sepression" (spontaneous literature). This is the beauty of correspondence. Perhaps the chief harvest of Chinese literature in the mainland during period is "the literature of correspondence"!

The section of novelettes consists of five pieces of work. Apart from "Shen Ping" mentioned above, the other four novels deal with wider subject matters. In "The Personal Writings of a Psychotic", the first person is used and the author relates her political persecution complex as a disciple of God who has participated in the revolution. The author attempts to use an overlapping technique to portray four main themes: the past conflict between human nature and revolution, the conflict between God and His world, the conflict between man and himself, and the conflict between generations. At the same time, the novel is a strong and damning accusation against totalitarian dictatorship.

"Revolution is great. Has it lofty aims? The aims are great. Are the fighters pure? God has not granted it unity. Yet I can't be at a distance from this world! There's always a way. It can't be nothingness."

He fell back to his reclining chair. He had totally lost hope.

'Son, are you insisting on leaving God?'

I walked close to him and asked. He nodded his had and with much effort he said, 'I understand; your God, my God and their gods. I only love mine – a man must be so.'

'We are separated by a whole world.'

I felt that he was a stranger to me."

(The Personal Writings of a Psychotic)

The emphasis is on the expression of thoughts and not the description of visions.

"Yu Lan" is a complete and moving story about Yu Lan from the moment she started to understand things to the moment of her death. That was exactly the period from when the Chinese communists established their regime to the time of the Great Cultural Revolution. There has not been a non-"message-preaching" novel with this period of time as background. "The Song of Rice Planting" by Chiang Oi Ling is about the peasants after land reforms. It is one hundred thousand words long, covering a period of two winters and Chiang has managed with great ease. "Yu Lan" is but thirty thousand words, covering so many episodes which have taken place over nearly twenty years. It was very difficult to tailor the story and as a result, the last half appears to be somewhat cramped. Although the story is concentrated on the person of Yu Lan, it portrays in a vivid and lively manner the society of China today: the personal relationships, the creation of values, the psychology of the masses during the movements. The image of Yu Lan represents the beautiful side of the tradition of the Chinese people, which can never be destroyed or interrupted either by force or by cultural domination. She will become more cleansed, purified and released from the filth and corruption to attain "manhood" and "love".

"The Curse of the Sea" describes escape and the life of prisons. The black cold of the sea and the horror of death are not as dark as totalitarian rule. The seed of rebellion is sown and spread although the sacrifice of life may be the price to pay.

Six chapters of the long novel "The Ages and the Poems" have been extracted and included in this book. This has been done because of particular circumstances and not because we would wish to submit an incomplete piece of work to our readers. On the other hand we would have been too miserly to leave it out. The good thing about it is that it directly depicts the young men and women after the Cultural Revolution; it reveals the "curse" of their lives, their personal destiny in connection with the destiny of China as well as the destiny of this age; and it shows how death and love become one in their soul . . . The readers who are interested may hope that this novel will appear in print soon.

If we compare the works of the youth of Mainland China with those of the May Fourth New Literary Movement, we could discover some similarities and yet there are also some differences. They are also very different from the works of Hong Kong or overseas Chinese youth. We shall not try to discuss the reasons. What is required is to summarise the characteristics of the literature of the "New Generation", some of which are collected in this book, as follows:

1. The manifestations of miseries (the tone is heavy-hearted but not rash; the style is angry but not decadent);

2. The colour of idealism (exhibiting the spirit of commitment and the desire to search);

3. The emotions of the ancient epics (intertwining joy and sorrow). We may call this the "literature of the awakening".

14th July 1974

AN INTERVIEW WITH AN ULTRA-LEFTIST

The following is a record of the interview originally published in Undergrad, issue 15, 1974/75.

Note from the editor of Undergrad: Wu Man was a member of the Red Guards in Canton during the Cultural Revolution. He fled to Hong Kong in 1973. The introduction to the book 'Revelations that Moved the Earth to Tears' was written by him. This interview consists of 2 parts, the first dwelling on the political views of Mr. Wu, and the second on the literary trends in China and the background of the book 'Revelations that Moved the Earth to Tears."

Q. Many of our students have read 'Revelations that Move the Earth to Tears" and have considered it representative of the literature of China after Liberation. The book should foster much discussion, but, its significance isn't limited to its function as a work of art, it leads us to an evaluation of the new China. It is a re-evaluation of China by the youths who went through the turmoil of the Cultural Revolution. It can rightfully be termed 'historical literature' as it carries with it the spirit of the times, and is basically different from the over done traditional anti-communist propaganda. Therefore before we go into the literary aspects of this book, we would like to know your views on China.

A. This is a formidable question. We could review what we know about China's revolutions. Previous issues of Undergrad have featured a series on New China in which Yu Shuet's 'The Dusk of Rationality' is representative of our views. The Cultural Revolution had a decided impact on us, in that youths who were generally idealistic about the revolution began to doubt their previous ideals.

Q. We all know that during the revolution, Sheng-wu-lien, the ultra left of the Red Guards had released an important essay 'Whither China?' which the 70s Biweekly had reprinted. Why was there a markedly different approach between the above essay and 'The Dusk of Rationality'?

A. There was a new view point in 'The Dusk of Rationality', and compared with 'Whither China?', it should be seen as a new stage. But 'Whither China?', appearing in the form it did at that time, had its limitations. During the Cultural Revolution, Mao Tse Tung assumed the guise of the liberator of the people from the clutches of the bureaucrats. In the latter part of the Revolution, the spontaneous movement of the people made Mao Tse Tung feel personally and politically endangered. In other words, Mao Tse Tung had to switch from one tactic to another.

The author of 'Whither China?' could grasp this point very clearly, but in view of the situation, had to make use of the promises Mao Tse Tung made to the people, as a cover for attacks on the bureaucrats. We could not interpret them solely by the terminology they used, for the bureaucrats used the same terminology, but the essence was quite different.

Q.   We should differentiate Mao Tse Tung from other bureaucrats as he himself advocated their overthrow. Maoism actually is idealistic as Mao Tse Tung personally sparked off the Revolution to eliminate bureaucracy. But the ultra left Red Guards had carried his ideals to the extreme so that Mao had to fall back on realism. Criticisms on Mao Tse Tung should be based on concrete analysis.

A.   This is a good way of looking at it. We should not just write him off as a bureaucrat, as he had his ideals also, although he was the chief representative of the class. Mao Tse Tung's power had been stripped before the Revolution and it was the bureaucrats who had victimized him, and therefore he had deep resentment and bitterness towards them. After weighing the pros and cons, and geared by his own stubbornness, Mao Tse Tung turned to the Cultural Revolution. He felt that in order to implement Communism, the 'new ideal man' must and should be moulded, for the Chinese society is basically different from the West. The Revolution had become an experiment to him.

If Mao Tse Tung's aspirations were the same as those of the people, it might work out, but regrettably, Mao Tse Tung, as all other rulers do, feared the people. This was due to his limited knowledge of Marxism and his need to keeping his position within the national political power structure. To guide the practice of the Revolution through Marxism, on one hand brought success but on the other resulted in a degeneration of the ideals. This was the tragedy of Marxism. Marxism had its roots in humanism, but through the conscious effort of making socialism scientific, rationalistic and realistic, had resulted in a 'political realism'. Throughout his lifetime, Karl Marx had few chances to put his ideologies into practice, therefore he could well have retained the humanistic element. But by the time of Lenin, Marxism had undergone a qualitative change. Lenin was more of a democrat, but he still could not help becoming autocratic. When Stalin took over, Marxism degenerated into utilitarianism, a "Marxism" which sneered at human ideals. Mao Tse Tung did not interpret Marxism through humanism in the endeavour to maintain its best qualities, but interpreted it as a tool for struggle with dialectics as the method. When he discovered that Marxism had failed on a world scale, he decided on an unprecedented act – to complete the communist revolution in China. He often found it easy to compromise with reality, for example, during the January Revolution, when the people rose to seize power aimed at setting up the People's Commune, Mao Tse Tung then indicated that it was not yet time for such establishments but suggested instead the establishment of revolutionary committees.

From a certain point of view, the Cultural Revolution could be said to have changed from idealism to realism. Mao Tse Tung exemplified this point in that at the onset of the Revolution, his beliefs were not yet consolidated but the Revolution taught him just as it had taught the people. Mao gradually came to realize the aspirations of the people just as they gradually came to see his. The people was not one homogeneous mass according to the ideal, but rather that they had individuality and were eruptive, with sentiments and feelings. The model Mao Tse Tung had set up to mould man could only destroy the nature of the people. This situation explains why during the latter stage of the Revolution the people were so oppressed and the revolutionary ideals discarded.

Q.   What is this humanism on which you have laid so much emphasis? Why does Marxism, containing this humanistic element, not work out in the end? Hasn't your criticism of Mao Tse Tung gone beyond the realms of reality into nihilism?

A.   Humanism is not the teaching of any scholar, any school of thought nor is it the teaching of any particular class. We believe that man is born with the ability to reflect on the complexities of his own life and that of the collective, to cherish the true and the good and discard the evil and decadent. Since history began, man has gone through numerous catastrophes to leave us an invaluable legacy — this bit of human spirit. This human spirit is reflected in all aspects of life, in the products of the field, in literary works, in scientific development; man is obstinate in keeping what is good. He can transcend his reality, for example, Reminiscences of Utopia by Tao Yuan Ming, and the uprising of Spartacus. In the history of man, all good revolutions were coloured by a healthy humanism.

As to whether the practice of Marxism brought about tragedy and the criticism of Mao Tse Tung I have just made is severe enough to be called nihilism, our views are as follows:

The practice of Marxism and its belief are quite different things. It could be clearly seen that humanism and agitation for class struggle were incongruent with each other. People have always believed that socialism is the obvious outcome of the revolution, that the revolution will certainly lead to a brighter future and prosperity. Compared to the misery of the people before the May 4th movement, this belief could be considered valid. But viewed from the history of humanity, by the tenth year after Liberation, China has left an ugly scar on humanity, marring her own progress to modernization. Our criticism was levelled at Mao Tse Tung not because he could not reach the Marxist ideals, but because his form of government was a bad influence on the future of China and the rise of a humanistic society.

Q.   There is still an unresolved question, the conflict between subjectivity and objectivity, idealism and realism, theory and practice. Was it the limitation of objective factors such as the economy, political structure of the society, that hindered Mao Tse Tung from putting ideals into practice?

A.   I recall that after the article, The Dusk of Rationality had been published in the Undergrad, there were many different responses. Some friends raised this point also, mainly pointing out that revolutionary ideals were necessary, but during this 'transitional period', Mao Tse Tung just couldn't realize his ideals. We could not accept this 'transitional period' as excuse, for if we accepted it, many problems would disappear. We deliberated on this point and felt that 'can't be helped' was only an excuse. Suppose we refrain from criticising Mao Tse Tung from an individual, minority or even the people's point of view, and take a more 'objective' view (the mere mentioning of objectivity will certainly solicit a torrent of criticisms) — and evaluate him through his own philosophy. At any time, rulers have used the same excuse — monarchists are forced to foreign invasion for the sake of keeping peace; it 'can't be helped' if demonstrators are arrested by colonial governments etc. We do not need any theories to back us up in handling these kind of problems except we don't want 'transitional periods'. Who would dare to say that India is not on the way to Communism?

You may ask what are the solutions to this problem? Many feel it is difficult to answer. We feel that there cannot be a complete answer for every group or every one of us. An example can be seen from the socialist revolution of the peasants in Ji Shui, Hupeh mentioned in "The Dusk of Rationality". It would be seen that the people can find their own directions.

Q. Enough of politics. Shall we move to literature? The Introduction of 'Revelations that Move the Earth to Tears' criticised the Chinese Communists, since their takeover of the country, for practising the 'new-religious literature', 'regal eight-legged-literature' 'propaganda literature', which is more political than anything, instead of realism in literature. It is generally referred to as the "neo idealistic heroism" in literature. What actually is it? To our understanding, literary work was markedly different after the Cultural Revolution. This Neo Idealistic Heroism trend refers to officially-recognised works published after the Cultural Revolution. Could you further explain literary trend after Liberation? The content, style and technique employed in the 'Revelations that Move the EArth to Tears' is definitely different from other literary works published after Liberation. What are your views on its nature and function?

A. Many people are of the opinion that literature is basically free and unique. This neo idealistic heroism should be considered within its Maoist context. Mao Tse Tung had made it very clear in his lecture at the Yenan Conference on Literature and Art that he regarded literature as a means, a screw in the machine. This concept was picked up from Lenin. Marx and Engels had little to say on literature, but Marx personally loved literature, especially the work of Heine. Everyone knew that Heine was not a revolutionary although he was sympathetic to the revolution. Lenin criticised Gorki for not conforming to the revolution. Mao Tse Tung used this point to stress the usefulness of literature in revolution. Everyone disobeyed him on the sly before the Cultural Revolution: the literary field was still able to ignore Mao Tse Tung's directives. It was through the Cultural Revolution that Mao Tse Tung was able to consolidate his literary influence.

The term neo idealistic heroism was in fact a very narrow term and was used because we could find nothing better. Literary trends since the May Fourth Movement were influenced by writers like Gogol, Tolstoy. Critical realism in literature was very popular then and writers from Lu Hsun to Mao Tun were affected by this trend, and what was called 'literature from life' and the 'people's literature' came into being. After Liberation, people felt that critical realism should be the trend literature should take. Camus could not find a suitable term to describe the trend in his discourse on literary works in socialist countries and simply used the term 'socialist realism' whereas in actual fact literary works after Liberation had nothing to do with realism. It could be said to be 'anti-realism', for allowing realistic portrayals to appear in literature would be allowing the political world to be ridiculed. Realism in literature tended to be controversial as it brought to light an undemocratic society, inequality and a deformed reality. Writers who were in fact loyal to the Party and country were criticised after Liberation because they were advocates of realism.

This trend, the neo idealistic heroism advocated by the communists, also influenced us. We have been educated in an idealistic spirit and tend to write everything down as 'transitional'. We always looked forward, neglected and despised reality, so therefore the works found in this volume of literature are strongly idealistic. I recall a reporter from the New York Times asking me whether life in the country had been difficult, and why hadn't it been reflected in the book. It was entirely the result of idealism making one oblivious to reality. What was painful to us while we were in the countryside was not that life was hard but that we were disillusioned. The lower middle strata of the peasants had not conformed to the image as publicised. Private plots were tilled with greater care than the communal land. They were not the heroes depicted by Mao Tse Tung. It was in discovering all these facts that we felt the greatest anguish.

Q. If your works were merely depicting reality, displaying the dark side of socialist China, your work might have degenerated into rightist anti-communist anti-Chinese formalism. It was because your work reflected an insistence on searching for the ideal that made them works of art.

A. I am not saying anything against idealism. Many great works of literature contain idealism, like Cervantes' Don Quixote. But we would reject the neo idealistic heroism because it was created by tailoring it to the concept of one man and one party. Mao Tse Tung's idealism had strangled literature. We wanted an idealism that is not a doctrine nor a vacuum but an integral part of life, unique and with passion. We don't want idealism that comes as a screw in a machine.

Q. Then idealism should be part of life.

A. That's right. I can tell you a story. One of the authors of the poetry section, L, was almost a fanatic in search of idealism. She thrived entirely on the intellectual sphere. After the Cultural Revolution, she also went into the countryside taking with her many questions. She feverishly studied the works of Marx and Lenin day and night with the intention of evaluating Marxism. This was a dangerous thing to do. Yang Hsi Kwang's "Whither China?" had brought him 20 years of imprisonment and actually no one really knew whether he was alive or dead. L was prepared to sacrifice herself in putting her thoughts to paper, so that others coming after could benefit from it and then she would willingly die for her cause. But she could not even accomplish this. None of her comrades would agree to safeguard her papers. One female officer of some rank finally took pity on L but she only made a double layer leather case for L to hide her papers, and told her to take it with her to the countryside. Up to this point, before L had a mental breakdown, she could not sleep and it suddenly dawned upon her that her idealism was out of touch with reality. She should have sought idealism from life. In the 'Song of Man' she wrote 'I finally understood: there is no such thing as abstracting oneself from reality. Ideals and beliefs should be obtained from life and yet I have forsaken it.' She completed her work with all her energy.

Q. We feel that this book is strongly individualistic, that it has swung from one extreme to another, as illustrated in the love stories. We know that Russia has produced a writer Solzhenitsyn whose works represent an accusation against Russian autocracy, but some Marxists from the West point out that this is an reactionary aspect of Solzhenitsyn's work. What are your thoughts on this point?

A. Firstly I would like to point out that this sort of manuscript is plentiful in the underground in China. The point is how can we understand the personal feelings of the authors. After Liberation, everyone refrained from writing realistically for this trend had become a grave offence. Why was it that everyone felt that Mao Tse Tung was being criticised when they read 'Hai Jui's Dismissal from Office'? It could be that everyone could not and avoided expressing their opinions frankly under the long-term autocracy. This situation extended through all levels of the society. Just take a look at the "Red Flag" Magazine in which one attacked the other. Everyone understood that 'temporary officers' 'being spoilt' and 'pacifist' were euphemisms launched at each other by the two parties. This was the spirit which was permeating the whole country and naturally, appeared in writings. For example, there is a line in 'Dialogue and Subtitles in the Deserted Land' which said 'someone committed a monstrous offence'. Outsiders can see nothing in this phrase, but actually it is hinting at the Lin Piao incident. Some friends asked me to decypher the incidents one by one, but it is impossible, for there are far too many metaphors and understatements. Love poems reflect the reality that a lover was no more than the projection of an ideal. "I Fear What I Love is Only the Beauty in My Heart" illustrates this point very clearly. Ideals were generally expressed in feminine forms often as goddesses.

I cannot comment on Solzhenitsyn as I have only read "One Day in the Life of Ivan Denisovich". Individualism is of course something very natural. After Liberation the Chinese communists severely repressed individualism, but after the Cultural Revolution, it grew to enormous proportions. It was understandable within the context of its socio-psychological background, as people had no way to balance out their needs, except through an impulsive release of feelings or sublimation. Viewed from this context it is possible to understand the individual in the works in this book. Letters and poems are an expression of the individual but in fact they incorporate and reflect the plight of the whole generation. It is different from the individualism expressed by young people abroad, as the works in this book are the condensation of thoughts on the meaning of life by Chinese young people of this generation. After going through considerable psychological upheaval, they can scarcely look after themselves let alone reflect the aspiration of all the Chinese people. Was it not the same situation for Lu Hsun after the 1911 Revolution? He was copying epitaphs alone under a wattle tree, oblivious to the cold and clammy caterpillars falling upon his neck. Therefore the poetry section contains one piece:

– I have been
feeding my life's loneliness
on the blazing fire!
The green flames, leapt endlessly
– Then it froze, and turned into three feet of ice.

In China the ideal was not accomplished by the collective character of the people but by strangling the life of the individual. In clinging to our individual ideals, we are rebelling against autocracy. This is invaluable to us, as it is the future hope for China.

Q. This leads to another question – how does the individual reconcile with the group? What are your views to this large and somewhat philosophical question?

A. I have always felt that insisting that the individual fit in with the group is perfectionist; we should rather expect unending search for a balance between the individual and the group, to maintain a suitable distance between the two. To my understanding, subjectivity can always transcend the objective environment. Struggles are only the unwholesome and debased price we had to pay. In the hands of the politician the revolution is tainted, but that does not mean that we are against the revolution. This is a distressing situation but we would have to throw ourselves into it. The individual and the group are so different yet cannot be separated. No man is an island. There are no Robinson Crusoe's, but we must admit that man has to reserve some living space for himself.

Q. There is a quite interesting question. One journalist asked me to get her a copy of this book as she was anxious to read it but doubted its truthfulness. We also have some doubts as the works in this book reflect a lot of reading and understanding of foreign literature, which we believe is difficult to come by in China. Could you tell us about the general reading habits in China?

A. This is a question of interest to many people. We must not be biased by the anti-communist propaganda that the people are all ignorant and the Mainland is a hell. In fact before the Cultural Revolution, China had published a number of works by Western writers, especially Russian ones. That was a fine series of very high standard. Therefore many students were familiar with foreign culture. I have met some young people from China in Hong Kong, who have a very deep understanding of Russian culture.

The Cultural Revolution is also an important reason why we could read so many books. This might seem unbelievable. The one thing the general public abroad could not forgive China was that the authorities encouraged Red Guards to 'destroy the four ancients' thereby destroying Chinese culture. Actually we did not destroy it – we rushed into the national libraries and confiscated the books which we then read in private. Professor Fung Nai Chao of Chung Shan University had a personal collection of books which we confiscated. After the Cultural Revolution, a document issued by the Sheng-wu-lien "Whither China?" further stimulated our desire for reading. "Whither China?" affected us very deeply, for which we have the Communist leaders to thank. When they issued an order to criticise this essay, the whole country was in an uproar. All the Red Guards fought to get a copy of it. The method they used was to attack it on the surface but to promote it on the quiet, like putting a comment on each publication saying that this essay was being criticised by the Central Committee therefore everyone should read it in detail; once was not enough, it must be read at least three times over. The mere title 'Whither China?' was challenging enough, and the "Dictatorship of the Proletariat and Our Mission', "The Program of Sheng-wu-lien" all stimulated us to think. We needed a lot to read, to provide a basis for discussion. Our discussions went really deep, for some had already raised such questions as 'the revolutionary could remake the world' but could he 'maintain his hold on it'; the validity of Marxism etc. The fervour with which the Red Guards devoured books had to be seen to be believed. Because it was forbidden to read the banned books in public, we established underground libraries in which we circulated our books and discussed problems. The learning potential of the Red Guards went far beyond anything this book can express. A large number of masterpieces were composed, eg. some wrote articles discussing Marxism, the Cultural Revolution, the revolution in China, and there was a script for a movie in which the film started with a flutter of leaflets from a train leaving Wu Han. The technique fitted a montage and it was a pity that these compositions could not pass out of China for they would open a new page in the history of Chinese Culture.

There is one more point I would like to raise, that is we have been raised in different environments and the problems we face are different. We former Red Guards are in better position in a way, for we could feel and get to understand the oppression and alienation you experience in bourgeois society. We can also have direct access to what you write. Your situation is different. You have not lived in China. One of the purposes of publishing this book is, hopefully to bridge the gap between young people abroad and ourselves. We are Chinese despite all our differences. There are many areas in which we need to fight side by side. Long-term separation would only increase our rejection of each other and make us strangers. Let's hope that we can exchange views more often.

CONCERNING SOCIALIST DEMOCRACY AND LEGAL SYSTEM —

DEDICATED TO CHAIRMAN MAO

AND

THE FOURTH NATIONAL PEOPLE'S CONGRESS

By Li I-che

A spectacular sight appeared recently on Peking Road in Canton. A big-character poster was displayed, which defiantly extended for a hundred yards in length. Crowds of attentive readers mingled with the omnipresent Maoist cadres; all were marveling at, pondering, and busily copying this significant political writing. The sheer size of this "revolutionary," or in Maoist terms "counterrevolutionary," poster was impressive, for it contained no less than twenty thousand Chinese characters and occupied no less than sixty-seven sheets of news-print paper.

Li I-che, the name appearing under the title of the poster, is, in fact, a collective pseudonym of a group of three ex-Red guards. The Chinese authorities identified the real name of the writer and the leader of this "counterrevolutionary" group as Li Cheng-t'ien, a youngman from Wuhan

Reflecting on the Great Proletarian Cultural Revolution, Li wrote this article which according to his own statement could be publicized only in the form of big-character poster.

The first draft was completed on September 13 and the second one on December 12 of 1973. Because of the political situation, particularly the delay of the convening of the Fourth National People's Congress and criticism from some "revolutionary friends," the final version was not completed until November 7, 1974, apparently with considerable modifications plus a preface more lengthy than the main body. Stenciled copies of the poster were circulated. Before long, this document has found its way to other places on the Chinese mainland and even overseas.

According to some sources, the local Maoist cadres were stunned by the poster; and they referred the incident and the contents of the poster to the CCP Central Committee for instruction. Li Hsien-nien, vice-premier of the State Council of Communist China, handed down his verdict that the poster was "Reactionary through and through, vicious and malicious to the extreme."

The fate of the author was thus sealed. Public security authorities in Canton put Li I-che under arrest and temporarily detained him. As a counter-revolutionary culprit and a "negative teacher," Li was brought to various units and mass meetings for public criticism and humiliation. He was also required to write reports of self-criticism for perusal by the authorities.

Since the poster has been so influential and has generated so much debate, a simple self-criticism by Li was, in the opinion of Communist authorities, not sufficient to put the matter to rest. Following past examples, another orthodox poster under the pseudonym of Hsüan Chi-wen appeared in Canton, which was supposed to deliver a coup de grace to Li I-che, or the Li Cheng-t'ien group, and his poster. Although the orthodox criticism was probably penned out by the Propaganda Department of the CCPCC — the highest official organ for dealing with such matters — the quality appeared much inferior to the poster of Li I-che. As a result, the editors do not see the necessity of reproducing Hsuan's poster here. However interested readers may be supplied with a copy of it on request.

Like Rationality at Dusk, the Li I-che poster represents the development of the ultra-left stream of thought among Chinese youths since Sheng-wu-lien's Whither China? The whole tone of the poster is "reformist" but the "reformism" must be seen not only in the light of the inadequacies of its authors but also in the light of the extremely repressive nature of the Maoist regime.

PREFACE

Since August of last year [1973], the Fourth National People's Congress, which the people thought would soon be convened, has not been held, while, on the other hand, our article, which is a dedication to it [the Congress], has been regarded as a "system" of ours.

In this article, we have primarily criticized the Lin Piao system. And the criticism has been further continued in subsequent articles. Quite unexpectedly, some of our friends have thrown back this "system" to us as something "frightening." Perhaps, the extensiveness of our criticism and the completeness of our self-exposure can indeed validate themselves to become a "system." But, this kind of "system" – even if we may rightly acknowledge that we do have a certain system, is not heretical to the Marxist system. We only attempt to use the ideological weapons of Marxism to make a serious improvement in the spheres which have been influenced and damaged by the Lin Piao System. In fact, we have not accomplished this yet.

There are no contradictions between this new exposure of the Lin Piao System and our comments on it made one year ago. On the contrary, what surprises us is that our comments have been proven to be valid in many respects. In the present version (the third draft) being posted on the streets, only some slight modifications are made in the first five parts, while the sixth part – our expectations for the People's Congress and our recommendations concerning the legal system – has been rewritten because we were no longer satisfied with the original writing due to developments of the situation in the current year, which made us feel that some deepened exposition was necessary. More numerous are those questions which were only briefly touched upon in last year's paper and thus need further efforts, as well as those such questions recently involved. About these, we wish to talk a little in this preface.

The reason that our "system" makes some feel "frightened" is, in the first place, the main subject of our discussion.

Allegedly, anyone who has a little bit of Marxist-Leninist common sense will not talk about the so-called "socialist democracy and legal system". Admitting that we are the ones who do not have an *iota* of Marxist-Leninist common sense, we do know several events which have happened since the 1960s: First, most socialist countries have had a restoration of capitalism, and more than a hundred parties no longer believe in Marxism-Leninism; second, there emerged in our country, China, the Great Proletarian Cultural Revolution which was, and is, not fully understood by many people; and third, Comrade Mao Tse-tung has summed up the experience from the half century's practice of socialism and thus brought forward the basic line for the whole historical stage of socialism, which we must quote here in full:

> Socialist society covers a fairly long historical period. In the historical period of socialism, there are still classes, class contradictions and class struggle, there is the struggle between the socialist road and the capitalist road, and there is the danger of capitalist restoration. We must recognize the protracted and complex nature of this struggle. We must heighten our vigilance. We must conduct socialist education. We must correctly understand and handle class contradictions and class struggle, distin-

guish the contradictions between ourselves and the enemy from those among the people and handle them correctly. Otherwise a socialist country like ours will turn into its opposite and degenerate, and a capitalist restoration will take place. From now on we must remind ourselves of this every year, every month and every day so that we can retain a rather sober understanding of this problem and have a Marxist-Leninist line. [Mao's words quoted by Lin Piao in his "Report to the Ninth National People's Congress of the Communist Party of China," *Peking Review*, No. 18 (April 30, 1969), p. 20.]

Thus we know that the socialist system still needs improvement and that it is not yet perfect. The fact that, in so many countries, it has not beaten the new bourgeois class and there have thus emerged capitalist restorations, as well as the fact that in China there was a "second revolution," all clearly prove that the proletariat must, in this "fairly long historical period," conduct many cultural revolutions to make the socialist system become better and better day by day.

These viewpoints are, of course, not exactly Marxist-Leninist common sense. But we can assert, based on them, that included among the questions in various aspects of socialism also are the questions of socialist democracy and legal system, which entirely deserve discussion and should be discussed. What is so "frightening" about a heresy? Truth is developed out of the struggle with fallacies.

Lenin has put it aptly: "We do not regard Marx's theory as something completed and inviolable; on the contrary, we are convinced that it has only laid the foundation stone of the science which socialists must develop in all directions if they wish to keep pace with life." (quotation from Lenin's *Collected Works* [Chinese-language] Vol. 4, p. 187. [V. I. Lenin, *Collected Works*, Vol. 4 (Moscow: Foreign Languages Publishing House, 1960), pp. 211-12.])

The reason that our "system" is so frightening to some is, in the second place, that in this article, which was first made public one year ago, we have, based on the revelation of cruel facts of class struggle and the basic line, put forward the question of the newborn bourgeois class and the mode of possession by the new bourgeois class as well as how to struggle against them.

When our article's illucidation of the social base of the capitalist-roaders and the careerists was criticized by some friends, a youth in the stratum which enjoys all kinds of preferential treatment rebeled with the kind of courage impossible for a Chia Pao-yu [the leading character in the *Dream of the Red Chamber* who was good-natured, well-bred and spoiled in an old-fashioned feudalistic family]. Although student Chung Chih-min's withdrawal from school [See *People's Daily*, January 18, 1974] is only a feeble echo from the privileged stratum, this echo has caused repeated shocks among the masses of people. This rebellious action has frightened some persons badly, but has encouraged some others. Some vehemently hate it, and some welcome it wholeheartedly. Are not these mutually different reactions exactly the reflections in profile of the change of class relations and the new class contradictions in our country?

The essence of the new bourgeois mode of possession is "changing the public into private" under the conditions of socialist ownership of the means of production. When the leader of the state or an enterprise redistributes the properties and powers of the proletariat in a bourgeois manner, he is, in fact, practicing the new bourgeois private possession of these properties and powers.

This redistribution of properties and powers in a bourgeois manner is chiefly manifested in two respects:

What has been commonly observed is that some leaders have expanded the necessary preferential treatment granted by the Party and the people into political and economic special privileges, and then extended them boundlessly to their families and clansmen, relatives and friends, even to the degree of exchanging special privileges [among themselves], of obtaining for their children factual inheritance of political and economic positions through such channels as "taking the back door," and of changing the socialist direction of the enterprise in favor of their private interests in order to practice cliquism and cultivate an "upstart" faction and force which is differential and opposed to the interests of the people.

More important is that they must, to maintain their vested privileges and obtain more preferential treatment, attack the upright revolutionary comrades who insist on principles, suppress the masses who rise to oppose their special privileges, and illegally deprive these comrades and masses of their political rights and economic interests.

Thus they have completed the qualitative change from "public servants of the people" to "masters of the people," becoming what we call "power-holders taking the capitalist road." This is exactly what we mean in this article that "the base of the capitalist-roaders and careerists in the Party is the newborn bourgeois class hatched out of special privileges."

According to the exhortations of the basic line, for several hundred years to come the new bourgeois elements will rise generation after generation, and this is something that will not be altered by men's will. Acknowledging or not acknowledging that [the existence of] this new-bourgeois class (which is represented by the capitalist-roaders) is the main danger of a capitalist restoration is the demarcation between the current proletarian revolutionaries and the conservatives, as well as the basic theoretical question affirming or negating the Great Proletarian Cultural Revolution. If you do not acknowledge it today, that is all right because there are Ch'ien Shou-wei, Huang Kuo-chung and their ilk who will give some help while Chiang Kai-shek also frequently sends his men here. Perhaps it would be all right for you not to acknowledge it in the next twenty years; but what would happen after fifty or a hundred years of stalling? One has to acknowledge it ultimately.

The reason that our "system" is frightening is, in the third place, because we assert that "This Great Proletarian Cultural Revolution has not accomplished the tasks of a great proletarian cultural revolution because it has not enabled the people to hold firmly the weapon of an extensive people's democracy." [One might ask:] Is this not a negation of the Great Proletarian Cultural Revolution? And what are the bases of such an assertion?

When we are once again confronted with this article, the revolutionary mass movement in Kwantung has risen, once more, for about half of a year. What is interesting is that as a prelude to this movement there was a struggle of posting up and tearing down big-character posters, just like what has happened in Wuhan.

In the eyes of the foreigners, China should never have had such a struggle. When handbills written in big letters were posted on walls in front of the Ethiopian palace, Western news agencies unhesitantly called them "Chinese type big-character posters."

But, the "Chinese type big-character posters" have met disasters in China. Not mentioning what happened several years ago, in May this year, the "City-Political-Appearance Cleaning and Sweeping Teams: cheng-chih shih-jung ch'ing-sao-tui" organized by the Canton Municipal Committee were equipped with water hoses and brooms to remove at any time big-character posters appearing on any street or alley. If they did not remove all the posters, it was because the big-character posters emerged continuously, and an endless column of successors followed behind the fallen.

Is the Great Proletarian Cultural Revolution not still continuing? And who has announced the completion of the tasks assigned to the big-character posters? Is not Chairman Mao's passage in his "Introducing a Collective,"' which says that the big-character poster "should be forever used," also a "highest instruction" to be "resolutely implemented" and "resolutely observed"? But when the suppressed revolutionary masses are trying to rise and attempting to use again this weapon to criticize the Lin Piao line and struggle for their own political and economic interests, they still have to first wage a bitter fight for this democratic right which they originally held! When an entanglement of big-character poster removal and replacement was raging in the streets of Canton, Document No. 18 came down, by which the Chairman has once again made plain his attitude toward the big-character poster. After several years of dumbness for ten thousands horses [classical Chinese parable for "silence of all the people"] under the excess of the Lin Piao Line, the big-character poster was pronounced anew as legitimate. The far-reaching significance of Document No. 18 has not so far fully unfolded itself to the people; but, if some people fail to perceive this, they are making a very great mistake. The most fundamental right of the people in a socialist society is the right to manage the state and the society; and, Document No. 18 has just opened up a vast horizon for the people's right of management and their right of criticism. Even if the people fail to achieve most of their original aspirations which have been rekindled by this revolutionary mass movement, their possession of Doceument No. 18 alone is a great victory. If someone says that our conclusion, which was arrived at the second half of the seventh year of the Great Proletarian Cultural Revolution, that the Cultural Revolution "has not accomplished its tasks" is premature, we will be glad to acknowledge it because now, i.e., the ending of the eighth year of the Great Proletarian Cultural Revolution, the right to use this weapon of extensive people's democracy – the big-character poster – is finally comfirmed by the historical Document No. 18. Just one year ago, how many persons would admit that the Great Proletarian Cultural Revolution had entered the eighth year? Even today, if Chairman Mao had not spoken, no one would admit it either. Are there not some very complicated contents in this?

The reason that our "system" is frightening to some is, in the fourth place, that we have pointed out [the existence of] the "Lin Piao system" and the fact that that system has been established firmly in the Great Proletarian Cultural Revolution.

What is a "system"? It is the total entity of related things – thus a complete system. The Lin Piao System is the whole lot of Lin Piao's theories, programs, roads, lines, policies, measures, style of Party [management], style of study, and style of work which has, in various spheres of politics, jurisprudence, military affairs, economy and culture, opposed the Party Central and Chairman Mao and thus brought great disasters upon the people and spread poison over the whole country.

The erection of Lin Piao's entire "system" six years ago undoubtedly sabotaged or even replaced the whole of Chairman Mao's ideas. It was not until the "September 13" incident (which is the manifestation of the absolutely and irreconcilably intensified contradictions between the whole set of Lin Piao's ideas and the ideas of the Chinese people) that the whole of Lin Piao's ideas were gradually destroyed and rejected in a marked way. Are not historical events just like this?

Let us make some retrospection about the scenes when the Lin Piao System was "flourishing"!

218

We have not forgotten the giving prominence to (empty) politics which rewarded the lazy and punished the diligent, the "daily reading [of Mao's works and quotations]" which resembled the incantation of spells, the "discussion-application [of Mao's works and thoughts]" which became more and more hypocritical, the "revolution erupts from the depth of the soul" which become more absurd, the "manifestation of loyalty" which encouraged political speculation, the grotesque "loyalty dance," and the excruciatingly multitudinous rituals of showing loyalty — morning prayers, evening penitences, rallies, falling-in, reporting for and quitting work and making duty shifts, buying and selling things, writing letters, making phone calls, even taking meals — which were invariably painted with violent religious colors and shrouded in such an atmosphere. In short, loyalty occupied one hundred percent of the time and one hundred percent of the space. The movements of this "good" and that "good" were, in fact, competitions of "left! left! and more left!" and contests for "the most . . . the most . . . and the most." The innumerable "meetings of representatives of active elements" were, in fact expositions of hypocritical, evil and ugly behavior and a gambling house which offered "10,000 times profit for one unit of capital."

We also have not forgotten the "wind of public property" which jeopardized the basic interests of the worker and peasant masses, the style of Party [management] which permitted that "when one man has understood [or possessed] the way, chickens and dogs also go to heaven with him [Chinese folk saying]," the style of study which trumpeted "what is useful is truth" and "a pole casts a shadow as soon as it is set up,' the "new stereotyped writing style" which encouraged lying, the theory of "small details [mistakes] do no harm" which promoted a corrupt and villainous style of work, and "the wind of taking the back door prevails in the present society . . ."

More so, we have not forgotten the formula "preachings" of class struggle, and the "scum hole" type of cow pens [meaning the detention camps] which were more so and no less [inhuman] than the massacre of the historical incidents such as "March 18," "April 12," "May 30," and "June 23," because in Kwangtung Province alone nearly 40,000 revolutionary masses and cadres were massacred and more than a million revolutionary cadres and masses were imprisoned, put under control, and struggled against.

But there are some people who shut their eyes and do not admit the fact that the Lin Piao system, which has been witnessed by 800 million people, has been firmly set up; and with thickened faces they stubbornly say that Chairman Mao's revolutionary line has, "at all times and in all places," occupied the ruling position. Is this not to say that all these bloody butcheries and unreversible cases of long standing are based on decisions made by the "revolutionary line"?

If there was not the firm establishment of the Lin Piao System, then why has the call for "taking concrete measures to ensure the fulfillment of policies" only been implemented in the case of Comrade Ho Lung after being enjoined more than thirty times and fifty reiterations?

If there was not the firm establishment of the Lin Piao System, why did the "big joke of Lushan" occur?

The diehards who have insisted on the Lin Piao System have sworn that they will not let the Communists who were struck down by them rise again from the dirt. For this, they have found a knack of doing things, that is, to use "not necessarily available" indiscriminating evidence to accuse the revolutionary comrades who are more dangerous to them because they [the diehards] can accuse them of being "big counterrevolutionary black hands," "bad counterrevolutionary chieftains," "May 16's," "active counterrevolutionary elements" and "traitors" etc. When they fail to produce evidence against others after protracted periods of imprisonment and licentious maltreatment, they confuse a clear case further into an insolvable mess and then use this as an excuse to continue the case for yet a longer time, waiting for a chance to try again. Are not a great number of cases just so?

The emergence of the Lin Piao System is [a natural product] developed within the historical conditions of the Chinese society.

Our China has been transformed into a socialist society directly from a semi-feudal, semi-colonial society. The feudal rule which continued for more than two thousand years has left its ideology deeply rooted. A destructive blow has not been dealt to it in either the period of old democracy nor in the period of new democracy. The bad habits of autocracy and despotism are deeply imbued in the minds of the masses, even in those of the Communists in general. Are not these the factors that provided the conditions for the Lin Piao System to flourish for a certain period, even to the degree of "forcing" Chairman Mao "to join the Liangshan rebels"? Are not these the factors that allowed Lin Piao's cohorts to announce in their spheres of influence in "all-out victory" by way of suppressing the people's democracy?

When we are pointing out the Lin Piao system, we also have made plain that the statement which asserts that "the historical concept of genius is its guiding principle" is to say that it also is its ideological foundation. Why so? Because it says that there would only be a "genius" in a period of several centuries or several milleniums; thus, everyone must worship this "genius," be absolutely loyal to this "genius," and do everything according to the will of this "genius." Furthermore, whoever opposes this "genius" will be struck down. Is this not an extremely encompassing ideological and political line? No one is allowed to think; no one is allowed to study; no one is allowed to do research; and no one is allowed to "ask a single why" on any question. The "historical concept of genius" has indeed liquidated 800 million brains.

Now, people can see very clearly that they [Lin Piao and his cohorts] have cooked up this "system" based on the foundation of the historical concept of genius. This is a set of modern "rites." And they have used this set of "rites" to "rule" the Party, to "rule" the state and to "rule" the army. As a result, our Party has thus been molded into a ruler-vassal and father-son party, our state has been molded into a state under a feudalistic social-Fascist dictatorship, and our army has been molded into a group of soldiers like that of Yuan Shih-K'ai's Northern Armies. Is it not so? Lin Piao had in Peking his own Feng [Kuo-chang] and Tuan [Chi-jui] and in local regions his own Military Governors. These "big generals" and "military governors" have done almost everything, with the only exception that they did not have the time to lead their soldiers to attack Peking.

People may ask: "If 'the Great Proletarian Cultural Revolution has not accomplished its tasks but on the contrary affirmed the Lin Piao System, which has not been liquidated up to this date,' then what are the positive fruits of the Great Proletarian Cultural Revolution?"

We answer: "No! When we say that the Lin Piao System has been affirmed in the Great Proletarian Cultural Revolution, that does not mean that Chairman Mao's revolutionary line has been absolutely replaced by it. What we say is that during that time there appeared to be a temporary dualism (this fact is determined by the existence of two head-quarters) which resembled the historical situation as when Tung Chung-shu affirmed the position of the Confucian scholars but did not immediately cancel the Legalist line taken by Han Wu Ti."

Moreover, at the time when we put forward the assertion that the Lin Piao System has been affirmed, we also have pointed out: "This is only one of the aspects. The aspect which is more important is that it has created its opposite, that is, a newly emerged social force." Here, we would like to quote a very significant saying of Marx:

The revolution made progress, forged ahead, not by its immediate tragicomic achievements, but on the contrary by the creation of a powerful, united counter-revolution, by the creation of an opponent in combat with whom, only, the party of overthrow ripened into a really revolutionary party. (The Class Struggles in France: 1848-1850)

With the above, we do not have to dwell.

In those days when the Lin Piao System was quite secure and appeared to be permanent, the Communists who were loyal to Marx were dispassionately observing, in conformity with Marx's instructions, such an historical phenomenon; thus, they knew that it was only something ephemeral and, with confidence of a sure victory, they unflaggingly waged struggles against it.

We see, now, how important to the future development of our party is this unprecedentedly violent and complicated struggle being waged since 1968 between our Party and this new-fangled enemy of the Lin Piao System! Without an unprecedentedly strong enemy, there would not be an unprecedentedly violent struggle and the creation of an unprecedentedly strong revolutionary force as well as the accomplishment of the unprecedentedly difficult and great revolutionary missions of the historical stage of socialism. History's way of getting things down is just so.

The reason that our "system" is so frightening to some is, in the fifth place, because we have touched upon the question of whether Lin Piao's line is rightist or "leftist."

After the "September 13" incident, the whole Party and all the people, by applying their personal experiences and observing the series of Chairman Mao's instructions of criticizing Lin Piao and his cohorts, criticized Lin Piao, the "leftist" friend "who spoke nice things to our faces but stabbed us in the back." They criticized Lin Piao's cliquism of "cruel struggle against and merciless attack [rivals]"; they criticized "politics have an impact on everything," the "public property" the "climaxism" and the "absolutism." This criticism has, however, finally touched on those persons who are related to the Lin Piao System in a manner of "I am one among you; and you are one among us." Thus some people come forward and say that no more criticism is allowed because you "criticized the masses."

The masses have been subject to three solid years of criticism and three years of struggle; but no one comes forward to say a single word or offer any protection. Now, all of a sudden some people say that no more criticism against the ultra-left is allowed; and the masses who suddenly enjoy some protection are indeed agreeably surprised by this great favor! Here, we really wish to have some discussion with those theoreticians who protect the masses from being criticized.

The theoreticians have asked: "Is the essence of the Lin Piao line 'leftist' or 'rightist'?" This question is indeed solemnly absurd. The essence of all the opportunist lines in the Party is rightist, no matter whether its appearance is leftist or rightist, because they will ultimately lead to losses, or even failure, of the revolution. To this matter, there is no distinction between "leftist" and "rightist". Do our theoreticians really lack this bit of common sense?

221

Furthermore, has any one of the historical opportunists in the Party not appeared to be "leftist" at some time and "rightist" at another?

Our theoreticians! Has Lin Piao not propagated the doctrine of Confucius and Mencius? How can we say that he is "ultra-leftist"? But, on newspapers and documents published from 1960 to 1971, can we find any instruction issued by this "the highest, the highest" Vice-Chairman Lin which called us to learn the doctrine of Confucius and Mencius? They wanted people to emulate Tung Chung-shu, but they also wanted people to worship the Mao Tse-tung Thought as a kind of religion! Was it not that the new principle of rites − "whoever opposes the Mao Tse-tung Thought will be struck down" − which has enabled us to see the feudalistic nature of Lin Piao? On the other hand, was Lin Piao not, as an opposite side to Liu Shao-ch'i and Chou Yang and their ilk who intensely hated the Mao Tse-tung Thought, very "leftist"?

This [questioning the nature of the Lin Piao line] is to cook "Yenan" and "Sian" in the same pot, the more the cooking the more the mass. "The Outline of 'Project 571'" can only show that the Lin Piao clique was a counterrevolutionary banditry. How can it tell his opportunist line in the Party?

One must distinguish the counterrevolutionary double-dealer's opportunist line in the Party from his counterrevolutionary activities. Whereas Stalin has made such a distinction in Trotsky (reference Note 30, p. 153 of Mao's *Selected Works,* [For English translation, see Note 31, p. 177 of *SW.* Vol. I (Peking: Foreign Languages Press, 1967]), and Chairman Mao has made such a distinction in Chang Kuo-t'ao (reference Note 10, p. 258 of Mao's *Selected Works* [For English translation, see Note 13, p. 294, *op. cit.*]). Why cannot people make such a distinction in Lin Piao?

This is a fraudulent substitution of concepts and a confusion of two [different] categories of contradictions, which are made in a very flagrant manner. This act itself has concretely embodied Lin Piao's line in the Party which is "leftist" in form but rightist in essence.

Now we have witnessed that those diehard cohorts who participated in the plots of Project 571 and responded to the *coup d'etat* are enjoying exemption from punishment on the grounds that they only commited the so-called "errors in line," while, on the other hand, not a few good cadres who used to carry out the erroneous line which were put through the Party by Liu Shao-ch'i and Lin Piao are continually regarded as enemies and thus mercilessly dealt with. Are such facts not sufficient for stimulating some deep reflection?

Marx has said: If phenomenal forms of things were directly associated with their essence, all sciences would become superfluous. (*Capital*)

Our theoreticians! Why have you been so shy about the question of the line which was ultra-rightist in essence and ultra-leftist in form and which had been carried out during the period (1966-1971) when Lin Piao was the supreme chieftain of that opportunist line? Whereas we can cite a hundred or even a thousand phenomenal forms to illucidate Lin Piao's "leftist" essence, how many can you single out to show the rightist essence of Lin Piao in the Party when he was the supreme chieftain of the opportunist line?

When appearance is taken for reality, reality becomes appearance,

Where nothing is taken for something, something becomes nothing.

This couplet, hung in the Phantom Realm of the Great Void as depicted in Chapter 1 of the *Dream of the Red Chamber,* is rather full of realistic significance!

Hegel remarks somewhere that "all facts and personages of great importance in world history occur, as it were, twice." He forgot to add: the first time as tragedy, the second as farce . . . (Marx, *The Eighteenth Brumaire of Louis Bonaparte*)

If Wang Ming's opposition to Li Li-san's "leftist inclination" were the first, then who would be glad to play the role of a Wang Ming who is to appear for the second time?

The reason that, to some people, our "system" is frightful by mere appearance is, in the sixth place, because of our comments on the slogans of "anti-restoration" and "anti-reverse tide." But, the judgements made in our comments of last year have been proved to be true.

When did the "restoration" occur; and when did the "reverse tide" occur? Since this year, some VIPs and authoritative articles (such as the "Comments on Hunan Opera 'Song of the Gardener,' " [*Kuang Ming Daily*, August 11, 1974]) have told us that the "restoration" and "reverse tide" occurred in 1972. In March of this year, the so-called "going against the tide" big-character poster written by the 1st Municipal Hospital, which was trumpeted loudly as headline news in the *Canton Daily*, even put the year 1971 as a "hot blood seething [meaning seething with enthusiasm]" and "flaming red year" whereas the time after 1972 is almost an "era of restoration."

When did Lin Piao collapse? Autumn of 1971. Then, why at the time when Lin Piao was prominent everywhere was there "a span of redness" and "all-out victory" and when Lin Piao did collapse there followed "restoration" here and "reverse tide" there, and the year was no longer flaming red and the hot blood was no longer seething? What a queer story this is!

Does it mean that the direct results of the great victory in the 10th line struggle in the autumn of 1971 were not a further liberation of the people and the consolidation of the dictatorship of the proletariat but, on the contrary, an opening up of road for the "restoration" and the "reverse tide"? This is indeed a mockery of the tenth line struggle.

Without the slightest doubt, the masses of people are opposed to restoration, but the blood dripping and blood thirsty activities of restoration they have witnessed by their own eyes were started in the later half of 1968 and the restoration reached its climax when Lin Piao was legalized as the successor. (This is the thing which makes some people's "hot blooding seeth.") After the decisive battle from August 1970 to August-September 1971 which was followed by Lin Piao's collapse, these restoration activities almost ceased in full-scale in 1972; then, the counter-offensive by the masses of the people began. Some people have just called the people's resistance as "restoration"; and, therefore, their "anti-restoration" is in actuality anti-anti-restoration. Apparently, there are two kinds of people who are shouting aloud the slogan of "anti-restoration" but what they oppose is entirely different in content. But, the actual results of the slogan "anti-restoration" are better than what we originally anticipated, because in the people's revolution the people will not easily suspect revolutionary slogans and they in general did not become sensitive to the proposition that the "restoration" and "reverse tide" did start in 1972. As a result, even though there were fishes mingled with dragons [meaning a crowd of mixed people] and the question was in a tangled mess, "anti-restoration" has finally become, in the movement to criticize Lin Piao and Confucius in 1974, the banner by which the masses of people launch struggles against Lin Piao and his cohorts.

What needs some study here is why the diehards who insisted on the Lin Piao System also should shout aloud "anti-restoration" and "anti-reverse tide" under the situation of "the rites collapsed and the music deteriorated" which followed the collapse of Lin Piao?

223

It is quite clear that their current positions were affirmed in conjunction with the affirmation of Lin Piao's system; thus, to shake Lin Piao's system would undoubtedly shake their current positions. Their shouting "anti-restoration" is the reflection of sharpened contradictions between the "all-out victory" being stipulated in 1969 and the realities of deepened development of the Great Proletarian Cultural Revolution.

They are quite unwilling to part with those "glorious days — days when hundreds and thousands of the people's heads fell to the ground" — when the Lin Piao System was at its zenith. What they have gained in the "all-out victory" — positions, special privileges . . . even the lashes to drive and beat the slaves — are precious treasures glowing with a sacred halo and which cannot be desecrated by the slaves. The Chinese society of that time was their "paradise," and the social relations in that "paradise" cannot be changed in the slightest degree. If Lin Piao did not allow "the rightist forces to raise their heads," they will not allow it either.

Therefore, after the year 1972 when the sacred halo of these precious treasures became more and more dim, the attitudes of the slaves became more and more unreserved, the social relations in the "paradise" became more and more unstable, and invocation of the Scripture of the Tight Fillet [The rebellious monky in *The Adventures of the Monkey* was finally disciplined by putting a golden fillet — a head gear — around his forehead, when the spell was recited, an excruciating headache would make the Monkey behave. See Chapter XIV of Waley's English Translation.] became more and more ineffective (The "golden fillet" was put on the slaves' heads during the "all-out victory."), and they became exasperated. Then, murmuring some magic words on their lips, they dished up another very magic revolutionary piece which is called "anti-restoration"!

In the eyes of the diehards who insisted on the Lin Piao System, the years have changed from bad to worse since the 2nd Plenary Session of the 9th CC CCP, especially "September 13." This is because they are trying to turn back the wheel of history. In the first place, they wanted to turned it to back to the time before August of 1970; later on, they wished to turn it back to the time before September of 1971 and, having no alternative, they are now turning it back to March of 1974. Of course, they are not willing to abandon their goal to reverse four years of time. What is ridiculous is that they are condemning the people for being "restorationists" and "reverse tide-ists." Here, we would like to ask them: Should we not rehabilitate "the three working styles" and our army's excellent tradition of "the three main rules of discipline and the eight points for attention" which were wrecked and abandoned by Lin Piao and his cohorts? Should we not rehabilitate the true colors of our Party history and army history which were distorted beyond recognition? Should we not rehabilitate the lines of "taking warning from the past in order to be more careful for the future" and "unity-criticism-unity" which were replaced with suppression, apprehension, beating up and execution by Lin Piao and his cohorts? Should we not rehabilitate the guidelines for literature and art of "associating revolutionary realism with revolutionary romanticism which tampered with the mode of "from subjectivism to objectivism" and was pushed by Lin Piao and his cohorts? Should we not rehabilitate the guidelines for education of "all-out development of morality, intelligence and physical training" which was replaced by the line "politics has an impact on everything" of Lin Piao and his cohorts? Should we not rehabilitate the series of the Party's policies — the policy of relying on the working class and the poor and lower-middle peasants, the policy towards cadres, the policy toward intellectuals, the policy of "going up to the mountains and down to the countryside," the policy toward overseas Chinese, and all the economic policies . . . which were subverted and trampled by Lin Piao and his cohorts? Should we not rehabilitate "the five-dare spirit" which was suppressed by the concept of genius of Lin Piao and his cohorts? May not the hundreds and thousands of framed cases both in the Central and the local areas, which were fabricated by Lin Piao and his cohorts, be reversed and redressed? Can not great numbers of veteran cadres who committed this or that mistake but have proven loyal to the Party through a protracted test be employed again? Comrades such as Teng Hsiao-p'ing and Chao Tzu-yang should never be admitted into the Central Committee, should they? Even if a way-out should be provided for them, the cap [dunce-cap] must be placed in the hands of "masses" so that it could be put on their heads at anytime, is this not right?

In the eyes of the diehards who have insisted on the Lin Piao System, the act of our bringing forward in a very disrespectful manner a series of "provocative" questions constitutes in its own right the evidence of "restoration" and "reversal of decision," letting alone the whole piece of this preface and the main body of this article and the "What Should Kwangtung Do?" "The Ins and Outs of the Hall of A Single Spark Can Start a Prairie Fire," and "The Revolution Is Dead, Long Live the Revolution!" . . . which can be regarded in itself a "big poisonous weed" and are well qualified for a "manifesto of counterrevolution." If it were three years ago, we should have been long discredited as "counterrevolutionaries." Therefore they ruefully moan: "How good it would be if the time could be turned back three years!"

For three years, the Chinese people have really seen something which "appeared to be the answer to old things (Lenin)"; but who can help it? Things develop in accordance with their own laws (including the law of negation of negation); and the wheel of history is irresistible, it just does not care about anybody's face. "There is no help for the flowers that drop away/While the vaguely recognizable swallows have returned." We advise that the VIPs who feverishly followed Lin Piao and still retain their "high positions and fat emoluments" might as well try to pace back and forth and hum this couplet for a thorough appreciation of the significance contained in it!

Then, was there not any "reverse tide" in the year of 1972? We would say that there were a variety of manifestations of revisionism; but they could not be called "reverse tides," because the proposition of "reverse tide" is in itself a beautification of the period which affirmed the Lin Piao System — by calling it a "state without difference" in which there existed no revisionism.

"Whether the ideological and political line is correct or not determines everything"; of course, it also determines the educational line and the literature and art line. The ideological and political line of Lin Piao and his cohorts is reactionary, and their educational line and literature and art line cannot be revolutionary. If the Chang Yu-ch'in incident can be regarded a manifestation of a "reverse tide" of the revisionist educational line, it would be more appropriate to call it a reflection of the Lin Piao line on the educational battle front. Must the revisionist educational line be characterized by someone's death? The number of people who were put to death by the Lin Piao line was not limited to a few hundreds or thousands. Since veteran revolutionary cadres who had passed their forties and experienced all sorts of hardships were put to death, then how could a girl of only fifteen years old survive? Are those methods used by Huang Shuai's teacher to persecute Huang Shuai inherited from the revisionist educational line, or are most of them from the Lin Piao line? In later times, "Huang Shuai" endlessly raised standards [accusations] on revolutionary Comrade Wang Ya-chuo's different opinion; and, in an overbearing atti-

225

tude Huang condemned Wang for being a "force of restoration." Where do all these come from? Is it true that this kind of tyrannical style of first throwing a dunce cap on any opposition and then "struggling against it" really is something inherent in a teenage girl?

When discussing "going against the tide" in the educational line, we have mentioned Chang T'ieh-sheng. What is the tide that Chang T'ieh-sheng went against? Allegedly, it is the reverse tide that carried back the so-called "intellectual education first, academic ratings in command." To put it frankly, we can only find in his answer sheet the evidence of his compromise with the revisionist educational line, not the evidence of putting up a challenge. His turning in a blank answer sheet was in itself catering to the tide of "empty politics has an impact on everything" which was manifested on the educational battle front. Although there has emerged in this tide, when going toward its opposite, something like "intellectual education first and academic ratings in command," but it is far, far away from forming into a tide! Therefore, the reason for Chang T'ieh-sheng to become a "lucky boy" is that someone can use him as living evidence to prove that the reverse tide of "restoration" did occur after the year of 1972.

The reason that our "system" has frightened some people is, in the seventh place, that we do not show a respectful attitude to Ch'in Shih Huang. But, to look at it now, this is not so frightening. The criticism of the history of the struggle between Confucianism and Legalism is now undergoing a deepened development, while the affirmation of the Ch'in Dynasty's feudal system has become more principled. The *Wen Hui Pao* has just begun to develop some very significant discussions. Without the slightest doubt, the Legalist pioneers have made great historical contributions to the Chinese society's change from the slave system to the feudal system. But, is not the replacement of the primitive communal system by the slave system no less a great advancement in human history? Have not the bourgeois revolutionary democrats in the modern history of Europe also produced very revolutionary results? Since we have so mercilessly criticized the bourgeois class — from Cromwell to Robespierre, from the "encyclopaedists" to Belinsky and Chernyshevski, from Beethoven to Stanislavsky, then why should the bourgeois dynasty of Ch'in Shih Huang be regarded as so brillant? It is necessary to rehabilitate the original color of the history distorted by the Confucianists and to affirm the progressive role of Ch'in Shih Huang and his founding of a unified state, but this kind of affirmation must have, and observe, a strict boundary so that ruthless criticism can be conducted on them subsequently — this is something which is determined by the anti-feudal tasks facing our society, a society which is transformed from a semifeudal, semi-colonial society.

A very interesting fact is that we have found the great contradictions between the evaluation of historical figures made by our newspapers and journals in the period from late 1965 to early 1966 and the evaluation of historical figures made by our newspapers and journals now! "All ring-leaders of reactionary and opportunist factions are worshippers of Confucianism and opposed to Legalism." But, which one is a Legalist — is it the Hai Jui depicted by Wu Han or the Wu Tse Tien depicted by T'ien Han? However, the criticism of them had indeed become the direct stimulus to the first Great Cultural Revolution.

We believe that the evaluations of historical figures made today indeed possess more materialist spirit than the evaluation of historical figures made in 1965-1966. This is the fruit of the deepened revolution. But, whereas Wu Han was criticized by the first article of the Great Proletarian Cultural Revolution for his saying that Hai Jui "loved and protected the people," would it not really be a frightening "reverse tide" that there are now those

226

who say that "the Legalists loved and protected the people"? Hai Jui was doubtlessly a Legalist, and a Legalist who came from one of the minority nationalities which was rarely seen in history. Since, now, some people have made up a list, including from Ch'in Shih Huang to Sun Yat-sen, for "concretely implementing the policy," then why should they be so harsh and bitter about Hai Jui and thus refuse to "concretely implement the policy" on him and sternly cursing him in newspapers recently? This indicates that there still are some people who curse the Legalists. But we have not yet cursed Ch'in Shih Huang!

What we cannot understand is why there are some people who are inclined to dig out some ideas in the conceptual framework of "loving the country [patriotism]" and "selling the country," which have never had strict definition, historically? Where do they want to spread the fire? Why cannot [people] associate it with the realities of the lawlessness and recklessness, the gangsterism and killing, the kidnapping males and grabbing females, and the total rejection of the rule of law, which had been practiced by Lin Piao and his cohorts for so many years? Are there not very many such things? Would not the association with these be of very practical interests for winning over the people's support and for consolidating the dictatorship of the proletariat? What would be the use for the people if the reality of Lin Piao's crimes were not associated with this, but were exaggeratedly debated in terms of the history of struggle between Confucianism and Legalism?

From our point of view, as long as the feudalistic social-Fascist dictatorship is the main danger to our dictatorship of the proletariat and as long as anti-feudalism still is one of the important contents of our continued revolution, then the movement to criticize Lin Piao and Confucius should, in addition to studying the valuable historical experience of ideological and political line struggles in the great social change of our country's transformation from the slave system to the feudal system, emphatically criticize the ideological system of the feudal autocracy which was reformed by Tung Chung-shu. And if the May 4th Movement's "down with the Confucian shop" has advanced a thorough anti-feudal slogan, then today's movement to criticize Lin Piao and Confucius should be a thorough realization of the tasks of anti-feudalism on the ideological and political battle fronts. Unlike certain people, we should not strenuously laud the so-called reformists of the landlord class while we are at the same time criticizing the conservative faction of the landlord class. They [certain people] have completely forgotten that the so-called schools of Confucianism and Legalism after the Ch'in and Han Dynasties were invariably of landlord class ideology, while the struggles between them were essentially for maintaining the feudal autocracy. Having forgotten this point, have they not also forgotten the basic task that we should criticize Confucianism on the standpoint of the proletariat?

The reason that our "system" is frightening is, at last, because it has allegedly picked up the rubbish of the 1957 rightists.

Yes, the slogans of "democracy" and "legal system" were once shouted loudly by the rightists. But, since 1966, have there not been a great many slogans shouted by the revolutionary rebels and the masses of people that were once shouted by the rightists? Do the slogans of "Bombard the Black Provincial Party Committee" and "Oppose Persecution, Oppose Suppression" still make the opposition faction to the Great Proletarian Cultural Revolution regard the Great Proletarian Cultural Revolution as "overturning the sky by the rightists"? There is far more "rightist opinion" expressed in Li Ch'ing-lin's letter than that expressed by the 1957 rightists. Some of our friends have not given a single thought to the facts as why did the slogans of "democracy" and "liberty" gather together in Budapest counterrevolutionaries in 1956 whereas the same slogans became the battle banners of the Polish working class on the south coast of the Baltic Sea in 1970; and why had the Soviet Union's sending troops to Hungary in 1956 been met with the opposition from the rightists in our country, whereas the Soviet Union's sending troops to Czechoslovakia in 1968 was met with the protests from the Chinese people!

The friends who have criticized us have completely failed to make, in accordance with the basic line, an analysis of the changes of social relations in foreign countries and in China since the 1960's. They are not aware that during the late 1950's the main danger to our country's dictatorship of the proletariat was the bourgeois rightists left over from the old society, while after the early 1960's the main danger has been the capitalist-roaders in the Party. What these seemingly identical slogans oppose are of different content. The 1957 rightists opposed, under the slogan of democracy, the leadership of the Communist Party and the socialist road, while after 1966 the masses of people have opposed, under the slogan of democracy, the capitalistic counterrevolutionary line of the capitalist-roaders in the Party, especially the feudalistic social-Fascist line having an ultra-left appearance and an ultra-right essence, which was promoted by Lin Piao. Their [the people's] purpose is to consolidate the dictatorship of the proletariat. This is something not difficult to understand.

We do not want to dwell on the sixth part which has been rewritten, just leave it to others for comments and criticism. [We have presented these] as [our] expectations to the "4th National People's Congress," no matter whether they can fully materialize or not. More important are that the iceberg of the Lin Piao System is now melting away, that thinking is beginning to be liberated, and that the questions have been presented before those who are willing to study socialism. What can be added is that we wish that the delegates to the "4th National people's Congress" (regardless that we do not know how they are elected) would not forget the bitter lesson of the 1971's "big joke of Lushan."

We can only be grateful if the reader can read through this tediously long preface of ours and not feel bored. With a few more sentences, we are coming to the closing.

We are, allegedly, the youth who are "not afraid of tigers; but we are not unaware of the ferocity and cruelty of the tigers." We even dare to say that we are the survivors who were once bitten by that kind of animal but in the end could not be gnawed firmly between the teeth or swallowed; on our faces, there are claw marks so that we are not handsome figures.

Obviously, we have read very little Marxism-Leninism; but chiefly because we have been educated by cruel reality, we have come to know a little of it and wish to say something frankly. Here, we are merely trying to express our wishes and confidence to the "National Congress of the people" – among them we still can be regarded as part and to the subsequent revolutionary development of it; and we also are trying to find out what will happen when we have violated the "prohibition" of the newspapers and offended the "taboo" of the journals? It might also be called an act of testing the "rites" in one's own person! If we receive, for this reason, some special treatment from certain authoritative theoreticians, we can only regard it as something good and will learn more useful lessons from them, though we are not very eager in anticipation of them.

However, we place our anticipation for more lessons on the readers in the streets and wholeheartedly hope that the comrades would offer us criticism and corrective opinions, especially the generous instructions from the on-the-street theoreticians, experts of political science, jurists, philosophers, critics and observers. We hope that more and more comrades would openly discuss these questions.

We profoundly believe that on the soil being irrigated with the blood of the martyrs of the First Great Proletarian Cultural Revolution fresh flowers should grow.

Drafted November 7, 1974.

CONTENTS

(1) The New Question in the Socialist Revolution
(2) Lessons from the Great Proletarian Cultural Revolution
(3) Concerning the Lin Piao System
(4) Concerning the Situation Since the Criti ism of Lin Piao
(5) On Going Against the Tide
(6) Expectations for the Fourth National People's Congress

People are concerned about the convention of the 4th National People's Congress, especially about the legal system of the state, which is closely related to the fate of every Chinese.

Why should people be so concerned about it? What is the new question which has occurred during the revolutionary flux of the past twenty odd years that makes the people think that they have to be concerned with the new legal system of the state which is to be the newborn infant of the 4th National People's Congress?

(1) The New Question in the Socialist Revolution

There have been two great struggles since the advent of the Great Proletarian Cultural Revolution: one is the struggle waged by the proletariat and the revolutionary people against the Liu Shao-ch'i clique, and the other against the Lin Piao clique.

The essence of these struggles is to solve the question of taking the capitalist road or the socialist road, of furthering the dictatorship of the bourgeoisie or the dictatorship of the proletariat. In the anti-rightist socialist education movements in the past, similar struggles were conducted; and these movements wanted to solve the same questions. Then, what is the new question?

The new question is that what the Liu Shao-ch'i clique, and especially the Lin Piao clique, wanted to cook up was not an ordinary dictatorship of the bourgeoisie, but the feudalistic social-Fascist dictatorship.

The social base of the capitalist-roaders and careerists in the Party is hatched from special privileges. Under the conditions of the present Chinese society it is only possible for the newborn bourgeois class to cook up a feudalistic social-Fascist dictatorship, while impossible for them to share their vested profits with the old landlords and old compradors who were struck down. That the unhealthy flourishing of the counterrevolutionary changes made by the Khrushchev-Brezhnev clique did not restore for the white Russians their aristocratic heritage is the proof.

As early as in the beginning of the 1960's, Chairman Mao warned the whole Party and all the people in the country of the danger of social-Fascism. He has told us that if a restoration occurs in a country like ours, it will not be an ordinary dictatorship of the bourgeoisie, "but a reactionary, Fascist type of dictatorship." He has said: "This is a question which deserves vigilance, and I hope that the comrades will carefully think about it."

Ten years have passed and the Chinese people have thought about it for these ten years. Was it not the disasters that the Lin Piao line brought on the people which helped them really begin to understand Chairman Mao's warnings?

Since the specific feature in the current socialist revolution is the attempt of the

229

representatives of the bourgeoisie who have wormed into the Party to cook up a feudalistic social-Fascist dictatorship, then what weapon should the revolutionary people take up to resist them?

(2) Lessons from the Great Proletarian Cultural Revolution

In his profound study of the social, political and economic relations in contemporary China, Chairman Mao has discovered the Great Proletarian Cultural Revolution.

In its form, the Great Proletarian Cultural Revolution is actually a great revolutionary democracy of the people on the most extensive scale; it is to "mobilize the broad masses, in an open, all-out, and from the top to bottom manner, to expose our darkside"; and it is the weapon to prevent and oppose social-Fascism.

From the strategic point of view, it would be more appropriate to say that the Great Proletarian Cultural Revolution is for tempering the masses of people with the revolutionary democratic spirit to liberate themselves than to say that the chief task is to expose and destroy Liu Shao-ch'i's capitalist headquarters. "The revolution is to liberate productivity"; and what can be a more appropriate symbol than the discussion of important state affairs and the criticism of erroneous lines by the proletariat and broad masses of people in a rigorous and high-spirited way?

The freedom of speech, the freedom of press, the freedom of association, which are stipulated in the Constitution, and the freedom of exchanging revolutionary experience, which is not stipulated in the Constitution, have all been trully practiced in the great revolution and granted with the support by the Party Central headed by Chairman Mao. This is something which the Chinese people had not possessed for several thousand years, something so active and lively; and this is the extraordinary achievement of the revolution.

But, this Great Proletarian Cultural Revolution has not accomplished the tasks of a great proletarian cultural revolution, because it has not enabled the people to hold firmly in their hands the weapon of extensive people's democracy.

In the summer of 1968, the socialist legal system "suddenly became inoperative," while, on the other hand, "the state power is the power to suppress" became operative. All across the land, there were arrests everywhere, suppressions everywhere, miscarriages of justice everywhere. Where did the socialist legal system go? Allegedly, it was no longer of any use because it belonged to the Constitution established by the old People's Congress whereas the new People's Congress was not convened yet. Now, there was no law and no heaven!

This was a rehearsal of social-Fascism in our country; and the commander-in-chief of the rehearsal was Lin Piao.

"To the broad masses of people, should there be protection or suppression?" Chairman Mao indignantly voiced such a question.

To worship the Lin Piao system as the orthodox Mao Tse-tung Thought is the unavoidable historical mistake committed by the Chinese people in the Great Proletarian Cultural Revolution.

Lin Piao and his cohorts exploited the people's revolutionary movement as the "borrowed force" for his carrying out usurpation of power and restoration [of capitalism]. Thus the criterion of one's attitude toward "genius" substituted the criterion of whether taking the socialist road or the capitalist road. The principles of "together [we] eradicate them," "together [we] punish them," and "whoever resists will be struck down" challenged the legal system; and they became the Imperial Sword which protected the absolute worship of the "genius." Once his position was established and when the Party announced that the affirmation of his position was the landmark of the "all-out victory" of the Great

Proletarian Cultural Revolution, he immediately wanted to establish the "new order" and to "correct the terms." In this respect, he also had his Tung Chung-shu!

What is the "new order"? It is the "theory of the final victory," "theory of the four-obsoletes," the "theory that state power is suppression," and the "theory of the military-Party." In short, it is the theory of social-Fascism which intends to cook our Party and our army into a relationship of "ruler-vassal and father-son; no one is allowed to be impertinent to his superiors." The lessons from the Great Proletarian Cultural Revolution have taught us that the people's Great Democracy cannot drift away from the correct line; otherwise, not only the revolution will fail to accomplish its missions but it will also be exploited by the bourgeois careerists. The masses of people will get nothing but new fetters.

(3) Concerning the Lin Piao System

What is the Lin Piao System? It means the whole lot of things which was promoted by Lin Piao, when he was the general chieftain of the opportunists in the Party, to oppose the Chairman and spread poison in the whole country. It consists of the "theory of absolute will" in the sphere of philosophy, the concept of genius in the sphere of history, the theory that state power is suppression in the sphere of politics, the theory of "public property" in the sphere of economy and big-nation chauvinism in foreign relations etc., with the historical concept of genius as its guiding principle.

Chairman Mao has, from the beginning, been in opposition to the Lin Piao System. Before the Lin Piao System was affirmed, Chairman Mao's letter to Comrade Chiang Ch'ing had manifested this contradiction. And once the Lin Piao System was affirmed and rendered the Chinese revolution and even the world revolution in great crises, this contradiction unavoidably became sharpened.

If we are not to understand Chairman Mao's extreme opposition to and complete disassociation with Lin Piao's social-Fascistic suppression of the people's democracy, how can we come to understand why Chairman Mao brought forward at Lushan the question that "Is it the heroes who create history or is it the slaves who create history"; how can we come to understand the profound crisis in the whole Chinese society which were reflected by the great struggle at Lushan; and how can we come to understand the lessons that the big joke at Lushan should bring to us?

The reason the propositions that "the line struggle is unknowable" and "the line struggle is nothing but a domestic power struggle in the Central" are erroneous is because they have, based on the foundation of an idealistic historical concept, rejected the direct damage brought along by the benefits which were offered to the masses of people by all erroneous lines — no matter whether they were "leftist" or rightist. The masses of people will, for maintaining and striving for their own interests, use all forms of action (even including passive or "reactionary" forms of action) to resist and oppose. The struggle in the Central is nothing but a concentrated manifestation of the social struggle.

(4) Concerning the Situation Since the Criticism of Lin Piao

The Lin Piao System reached its highest peak in the Great Proletarian Cultural Revolution. But this is only one of the aspects. More important is that it has created a reaction to itself, i.e., a newly emerged social force — the people who have gradually come to understand, under Chairman Mao's enlightenment, Marxism-Leninism-Mao Tse-tung Thought in this great revolution. The universal upsurge of the democratic spirit since the collapse of Lin Piao has further formed a mass base for them. They are mostly the victims of the Lin Piao System. They have a deep hatred of the Lin Piao System. They demand the continued revolution; they demand the Great Democracy; and they demand the restoration of the socialist legal system.

This time, the people's demands were brought forth under the cloak of history. A philosopher has played the role of the pioneer for new political changes, and this man is Yang Jung-kuo.

When the deep scar left on his neck by hanging a board inscribed with "Counter-revolutionary Black Hand" was not completely healed, and when they still were in the "oxen team," Yang Jung-kuo and his assistants began their study of criticizing Confucianism and the new Confucianism. This white-haired professor is a real rebel. For the first time, he unmasked the secrets to the "rule by rites." "Their will was law," Comrade Yang Jung-kuo accused, "they could, following their own inclination, suppress and exploit the slave, even to the degree of massacre; on the other hand, the slaves could only be absolutely submissive and were not allowed to resist. This is the so-called 'rule by rites'."

Yang Jung-kuo has repeatedly criticized the "rule by rites" and repeatedly criticized Confucius' execution of Shao Chung-mao. What crimes did Shao Chung-mao commit? He only "gathered together some people for free assembly and association, and randomly criticized the authorities." Does this warrant execution?

Chairman Mao has given support to the Yang Jung-kuo faction's voice for revolution and democracy. And how greatly his reply to Li Ch'ing-lin's letter, which has been called everywhere as the "reactionary letter of accusation," has encouraged the masses of people! Indeed, it has never been observed since 1968 that the masses of people are "so full of spirit and elated." "I called heaven for help but heaven did not answer; and I called the earth for help but the earth did not respond." What a cry which expressed so many people's long penned up hatred to Lin Piao's Fascism!

But, the excitement vanished very quickly. Following it was the widespread black-out of threats and suppression to the Li Ch'ing-lin type of letters. Li Ch'ing-lin's fate has aroused sympathy and anxiety among the broad masses. They say: "It's fortunate that Chairman Mao did receive the letter"; and they are wondering about what has suppressed their democratic rights!?

Lin Piao's collapse does not mean the end of his system. The process of the affirmation of the Lin Piao System has created a force of the civil officials who share vested interests; and they are afraid of the upsurging masses of the people. The waves of liquidating the Lin Piao system have destroyed the foundation of their vested interests. Therefore, they have been playing with a sophistic trick and distorted the Chairman's Thought, calling the ultra-rightist essence of the Lin Piao System something "right-inclined" or shying away from the whole lot of things which Lin Piao promoted, when he became the general chieftain of the opportunist line, to oppose Chairman Mao and to spread poison in the whole country, or using Lin Piao's shameless reactionary utterances to cover up Lin Piao's shameful demagogic pronouncements. They have taken the stand opposite to the people who demand, seething with enthusiasm, to criticize the Lin Piao System and have struck down the criticism of Lin Piao. They condemn the masses of people for being "restorationists" and "reverse tide-ists." They wave the banners of "anti-restoration" and "anti-reverse tide," as if they were themselves the revolution and no one could touch them.

What is ridiculous is that they also have come forward to criticize Confucianism. They have tried in a thousand and one ways to cover up the secrets of the "rule by rites" which are exposed by Yang Jung-kuo and described the blood dripping "rule by rites" as a kind of sham benevolence and sham righteousness. The affirmation of the revolutionary role of the burning of books and burying scholars alive makes them think that this is an exploitable chance. They have unscrupulously boasted and lauded the feudal dictatorship of the Ch'in Dynasty and unhistorically trumpeted the theme of bodily eliminating all opponents. This is, in fact, to prepare public opinion for social-Fascism in order to complete Lin Piao's unfinished business. They dare not touch upon the two negations which the Ch'in Dynasty faced: the reactionary negation from the old autocrats of the six States and the revolutionary negation from the peasants of Ta-tse *hsiang*. Why did the peasants oppose the Ch'in Dynasty? When Ch'in exterminated the six States, the Peasants "without exception humbly respected the [imperial] court." Were not they all supporters of it? The reason is that the Ch'in Dynasty in the end harmed the peasants. Why do the masses of people oppose the Lín Piao System? Did not the Red Guard movement, which swept over everything, shout aloud Lin Piao's slogan of "Whoever resists will be struck down" in its gallant fighting? The reason also is that the Lin Piao System in the end harmed the masses of people. For several millenniums, the ones who harmed the interests of the people have been in the end struck down by the people; and this is called "the slaves create history."

Those "who enjoy vested interests" condemn the so-called "restorationists" and "reverse tide-ists" for rehabilitating the old. Yes, there are not a few among the masses of people who have, in the face of the Lin Piao System, nursed a kind of nostalgic sentiment. But this is because the current Lin Piao System has brought direct harm to them; thus, they objectively demand progress, while subjectively failing to know what progress is. This is almost an historical law. Did not Ch'en Sheng and Wu Kuang, who are praised by Chairman Mao as geniuses, either pretend to be Fu Su [Ch'in Shin Huang's elder son who should have been the successor of the Ch'in Dynasty but was forced to commit suicide] or self-entitled as the King of the State of Ch'u, and thus launch their revolutionary uprisings under the flag of a reactionary restoration? Since we proletarians have given high historical positions to peasant uprisings which waved such a flag, why should the broad masses of people, who nursed some nostalgic sentiment during the struggle to criticize Lin Piao, be dealt with so harsh a punitive force? Further-more, is not that negation of negation "appears to be regression to old things" also the dialectics of Lenin? That the revolutionary road must be thoroughly straight is Wang Ming's metaphysics. To render dialectic negation to the revolution is not a regression in history but an advancement in history.

Of course, if true counterrevolutionary restorationists like K'ung Fu [Confucius' ninth generation descendant] and his ilk could worm into the revolutionary ranks which marched out from Ta-tse *Hsiang,* it is more possible that there is a mixed lot of fishes and dragons [of different kinds of elements] in the counter-offensive and dialectic negation which today's Great Proletarian Cultural Revolution is facing. We must oppose the elements of counter-offensive and reverse settling of accounts in order to defend the fruits of the Great Proletarian Cultural Revolution. But, the main danger in the current struggle to criticize Lin Piao is the erroneous tide of defending the Lin Piao System under the flag of "anti-restoration of old."

In short, after a panoramic review of the situation since the advent of the struggle to criticize Lin Piao, it is believed that the struggle is acute; and the criticism of Lin Piao and rectification of the style of work is still the main task. The 10th line struggle still continues in a basic way, perhaps conceived in this deepened continuation is the 11th line struggle!

(5)   **On Going Against the Tide**

The "10th National Party Congress" has abolished the principles of "together [we] eliminate them" and "together [we] punish them," which were crammed into the "9th National Party Congress" by Lin Piao, and replaced it with the principle of going against the tide. This is a great achievement of the "10th National Party Congress."

But, the current situation is that this slogan has become a clarion; and everyone is shouting: "Going against the tide!"

In August this year (1973), was there not a Chang T'ieh-sheng who also stepped forward to "go against the tide"? The ending is that neither did he get his head chopped off nor get himself imprisoned; and, in the third place, there was not a wife who demanded a divorce. On the contrary, he has been flying high with the wind; and it is reported that he has been sent to a certain academic institute to take advanced study of the secrets and marvels of the "going against the tide." But, among the revolutionaries who put up real fights to oppose the Lin Piao System, not a few had their heads chopped off; and so they are headless; those who were imprisoned are still in the prison; and those who were dismissed from office are still suspended. They are not that lucky and happy. Some people condemn us, saying, "You are reversing the correct verdicts for the struck down freaks & monsters" and "you are the 571s [participants in Project 571] and thus you are wrong." Lin Piao's [Project] 571 was only intended to exploit the masses of people who were victimized by his system as a kind of "borrowed force" to attack the proletarian headquarters. What is the crime in "using a B52 [code name for Mao in Lin Piao's *Project 571*] to attack a B52"? Even the 571 [meaning Lin Piao] himself knew that the victimized masses of the people are Chairman Mao's strength, not his force!

The masses of people are not A-tou [nickname of the crown prince of the State of Shu in the period of the Three Kingdoms who was notorious for his innocent ignorance and good-for-nothingness]. They are fully aware of the source of their misfortune. The cutting edge of their attack is directed at the Lin Piao System. No one of them has manifested hatred of Chairman Mao's revolutionary line and policies. On the contrary, they hate Lin Piao – the one who distorted and hindered this line and these policies – and those who enjoy vested interests from the Lin Piao System. They demand democracy; they demand a socialist legal system; and they demand the revolutionary rights and the human rights which protect the masses of people. "What? You demand democracy? You are reactionaries! Because you are reactionaries, we'll give you no democracy." They talk loudly and fluently; and are fond of quoting Chairman Mao's passages in connection with the people's democratic dictatorship.

But, on the foreheads of the reactionaries there inscribed no signs of "reactionary." "Only give democracy to the people" is very right. But, while you are shouting and crying aloud for the sake of the Lin Piao System, have you given the slightest bit of democracy to the people who are opposed to that system? What they have been given are cruel struggles and apprehension! "Give no democracy to the reactionaries" is correct. But do not forget the fact that the Lin Piao System had been flourishing for a certain period and that on Lushan about one hundred Central Committee members followed it. Was that not democracy serving the reactionaries? He has that kind of democracy without your giving, first because he has the power, and second because he has the revolutionary banner. If you do not give it to the masses of people, they will not have it, first because they do not have the power, second because they sometimes could not raise a revolutionary banner.

History has taught us that even under the conditions of the proletarian dictatorship the revolutionaries are sometimes regarded as reactionaries and deprived of democracy, while, on the other hand, the reactionaries are sometimes regarded as revolutionaries and allowed to possess democracy; and sometimes there have emerged the abnormal situations in which the revolutionaries are suppressed while the reactionaries soar higher and higher. We must make a serious analysis of who are the revolutionaries, who are the false revolutionaries, who are the reactionaries and who are the ones being framed as "reactionaries." The criterion for such an analysis can only be based on the fact that one's social practice has represented the basic interests of the broad masses of people, nor on one's attitude toward the so-called "genius."

In this world, there is no such thing as a democracy beyond class. The great masters of Marxism have advanced numerous discourses on class democracy in which they examined the whole revolutionary class in contrast with the whole counterrevolutionary class.

Since the Great Proletarian Cultural Revolution, the experience of class struggle reflected in the factional struggles among the people has prominently brought the factional democracy to the attention of the Marxists who are willing to study new questions. Because the two sides which reflected this class struggle should both have democratic rights, to have one faction overcome the other will not work. Are there only a few such aftermaths? Thus, this makes us understand that if the previous relationship of the oppressing and the oppressed, or, the suppressing and suppressed, existing between those may be now termed as the "[following the] tide faction" and the "going against the tide faction" cannot be changed into a relationship of the critics and the counter-critics which is based on unity, class democracy would not exist. The people's democratic dictatorship will then become the people's factional dictatorship. If the faction which holds the dictatorship is "correct," it still would not be able to unite the broad masses of people; if it is erroneous, it would be the beginning of social-Fascism.

Comrade Wang Hung-wen's report calls the people to exert the "five fear-nots [removal from one's post, expulsion from the Party, imprisonment, divorce and guillotine]" to go against the tide. The present situation is, however, that without the sanction and propagandization of the "VIPs" and the Central newspapers and journals, any kind of thinking cannot form a tide, especially an upsurging tide. From ancient times to the present, there has always been in China some people who are not afraid of having their heads chopped off for the sake of speaking out. Lu Hsun was naturally one of those who was not afraid of beheading. But Lu Hsun could go to his Japanese friends and get his articles published; and, where can today's "five fear-nots" people go to have their articles published? The apparitions of the Great Proletarian Cultural Revolution are still lingering around them. More than once, they have thought to restore the authority of the big-character poster. But the Lin Piao System is still threatening them; the stern rites which are saturated with "loyalty" are still fettering them; and shackles, iron-bar windows, leather whips, and bullets are waiting for them.

The reality in China since 1968 has thus grimly brought before the people this question: Is the Great Proletarian Cultural Revolution "dead"?

(6) Expectations for the Fourth National People's Congress

Revolution is doubtlessly the most authoritative thing in the world. The penetrating shocks and far-reaching significance rendered to the Chinese society by the Great Proletarian Cultural Revolution, which once left the whole world wide-eyed and open-mouthed, will in the future influence the whole historical stage of our socialism.

How will the "Fourth National People's Congress," to be convened soon, reflect the

Great Proletarian Cultural Revolution which is called by people China's "Second Revolution"? Law is the manifestation of the will of the ruling class. Then, how will the fundamental law of the state — the new Constitution — which the coming Congress is going to formulate, manifest the will of the Chinese proletariat and the broad masses of people who have gone through the Great Proletarian Cultural Revolution?

What are the masses of people thinking about right now? What do they demand? And what expectations do they have for the congress of "the people of the whole state"?

1. Legal system, not the "system of rites"

The basic content of the Great Proletarian Cultural Revolution is, in fact, "to rebel against the capitalist-reactionary line" and "to seize the power in the hands of the capitalist roaders." But one may say that suppression (for the people's democracy) and resisting the suppression (from the capitalist-reactionary line) have been the main activities throughout the whole course of the Great Proletarian Cultural Revolution. Moreover, the numerous movements since 1968 have all been designed to deal blows to the people, who rose in the Great Proletarian Cultural Revolution to make rebellion to the degree that they had to be beaten and sent down to the 18th hell [in Buddhism, the lowest level of hell where the souls of evil persons are tortured]. It was just when the mass movements in the Great Proletarian Cultural Revolution were suppressed that the Lin Piao System got the chance to be affirmatively established, that they [Lin Piao and his cohorts] were able to cram the feudalist and patriarchic terms into the "new Constitution" (draft) of 1970.

This crude fact illustrates that the feudalistic, social-Fascist dictatorship is the main danger to our dictatorship of the proletariat.

Our country has been transformed into socialism from a semi-feudal, semi-colonial society; thus, the tradition formed by the feudal autocracy of several millenniums is stubbornly entrenched in all domains of the superstructure such as ideology, culture, education, and law etc.

Are the strong elements of feudalism and patriarchism manifested in Liu Shao-ch'i, and especially in Lin Piao, not sufficient to prove that anti-feudalism is still an important factor in our continued revolution?

What could be a more sacred pillar to support the "rule by rites" of the Lin Piao System than the principle of "Whoever opposes Mao Tse-tung Thought will be struck down"? In name, they are upholding the others, in fact, they are upholding themselves. If Lin Piao could rightfully step onto the stage and speak up, then would it not be "whoever opposes Lin Piao will be struck down (in reality, he had done just that)"? Furthermore, any one of the VIPs can become something sacred as long as he claims for himself the incarnation of Chairman Mao's revolutionary line, whereas "the handful" of revolutionary masses who dared to affront his dignity will thus never be recognized as the objects which the law protects!

If we are not going to oppose this feudalist principle of the "system of rites" which stresses that "ruler-vassal and father-son, no one is allowed to be impertinent to his superior," can we really carry out the rule by law of the dictatorship of the proletariat which emphasizes "suppressing the enemies; protecting the people"?

This is an extememly great contradiction. On the one hand, the Party's centralized leadership must never be shaken, while, on the other, "the emphasis of the movement is to rectify the capitalist-roaders in the Party" with these capitalist-roaders being exactly the embodiment of the centralized leadership in areas and departments which have been monopolized by them.

236

How should the rights of the masses of people to struggle, under the Party's centralized leadership, against the capitalist-roaders in the Party and their erroneous line be protected? This is a great task confronting the "4th National People's Congress."

It would be superfluous to say that the Party leadership should listen carefully to the opinions of the masses; it would be equally superfluous to mention the rights of the masses of people to exercise revolutionary supervision over the Party leadership at various levels; and it would be more so to say that it is justified to rebel against the capitalist-roaders. Even if the opinions of the masses are erroneous and excessive, or, they are, out of their ignorance, discontent with certain aspects of the Party's policies, should they be "supressed when persuasion fails, and apprehended when suppression fails"? Moreover, it is not always easy to distinguish between fragrant flowers and poisonous weeds, between the correct and the erroneous, and between the revolutionary and the counterrevolutionary. There must be a process; and the distinction must be tested by time. Therefore, we should not be afraid of the upright and honest opponents as long as they limit themselves by not making intrigues and conspiracies.

The "4th National People's Congress" should stipulate in black and white that all the democratic rights which the masses of people deserve should be protected, and that dictatorship will only be exercised over the criminals who committed murder, arson, gangsterism, robbery and theft and the elements who incited armed struggles and organized conspiratorial cliques.

2. Restriction on special privileges

Whether or not acknowledging that there is emerging in China a Soviet Union type of privileged stratum (of which Liu Shao-ch'i and Lin Piao etc. were the political agents only) is the fundamental theoretical question of affirming or negating the Great Proletarian Cultural Revolution.

It must be pointed out at the beginning that most of our Party members are good ones and comparatively good ones. However, this privileged stratum is an objective being that is generated out of our country's socio-economic conditions and cannot be changed according to men's will.

Whence is the reality "in the present society, the wind of taking the back door prevails"? Whence are the indulgent quandaries of the products of the society and the shockingly high-class luxuries? Whence are the disguised heritages of a considerable number of children of the high-ranking cadres who have matter-of-factly enjoyed the rights of possessing property? What are the recourses of the mode of possession of the new bourgeois class and the political measures which protect this mode of possession? In literature and art, in education, in the "May 7 Cadre School," in Going up to the Mountains and down to the Countryside, in Getting Rid of the Stale and Taking in the Fresh, in attending universities, and in cultivation of the successors, in short, in almost everything which is called a "newborn thing," the privileged can use their divine presence and demonstrate their divine power.

May we not say that the Soviet Union's change [to revisionism] began with the practice of a high-salary system for its high-ranking cadres, which was intended to keep up with the [payments to] bourgeois experts? In our China, even if the tradition permits, and the people do not object, the practice of providing certain preferential treatment to the veteran cadres who have allegedly shed much blood and sweat for the revolution, can we thus belittle its corruptive effects on the regime as well as its influence over the new social relations?

We are not Utopian socialists; therefore, we acknowledge that there exist in our society at the present stage various kinds of differences which cannot be eliminated by a single law or decree. But, the law governing the development of the socialist revolutionary movement is not to enhance the differences but to eliminate them, and more, so not to allow these differences to be expanded into economic and political privileges. Special privileges are fundamentally opposite to the interests of the people. Why should we be so shy about the criticism of special privileges? Why should the right and wrong on this issue of importance, which is reflected in the "taking the back door," be stealthily substituted by the so-called question of "good people" and "bad people"?

The 4th National People's Congress should write in black and white the clause which restricts special privileges.

3. Guarantee of the people's right of management of the state and the society

The fact that both the "new Party Constitution" of 1969 and the "new Constitution" (draft) of 1970 have all legalized Lin Piao, the prince of evil, as the successor makes the Chinese people see a very frightening shadow. At the same time, it also has posed a very important question to the people. How can we guarantee that the power of the party and the state will be held in the hands of the Marxists? How can the successors to the proletarian enterprise surge out in "thousands and millions"?

What has enabled "a great number of unheard of youth to become revolutionary pathbreakers" is the Great Proletarian Cultural Revolution; and what has antagonized Chairman Mao and the broad masses of people are the "activists' congresses" purported for "creative study and application [of Mao's thought and works] (i.e., speculation and manipulation)."

Chairman Mao has brought forward five requirements for the successors, and Lin Piao also brought forward three requirements of his own. In the several years wherein the Lin Piao System was affirmed, selection and cultivation of cadres had been chiefly based on Lin Piao's three requirements. Are the successors to the enterprise of the proletarian revolution to be selected from the seedlings of the families of geniuses, or to be these who have grown up in strong winds and heavy waves and surged up in class struggles? How contradictory this question has been between theory and practice even to this date!

"Who gives us the power?" The people do. Thus, our cadres should not be Mandarins but errant runners of the people. However, power is the most corruptive agent of men. A man's ascension in status is the most trying test to see if he is working for the benefit of the majority, or for the benefit of a minority. Whether or not one can preserve his spirit of serving the people is chiefly dependent upon the revolutionary supervision by the people, in addition to his own efforts; whereas the mass movements are the richest sources for a revolutionary to preserve his revolutionary spirit.

How should the rights of revolutionary supervision of the masses of people over the leadership at various levels in the Party and the state be stipulated? And how should it be explicitly stipulated that when certain cadres (especially the high-ranking cadres in Central organizations) have lost the trust of the broad masses of people, the people "can dismiss them at any time"?

The "4th National People's Congress" should answer these questions.

4. Consolidation of the dictatorship of the proletariat and sanction against reactionaries

Are the people's democratic rights not written in our Constitution and Party Constitution and Central documents? Yes, they have been written down. Not only that, but there also are the stipulations of "protecting the people's democracy," "not allowing malicious attack and revenge," and "forbidding extracting a confession by torture and interrogation." But, these protections have been, in fact, always unavailable, while, on the contrary, Fascist dictatorship has been "allowed" to be practiced over the revolutionary cadres and masses — some of them were imprisoned, some executed, and some framed in fabricated cases; even the unlimited practice of savagely corporal punishments cannot be "strictly forbidden."

The basic task of the Chinese people in the entire historical stage of socialism is to consolidate, under the guidance of the direct line, the dictatorship of the proletariat. However, this revolutionary program of the dictatorship of the proletariat, when placed in the hands of the reactionaries, becomes a mockery of the revolutionary aspirations of the masses; and thus it further becomes the most ferocious murdering weapon in the hands of our irreconcilable enemies.

If we do not punish the Chiang [Nationalist] gang who have aroused great popular hatred by insisting on the counterrevolutionary line, by turning the proletarian dictatorship into a Fascist dictatorship, and by bloody suppression and massacre of the people, the socialist democracy and legal system will not be established and the proletarian dictatorship cannot be consolidated. The ones who suppress the people must be suppressed. The "4th National People's Congress" should stipulate in black and white the terms to punish the "ministers" who have committed the heinous crimes of transgressing the law knowingly, violating the law while enforcing it, creating fabricated cases, using the public to avenge personal grudges, establishing special cases without authorization, instituting prisons without authorization, using unlimited corporal punishment, and practicing wanton murder.

5. Taking concrete measures to ensure the fulfillment of policies

The "9th National Party Congress" in 1969 has already announced that "the current main task is the concrete fulfillment (of policies). Since then, five years have passed; and Lin Piao has been destroyed for three years. Why have so many important proletarian policies not been concretely fulfilled?

Moreover, in recent years the policies have been changed frequently, even to the degree that "orders issued in the morning are changed in the same evening" (there are the reasons of [someone's insufficient or incorrect understanding of these policies], but it is chiefly a reflection of the violent class struggle.) In addition, there has been an endless emergence of indigenous policies, which make the people very much confused, even to the degree of doubting the Party. We believe that the "4th National People's Congress" should reiterate those policies which have been proven to be the correct ones that should be practiced for long periods in this historical stage of socialism; and embody them in appropriate forms through legalization. Policies and strategies are the lifeline of the Party. Therefore, those who seriously sabotage the Party's policies must be sternly handled.

6. From each according to his ability, to each according to his work

Since the summer of 1968, and owing to suppression of democratic rights in the political sphere, especially by Lin Piao's Fascist organizational line and their nepotism as well as personnel transfers and reshuffles of the disobedient based on punitivism, the principles of "from each according to his ability" and "employ only the competent" have been sabotaged and the people's socialist initiative trampled underfoot.

At the same time when we see that the special privileges are expanding we also see clearly that the worker and peasant laboring masses are deprived of many of their reasonable economic benefits under slogans of "public property-ism." For many years, the workers have not had their wages raised, but had the reasonable monetary rewards which were part of their wages abolished; while the peasants suffered even greater losses as a result of the movements of [turning in] uncompensated "loyalty grains," high quota requisitioning of grain, and "cutting off the tail of private ownership." Now, the dangerousness of Lin Piao's "ultra-leftist" line becomes more and more manifested.

Has Lenin not lauded the "Communist voluntary service on Saturday" as a "great unprecedented undertaking"? Have there not been innumerable self-sacrificing and selfless revolutionary heroes who emerged from the Chinese laboring people in the period of revolutionary war, in the high tide of socialist construction, and in the Great Proletarian Cultural Revolution which were characterized by rigor and vitality? This is exactly the invaluable historical initiative of the masses of people. But, can it be said that it may be thus absolutized and that spirit can substitute for everything, even the principle of "from each according to his ability and to each according to his work" in this historical stage of socialism? Obviously, this is extremely absurd. It will be punished by the law of history; and so it was.

In the Great Proletarian Cultural Revolution, we have opposed high wages, high monetary rewards and high payments; but should we absolutely negate the role of monetary rewards? Why could a worker who is more enthusiastic, more conscientious and responsible, and has overfulfilled the set production quota, or invented or created something, not get more appropriate rewards than his colleagues of the same grade of wage? Why could a worker, a peasant, a revolutionary intellectual who has engaged in creative writing in addition to his assigned works, or made new discoveries or new inventions, not get appropriate material incentives? The principle of empty politics is the principle to reward the lazy and to punish the diligent. The principle of "from each according to his ability and to each according to his work" under the proletarian politics in command is the principle of bringing into play and protecting the socialist initiative of the masses of people; moreover, conscientious practice of this principle also is the most effective measure to restrict special privileges!

The 4th National People's Congress "should stipulate in black and white" the clause of from each according to his ability and to each accordng to his work.

We have nursed very great expectations for the "4th National People's Congress." We hope that it can be a congress of unity, a congress of victory, and a congress which reflects the united will and wishes of the broad masses of people who have gone through the Great Proletarian Cultural Revolution.

But, the tragically heroic *Internationale* which was sung aloud by Chairman Mao when he was waging violent battles against the Lin Piao anti-Party clique has deeply shocked and moved the broad masses of people. They know that the stipulations in the new Constitution would once again give us a weapon. To really practice them [these stipulations] will depend on the struggle waged by the broad masses of people themselves.

Has the Constitution of 1954 also not made stipulations of the people's democratic rights? Has Chairman Mao not said many times that: "Without extensive people's democracy, the dictatorship of the proletariat cannot be consolidated"? But, partly because there exists the anti-democratic force which was represented by Lin Piao, and partly because the masses of people have seldom made use of these democratic rights (owing to the deeply entrenched feudalist tradition in China and a lack of democratic spirit resulting from our country's comparatively backward production and the limited cultural level of the people), the objective of "creating a lively and vigorous political situation" brought forward by Chairman Mao many years ago has been far, far away from being achieved.

Just like a traveller from the well rivered south who treasures water only when he comes to the desert, the masses of people appreciate more the value of the democratic rights when they were deprived of them during the Great Proletarian Cultural Revolution. Although the broad masses of people were cruelly suppressed in 1968, "in the current tides in the world, the anti-democratic reactionary faction is simply a reverse tide." A mass movement to thoroughly destroy the Lin Piao System will come in the not too remote future, it will restore and develop all the spirits of the first Great Proletarian Cultural Revolution.

First draft: September 19, 1973
Second draft: December 12, 1973
Finalized draft: November 7, 1974

POSTSCRIPT

In response to the suggestions proffered by a few comrades, we intend to mimeograph this article so that many more people can study, criticize and comment on the viewpoints presented in this poster. Due to the shortage of paper, we sincerely request that the broad masses of revolutionary comrades provide us with as much paper as possible, for instance, ten, one hundred, a thousand, or ten thousand sheets of paper, no matter how few or many they are.

Those who are willing to help should keep in touch with Li Cheng-t'ien whose address is Hsinkang Road, Kwangtung People's Arts College (originally Canton Fine Arts College), Canton. And to those we render our

Sublime revolutionary Salute!

November 11

Li I-che

APPENDIX

Some Thoughts on the Chinese Revolution

By Lee Yu See and Wu Che (Two Chinese anarchists)

1.   From the beginning, the Chinese Communist Party was a bourgeois organism. The party was structured along hierarchical lines. It was a miniature state. It assimilated all the forms, techniques and mentality of bureaucracy. Its membership was schooled in obedience and was taught to revere the leadership. The party's leadership, in turn, was schooled in habits born of command, authority, manipulation and egomania. At the same time, the party was the spineless follower of the Comintern directed by Moscow.

2.   The rigid dogma adopted by the Chinese Communist Party was that of Leninism-Stalinism, an ideology which had led to the consolidation of a system of state-capitalism in Russia. Not by deviating from but by following Lenin's ideas, a new dominating and exploiting class came into power over the working masses.

3.   China was an economically backward country in which the the old ruling classes were incapable of carrying out industrialisation. The young native bourgeoisie had neither the strength nor the courage to revolutionise the old social structure, in the way that a genuine modernisation would require. The "bourgeois tasks" were to be solved by a bureaucracy.

4.   In pursuing the strategy of encircling the cities from the countryside in its attempt to seize state power, the Chinese Communist Party built up a peasant army. But such an army, organised by a bourgeois party, became a tool of the party and therefore a capitalist machine.

5.   The so called 1949 revolution was nothing in common with a genuine socialist revolution. It was simply a violent take-over of the state by a bureaucracy better-placed to manage the national capital than the old ruling clique.

6.   Having won control of the state machine, the only way to move forward for the Maoist bureaucracy was to impose a regime of ruthless exploitation and austerity on the working masses.

The bureaucracy began to carry out the task of primitive accumulation. Because of the lack of capital-intensive industry, economic development depended on the most primitive methods of extraction of surplus value: in the countryside, mobilizing

242

millions of peasants and semi-proletarians around the construction of public works and irrigation projects, built almost bare-handed by the rural masses; in the cities, forcing the workers to work long hours for extremely low wages, banning strikes, putting restrictions on the choice of employment and so on.

7. The new bureaucratic capitalist class in China did not emerge because of the development of new modes of production. It was on the contrary, the bureaucracy which brought the new mode of production into existence. The Chinese bureaucracy did not originate from the industrialisation of the country. Industrialisation was the result of the bureaucracy's accession to power.

8. Soon after the accession to power of the Maoist bureaucracy, intraparty feuds occurred. Such feuds originated out of two different conceptions of how China was to modernise in agriculture, industry, science and technology.

9. The Maoist-radical faction (led today by Chiang Ching, Wang Hung-wen, Chang Chun-chiao and Yao Wen-yuan) advocated self reliance, the active mobilization of the "popular masses" behind the state and the economy to promote production by ideological rather than material incentives, "redness" over "expertness", the "infallibility" of the thoughts of Mao Tse-tung, hostility towards Soviet Union, "revolutionising arts and literature to serve the single purpose of propagating the official ideology, the need for endless mass movements and struggle because "in the long historical period of socialism, the principal internal contradiction is the contradiction between the working class and the bourgeoisie "[1]

The so-called capitalist roaders (Liu Shao-chi, Teng Hsiao-ping, et al) favoured the retention of wage differentials and the extension of material incentives for increased productivity. They also stood for a more efficient technological apparatus, rapprochement with the Soviet "revisionists", liberalisation of policies in relation to the arts, rejection of the personal cult of Mao, the priority of national construction over endless "class struggles".

Both lines represented different strategies designed by the different factions of the bureaucratic capitalist class for attacking the working masses, for intensifying their exploitation.

The Maoist-radical road was leading to a "feudalistic social-fascist dictatorship". The road of the "capitalist roaders" would bring a "destalinised Russian type of society" like today's Russia.

10. Mao's way to develop and to modernise the Chinese economy had the opportunities to be tried out fully in 1958. From "top to bottom", the Party announced its policy of the "Three Red Banners".

The first "red banner" was the "general policy of socialist construction."

The second "red banner" was the "great leap forward".

The third "red banner" was the formation of "peoples' communes".

As a result, China experienced three years of economic difficulties.

11. The Great Leap Forward failed dismally and the intra-Party conflicts of the two lines grew into sharp political struggles.

Mao's influence was reduced in December 1958 when he resigned the State Chairmanship, though retaining the Chairmanship of the Party. Mao said, "I was extremely discontented with that decision, but I could do nothing about it."

12. With Mao's weakened control over the country, the "capitalist roaders" adopted a series of policies to minimize the economic crisis ———— in part created by the Great Leap Forward and in part created by natural disasters of various sorts. The

"capitalist roaders" proceeded to develop and to modernise the economy according to their own perceptions.

13. Mao initiated the Great Proletarian Cultural Revolution in 1966.

It was a power struggle between the two factions of the bureaucratic capitalist class and also an attempt to mould the Chinese people and their thoughts according to the cast of Mao.

The immediate and tumultuous response of the masses to Mao's call for rebellion pointed to the extreme discontent towards the policies of "capitalist roaders" and the system that have been set up since 1949.

The masses ended up opposed to, not just the "capitalist roaders", but to the bureaucracy.

14. A pseudo-revolution had turned into a real revolution.

"90 percent of the senior cadres (of the Party) were made to stand aside. In Hunan, Chang P'ing-hua, Chang Po-shen, HUA Kuo-feng and the like had their power reduced to zero. At the Centre (Peking), power seizure (by representatives of the Cultural Revolution) took place in the Ministry of Finance, the Radio Broadcasting Administration Bureau and other departments; and the power of people like Li Hsien-nien, Ch'en Yi, T'an Chen-lin, as well as that of Chou En-lai who represented them, was greatly diminished. Into whose hands did the assets go at that time? They went into the hands of the people, who were full of boundless enthusiasm, and who were organised to take over the urban administrations and the Party, government, financial and cultural powers in industry, commerce, communications and so forth."[2]

The masses had risen to take hold of their own destiny.

Mao ignited the revolution but he could not control it.

With the aid the Lin Piao and the military, Mao suppressed the revolutionary masses.

15. The bureaucracy, now temporarily controlled by Mao Tse-tung, led China further drifting down the road of "feudalistic social-fascist dictatorship."

16. Some phenomena under this "feudalistic social-fascist dictatorship" include "giving prominence to (empty) politics which rewarded the lazy and punished the diligent, the "daily reading (of Mao's works and quotations)" which resembled the incantation of spells, the "discussion-application (of Mao's works and thoughts)" which became more and more hypocritical, the "revolution erupts from the depth of the soul" which became more absurd, the "manifestation of loyalty" which encouraged political speculation, the grotesque "loyalty dance", and the excruciatingly multitudinous rituals of showing loyalty — morning prayers, evening penitences, rallies, falling - in, reporting for and quitting work and making duty shifts, buying and selling things, writing letters, making phone calls, even taking meals — which were invariably painted with violent religious colours and shrouded in such an atmosphere. In short, loyalty occupied one hundred percent of the time and one hundred percent of the space. The movements of this "good" and that "good" were, in fact, competitions of "left! left! and more left!" and contests for "the most . . . . . the most . . . . . and the most." The innumerable "meetings of representatives of active elements" were, in fact expositions of hypocritical, evil and ugly behaviour and a gambling house which offered "10,000 times profit for one unit of capital;" "the formula 'preaching' of class struggle, and the 'scum hole' type of cow pens (meaning detention camps) which were more so and no less (inhuman) than the massacre of the historical incidents such as 'March 18', 'April 12', 'May 30' and 'June 23' because

244

in Kwangtung Province alone nearly 40,000 revolutionary masses and cadres were massacred and more than a million revolutionary cadres and masses were imprisoned, put under control, and struggled against."[3]

17. Lin Piao, officially designated Mao's heir apparent and the closest comrade in arms of Mao, became the "arch traitor, renegade, political swindler and double dealer". "On September 12, 1971, Mao was returning to Peking from Shanghai by train. Lin had arranged to blow up the train somewhere north of Nanking." And when the plan was thwarted, Lin fled on a plane which "ran out of fuel and crashed in Mongolia, killing everyone who was still alive by the time it crashed."[4]

Once again, the bureaucrats manoeuvred above the heads of the masses who were not informed of the "Lin Piao affair" until months later.

18. By 1973 Teng Hsiao Ping, the capitalist roader during the Cultural Revolution, was re-instated and became one of the most powerful men in the Chinese Communist Party hierarchy. Closely aligned to Chou En-lai, Teng was soon seen as the person to succeed Chou, who was Premier and first Vice Chairman of the Party, one of the most efficient bureaucrats to have administered China. Chou also richly personified the most opportunistic elements that genuine revolutionaries despised – with little principles, Chou always sided with the faction commanding a position of greater strength.

19. However, Chou seemed to be the target of the Movement of Going Against the tide & the Anti-Confucius movement waged by the Maoist radical faction of the bureaucrats, but skilfully Chou "adopted the soft, supple Taoist strategy of non-interference and non-resistance: like a judoka, he never opposes the adversary's impact, he yields – and then manipulates the switches so as to send the enemy rushing under his own steam onto a sidetracking leading nowhere."[5] Chou managed to divert, control, distort and neutralise the movement aimed at him by identifying the "erroneous current" as the Lin Piao current. The movement was circumscribed to the innocuous denunciation of an already discredited corpse.

Thus the anti-confucius movement was successively designated by three names. first, "criticising Confucius" (pi Kung), then "criticising Confucius and Lin Piao" (pi Kung pi Lin) and finally "criticising Lin Piao and Confucius" (pi Lin pi Kung).

Unlike Liu Shao-chi and Lin Piao, Chou En-lai managed to die as a member of the Chinese Communist Party.

19. The masses were unenthusiastic about the "criticising Confucius and Lin Piao" movement, because "China is no longer the China of yore, and the people are no longer wrapped in sheer ignorance."[6] The "criticising Confucius and Lin Piao movement", the movement of "Going Against the Tide", the "Study of Proletarian Dictatorship Campaign", the attack on the 14th century classic Water Margin, the movement "to counterattack the Right Deviationist Attempt to Reverse Correct Verdicts" are only struggles between the different factions of the ruling class. The masses understand that such mobilizations are to ensure their own servitude and to promote production, ie. intensifying their exploitation.

20. According to the "Renmin Ribao", (People's Daily), "Early April, a handful of class enemies, under the guise of commemorating the late Premier Chou during the Ching Ming Festival, engineered an organised, premeditated and planned counter-revolutionary political incident at Tien An Men Square in the Capital. They flagrantly made revolutionary speeches, posted reactionary poems and slogans, distributed reactionary leaflets and agitated for the setting up of counter-revolutionary organisations. By means of

insinuation and overt counter-revolutionary language, they brazenly clamoured that "the era of Chin Shih Huang is gone," Openly hoisting the ensign of supporting Teng Hsiao-ping, they frenziedly directed their spearhead at our great leader Chairman Mao, attempted to split the Party Central Committee headed by Chairman Mao, tried to change the general orientation of the current struggle to criticise Teng Hsiao-ping and counterattack the Right deviationist attempt to reverse correct verdicts, and engaged in counter-revolutionary activities.

The counter-revolutionary activities culminated on April 5. At about 8 am, a loudspeaker car of the municipal Public Security Bureau was overturned, the body of the car and its loudspeakers smashed. After 9 am, more than 10,000 people gathered in front of the Great Hall of the People. At its maximum the crowd at Tien An Men Square numbered about 100,000 people."

The "Renmin Ribao" also reported that people broke into the barracks of the People's Liberation Army and occupied it. They overturned cars and set them on fire. Windows and doors at the barracks were smashed. Then they set the barracks on fire. Members of the fire-brigade and policemen were beaten up. Several hundred worker-militiamen who went up the flight of steps leading to the Great Hall of the People to stand guard were broken up into several sections. More than 100 Peking worker-militiamen were injured, a dozen of them seriously wounded. The riot continued. At 6.30 pm, Wu Teh, the chairman of the Peking Revolutionary Committee, made a broadcast Speech at Tien An Men Square. "Most of the onlookers and the masses who had been taken in quickly dispersed. But a handful of counter-revolutionaries continued their desperate resistance and again posted some reactionary poems around the Monument to the People's Heroes. Three hours later, on receiving an order from the Peking Municipal Revolutionary Committee, tens of thousands of worker-militiamen, in co-ordination with the people's police and P.L.A. guards, took resolute measures and enforced proletarian dictatorship."[7]

On the 7th April, 1976, the Central Committee of the Communist Party of China announced that "on the proposal of our great leader Chairman Mao, the Political Bureau of the Central Committee of the Communist Party of China unanimously agrees to appoint Comrade Hua Kuo-feng First Vice-Chairman of the Central Committee of the Communist Party of China and Premier of the State Council of the People's Republic of China,' and that "having discussed the counter-revolutionary incident which took place at Tien An Men Square and Teng Hsiao-ping's latest behaviour, the Political Bureau of the Central Committee of the Communist Party of China holds that the nature of the Teng Hsiao-ping problem has turned into one of antagonistic contradiction. On the proposal of our great leader Chairman Mao, the Political Bureau unanimously agrees to dismiss Teng Hsiao-ping from all posts both inside and outside the Party while allowing him to keep his Party membership so as to see how he will behave in the future."[8]

The acts of appointing Hua Kuo-feng and dismissal of Teng Hsiao-ping are apparent contravention of the provisions in the constitution of the People's Republic of China.

21. Contrary to the pronouncement of the official New China News Agency, the demonstration and riots were clearly not "organised, premediated and planned". All other eye witness accounts pointed to the opposite.

The "Renmin Ribao" refused to admit that the direct and immediate cause of the riots was the premature removal of the Ching Ming wreaths for Chou En-lai.

It was in fact a spontaneous mass demonstration with the participation of the majority of the 100,000 people at Tien An Man Square. If it were an action of a minority, how could the several hundred worker-militiamen standing guard at the Great Hall of the People be broken up into several sections? How could the riot last through the whole day? And why was the need to send in "tens of thousands of worker-militiamen" in addition to the people's police and the P.L.A. guards?

The "Renmin Ribao" report said that the rioters were "openly hoisting the ensign supporting Teng Hsiao-ping", but eye-witnesses said that they neither heard nor saw any direct references to Teng. And what gains would be made by Teng and the "capitalist roaders" by organising a mass demonstration without corresponding actions to attempt to seize power?

22. The spontaneous demonstration of the 100,000 at Tien An Man Square (and similar demonstrations reported to have occurred at Chengchow, Kunming) signified that the Chinese masses are formulating their answers to the question "Whither China?", that they have intense hatred for the existing system and the ruling class, that they want to control their own destiny, that they want an end to "Chin Shih Huang's feudal society."[9]

For the first time since the Cultural Revolution, the masses asserted themselves in a big scale.

Were the masses supporting the "capitalist road"? No! The masses had passed their verdict during the Cultural Revolution.

When the masses paid their homage to Chou, they were making their protests in a round about way. This was necessitated by the extremely repressive nature of the existing system of rule.

23. In face of self actions of the masses, the bureaucracy acted swiftly. Reaching a compromise to sack Teng Hsiao-ping (but keeping him as a party member), the Maoist-radical faction joined hands with the "capitalist roaders" in suppressing the masses. Ignoring the violations of the constitution of the state, the ruling class shows nakedly that it will stop at nothing to perpetuate its continued rule. The bureaucrats, Mao, capitalist roaders and all, trembled at the self-action of the masses.

24. The socialist revolution is a long and tortuous road, but the end of the barbaric era of Mao Tse-tung is in sight.

Note 1:   Quotation of Mao Tse-tung
Note 2:   "Whither China?" Shengwulien document; reproduced in full in Section Three of this book, pp 180-200.
Note 3:   Li I Che's Big Character Poster – "Concerning Socialist Democracy and Legal System", reproduced in full in Section Three of this book, pp 249-283.
Note 4:   For details of the Lin Piao Plot, refer to the famous article by Wilfred Burchett published in August 1973 in the American Maoist paper, the Guardian weekly. The same article was also carried in the August 20, 1973 issue of the Far Eastern Economic Review.
Note 5:   "The Grand Master's checkmate" by 'Simon Leys, anarchistic author of "Chairman Mao's New Clothes." December 3, 1973 issue of the Far Eastern Economic Review.
Note 6:   Poem at Tien An Men Square Incident. April 5, 1976.
Note 7:   For full text of the "Counter-Revolutionary Political Incident at Tien An Men Square," refer to no 15, Peking Review, April 9, 1976.
Note 8:   Refer to No. 15 Peking Review, April 9, 1976.

WORLD INEQUALITY

edited by
Immanuel Wallerstein

What has changed with the advent of the modern world since the 16th century is neither the existence of inequalities nor the felt need to justify them ideologically. What has changed is that those who defend the "inevitability" of inequalities argue that eventually, inequality will diminish. This factor is at the base of the debate on "international development."

The current debate however is a variant of the classic debates but a number of new issues have outdated these considerations. The thesis of the contributors to this book is that the modern world comprises more than ever before a single world capitalist economy. It follows from this that nation-states are not societies that have separate, parallel histories, but parts of a whole reflecting that whole. To the extent that stages exist, they exist for the system as whole. To understand the internal class contradictions and political struggles of a particular society, we must first situate it in the world-economy. We can then understand the ways in which various political and cultural thrusts may be efforts to alter or preserve a position within this world system which may be to the advantage or disadvantage of particular groups within a particular society.

Prof. Wallerstein brings together in an impressive international discussion of leading authorities to examine various aspects of development and inequality. These include: Richard D. Wolff, Mohamed Dowidar, Jean Piel, Ervand Abrahamian, Albert-Paul Lentin, Mohamed Harbi, Cary Hector, Bogdan Denitch, Denis Brutus, Jorge Niosi, Mahamed-Salah Sfia and others.

Prof. Immanuel Wallerstein is author of the internationally acclaimed book, *The Modern World-System: Capitalist Agriculture and the Origins of the European World-Economy in the Sixteenth Century.*

225 pages | Hardcover $12.95 | Paperback $3.95
ISBN: 0-919618-66-9/ ISBN: 919618-65-0